Leadership at the Apex

Leadership at the Apex

Politicians and Administrators in
Western Local Governments

**Poul Erik Mouritzen and
James H. Svara**

University of Pittsburgh Press

This book is dedicated to our children

Christoffer and Sofie; John and Kevin

Published by the University of Pittsburgh Press, Pittsburgh, Pa., 15261

Copyright © 2002, University of Pittsburgh Press

Manufactured in the United States of America

Printed on acid-free paper

10 9 8 7 6 5 4 3 2 1

LIBRARY OF CONGRESS CATALOGING-IN-PUBLICATION DATA

Mouritzen, Poul Erik.

    Leadership at the apex : politicians and administrators in Western
local governments / Poul Erik Mouritzen and James H. Svara.

      p.   cm.

    Includes bibliographical references and index.

    ISBN 0-8229-5785-X (pbk. : alk. paper)

    1. Municipal officials and employees.   2. Leadership.   3. Municipal
government.   I. Svara, James H.   II. Title.

JS141 .M68 2002

320.8'5—dc21

2002005254

Contents

Foreword

THIS BOOK IS ABOUT PART OF OUR DAILY LIVES—local government and public administrators. In most countries, individuals and small groups feel that their roots, that is, what shapes their respective identities, to a very large extent are embedded in subnational territories. In what city do I live, from what region does my family come, which public goods and services are provided to ease my life, what symbols help to map the physical landscape around me?

The twentieth century was tough for local government. What was local came to be considered old-fashioned, conservative, and stuffy. Large territories and the nation-state were considered the main vehicles for more equality, better effectiveness, and enhanced citizen participation. Progress for the inhabitants of Peoria or Caltanisetta was to be exogenous to their respective communities; it was expected to flow down from Washington or Rome. In public affairs, outside and big—associated with national and global—were the right answers to good government and democratic governance. The process by which the welfare state was built in many countries, especially in the 1950s and 1960s, was clearly a centralization process. Even neo-liberal leaders like President Reagan and Prime Minister Margaret Thatcher, while rhetorically criticizing the role of the state, reinforced the marginalization of subnational levels and authorities. It was more attractive to make a career as a bureaucrat or to serve the public interest as a politician in ministries than in city halls. Local authorities were still needed, but as mere functional agents of a principal—the state or the world economy.

Today, the periphery not only has survived, but its role is becoming increasingly crucial. Principles that were once accepted without question now appear to be groundless preconceptions. Countries such as France and Italy, historically considered as archetypes of political and administrative centralization, have taken the lead in transferring powers and in allocating financial autonomy to subnational levels such as communes and regions. "Subsidiarity" has become the new motto in the European Union. Most of the wealth deriving from public policies has its origins in local authority initiatives. Cities take care of sewage, law and order, roads, housing, culture, jobs, education, and so on. As suggested by the bumper sticker Think Globally, Act Locally, successful globalization requires a strong localization. Subnational territories that are well administered by their respective public authorities are providing the key resources to their population and basic competitive advantages to their firms. The market and the public sector are partners, not foes. Bureaucracy is not at its core a monument to obsolete principles of "good government." In specific circumstances it may even outperform other systems of collective goods and services delivery such as kinship, neighborhood, not-for-profit associations, or the market. Political progress and democratic participation maintain their roots in local communities, despite the fact that their residents increasingly divide their lives across the places where they have their residences, where they consume, and where they work. In the final analysis, people identify themselves with multiple references: local, regional, national, European in fifteen countries, city, county, and state and federal in the United States. Most of us feel we are citizens of several communities and polities, including the whole planet, but we remain rooted in a place—for the bulk of the population a municipality—and this place retains its importance.

There are good reasons to pay close attention to this book. Poul Erik Mouritzen and James Svara offer a variety of contributions to knowledge and to practice. They bring local government to the forefront, they underline the rather sophisticated level of city management in advanced Western countries, and they discuss how administrative machines and political arenas may cooperate within a democratic context.

The importance of bringing back local administration is not a rhetorical exaggeration. Personal experience suggests how great are the misperceptions about where important work is done in government in many countries. A few years ago, I was considered for a position in a very distinguished Anglo-Saxon university. During the interview, one panel member made the following comment about my research foci. "You are a professor in a major business school, INSEAD. . . . For sure you may have fun working with all these multinational executives! I envy you. I realize that you also teach at the famous Ecole Nationale d'Administration. . . . That is rather prestigious, you see other kinds of elites. But, tell me, why the hell are you training city managers? . . . Do you really need to do that?" I realized that this latter aspect of my work was considered a second-class academic activity. Serious issues and serious persons are not local government centered.

One major research discovery presented in this book is related to the issue of convergence or divergence between countries. Does local government at the local level look the same or not across the Western democracies? On one hand, nothing seems more representative of national identities than political and administrative institutions. On paper, not one single country really shares the same legal and organizational blueprint with any of the other thirteen. On the other hand, societies and economies have for more than two hundred years evolved toward the same ends. Today, the case spectacular is the European Union. What the book underlines is that, in fact, Western democracies share some common principles and have a choice among four different types of organizational solutions and institutional designs. At least two reasons for optimism derive from such findings.

Local systems can be improved or changed. There is room for voluntary action. In other words, countries are not prisoners of specific Volksgeiste, functioning as a kind of iron cage that prevents any move not fitting basic cultural values. While the authors show that national and regional patterns exist, I am impressed by the rather weak impact of cleavages such as North versus South Europe or United States versus Europe. These findings suggest that despite national differences linked to history, religion, or whatever, some dynamic is at work that, beyond differences in legal and formal structures of municipalities, reflects convergences and commonalities inside a collective and professional field. This dynamic opens the way to something called management, but not to the exclusion of democracy.

Western countries have found stable and reliable ways to avoid two sins: clientelism, the triumph of political corruption over professional values, and technocracy, the triumph of self-proclaimed experts over representatives of the people. Leadership in municipalities combines democratic mechanisms and bureaucratic excellence. Politicians and elected bodies matter. So do administrative agencies and their appointed heads. Like firms, local bureaucracies rely on an integration process that may be called chief executive officership, and its impact extends beyond the boundaries of the administrative organization.

This book should be to public management what two publications, considered today as milestones, have been to business administration: *The Func-*

tions of the Executive by Chester Barnard (1938) and *The Manager's Job: Folklore and Fact* by Henry Mintzberg (1975). They opened a new perspective for knowledge, for training, and for action.

Leadership at the Apex offers a rigorous inventory of job dimensions, managerial functions, and roles that the person at the top of administrative agencies fulfils. It illuminates a silent partner in local government—the CEO. The fact is that for too many years, leadership in public administration has been a kind of black box.

Academics conformed to research perspectives that had stemmed from a heuristic surprise. In bureaucracies, it was discovered that people at the bottom of the hierarchy do not behave like robots; they may even have a lot of autonomy. Therefore, the way frontline subordinates behave matters. Since the landmark study of the Tennessee Valley Authority by Philip Selznick (1949), leadership and leaders have not been the main items on the agenda of sociology of organizations. When city government and subnational authorities were studied by political scientists, politicians and elected officials were found to be important sources of influence in addition to economic elites, but the role if not the existence of administrative officers was minimized. Political scientists, such as Robert Dahl (1961) in his research on New Haven entitled *Who Governs? Democracy and Power in an American City*, focus primarily on the way some groups or political actors may influence some policies. Nevertheless, this scientific tradition has not considered administrative officers to be relevant actors in the influence games called politics.

Elected officials tend to underestimate the relevance of what goes on inside the local bureaucratic machines. After all, why should one care about local administrators? In the second half of the 1980s, acting as the "general rapporteur" of the conference that gathers the ministers of public administration of the member states of the European Union, I took the floor to suggest that the agenda of a common policy should discuss some guidelines about the training and mobility of subnational administrators. The idea was immediately turned down. A minister from a large country told me that in none of the countries was this an urgent priority. He added that "we do not expect these employees to have any impact on any policy." By contrast, the conference spent more than half its time discussing training and mobility of national top civil servants.

The arrogance of a few elected officials is shared by some academics. Many researchers studying local elites have not included local administrators as relevant actors. Even local politicians tend to believe that the world is subdivided into two different categories. One matters—politics. The democratic ethos is fully endorsed. By definition public policies supposedly express the discretionary will of the persons elected for office. The other one—administration—matters much less. Appointed managers are expected to behave like anonymous subordinates implementing silently and mechanistically the decisions made at the top.

As the book shows, the borderline is less than clear-cut. A rather extensive grey zone exists, with many overlaps and ambiguities. Politics and administration may each reflect rationales and values that are to some extent incompatible. Nevertheless, the linkage between both has been unknown territory, territory that Mouritzen and Svara explore and describe in detail.

The book goes even further. It discusses leadership inside and outside bureaucracy and, leadership being one of its main ingredients, public management. Do mayors and other municipal, elected top officials realize what it means to manage administrative agencies? Are they effective at setting the agenda for their governments and cities? The answer is far from being predominantly positive. There is evidence that mayors are satisfied when CEOs emphasize two skills. CEOs must be loyal and, if not supportive of their policies and interests, at least neutral. CEOs should solve problems, not increase them. A good CEO is a person who does not burden the mayor, who keeps the municipal agencies from being the source of any issue that may be sensitive and appropriated by the local political arena. In other respects, CEOs get a rather free hand. *Leadership at the Apex* is a book any mayor should read because it shows that what is at stake and what CEOs do is much wider that they realize.

Do CEOs themselves fully appreciate what it means to be the top officer of an administrative system? Certainly they must possess some basic skills in fields such as finance, law, or control. They also operate with nearly the status of general manager. But what the position implies in terms of training and in daily life remains a rather confused picture. Leadership is not a one-man show, being a charismatic figure or sensitive to human relationships and interpersonal communication. Just to mention one of its facets, leadership also implies that leaders help their subordinates to become leaders themselves.

Leadership, management, vision, commitment, and efficiency—such fancy words define the essence of a hero in the modern world. For many years, one idea has been hammered home. Business sets the standards. If such heroes exist in real life, it is within the companies and private sector. By contrast, the administrative and public sector tells us a story of the past, characterized by dysfunction, rituals, and errors. It is the merit of Poul Erik Mouritzen and James Svara to remind us of two lessons.

One is that local government as such provides opportunities for excellence. Some cities perform better than others. The credit for success cannot be given only to the politicians, and the blame for failure does not lie solely with the CEO. The second lesson is that public administration is not identical to business administration. Certainly some practices in successful firms may be imitated. What works (or does not work) for the good in the corporate world may also work (or not work) for the good of the local communities. But readers of *Leadership at the Apex* will get a clear message. In many ways, it is much easier to be a CEO of a company than to be a CEO of a city's administrative machinery. In both cases, short-term pressures to create value and the relationship to stakeholders are part of his or her daily life. But a company CEO may care only about efficiency (quality, reliability, and cost of goods and services delivered), whereas a public agency CEO is also accountable de facto for effectiveness (how great an impact the policy has on the external world). Publicness shapes a much more complex task environment for executives. Policymaking implies choices and processes in which politicians are highly involved when not in full control. Effectiveness implies criteria of performance evaluation that are not codified and that are not consensual inside a community.

Municipal CEOs may not be glamorous heroes who make the cover of management magazines. But they play a key role in helping public agencies to deliver and politicians to be legitimate. What may be considered as a book about micromechanisms—management in local government—helps in fact to understand macroconsequences—how Western countries improvise formal and informal compromises, use what in French is called *bricolage*—in order to solve what has long been considered a basic dilemma, namely the linkage between bureaucracy and democracy.

Jean-Claude Thoenig
*Professor of sociology of organizations at INSEAD,
Fontainebleau, and senior research fellow in policy
analysis, National Center of Scientific Research,
Ecole Normale Supérieure de Cachan, France*

Preface

THIS BOOK IS A TESTAMENT TO THE VALUE OF COLLABORATION.
It is based on the unique comparative research project developed initially in
cooperation with the Association of the European Local Government Chief
Executives. The French acronym for this association—U.Di.T.E (Union des
Dirigeants Territoriaux de L'Europe)—gave the project its name, The U.Di.T.E.
Leadership Study. The project was expanded beyond Europe and supported
by the International City Management Association (ICMA) based in the
United States and the Australian Institute for Municipal Management
(AIMM). The collaboration with and encouragement from the practitioners
who head the city governments in the fourteen countries was a critical contribution to the inception of the project and its success in securing the
lengthy responses from over four thousand CEOs. We and the other members of the international research group extend our warm thanks to the
U.Di.T.E. board of directors, to the ICMA and the AIMM, and to the national
associations of local government CEOs who have all recommended their
members to participate in the study. We would also like to express our gratitude to the Danish Social Science Research Council and The Local Government VAT Fund for the support they provided to the overall study.

The survey process was coordinated by a group of committed scholars
who came together to shape a common survey instrument, conducted the
surveys in their separate countries, and then helped to prepare the common
data set for analysis. There has been a substantial investment of time and resources in joint planning and coordination to insure high-quality research,
data preparation, and analysis. Seven meetings of the research group were
held between 1995 and 1998, including two meetings to discuss cross-cutting
themes that would be developed in books including this one. Most of the
coding of questionnaires was done by researchers working together in

Odense. The project has been a model in cross-national collaboration in pursuit of common research interests.

The U.Di.T.E. Leadership Study covers many aspects of the daily life of the *highest ranking appointed administrative officials in municipalities*—the local government CEO. These include work values, role perceptions, relations between administrators and political leaders, career and mobility, leadership styles, cultural values, administrative reforms, decentralization, networks, influence patterns, and social characteristics, only a portion of which are covered by this work. A substantial number of reports, articles, and books have been published as a result of the project in the native languages of the participants. In September 1996, the preliminary results from ten countries were presented at the third U.Di.T.E. Congress in Odense, Denmark. A report from the Congress is available in Danish, French, and English (Goldsmith & Mouritzen, 1997). The present volume is the third of four planned books from the U.Di.T.E. Leadership Study. Two books have been published so far:

Klausen, K. K., and A. Magnier, eds. *The Anonymous Leader: Appointed CEOs in Western Local Government.* Odense: Odense University Press, 1998.

Dahler-Larsen, Peter, ed. *Social Bonds to City Hall: How Appointed Managers Enter, Experience, and Leave their Jobs in Western Local Government.* Odense: Odense University Press, 2001.

The fieldwork on which the present study rests was carried out from 1995 to 1997 at the beginning of a period that according to many observers would be characterized by an increasing convergence of political and administrative structures and cultures in Europe. The results presented in this book as well as our previous research and conversations with practitioners from different countries at the U.Di.T.E. congresses and other settings have taught us that structural and cultural convergence is not just round the corner. On the other hand, there is also evidence of increasing commonalities among CEOs across countries. Whether or not convergence is going to happen, at what pace it is going to happen, and whether it is found to be positive or negative, this book is intended to kick off future studies. We hope that future generations of political scientists will replicate (and improve) our study at regular intervals. In other words, the design of the study and the methodology used will allow future generations to trace important aspects of the process of European integration, that is, the preconditions for effective cross-national interaction of political and administrative elites and for the exchange of ideas, models, and modes of thinking across the borders of the European nation-states. This book in particular, and the results of the U.Di.T.E. Leadership Study in general, contains historical knowledge as it describes the values, outlook, norms, dispositions, and activities of a European sub-elite at a particular point in time.

This book should also send a warning signal. We hope it will put a damper on the tendency of many Western researchers, consultants, and practitioners to engage in well-meant but often ill-placed efforts to help other countries design new institutions of local government. Often these "new designs" are gross replicas of the institutions with which they are familiar from their own country. Recently, there have been many such efforts in which Americans, Danes, Englishmen, Norwegians, Frenchmen, and others helped the Eastern European and Baltic countries establish new institutions of local democracy. Asian and African countries have over the years experienced a similar influx of well-intentioned advisors. Since institutions and cultures act as blinders, we all have a tendency to interpret new situations in terms of our familiar perspective. An American city manager would never recommend a strong mayor system like the one found in France. And his or her French colleague would probably not dream of emphasizing the advantages of the council-manager system. And neither of the two would recommend a Danish or Swedish committee-leader form of government.

Different forms of government bring together different concerns and principles. They represent different mixtures of representative democracy and the laymen rule, political leadership, and professionalism. They prescribe different roles for elected and appointed officials. They affect the ability of political and administrative leaders to act effectively to solve common problems. Finally, they affect the distribution of power and influence of politicians and administrators. All these effects, however, occur within a cultural context and interact with other political institutions (e.g., political party systems) that vary from country to country. The same institution can operate somewhat differently depending on the country in which it is found. In order for the consequences of choices to be anticipated, the possible effects of using various institutions should be laid out. As those consequences are to some extent dependent also on national cultures and political tradition, any professional advisor needs to focus on the characteristics of particular countries and how they may interact with structure. In short, this book is intended to guide reformers of government and help them reflect about the variety of possible outcomes in the process of institutional design. At a minimum, we hope the discussion raises awareness of the cultural traits of the countries in which they work and, maybe most importantly, about the impact of their own cultural blinders.

Readers will observe that there is some overrepresentation of Danish and American information when we go beyond the survey data in our analysis and interpretation. Obviously the authors know much more about their own countries, about local government research covering their own countries, and about cases and incidents that can be used to highlight some of the general patterns or problems found in our data. Some readers might even suggest that the authors carry within their minds a Danish/American frame of reference that brings a certain bias into the analysis and the interpretation that we present. We have our own blinders. To some extent this is unavoidable, although in our own defense, we can assert that engaging in comparative studies helps to reduce biases of this sort. When one studies other countries, one learns a great deal about the basics of one's own country.

Our viewpoints have been broadened considerably by our interactions with the other scholars involved in the overall project and in discussions about this book. During this study, the participating researchers have spent nearly three weeks together at seven meetings, including a week-long data confrontation seminar in Hanstholm on the northwestern coast of Denmark in January. At the seminar about twenty participants worked day and night on the survey results in order to develop a common understanding of the data and the problems associated with the analysis of the data. It has been a pleasure to work so closely and smoothly with thirty-five colleagues from the fourteen countries, and we owe every one of them great thanks for their excellent work and enthusiastic participation. They are all listed in the appendix. We have developed warm friendships during this project as well as establishing constructive professional exchanges.

For assistance in the preparation of this book, special thanks go to Marcel van Dam and Geert Neelen who helped organize a special study of political advice in the Netherlands and to James Brunet for organizing the study in the United States. Dam and Neelen also contributed to the development of chapter 4. Also we extend our warm thanks to Jean-Claude Thoenig with whom we spent several days discussing ideas and drafts and who persistently forced us to address the grand issues and not simply focus on the nitty-gritty of data analysis. Finally, we want to extend our thanks to Jørgen Grønnegaard Christensen, Geert Hofstede, Guy Peters, Richard Stillman, and an anonymous reviewer for University of Pittsburgh Press for their constructive comments on an earlier version of the manuscript.

Several young scholars who have joined or in the future may join the professoriat worked as research assistants and project coordinators on the U.Di.T.E. Leadership Study. Mads Rieper, Ulrik Kjær, Niels Ejersbo, Lene Anderson, and Steffen Petersen spent numerous days over a six-year period from 1994 to 2000 coding, communicating, registering, advising, and helping in many other ways. They made immeasurable contributions connecting the disparate parts and keeping the project on track to the creation of a first-class data set that all the researchers have used. We both benefited from the assistance of staff members in our respective offices. In particular, Vibeke Pierson in Odense and Carol Apperson in Raleigh helped to move the project along in a variety of ways. Students in our courses read drafts of the work and offered useful feedback. Finally, "our" faculty colleagues in Odense gave their time generously to read our papers and listen to our ideas and were insightful in their comments and suggestions.

We would like to express our appreciation to the editorial staff at University of Pittsburgh Press for their help. Niels Aaboe—familiar with both countries—guided this Danish-American project to completion, and Marilyn Prudente offered careful editing assistance that smoothed our writing. Dennis Lloyd, John Zaphyr, Craig Jennion, and Maria Sticco handled promotion.

We owe a great debt of gratitude to our wives—Lene and Claudia. Their support, encouragement, and tolerance of the time and effort devoted to this project helped to sustain us throughout the long process of research and writing. For their sake (and ours as well) we are pleased that the project has provided the opportunity for our wives and children to get to know each other.

Let us close as we opened by acknowledging the importance of collaboration. This book is the result of our own interaction and the extensive debating and sharing of ideas and perspectives that has occurred over the past four years. The book is a great example of how the whole can exceed the sum of the parts. Whether or not we have succeeded in meeting our objectives in this book, it is different and far better than two books we could have written separately.

CHAPTER 1

Studying Institutions
and Leadership Comparatively

ARE INSTITUTIONS CHOSEN FOR A REASON? Do they matter? Is leadership shaped by institutions at all, only generally, or in detail? If we change institutions, will practice change as a consequence, independently of the characteristics of the society and the acquired dispositions of its people? In this comparative study of the top local government leaders in fourteen Western countries, we explore these big issues in political science and public administration.

This book focuses on two interwoven questions. First, do institutions matter? What are the consequences of alternative political-administrative institutions? Second, do leaders matter? What impact do the differing individual and collective characteristics of officials have on their performance? We search for the answers to these questions in the intensive interaction of political and administrative leaders that occurs at the "apex"[1] of the governmental process in local government. In this interaction of top officials where the legislative meets the executive function, the political and administrative logics may converge or collide, the political and administrative levels of government may be tied together or remain separate, and the individuals who occupy political and administrative office may conflict or cooperate. The object of the study is to determine what happens at the apex of leadership where the two types of officials come together to shape local governance.

Cast in its most general form, the question, Do institutions matter? is as old as political science and political theory, dating at least back to Aristotle's classification of constitutions. Under the label "The New Institutionalism" it is now one of the most prominent and promising fields of inquiry within the discipline of political science (March and Olsen 1989, 1995; Hall and Taylor 1996; Peters 1999a, 1999b). It is the aim of our book to contribute to the theoretical and empirical literature on institutions. We show that institutions matter a lot.

Do leaders matter? is another enduring question in the study of society. In the study of history, some like Carlyle have placed great emphasis on the impact of leaders in shaping human events, whereas others like Marx have focused on the social and economic forces that sweep leaders along in their path (Gardner 1990, 6). In the current events of cities around the world, the question takes a different form. Are the individuals who occupy public office so completely constrained by the structure in which they operate or the circumstances of their community that their characteristics and behavior make no difference? We show that leaders vary in their behavior both within as well as across institutions.

They also vary across countries in part because of differences in national culture. Among the core questions for any reformer of political institutions, there are always two: Who has power to decide what? and What rules and procedures will be followed to attain desired ends? The Dutch scholar Geert Hofstede has studied how the answers to these questions differ across nations and regions of the world, reflecting some deeper dispositional structures of their people (see Hofstede 1980, 1997). Through the major institutions of society—the family, schools, and workplace—individuals learn that there are certain "natural" ways to respond to the two questions. What is natural, however, is different from country to country. In some countries power differences are expected and accepted. In others they are illegitimate. In some countries individuals learn to cope with complexity and uncertainty by relying on rules, structure, and stability. In others people do not feel threatened by the absence of rules, or they comfortably work around the rules. Despite the fundamental questions about power and rules raised and answered by Hofstede, his work is surprisingly unknown among political scientists. It is the aim of this book to demonstrate that the differences in national cultures have political and organizational significance. Institutions matter a great deal, but to a large extent they reflect, are embedded in, and tend to reproduce deeply rooted national cultural traits.

The focus of the study—the relations between politicians and administrators—is a relatively new theme that accompanied the emergence of the modern state and the rise of democracy. As an issue in institutional design, it dates back over a century and a half, and it has been a focus of scholarly inquiry for 100 years. The idea of separation of major functions of government has roots in the writings of Montesquieu, and the need for a division of politics and administration was directly stated by Vivien in 1853 (Martin 1987, 298). It underlay the Northcote-Trevelyan report of 1853 that laid the foundation for clarifying the distinction between political and administrative staff and for improving the professionalism and increasing the cohesion of the British civil service. It was the concern of Woodrow Wilson who sought to establish public administration as a field distinct from politics, and of Max Weber who advanced the idea of administrative organizations bound to observing impersonal rules based on law rather than the dictates of a political master.[2] The democracy-bureaucracy issue has been a recurring theme in the past century. This book contributes to the literature by expanding our theoretical and empirical understanding of the interactions between elected officials and appointed administrators. Are the latter neutral executors of the will of the former, or are administrators self-directed? Is there a clear division of labor between the two roles, or is the relationship characterized by extensive interaction, overlapping functions, and reciprocal influence? These focused questions are among the many we address in the book. We also use perspectives on institutionalism to help interpret our findings and suggest ways that our findings can clarify the different approaches to studying institutions.

Our focus is on the "constitutions" of local government, that is, their "form of government." It is a surprisingly disregarded problem in the comparative literature. Comparative studies of local government have focused on the position of local governments in the larger political-administrative system of countries (Gurr and King 1987; Bennett 1993), central-local relations (Goldsmith and Page 1987), the functions performed by local government (Goldsmith and Wolman 1992), the fiscal autonomy and capabilities at the local level (Newton 1980; Sharpe 1981; Clarke 1989; Mouritzen 1992), the rise and spread of the new political culture (Clark and Hoffmann-Martinot 1998), and democracy in big cities (Gabriel, Hoffmann-Martinot, and Savitch 2000). There have been extensive American writings on the strong-mayor form of government and the council-manager form of government (Banfield and Wilson 1963; Lineberry and Fowler 1967; Svara 1990a). Still, in the United States and other countries, the formal and informal rules that affect the way power is gained, maintained, expanded, and shared have almost exclusively been the occupation of scholars writing about their own country in their own language.

A few studies touch more directly upon the subject. Rose (1996) reports on a comparative study of local government CEOs in the four Nordic countries, Finland, Sweden, Norway, and Denmark.[3] The value system of local elites is the focus of the ongoing Democracy and Local Governance project, which has surveyed local leaders, mayors, council people, and party activists—but not administrators—in thirty-one countries all over the world (see, for instance, Eldersveld, Strömberg, and Derksen 1995). Finally, reforms of "the political executive" was the subject of a collection of articles covering five European countries (Batley and Campbell 1992).

Presently, there seems to be an increasing discussion about the possibilities of reforming local democracy through institutional changes. In some places institutional change has taken place. The Greater London Area has installed its first directly elected mayor, and British scholars are discussing the possibilities of reinvigorating local democracy by borrowing the idea of executive mayors from other countries (Clarke et al. 1996; Hambleton 2000). The British government has characterized the current committee system as confusing and inefficient and has pushed for alternative modes of political management of councils, including among others cabinets and directly elected mayors with a full-time manager appointed by the council (DETR 1998).

The Norwegian government has allowed municipalities to experiment with directly elected mayors also with an eye to increasing the interest of citizens in local affairs. So far there has been little success, maybe because there was no simultaneous transfer of real executive powers to the directly elected mayor.[4] In Germany, the city manager system is under increasing attack, and since 1990 an increasing number of localities have implemented a strong-mayor system with directly elected mayors.[5] In Denmark, three of the largest cities, Copenhagen, Odense, and Aalborg, changed their constitutions in 1998 from the traditional magistrate (or cabinet) form to the committee-leader form, which is present in all other Danish municipalities, apparently with a smooth subsequent change in behavior and procedures. And in the United States, at any time some cities are considering a change from the strong-mayor form to the council-manager form, or vice versa, or deciding what form to use when the city comes into existence through the act of incorporation. Even more cities consider revisions in their charter that will alter the relative authority of elected and administrative officials. At some point, as in a controversial charter revision in Cincinnati in 1999, it is difficult to determine whether changing specific provisions amounts to changing the form of government.[6] This book is intended to serve as a source of information and guidance for reformers of local government all over the world.

We contribute to the comparative literature on local government by the development and application of a typology of forms of government. Four forms are distinguished. First, the *strong-mayor* form is based on an elected executive as the central figure of the government. Second, the *committee-leader* form is based on the sharing of executive powers between a political leader and standing committees. Third, the *collective* form features the collective leadership of the executive committee of the council. Fourth, the *council-manager* form has a council headed by a non-executive mayor and an appointed executive—the city manager. It is demonstrated throughout the book that form of government makes a difference for what happens at the apex of leadership. Indeed, form of government has a greater impact than any other factor. Some findings are expected, whereas others are unexpected and provocative. The use of forms of government that differ substantially in their characteristics together with cultural differences would lead one to expect wide variation across countries.

The method used is comparative. There is comparison across the fourteen countries included in the study: Australia, Belgium, Denmark, Finland, France, Ireland, Italy, the Netherlands, Norway, Portugal, Spain, Sweden, United Kingdom, and United States. With the exception of Luxembourg, Austria, Greece, and Germany, all member countries of the European Union are covered.[7] We particularly regret the omission of Germany, the largest member state of the European Union. Its inclusion would have been interesting for the purpose of the book because two types of institutions are found in the different Länder (states): the strong-mayor type and the city manager type (Larsen 2000). It is regrettable that a larger number and greater diversity of countries could not be included in the study.[8] It does, however, encompass a sizeable number of countries with similar historical backgrounds along with variation across certain important characteristics. The sample of countries exhibits institutional and cultural variety along dimensions we want to measure, which allows us to replace country names with variable names that encompass aggregations of countries—a goal of comparative research identified by Przeworski and Teune (1970).

The study also examines the similarities and differences between local government CEOs and other types of administrative officials in higher-level governments and officials in lower-level positions in local government. The study focuses on the top administrators in local governments, whereas many of the models and findings of previous studies in political science and public administration have been drawn from research on national governments. As indicated later in this introductory chapter, there are some expected differences between patterns found in national and local government. In the conclusion (chapter 10), we consider whether generalizations about political behavior and political-administrative relations can be drawn from research on local government to be applied to governmental institutions generally. It is also important to consider how the top administrators compare with administrators who have lower rank in local government. It would be a mistake to assume that all local administrators are the same in their values and behavior. We do not have data for either officials in higher-level governments or administrators below the CEO in local government. We will seek to identify, however, which of our conclusions might be applicable to these other officials and which are not.

The Importance of Studying Local Government

Municipalities are the level of government closest to citizens. These governments respond to the most diverse populations and to the most intense social, economic, and political problems within each country. Although countries vary in the degree of ethnic heterogeneity and inequality, the greatest diversity and the widest range of conditions are usually found within the boundaries of cities. Conflicts over values and the distribution of resources have personal immediacy in local government with a variety of individuals and groups living, working, and politicking side by side. Municipalities are (along with other local governments in some countries) responsible for delivering a wide array of services. Some of these are developed locally and others are formed and funded at higher levels of government but delivered locally. The participants in city politics—elected officials and other politicians, administrators, and citizens—interact face-to-face. Constituents are potentially the neighbors or associates of elected officials. Citizens are real people who receive services often directly from a "street-level bureaucrat" rather than abstractions as they may be to administrators at higher levels of government. At the local level, there is also the greatest participation of a growing number of nonprofit organizations and nongovernmental institutions that seek to address social problems. Local governments have been at the forefront of new public management reforms with the most extensive experimentation with contracting out, privatization, and other new methods for providing "public" services. To a greater or lesser extent, municipalities have both the need and the capability to shape themselves and determine how they will develop. Thus, at the local level, it is possible to observe the process of working out issues of governance—how a society determines needs and goals and seeks to deal with them through collective, although not necessarily governmental, action.

The range of municipal services varies greatly by country reflecting cultural traits, prevailing ideas about size and role of government in general, and the approach to intergovernmental relations and how responsibilities are divided among governments. Countries differ in the size of the public sector, the degree of decentralization of service provision, and the extent of governmental consolidation. As discussed in chapter 3, there are three clusters of local governments represented by the countries in this study. There are municipalities that are major contributors to the welfare state (particularly in Scandinavia) or to high levels of collective consumption goods, such as in Britain. There is a blend of "clientelistic" provision of specific public goods to small constituencies and broadly provided welfare services in the cities in Southern European countries. Finally, some governments focus on supporting the development of the municipalities and providing the physical, security, and cultural services needed or demanded by people living in the concentrated residential patterns found in cities, for example, the municipalities (as opposed to the county governments) in the United States. Thus, it is important to study local governments for their variation in size, their policy orientation, and their scope of services.

The Apex and the Objects of the Study

At the core of our study is an interest in officials. We examine how they are shaped by the institutions in which they operate, how they are impacted by the political environment and culture in which they work, and how they fill the positions individually and in combination with each other. The core concern is how officials, who sit atop the political and administrative spheres of government, interact with each other.

The *apex of leadership* is where the top-level officials come in contact with each other. It is possible that the contact could produce friction with one set or the other seeking to achieve dominance. It is possible that the two sets of officials could maintain their distance and carefully regulate their exchanges to reduce interference in the sphere of the other official. Finally, it is possible that a positive linkage of the political and administrative dimensions of government could occur and that combined leadership would emerge among top officials.

The idea of the apex comes from Peter Self (1972, 150–51) whose view of what happens at the apex reinforces the expectation of a blending of leadership. He visualizes the governmental process as an arch with the left arc representing the political process and the right arc the administrative process. There is a "junction" at the top of the arch that represents the critical point at which political will flows into and energizes the administrative systems. It is also the point at which influences that have been generated within the administrative process flow back into the higher levels of the political process. There is thus, at the apex of the arch, a fusion of political and administrative influences that have been generated lower down the two arcs.

We examine in depth this joining and blending identified by Self. In the analysis, we consider how the political and administrative leaders at the top of each sphere—usually the mayor and the CEO in local government—relate to and impact each other as they meet at the apex of the governmental process.

As Self anticipated, we demonstrate that there is closeness between the two types of officials, extensive exchange, and mutual impact, although there is also variation in these characteristics related to governmental structure, culture, nature of leadership, and individual and community characteristics. Indeed, this work is a major addition to the limited number of studies of what we are beginning to recognize as the complementary—but still potentially contentious—relationship between politicians and administrators (e.g., Aberbach and Rockman 2000).

The Primary Object of the Study: The Local Government CEO

Understanding the nature of leadership provided by the appointed executive in local government has been an intellectual challenge for scholars and an ongoing puzzle for practitioners. It is apparent to any close observer that top administrators are important figures in their cities. Still, little is known in a systematic way about the nature and extent of their contributions to the political process or the factors that might explain variations in their contributions.

The official surveyed was the highest appointed administrator, identified by titles such as chief executive officer (CEO), city manager, secrétaire générale, ràdmann, municipal secretary, stadsdirektör, kommunaldirektör, segretari comunali, or chief administrative officer in different countries. For simplicity, we refer to these officials as chief executive officers or CEOs.[9] Although objections might be raised to the use of this term, it is better than the alternatives. "City manager" implies a particular form of government used only in a few of the countries under study. "Top administrator," "city administrator," or "chief administrative officer" do not clearly convey the executive dimension of the position.

To be precise, we should always refer to this official as the "appointed CEO," to prevent confusion with the mayor in strong-mayor cities in which mayors have more executive authority than the top administrator. Even in these countries, however, the term CEO is not inappropriate. The term implies a staff member rather than an elected official, as in the British convention of distinguishing politicians from officials in government office. Purists might want to think of the CEO as chief executive "official." The official under question has executive as well as administrative authority and is the "chief" among administrators, that is, the first among equals even in cities with other important administrators.[10] The term does not suit the mayor in these cities (or in cities with other forms in which the mayor has executive authority). Such mayors are more than a CEO; they are analogous to the head of state or the political chief as well as being the head of government. There are differences in the amount of executive authority that CEOs have and in the extent to which executive authority is shared between the top administrator and elected officials. Still, all the officials included in the survey exercise at least de facto a substantial part of the executive authority in their jurisdiction and occupy a central position in which they interact directly with the top elected official and some or all council members. Thus, they occupy a position that is clearly at the apex of leadership.

The Job of the Local Government CEO

The appointed CEO stands at the interface of the political and administrative spheres in government. He or she interacts closely with top politicians, staff, the media, and the public in shaping the municipal agenda and assuring that approved policies and programs are carried out appropriately. He or she is concerned about the interactions with higher-level governments as well as other local governments, particularly in the surrounding area.

Similarities and Differences between CEOs and Other Administrators

When compared with other high-ranking administrators, municipal CEOs are distinctive for three reasons. First, unlike career administrators at other levels of government, they interact directly with elected representatives without the mediation of other politicians or politically appointed, short-term administrators. This condition makes local government a propitious venue in which to observe the apex of leadership between top officials from the political and administrative spheres. Second, the CEO has the authority to directly control at least part of the governmental organization—and in some countries all of the organization—as opposed to being only the assistant to the political executive as is true at other levels of government. This condition makes it possible to examine how CEOs define their administrative responsibilities and balance these with other aspects of the position. Third, by virtue of a municipal government's proximity to the citizens it serves, the CEO has extensive opportunities for contact with the citizens, interest groups, and other key actors who head agencies, businesses, institutions in the locality, other local governments, and higher-level governments. Variations in networking—what external actors are considered to be important and how much contact the administrator has with them—can be measured.

Furthermore these unusual features are simultaneous and interrelated. Because of their access to individual political leaders, organizational control, public contact, and intergovernmental relations, the potential influence of CEOs is enhanced as they interact with the mayor and the city council. Not all CEOs are equally engaged in all the dimensions of the position, but all have the possibility of actively filling these roles. As we shall see, they are constrained by a number of factors, but within parameters set by institutions, political culture, and community characteristics, they are free to fashion a potentially extraordinary leadership position. Once we understand how local CEOs put together the elements of their position and how they use their resources, it may be possible to discern variations of the same behavior among other types of administrators.

There are some other potential differences between the local top administrators and administrators in higher-level governments or at the departmental level in local governments that may affect the generalizability of findings from this study. First, the politicians with whom administrators interact may be weaker. Whereas the party leaders in parliaments have their hands on "the levers of power in the modern state" (Aberbach, Putnam, and Rockman 1981, 3), at the local level, the mayor who is usually the leading politician is not necessarily a party leader nor a powerful leader. Second, it is common to view administrators as focused on a particular functional area or sector. Aberbach, Putnam, and Rockman (1981, 11) assume that at the national level "cross-sector aggregation of interests . . . is typically the province of politicians." This generalization, however, would not apply to the staff in the office of the prime minister or the finance ministry, and CEOs are more like these officials than their own department heads. They are necessarily generalists who seek to bring together the diverse functions provided by their governments.

Other perceived differences between politicians and administrators seem less plausible when viewed from the local perspective or may simply be less appropriate now than previously. Aberbach, Putnam, and Rockman (12) view bureaucrats as having a narrow range of value commitments. Although administrators do not have the "partisan passions" of politicians, there would be substantial disagreement with their assertion that administrators generally at every level of government are lacking in "ideals." A large body of literature in American public administration (e.g., Marini 1971; Frederickson 1996; Wamsley et al. 1990; Terry 1995; Cooper 1998) stresses the value commitments of public administrators. Evidence presented in chapter 4 shows that local government CEOs are committed to action and advocacy. Aberbach, Putnam, and Rockman (1981, 12) also asserted that administrators focus solely on "short-term feasibility," but top local administrators would not necessarily share this perspective. Long-term sustained efforts are often required to accomplish objectives in local government. Commonly, it is politicians who seek to promote short-range interests and administrators who press for long-term solutions or the maintenance of effort to achieve prior commitments. A former English CEO attributed this remark to one of the persons who had served as council leader in his city: "Terry, you look after the long-term strategies. We will make the decisions which really matter," meaning the week-by-week decisions on which the council leader's reelection depended.[11]

Given these differences, it is possible that local government CEOs will bring a different orientation to the governmental process than has been found in national level studies. They may be broader in their views, more committed to ideals, and more oriented to long-term goals than bureaucrats at other levels of government.

CEOs apparently are different from other top administrators in some respects and similar in others. Some generalizations drawn from studying CEOs may be applicable to administrators at other levels of government when their circumstances approximate those of the CEO. For example, other administrators may offer similar levels of policy and political advice when they have a generalist position, proximity to key politicians, and sufficient trust. CEOs may seem atypical because they operate on the boundaries of their profession at the point of transmission between the political and the administrative realms. These characteristics may make CEOs prototypical rather than anomalous. By observing these extraordinarily engaged administrative leaders, we may be able to achieve new insights about the contributions that professional administrators can make to policy making and public management and better general understanding of the relationship of politics and administration at the apex of leadership in general.

At the local level, CEOs diverge from other administrators in their own governments in some respects and share other characteristics. One potential difference stands out. As top-level administrators, they may have different incentive structures than lower-level staff. As Dunleavy (1991) suggests, the CEO is quite unlikely to pursue private interests through budget expansion. Administrators at the department level and below, on the other hand, may be more inclined to be budget maximizers because they focus on their part of the organization rather than on the whole city. In other respects they may be similar. Other high-level administrators in local government have some of the contact with elected officials that CEOs do, share their close interaction with citizens, and help formulate and interpret policy from the perspective of their department. They may have exchanges with elected officials about sensitive political matters regarding service delivery to constituents or the details of implementing programs. Self (1972, 151) suggests that the amount of interaction between the political and administrative processes declines as one moves away from the apex: "the great bulk of administrative operations continues in political obscurity, and the main interactions between politics and administration occur at the top levels of government." Still, at the local level, obscurity may be overcome by proximity for officials throughout the organization because "political activity is like lightning, in that it may suddenly strike into any corner of the administrative system, but only rarely does" (Self 1972, 151). Thus, the apex of leadership includes those with high position, but lower-level administrators share many behaviors with the CEO and experience some of the same pressures from the political environment.

The Secondary Object of the Study: The Mayor

We are also interested in studying top political leaders. Even though we have surveyed only the CEO, many of the questions also provide information about the nature of leadership provided by the highest elected official. For most countries, without question the top official is the mayor. In some countries, the mayor may merely have ceremonial functions and preside over meetings of the city council, but he or she is still the top politician. There are three exceptions to this generalization that are fully explained in chapter 3:

there are two contenders for the political leader designation in Finland, the council leader rather than the mayor is the key political leader in Britain, and the mayor in Holland is not an ordinary politician. For simplicity, we use the term mayor throughout the book but the top politician is not always the mayor.

Conceptual Framework

No particular school or theoretical approach guided the U.Di.T.E. Leadership Study. A rather open conceptual framework was established early on to accommodate different substantive interests and modes of inquiry among the participating researchers. This research group consisted of political scientists (the largest segment), sociologists, and public administrationists.[12]

The framework indicated the major categories of variables to be investigated and the relations between them. Five foci of research—sets of dependent variables—were identified:

- roles of administrative and political leaders
- decision making and distribution of influence
- networking activities of CEOs
- organizational change behavior on the part of the CEO
- job motivation

This book explores aspects of the first three of these foci of research.[13] The behavior, attitudes, and outlooks of local government CEOs were expected to be a function of three sets of factors:

- characteristics that can be attributed to the individual chief executive officer (social background, education, and career)
- characteristics attributable to the particular local government or community in which the CEO works (social, political, organizational, and economic environment)
- country characteristics (form of government, scope and autonomy of local government, and national culture)

A modified version of the original framework underlies the analyses in the present volume (see fig. 1.1). At the center of our focus are top officials, and the investigation examines five aspects of what happens at the apex: the activities of the CEOs, their involvement in political advice, their definition of the ideal politician, their levels of influence, and the types of partnerships between them and the key politicians. (These five aspects are analyzed in chap-

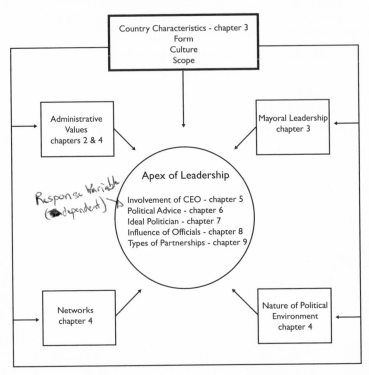

Figure 1.1 Conceptual framework

ters 5–9.) How do CEOs differ in the importance they assign to policy innovation and administrative functions? Why is it that some top administrators are heavily involved in giving political advice while others shy away from such activities? Or why do some CEOs accept political interference in administrative affairs while others try to keep politicians at arm's length? Why do some CEOs "penetrate" the political sphere from below? And why do some accept "penetration" from above by politicians? These are a few examples of the kind of questions we seek to answer in our analysis of the activities at the apex.

At the most general level, the answers can be found in differences attached to the country level. These are factors that may vary across countries but are constant for all CEOs and local government units within a particular country. Chapter 3 focuses on three such country variables: form of government, scope of government, and national cultures.

What differs within countries and between CEOs and localities are four sets of variables that potentially may have important implications for what happens at the apex of leadership. First, mayors differ. Some occupy office at the mercy of a fragile coalition of parties, whereas others have consolidated their power over decades in office. Some are proactive, visible, and deeply engaged in policy making and administrative detail, whereas others are reactive, invisible, and detached caretakers. Formal structure defines the overall parameters of the office. Form of government and national culture are likely to affect mayoral leadership, but offices are filled in particular ways, in some instances to the extent that the structure seems to be transformed by leadership. The type of leadership provided by mayors may as a consequence differ within the same form of government. The activities at the apex are likely to be affected by the type of mayoral leadership. Weak mayors may create a vacuum to be filled by a strong administrator. Or it may be the other way around. A powerful administrator may be enabled by an effective mayor. (Mayoral leadership is introduced in chapter 3.)

Second, CEOs may bring different values with them based on their educational background, previous experience, and the like. In chapter 4, values concerning neutrality, advocacy, and political responsibility are introduced. Are administrators committed to political neutrality and does this commitment preclude or coexist with a desire to make government a force for change and to help the disadvantaged in society? Should CEOs be responsible primarily to the political leadership or to citizens? Should they have the same political opinion as the majority of the local council? From the answers to these questions, it is possible to distinguish contrasting attitudes about how CEOs relate to the political process, including stances of accountable responsiveness and independent neutrality.

The third set of intervening variables relates to the nature of the political environment. Political parties may be at war with each other, or all decisions in a municipality may be made in a consensual atmosphere with political battles being nonexistent or confined to the electoral arena. Signals from the political leadership may be clear and unambiguous or they may be absent or confusing. Pressures from the local community or other levels of government may overwhelm the CEO with demands that far exceed the economic resources of the community. These factors are introduced in chapter 4.

Finally, CEOs can exercise some choice about how much communication they have with certain actors within government (other relationships are essentially fixed by structure) and with a wide range of actors in the community. CEOs may be internally oriented or be active "networkers." These issues are also covered in chapter 4, and in subsequent chapters these characteristics as well as the other environmental factors are considered possible factors that affect the behavior of CEOs. The conceptual framework is designed to identify differences across localities, countries, and forms of government. To explain these characteristics, we can utilize factors measured by the survey such as the leadership style of the mayor, the characteristics of the CEO, and the environment in which they work. Certain commonalities, however, in outlook, values, and activities stand out. For example, CEOs are heavily involved in policymaking and they generally want the elected officials to set broad goals. Can these results be explained by the common location in the apex or by a cross-national professional consciousness? To explain commonalities, as well as some of the differences, it is necessary to go beyond the factors directly measured in the study and consider the nature of institutions and their impact on the attitudes and behavior of persons who work in them.

Thinking about Institutions and Their Impact on Behavior

The term "institution" has been used in a variety of ways. It can refer precisely and concretely to specific governmental structures such as forms of government. Defined broadly in the new institutionalist research, an institution is a collection of interrelated rules and routines that constitute a formal or informal structure with stability over time and affect the behavior of individuals (Peters 1999a, 18).

In order to explain the relationships among variables used in this study, some behavioral assumptions that connect the individual with the overall institutional framework are required. We will use a simple scheme for understanding institutions based on four perspectives that are borrowed from Peters's (1999a) incisive analysis of the variants of "institutionalism." The four are old institutionalism, empirical institutionalism, rational choice institutionalism, and normative institutionalism.

First, there was an emphasis on the old institutionalism in the early stages of the development of political science and public administration, imposing a legalistic, structuralist, and normative perspective on institutions. It was legalistic because it emphasized law as the essential element of government; it was structuralist because it assumed that the behavior of individuals was determined by structure; and it was normative because its proponents had a concern for good government. Theorists and activist reformers sought to design ideal structures and vigorously advocated them. The American municipal reform movement, which was closely aligned with academic political science, reflected the old institutionalist perspective. This approach was dismissed in later times as prescriptive and simplistic. The former characteristic was apt but the "model" institutional arrangement proposed for cities was more complex than is usually recognized. (This issue is explored more fully in chapter 2.) The interest in institutional design was linked to simple atheoretical research efforts to describe the differences between institutional arrangements. Presumably, the underlying explanatory premise was that institutions determine behavior and promote intended outcomes.

There were early empirical critiques of the prescriptive model—"that's not the way things work in practice"—and the identification of factors that could explain the discrepancy between the supposed ideal and reality. These critiques merged with the behavioral revolt in social sciences and the denigration of a narrow "institutional" emphasis in public administration as implied by the old institutionalists.[14] A new *empirical institutionalism* shares some of the characteristics of the traditional approach; however, its proponents leave it open for empirical investigation if and to what extent structure affects the behavior of individuals. A great deal of comparative research on governmental structure is based on an interest in comparing the impact of structures on behavior and outcomes, for instance, the difference in performance between presidential and parliamentary systems of government or the ability to govern in majoritarian and consensual systems (Peters 1999a, 80 ff). In many respects, our study may be characterized as empirical institutionalism. We maintain that institutions matter only if we can demonstrate through the use of methods accepted by empirical social science that different institutional arrangements lead actors to behave in different ways. It is one thing, however, to demonstrate the impacts of institutions. Another is to explain how they affect individuals. Empirical institutionalism has been criticized for producing "credible findings without a strong theoretical basis for explanation" (Peters 1999a, 80). Rational choice institutionalism and normative institutionalism offer such explanations.

Rational choice institutionalism builds on three assumptions. One, individuals have a fixed set of preferences, that is, preferences are exogenous. Two, individuals seek the biggest possible benefits and the least costs in their decisions, that is, they behave rationally. Three, they try to maximize their personal welfare, that is, they are driven by egoistic motives. The calculus of benefits and costs is framed by institutions whose rules forbid, require, or permit some actions or outcomes (Ostrom 1986, 7). As North (1990, 26) puts it, "Institutions alter the price paid for one's convictions and hence play a critical role in the extent to which nonwealth-maximizing motivations influence choices." The rational types of explanations are based on a logic of consequentiality: Courses of action are chosen because they have certain beneficial consequences for the decision maker (March and Olsen 1989). We assume that local government CEOs seek to advance their interests broadly defined, including a preference for stability, autonomy, and personal gain.

The fourth perspective is *normative institutionalism*, the approach propounded by March and Olsen in their call for a new emphasis on institutionalism in political science. In this approach, behavior is based on premises that are shaped by institutions rather than being fundamentally based on a pursuit of self-interest. In the view of March and Olsen, "Human action is driven less by anticipation of its uncertain consequences and preferences for them than by a 'logic of appropriateness'"(March and Olsen 1995, 28). When following this logic, officials act in ways that will meet expectations. "Institutionalized rules, duties, rights, and roles define acts as appropriate (normal, natural, right, good) or inappropriate (uncharacteristic, unnatural, wrong, bad)" (March and Olsen 1995, 31). Appropriateness is shaped not only by the norms of a particular government but also by the standards of organizations that span governmental boundaries, for example, city administrators as a professional group, and by national cultural traits. Expectations about how individuals should relate to each other are affected by values regarding power and rules that are widely held in a society.

Our research was not designed to sort out institutional models. Still, we will examine the findings to answer some key questions that are derived from the alternative perspectives. Following the longstanding interest in comparing institutional structures, we will elaborate with care how different structures—particularly forms of government and alternative ways of designing the positions of mayor, city council, and chief executive—affect attitudes and behavior of officials. For example, we are interested in knowing how different institutional arrangements create conditions for official actors to have more or less involvement and more or less influence. We shall also use the rational choice institutionalist and normative institutionalist perspectives to interpret our findings throughout the book and in the concluding chapter. Do officials act with an eye to promoting their personal interests, guided by the logic of consequentiality, or do they seek to meet normative expectations, guided by the logic of appropriateness?

Data and Methods

Leadership at the Apex is based on data collected as part of the U.Di.T.E. Leadership Study. The title of the study signifies the close collaboration that has occurred between academic and leading practitioners throughout. The study was also supported by the International City Management Association based in the United States and the Australian Institute for Municipal Management. A common survey developed by an international team of researchers was completed by over forty-three hundred CEOs during 1995–97 in the fourteen countries. A more detailed description of the survey is presented in the technical appendix. The complete questionnaire can be found in the first book from the project, *The Anonymous Leader* (Klausen and Magnier 1998).

A second source is information from intensive interviews conducted in eight of the participating countries. Most of them were taped and transcribed, and in some cases English resumes were developed and shared among participants. A special data-gathering project is the basis of chapter 6, in which we enter the normally unapproachable "smoked-filled room" where politicians work out power positions. Are administrators allowed to enter this room? Are they asked to come in? And are they willing to enter the room? After finding that CEOs reported a surprisingly high level of political advice, we decided that a special study of political advice was needed. A group of CEOs in Denmark, the Netherlands, and the United States responded to a questionnaire containing a series of hypothetical situations covering various aspects of political advice. Subsequently, the questionnaires were analyzed and the respondents were invited to a half-day seminar in which the ideas behind the survey and the results were presented briefly and the results discussed.

The large multinational dataset and a multilevel analytical plan make this project unique. The dataset has been prepared as a sample of national CEOs from the fourteen countries. Within each country, respondents have been weighted to match the distribution of cities of different sizes in that country, that is, to adjust for higher or lower response rates from cities in a certain size category. Across the countries, respondents have been weighted so that there is an equal number of respondents from each country. This approach creates, first, a sample of Western countries in which each country has equal weight and, second, a sample of CEOs by country in which each CEO respondent case has equal weight with every other CEO within or outside his or her country. By preparing the data in this way, it is possible to make comparisons across countries without the relative size of the country sample or the absolute size of the country population distorting the results.[15]

Analysis of data was conducted at three levels. There are comparisons of countries, analyses at the individual level, and analyses of individual characteristics removing the effects of country differences.[16] The results presented may be based on country-level analysis, individual-level analysis, or difference from the mean analysis.

The first analysis is straightforward. Countries are compared using the mean value of responses from all respondents in each country or, in some cases, the distribution across a typology of respondents from each country.[17]

The second level is also easy to interpret. The individual scores are analyzed in terms of individual or community characteristics. When individual scores are used, however, they often are grouped by a factor that eliminates country variation, for example, grouping respondents by form of government. For instance, if differences in the influence of the CEO are related to the activity level of the mayor, the finding would be misleading if the influence level of the CEO and the activity level of the mayor were both affected by the form of government used. If the responses are grouped by form of government, on the other hand, it will be possible to determine whether the mayor's activism affects the CEO's influence among cities that use the same form.

The third level of analysis assesses the relative level values for a variable within a national context by subtracting the score of an individual respondent from the mean value for his or her country. CEOs in one country may be more influential than those in another country, but what factors explain deviation from the norm within each country? This kind of analysis makes it possible to remove the effects of characteristics that are associated with a country to examine CEOs in comparison to their national peers. In practice, it turns out that this form of analysis produces only modestly important results. The impact of form of government and culture—both country characteristics—is substantial. When the effects of these factors are removed by converting variables into the value of the difference between the individual score and the country mean, there are few variables left that are important at explaining variation across all countries. Still, the analysis adds some interesting insights about the impact of the characteristics of individual CEOs and specific communities.

We use standard statistical techniques such as multiple regression analysis, factors analysis, and cluster analysis. The application of such techniques can be intrusive on the lay public. We find it important that the book, on the one hand, live up to the normal requirements for scientific inquiry and documentation. On the other hand, we find it important that it can be comprehended by the people it studies, the local government administrators. We keep the statistical elaborations at a minimum in the body of the text and use indices, frequency distributions, scattergrams and bar graphs to present our results. In notes and in the technical appendix at the end of the book we document the statistics in detail.

Many of the questions posed in the survey involved five response categories. In order to simplify the presentation of the results and the comparison across countries, indices ranging in values from 0 to 100 were constructed. For example, CEOs were asked to indicate how much emphasis they assigned to different tasks in their daily work (see chapter 4). They were also asked to respond on a five-category scale ranging from "of utmost importance" to "of very little" or "no importance." The first category was assigned a value of 100, the intermediate responses "very important," "moderate importance," and "of little importance" were assigned values of 75, 50, and 25, respectively, and the last category was assigned the value 0.[18] In some cases, the percentage that describes a particular response will be presented, for example, the percentage of respondents who consider an activity to be important. More often, a mean value for the index is presented to summarize the full range of responses with a single number.

There are some important limitations of the data. First, although elected official-administrator relations are central to the discussion, data from elected officials are available in only a few countries. Normally, we rely on the survey responses of the chief administrator alone. Second, it is not possible to measure trends directly because we are using data collected at one period of time in each country. Reference will be made to the country studies completed as part of this project that incorporate historical information and to other secondary sources. Third, comparative survey analysis always has some inherent problems of reliability and validity. First, we have to rely on fourteen persons' translations of more than fifty questions, some of which involved fifteen to twenty items. In order to reduce the loss of reliability in the coding process, the student assistants who were responsible for the coding in each country spent a week together in Odense, Denmark, with members of the project group. This collaboration has greatly enhanced the homogeneity of the data. After the completion of the coding, the Odense team scanned all variables for invalid codes or extreme values and communicated intensively with the national teams to correct mistakes. These validity issues are fully explained in the chapters where they arise.

As a conclusion to the analysis and interpretation of results, we reexamine the findings to help illuminate the major questions in the research. Do institutions matter? Does culture matter? Do leaders matter? We are able to answer each question in the affirmative and reconsider the interrelationship between the three questions. We describe the characteristics of the apex of leadership in local government, and provide a general framework for understanding the nature of interactions. Although the generalizations based on the local government context are not transferable in their entirety to political-administrative relations at other levels of government, the results of this study should stimulate research on the apex in other settings as well. Often, we believe, researchers will be surprised at what they discover there.

CHAPTER 2

Politicians and Administrators in the Political Process: The Theoretical Issues

Long gone—if they ever existed—are the days of the pure split between councils making policy and managers never making policy, and councils never administering and managers only administering. In many communities there's a blend between policymaking and administration.

American City Manager

WHO IS IN CHARGE IN CITY HALL? is a key question in this study and one that is often asked by citizens and observers of city government. Are the leaders chosen by citizens in elections, are they the administrators who operate largely behind the scenes, or are the leaders some combination of the two sets of officials? An exploration of leadership at the apex is concerned not only with the individual contributions of mayors or top administrators but how they relate to each other and how the work of city government is divided between them.

There have not been many empirical studies of the involvement and influence of CEOs in the political process and even fewer that examine the relative contributions of key political and administrative officials, but a great deal has been written about what the roles of CEOs should be and how they should relate to elected officials. If the leadership in local government reflects some combination of the contributions of elected and administrative officials, there are four hypothetical possibilities. One, each handles specialized tasks and operates in separate spheres. Two, the elected official dominates the relationship and gets involved in the administrative sphere. Three, the administrator maintains distance from elected officials and is self-directed. Four, they jointly lead through a partnership with extensive sharing and interaction.

As noted in chapter 1, there are some important differences between the national and local political process in the perspectives and behaviors of officials, and these differences are likely to affect how politicians and administrators interact with each other. Still, in examining the relationship between CEOs and politicians in local government, it is possible to gain new perspectives on the relationship of politics and administration in general. Two related issues have been central to efforts to define the field of public administration and connect it to the general study of politics. First, what is or should be the hierarchical relationship between elected officials and administrators? Is there a clear superior-subordinate relationship, or do administrators possess influence that approximates or exceeds that of elected officials? Second, what is the boundary that demarcates public administration from the larger political process, and is the boundary closed or porous? Do the two sets of officials fill separate roles and occupy clearly separated spheres, or do they have overlapping roles and operate in each other's spheres? If the latter, are the officials still differentiated or completely intermixed? These questions have been important in both research and practice in local government. In fact, one could argue that scholars and practitioners in local government have led the debate over relationships and boundaries.

This has been the case in the United States where the council-manager form appeared as a major reform in the early twentieth century. This new form was intended to be an institutional remedy to the perceived problem of excessive political interference in administrative matters and the lack of coherence and competence in municipal governance. It was also designed with the explicit intention of refashioning the relationship between elected officials and administrators. Exactly what that relationship is in theory and in practice, however, has been the subject of extended debate. Some have argued that the city manager is supposed to be strictly separated from elected officials in a dichotomous relationship, and others have contended that the manager is a "politician" who has a coequal relationship with elected officials. Thus, even in the cities of one country where official roles are clearly demarcated by institutional arrangements, the nature of roles and relationships is unclear. Even greater uncertainty is likely in other countries with a variety of other forms of government in which the authority conferred to elected officials is greater than in the council-manager form and the formal position of CEO is more ambiguous.

Alternate approaches to conceptualizing the relationship between politicians and administrators are presented in this chapter. These approaches serve as a foundation for the empirical analysis in subsequent chapters.

Conceptualizing the Relationship between Politicians and Administrators

It has been common practice to think of local government as divided into two spheres with separate roles assigned to elected officials and administrators—two sets of officials who operate in terms of different norms of behavior. Three other models, based on the autonomy of administrators, the political responsiveness of administrators, and overlapping roles of politicians and administrators, have also received attention in the literature. The four models represent a combination of choices on the two dimensions used to analyze interactions noted above—the nature of the hierarchical relationship on the one hand, and the differentiation of roles, distance between spheres, and choice of norms on the other.

The nature of the hierarchical relationship refers to the extent to which the administrator is subordinate to the elected official de jure or de facto. In all local government structures, elected officials occupy a formally superior position to the top administrator. The actual working relationship can vary along a continuum from high administrative subordination through parity of influence to high administrative independence. When the CEO is clearly subordinated, elected officials direct the CEO either through their instructions or through the policies or laws they establish. The flow of influence between the two sets of officials is unidirectional. Elected officials determine directly or indirectly what administrators do. Subordination does not necessarily mean political interference in administration, nor subjecting administrators to the personal whims of the politician. In orthodox administrative models, administrators are subordinated to impersonal rules that entail a constrained but protected status for the administrator. These distinctions in the nature of political penetration are addressed in the discussion of the second dimension. Regarding the degree of hierarchy, it is also possible that the two sets of officials are both influential and that they interact in a reciprocal way (Farazmand 1997, xi). There can be, as Krause (1999) puts it, a "two-way street" between elected officials and administrators.

The determination of separateness comes from examining roles and norms for behavior. Roles refer to functions that an official performs. Making policy or implementing policy and managing resources are the major roles that concern us here. When roles are separate, each function is performed by a different set of officials, for example, elected officials make policy and administrators implement it. When roles overlap, both sets of officials perform one or both of the same functions. Norms refer to the values and standards that guide choices. Officials act on political norms when they seek to advance individual or party advantage, to promote personal agendas or party positions and policies, and to secure benefits for their supporters. Administrative norms stress general values (such as fairness, impartiality, and objectivity), the values of professional groups or technical experts, and/or impersonal rules based in the law as bases for decisions. These are universalistic administrative norms that are generally accepted as values that advance the public interest. Administrators may also demonstrate agency-serving norms when they skew these values toward protecting resources and power or their personal well-being in combination with or instead of advancing the public interest.

If "outsiders" enter the arena of the "other" official, they may act according to their own norms or the norms that prevail in that arena. For example, an elected official operates in the administrative arena as the council committee chair who oversees a department in city government. She would be following political norms by trying to get benefits distributed to party supporters or following administrative norms by ensuring that benefits were distributed according to objective criteria of eligibility established in policy. On the other hand, a CEO who develops a policy proposal would be following administrative norms by developing a program that attempts to meet long-term community needs or acceding to political norms by proposing a program favored by a key politician who could affect the future employment of the CEO. The CEO could blend norms by incorporating elements of the politician's proposal with features that meet administrative criteria. The degree of distinctness between elected officials and CEOs depends on the extent to which roles are differentiated and whether norms that are appropriate to each official position are followed.

The variations between the four models based on the extent of a hierarchical relationship and the relative distinctness of officials can now be elaborated.[1] The models and key distinguishing characteristics follow:

- *Separate roles:* clear subordination of administrators to politicians and separate roles and norms
- *Autonomous administrator:* equal or greater influence for administrators and separation of politicians from the administrative role
- *Responsive administrator:* subordination of administrators to politicians and dominance of political norms over administrative norms

• *Overlapping roles:* reciprocal influence between elected officials and administrators and shared roles

We will examine each model in detail. The discussion begins with a discussion of the separate roles model. This approach has been particularly important in shaping thinking about relationships in public administration, although it has often been stated in an exaggerated way that presumes great distance between types of officials and complete confinement of administrators to the administrative role. The responsive administrator and autonomous administrator models raise two distinct questions. First, how is administrative responsiveness reconciled with administrative competence? Second, how is administrative autonomy reconciled with democratic control? The overlapping roles model potentially reconciles these tensions but raises new questions about the consequences of ambiguous authority relationships and unclear separation of spheres.

Before we explore the development of the four models, it is useful to examine a factor that may be common to them all. The commitment of administrators to neutrality and neutral competence, when defined broadly, may be present in all the models.

The Meanings of Neutrality and the Distinctness of Administrators

Neutrality and neutral competence are commonly viewed as the bedrock characteristics of administrators in the separate roles model. Is it safe to conclude, therefore, that they are missing from the other models that involve more overlapping roles or greater parity between politicians and administrators? The answer is no. This conclusion is not warranted when broader definitions of concepts are considered. All administrators are not necessarily neutral or neutrally competent in the same way, but we would argue that all share these characteristics and that this is an important common element across the four models of political-administrative relations.

A narrow view of neutrality stresses the instrumental position of the administrator—one that seems consistent with the separate roles model and, in a perverse way, with the responsive administrator role but not the others. When neutrality is defined most narrowly, it would presume that administrators exercise no independent judgment about the rightness or appropriateness of the actions of government (Thompson 1985, 556).[2] This orientation is reinforced by a "technocratic formulation that states that public servants should apply value-neutral techniques derived from science and the professions to achieve the ends prescribed by law" (Green 1998, 92). Competence is applied to accomplishment of any task. Critics of administrative behavior contend that administrators divorce technique from purpose and can cause great harm to the public (Adams and Balfour 1998). Such views of neutrality may even be consistent with an extreme form of the responsive administrator model in which administrators do whatever they are told, abandoning principle and sound practice to advance the political goals of current incumbents. This would be neutrality without competence.

Such a view is disputed by practitioners and scholars alike. An American city manager expressed this opinion: "In the council-manager form of government, both the council member and the city manager are constitutional or charter component pieces of the government. There is no question about the city manager working for the council, but the manager is not just a grafted-on lackey to whomever happens to be holding office at the time" (Gaebler in Nalbandian and Davis 1987, 79). Aberbach and Rockman (1993, 1) suggest that the neutrally competent administrator is "a skilled practitioner who makes the best possible effort to carry out the task at hand without regard to party or other loyalties." This view emphasizes impartiality among political contenders but is silent on the extent to which administrators assert their own views of preferences regarding the options considered by politicians. As a former British minister summed up the desired qualities, "I believe in the principle of a non-political career civil service, available to service with efficiency and commitment the government whom the people have chosen to elect" (Smith 1991, 519).

In a still more complex view of neutrality, there is tension between obedience, expertise, and principle. To some extent, the administrator is an instrument of the political superior who follows instructions. To some extent, the administrator is a repository of professional knowledge or technical expertise and accompanying values that support judgments that cause resistance to instructions. To some extent, the administrator is an independent and objective interpreter of the law who refuses to accept the idea that a politician is above the law or deserving of special treatment or absolute deference. The Northcote-Trevelyan report in 1853 (British Council 1999) captured the complexity of the concept. It advocated having "permanent officers subordinate to Ministers yet possessing sufficient independence, character, ability and experience to be able to advise, assist, and to some extent to influence those who are from time to time set above them."

Max Weber (Gerth and Mills 1946) expresses all these perspectives. Weber stressed on the one hand that the administrator is subordinate and that bureaucracy is instrumental. The bureaucrat demonstrates "readiness to subordinate himself to the chief without any will of his own" (208). The bureaucrat is part of a hierarchical organization that obeys the directives of superiors. Once established, "the mechanism—in contrast to feudal orders based upon personal piety—is easily made to work for anybody who knows how to gain control over it" (229). On the other hand, there is a distance between the politician and the administrator that contributes to the independence of the administrator and the autonomy of the bureaucracy as an organizational system based on expertise. Weber argued that "the political official . . . is not considered to be the personal servant of a ruler" (199). Tenure for staff provides a "measure of 'independence'" (202). Ultimately, in the ideal typical bureaucracy, the bureaucrat is obedient to impersonal rules, not to the superior. The bureaucrat follows law and regulation and applies them with impartiality.

Although the idea of neutrality appears to stress the limitations of the administrator, independence and assertiveness can be implied. Heclo (1975, 81) refers to "a continuous, uncommitted facility at the disposal of, and for the support of, political leadership," but adds giving one's "best independent judgement of the issues to partisan bosses" to his definition of neutral competence. To Heclo, this kind of neutrality "entails not just following orders" and is, thus, a "strange amalgam of loyalty that argues back, partisanship that shifts with the changing partisan, independence that depends on others" (82). Rourke (1992, 545) argues as well that "independent expertise ensures that the administration's decisions are subject to informed criticism that will help anticipate and avert problems that may arise when the decisions are put into effect." Dunn (1997, 162) observes in Australian national government that neutral competence is consistent with active involvement in policy formation with elected officials, indeed, it is a condition for being invited to the "policy-making table." Wolf (1999, 163), in a case study of the executive budget office in American national government, concludes that the "neutral competence" of this office "was precisely the factor that made it so valuable to presidents and responsive to their needs."

Consistent with these views, an active definition of "neutral competence" is recognized as a conceptual possibility. "Neutral" means neither value-free (nor value-less) nor passive. Asmeron and Reis (1996, 8–9) come to the same conclusion in their review of studies in a number of countries: "Neutrality does not mean that top-level civil servants cannot or should not be involved in the articulation of public policy. Indeed, senior officials are professionally and morally obliged to provide their political leaders with the best policy alternatives based on sound arguments, relevant precedents, and suitability to the changing environment. The expectation that they will render these services from a non-partisan position is the crux of the matter."

Viewed in this way, neutral competence can be compatible with the overlapping roles or the autonomous administrator models. If the administrator is not simply an obedient agent, then it is possible to move beyond being independent to being self-directing. The former implies that the administrator brings knowledge and experience to the handling of public affairs and has a professional obligation to make these views known even if they counter those of elected officials. The latter involves resisting external control and promoting the interests of the bureaucracy as an organized entity. Heclo (1975, 82–83) observes that neutral competence promotes continuity of existing policies and protection of administrative interests. Neutral competence can be the basis and the rationale for the autonomous administrator model.

Thus, neutrality as an orientation to politicians can be found among all administrators regardless of their relationship to elected officials. A commitment to competence is also associated with all types of relationships, even perhaps the responsive administrator model. An examination of the attitudes of the respondents to the U.Di.T.E. survey indicates that the support for neutral competence is widespread. Over four out of five respondents believe that CEOs should be nonpartisan and base their recommendations on professional considerations only, and half strongly agree with this position. (These results will be examined in more detail in chapter 4.) Generally, CEOs see themselves as expert practitioners who are set apart from political parties and partisan considerations. Thus, there is no reason to presume that top administrators who have differing relationships with politicians necessarily have differing views about the importance of neutral competence. Although roles may overlap, administrators are likely to see themselves as different from politicians and to be inclined to act in terms of professional norms. There is a basic level of differentiation that is presumed, although in the empirical analysis in later chapters we will examine whether different types of administrators display a varying degree of commitment to neutral competence.

Four Models of Political Administrative Relations

The Separate Roles Model: Subordination and Separation between
Politicians and Administrators

The separate roles model carries a great deal of baggage because it has often been stated in such simplistic terms that it has served merely as a foil for other approaches. This phenomenon has been particularly common in the United States. After a short review of the place of strict separation in American thinking about the role of public administration in society, a restated version of the model will be provided that is more reasonable in its provisions.

In the United States, the "standard" model for describing the traditional relationship between elected officials and administrators is the dichotomy concept—the prototypical statement of strict separation. As it applies to local government, the model holds that the city council does not get involved in administration, the manager has no involvement in shaping policies, and the city manager occupies the role of a neutral expert who efficiently and effectively carries out the policies of the council. Presumably, administrators do not exercise discretion because to do so opens the door to interpreting policy and choosing how and to what extent it will be applied. The formulation of this concept is commonly attributed to Woodrow Wilson, who was a central figure in introducing ideas of modern public administration to the United States with his article "The Study of Administration" written in 1887. Goodnow (1900) is given credit for elaborating the dichotomy concept. This concept, in turn, is thought to be the basis for the council-manager form of government.

A careful analysis of the origins of the idea, however, demonstrates that the dichotomy concept was not what the founders of public administration in the United States or the originators of the council-manager form had in mind when they sought to separate politics and administration. The dichotomy concept of strict separation between policy and administration is associated with an "orthodox" approach to public administration that was prevalent during the twenties and thirties and essentially different from concepts of democracy and administration that preceded and followed it (Svara 1998a). The historical record shows that the dichotomy concept appeared after the founding period of public administration and the creation of the council-manager form. The early statements by Wilson and Goodnow were an attempt to define the field and to defend public administrators from interference by elected officials and party organizations, but their view of government does not match the features of the dichotomy model. The writings of political reformers before and for several years after the endorsement in 1915 of the council-manager form by the National Municipal League stressed the importance of "council government" with broad authority for elected officials, including administrative oversight and a clear acceptance of the policy role of the manager.

There are different versions of the dichotomy model with differing degrees of conceptual and empirical support. In Sayre's view of dichotomy, "politics and policy were separate from administration, which was concerned exclusively with the execution of assignments handed down from the realm of politics" (1958, 103), and his definition was very influential in shaping the definition of the dichotomy in the United States and its association with the early scholars in public administration (Svara 1999a).[3] Montjoy and Watson (1995, 231) characterize such a definition as a "strict version" of the doctrine, and they propose a "reinterpreted dichotomy" that permits a policy-making role for the manager, but still helps managers resist the forces of particularism. Similarly, as the concept was described prior to Sayre's article, it was permissible for administrators to propose policy but the dichotomy idea was deemed useful as it helped to focus public attention on elected officials and to shield administrators from interference (e.g., Lepawsky 1949). Kettl (2000) simply equates the dichotomy concept with an emphasis on separation of spheres and clear political control of administration and traces this definition back to Wilson. Frederickson uses a "sanitized" version of the dichotomy to remind administrators to pay attention to the day-to-day operations of public institutions and avoid engaging in policy making (1997, 227–29). In view of the variety of definitions and interpretations, it is not possible to resolve the "true" meaning of the concept. It does seem clear, however, that the version of dichotomy that needs to be reinterpreted or rejected on both empirical and conceptual grounds arose in the 1950s rather than in the 1880s. The founders of public administration in the United States had a more complex view of the interaction of elected and administrative officials.

Defined in the strictest terms, the model is hard to defend. Indeed, one could argue that the model has often served as a straw man that could easily be torn apart. The orthodox dichotomy model entailed the dependence and compliance of administrators vis-à-vis elected officials and complete separation of their spheres. Administrators would have been confined to giving narrow technical advice to elected officials on policy matters and implementing the policy decisions of elected officials based on expertise but with limited discretion. Long (1954, 27) disparaged this approach long ago, noting that administration would have been "a neutral instrument solely devoted to the unmotivated presentation of facts to, and the docile execution of orders from, political superiors." This is not a workable relationship, nor does it match reality.

Peters (1995, 177–78) argues that the dichotomy concept has been perpetuated not because it is a sound model but because it serves a useful purpose for officials:

For administrators, this presumed separation of administration and politics allows them to engage in politics (organizational rather than partisan) without the bother of being held accountable politically for the outcomes of their actions. Further, they can engage in policy making—presumably using technical or legal criteria for their decisions—without the interference of political actors who might otherwise recognize political or ideological influences on policies and make demands on them for the modification of those policies. For their part, politicians can shift responsibility for decisions to administrators and claim that they were made for nonpolitical reasons.

Put in these terms, the relationship is not a strict "dichotomy" although it still appears to be based on maintaining separate spheres of activity. At this point it is useful to restate the model omitting the simplistic features that are easy to dismiss.

Restating the Separate Roles Model

In defining the first model, we will accept the underlying logic of the dichotomy concept but not its insistence on complete separation. The *separate roles* model is populated by elected officials who view themselves as detached governors, on the one hand, and by Putnam's (1975, 89–91) "classical bureaucrats," on the other. The elected officials are content with setting broad policy and providing general oversight. They are also likely to see themselves as trustees who act on their own view of what is best rather than being closely accountable to the electorate or a political party. The administrator, as described by Putnam, contributes to policy decisions and exerts influence. Still, there is a difference in worldview between the politician and the administrator together with a mutual attempt to maintain a clear differentiation of spheres. The classical bureaucrat thinks in terms of a "monistic conception of the public interest"—for example, the "national interest" or in local government the "interest of the community as a whole." Furthermore, this type of official "believes that public issues can be resolved in terms of some objective standard of justice, or of legality, or of technical practicality." Political problems are converted into administrative problems. Administrators view themselves as above politics, although this does not mean they have no impact on politics.[4] As a conceptual type, Putnam (1975, 89) suggests that this official tends to denigrate the contribution of the amateur politician and is not directly responsive to the public. "Such a bureaucrat may well find the ideal of pluralist democracy less congenial than the quieter, more ordered, less conflict-ridden world of a benevolent autocracy." The separate roles model also serves as a check to particularistic politics, that is, a protective shield against political interference in the actions of administrators, although legislative oversight is consistent with it.

Administrators are separated from politicians by their technical expertise and organizational position even though they are political actors who influence the policy process from their administrative sphere. When one considers the practical impossibility of specifying all details of implementation in the specification of a policy or program, some influence over the content of policy is inevitable in the exercise of administrative discretion. Furthermore, the policy recommendations of administrators in the form of technical or professional advice still influence policy formulation by elected officials. The separate roles model does not presume completely separate functions; in particular, it recognizes the contribution of administrators to policy making. The restated model does presume that administrators limit the scope of their policy involvement to technical advice and minimize efforts to be directly responsive to citizens while asserting that elected officials should keep their hands off administration. This view is an approximation of image II of Aberbach, Putnam, and Rockman (1981, 6–9) in which politicians bring values and administrators facts to the policy process.[5] Finally, the restated model presumes a broad and active definition of neutral competence that includes both the responsibility to implement directives from elected officials and also the responsibility to independently offer opinions and responses to elected officials based on expertise.

Thus, in the separate roles model, the administrator's behavior is shaped by technical expertise as well as organizational position and resources. Elected officials set broad policy and conduct general oversight of performance. Administrators stress separate roles and the subordination of administration to politicians. Although spheres are separate, clear control of bureaucracy by politicians is presumed.

The Autonomous Administrator Model

What if the control stipulated in the previous model is not achieved? The autonomous administrator as described in the literature also stresses distance from politicians but is self-directing to the point that subordination is questionable. Neutral competence is not lacking from this model, but political accountability may be absent. It is possible for administrators to separate themselves from elected officials to such an extent that they are beyond control. Gruber (1987, 92) describes local government administrators who consider themselves to be relatively free of democratic control and "do not perceive much need for it." She argues that administrators define policy in such an abstract way and administration in such an expansive way that they claim the right to make virtually all decisions even when they limit themselves to "administration" (1987, 109–110). Problems with control result from the imbalance or asymmetry in experience and specialized knowledge between the elected principal and the administrative agent (Banks and Weingast 1992). Often it is suspected that administrative agencies are "bureaucratic fiefdoms . . . that cannot be held accountable through the normal mechanisms of representative democracy" (Stein 1991, 1).

Weber (Gerth and Mills 1946) recognized that the bureaucracy can be resistant to control and change: "Once it is established, bureaucracy is among those social structures that are hardest to destroy" (228). Officials "have a common interest in seeing that the mechanism continues its functions and that the societally exercised authority carries on" (228–29). Although in theory the servant of elected officials, Weber recognized that in practice the power relationship may be reversed. "Under normal conditions, the power position of a fully developed bureaucracy is always overtowering. The 'political master' finds himself in the position of the 'dilettante' who stands opposite the 'expert,' facing the trained official who stands within the management of administration" (232).

The "power-wielding bureaucracy" (233) seeks to limit release of information and resists external investigation. "Bureaucracy naturally welcomes a poorly informed and hence a powerless parliament—at least in so far as ignorance somehow agrees with the bureaucracy's interests" (234). Specialized knowledge enhances the "power position of the officeholder" (235). Anticipating the work of later analysts, Weber noted that when bureaucratic bureaus incorporate interest groups in advisory bodies, "it further increases the power of bureaucracy" (239). The servants can become the masters.

Public choice theorists argue that administrators act in terms of their own interests rather than the public interest (Tullock 1965; Niskanen 1971; Dunleavy 1991). In some respects, to consider the autonomous administrator as maintaining separate roles is misleading because administrators are active (perhaps even dominant) in the policy making that is also the key role of politicians. Still, the central element in this model is that administrators are "separate" or distant but not subordinate.

The Responsive Administrator Model: Administrators Being Supportive of Politicians

This approach is like the separate roles model in its emphasis on the subordination of administrators, but it differs by stressing a political nature of the roles and relationships between officials. Under the responsive administrator model, politicians operate within the administrative sphere and directly fill administrative roles, or administrators anticipate political norms and preferences and accede to them. Administrators act as the political agent of the mayor (or party majority), but not simply in the detached, passive approach of the separate roles model. This model is based on the presumption that politicians are looking for politically "responsive competence" from administrators. In his analysis of American presidents, Moe (1985, 239–40) explains the distinctive elements of responsive competence. "With neutral competence there is no mechanism to guarantee that what the organization potentially has to offer is willingly made available in an appropriate form and timely fashion to the president. Nor is there a mechanism to guarantee that the types of competence the organization is equipped to provide are well suited to the president's needs—a problem that has less to do with willful resistance than with organizational myopia, parochialism, insularity, and other pathologies of a systematic nature. . . . Ideally, it (responsive competence) is competence that is developed and adapted in light of his political needs and willingly made available to him." Thus, politicians may want administrators who not only do what they are told, but believe in the political aims of elected officials—a quality not found among neutral bureaucrats.

For their part, administrators seek a closer affiliation with the mayor or political parties. This relationship may be reinforced by process, structure, or a combination of the two. In the former case, elected officials are highly determined to push through their agenda and to secure rapid and highly compliant implementation from staff. Some observers (Aberbach and Rockman

1993; Rourke 1992; Eggars and O'Leary 1995; Aberbach and Rockman 2000) note that politicians increasingly expect a high degree of loyalty from their administrative subordinates. They want programs implemented quickly with attention to the political interests of the politicians. The governmental structure may also increase the emphasis on political responsiveness when administrators are appointed by and directly answerable to the elected executive. Politicians are likely to prefer administrators who share their values. Legislators use oversight to ensure that programs serve the interests that were part of the winning coalition that created the program in the legislative body (West 1995, 145–46).

Administrators as well may feel it is appropriate and advantageous to have views that are congruent with those of politicians. Among administrators, the interests of those directly controlled by politicians, for example, the political appointee, are obviously linked to the electoral success of the politician. Moe (1989) has observed, however, that even career civil servants are concerned about "political uncertainty." In order to reduce uncertainty about potential negative changes in resources or assignments, "one attractive strategy is to nurture mutually beneficial relationship with groups and politicians whose political support the agency needs" (283). Under these circumstances, the administrator is likely to identify more with elected officials and give less attention to bureaucratic or professional considerations. Administrators are actively compliant partners with elected officials and behave in a supportive way. Either as a result of political pressure or administrative compliance, competence may be sacrificed to responsiveness (Aberbach and Rockman 1993). In governmental forms with strong elected executives, administrators may even abandon neutrality to promote the interests of incumbents.

Thus, in this model, elected officials occupy a superior position. They not only have final authority over major policy decisions as in the other models, but they also set the course and shape the terms of the relationship with administrators to a greater extent than in the other models. Elected officials may be activists committed to a political agenda or may be authorized by the formal structure to fill a dominant leadership role. Elected officials may also exert this active leadership through a cohesive and determined political party. Administrators are not merely compliant. They are supportive of elected officials who give direction to the political process. Although it is common to focus on the factors that impede the effective interaction of principals and agents, they are largely absent in this model. The politicians are assertive and/or powerful because of formal position or party support. The administrators are supportive and will adjust their behavior and their values to meet the expectations and preferences of the elected officials.

The Overlapping Roles Model

> My job is to collaborate with the mayor and city council in setting the strategy for the city which is not the textbook model where council makes policies and managers enact them. I don't think that model works at all today. I will argue that that is a dysfunctional model.
>
> (Interview, American City Manager)

Finally, there are a variety of approaches that share the characteristic of seeing administrators and elected officials as having roles that overlap each other and recognize the shared influence of politicians and administrators. Each set of officials has distinct roles and administrators respect political control, but there is extensive interaction, overlapping functions, and reciprocal influence. These approaches presume that administrators are active in a broad range of decisions including policy matters, and politicians are potentially involved in the detailed choices associated with administration. Self (1972, 149–52) has argued that none of the standard bases for distinguishing the roles of officials holds up in practice. Questions of policy versus questions of detail, generalized rules versus specifics, ends versus means, and higher versus lower value judgments can all be the province of either politicians or administrators, depending on circumstances. "British central and local government," he observes, "knows nothing of the distinction between policy and administration" (149).

One might conclude from these observations that the model of overlapping roles could assume no differences between politicians and administrators or the complete intermixture of activities. Aberbach, Putnam, and Rockman (1981, 93) propose as a conceptual category image IV of political-administrative relations that is a "pure hybrid" characterized by the bureaucratization of politics and the politicization of administration, although they find little empirical evidence to support it. Specifying the model as pure intermixture ignores the strong tendency of administrators to view themselves as politically neutral. Self (1972, 150) has argued that the most important distinguishing factor between politics and administration is the difference between the characteristics of politicians and administrators themselves and the offices they occupy. Administrators perform some of the same activities as politicians but they occupy career positions in an administrative organization and are guided by professional values and technical expertise. In constructing the overlapping roles model, therefore, we will assume that differentiation in values (and some specialization of functions) accompanies overlapping roles.

An example of the combination of overlap and differentiation is found in the original rationale for the council-manager form of government in the United States. Although commonly viewed as an example of a governance form based on the dichotomy concept, it is actually a prime example of complementary and overlapping roles (Svara 1998a). The form, endorsed by the National Municipal League in 1915 as part of the second edition of its model city charter, emphasizes distinct spheres with overlapping involvement and the concept of the controlled but broadly involved executive. Although the early reformers, who had views similar to those of Woodrow Wilson and Frank Goodnow, wanted to define a distinct role for administrators and protect them from political interference, they recognized the leadership provided by the city manager and expected extensive interaction between the two sets of officials.

The thinking of the originators of the council-manager form—whose commentary on the second model charter was published in *A New Municipal Program* (Woodruff 1919)—is particularly important in understanding the intended roles of officials. The council, which was to be the "pivot of the municipal system" (153), was given investigatory powers and authority to appoint the city manager. This latter provision, reflecting the concept of the "controlled executive," strengthened the council and the executive without either jeopardizing the role of the council or perpetuating separation of powers. The Model Charter distinguished "legislation" from "administration," naturally assigning the former to the council and the latter to the manager, but the theoreticians and practitioners of the council-manager plan did not adhere to a fundamental dichotomy between policy and administration. The charter stressed the insulation of administrators from interference by elected officials but not isolation. The council would exercise "constant and comprehensive" supervision and consider citizen appeals of administrative "rulings" (41, 18–19). According to the commentary, "administration is given a place apart, but it is not an independent place. It is subject to control but not to factious interference" (155).

Similarly, the manager was called upon to offer policy advice and recommendations to the council in its enactment of legislation. The commentary on the New Municipal Program contains numerous references to the manager's policy role. Overall, the manager must "show himself to be a leader, formulating policies and urging their adoption by the council" (130). The reformers did not intend to simply add an administrative technician who would take charge of implementation of policies only. An observer at the time (Story 1918, 220) remarked that the manager is "an active and influential factor in legislation" whose "judgment will rarely be considered lightly." Adrian (1987, 452) concludes that "by the 1920s, the city manager had become a firmly established community leader."

The scholars and activists who provided the rationale for the second model charter did not call for separation of politics and administration or of lay and expert elements. The commentary offers this assessment of the overall relationship of elected officials and administrators: "They are not two antagonistic elements, each seeking to enlarge its sphere of action at the expense of the other. They are not even independent powers in the government, each working in a distinct field, performing its appropriate acts, and having for these purposes an authority of its own. On the contrary, they are two parts of the same mechanism, or we may liken them to two elements in one chemical compound whose combined qualities give the character to the substance. In a sense, they take part jointly in every act performed" (Woodruff 1919, 37). These reformers envisioned a government with complementary and cooperative relationships between officials who reflected democratic accountability and professionalism (Svara 1999a).

A study of chief executives in British local government by Norton (1991, chap. 14) finds the same conditions as those advocated by the early American political reformers. Given their strategic position, it is "inevitable" that local chief executives "initiate change and balance this with the maintenance of continuity jointly with the chief officers and in association with political leaders." They balance working to achieve the "party manifestos" of the majority party, but also feel obligated to be responsive to "public wishes." The CEO is the local authority's "pilot," and the council "exercises its responsibility through a leadership which is largely dependent on the chief executive." But the administration is in turn "dependent on the co-responsibility with or acquiescence from the political leadership for its success." For the local government to be effective, "mutual understanding and joint working are essential" between political and administrative leaders.

There are a number of other strands that contribute to a model of overlapping roles. Putnam's "political bureaucrat" (1975, 90) is a person who is concerned about responsiveness to public sentiment and oriented to solving problems, someone who does not "shrink from advocating and even fighting for his own preferred policies." This administrator sees politicians not as a "troublesome or even dangerous antagonist" but rather as "a participant in a common game, one whose skills and immediate concerns may differ from his own but whose ultimate values and objectives are similar."

Aberbach, Putnam, and Rockman (1981) see the possibility of substantial overlap between politicians and administrators in policy and administration. In their image III, administrators are a force for stability—"equilibrium"—whereas elected officials bring change or "energy" to the policy process. As noted earlier, their image II also provides for administrators to contribute "facts" to the policy-making process to be combined with the "values" supplied by politicians. The drawback to these images is an excessively narrow view of the perspective and contribution of administrators. Administrators are also concerned with values, as the New Public Administration movement (Marini 1971; Frederickson 1980) in the United States stressed in the early seventies, particularly a concern for equity. Furthermore, CEOs in local government are commonly more actively engaged in identifying and framing the long-term mission of their governments than are city council members (Svara 1989), and this characteristic is becoming more pronounced (Svara 1999b). They are the strategic leaders of their government (Norton 1991). They are, therefore, a source of change or energy as well as stability. Finally, overlapping roles do not eliminate distinctive worldviews and perspectives on public affairs (Nalbandian 1994).

Other contributions to this approach can be noted. Krause (1999) argues that politicians and administrators can have impact on each other with either one side or the other being dominant or each adapting to the other. Farazmand (1997, xi) describes a "dual roles" model as an approach that "treats bureaucrats as integral parts of the policy process and governance in general. The relationship between bureaucrats and politicians is mixed and interactive, fluid and integrative, not dichotomous or hierarchical. According to this approach, bureaucrats and politicians should and must work together, and their relationship should be cooperative, not adversarial, to promote efficient and effective administration and governance."

In contrast to Gruber's arguments about the distance and self-direction of administrators noted earlier, Nardulli and Stonecash (1981, 83–84) found that the manager and administrators in a council-manager city have a "strong sensitivity to the climate of public opinion" and to the council's views on administrative actions. Officials evidence a "concern for both rationalistic and political considerations." Stein (1991, 61–62) finds a political-professional partnership in the delivery of most municipal services: with "mutual accommodation and mutual respect," administrators apply professional standards within "politically determined priorities." There is growing evidence that administrators are entrepreneurs who introduce policy innovation (Doig and Hargrove 1991; Schneider and Teske 1992). Cook (1996) has argued that administration fills a constitutive function—helping to shape the nature of government and guide the governmental process—as well as an instrumental function. Descriptions of and prescriptions for roles in local government are better grounded in a model of complementarity than of dichotomy (Svara 1999a)—an idea developed in more depth in the conclusion of chapter 9 and in chapter 10 of this book.

Expectations about Differences among CEOs

The four models represent different ways of looking at how politicians and administrators relate to each other and how administrators are connected to the political process. Table 2.1 offers a summary of the characteristics of each model and examines the implications of the models for expected differences among CEOs. In the discussion that follows, reference is made to four forms of government that were introduced in chapter 1 and are fully explained in chapter 3.

In the *separate roles* model, administrators are clearly subordinated to elected officials and there is a division of roles but not complete separation. The administrators in this model are unambiguously committed to neutral competence, although it can be expressed actively with assertions of independence and expressions of professional views that counter the predilections of politicians. Elected officials, on the other hand, focus on setting policy with advice from administrators and overseeing administrative performance without interference in the details of administration. The model is commonly associated with appointed executive systems, although the appropriateness of the connection is uncertain. As our discussion has indicated, the originators of the council-manager form of government in the United States describe a more active administrator than the separate roles model contains, but many of the later proponents and defenders of the form in the United States and other countries have stressed administrative subordination and strict separation. The top administrators in this model have low involvement in policy innovation—confining themselves to advice and comment—and low influence in policy making.

In the *responsive administrator* model, administrators are clearly subordi-

Table 2.1 Comparison of Models of Political Administrative Relations

	Separate roles	Autonomous administrator	Responsive administrator	Overlapping roles
Degree of hierarchy of politicians and administrators	Clear subordination	Administrators have equal or greater influence	Clear subordination	Reciprocal influence
Extent of separation of spheres	Clear division of roles and functions	Administrators shape policy; elected officials excluded from administration	Elected officials potentially involved in administration	Each set of officials involved in roles of the other
Nature of administrative norms	Commitment to neutral competence	Commitment to neutral competence and maintaining agency prerogatives	Commitment to responsive competence	Commitment to neutral competence and responsiveness to politicians and the public
Form of government	Uncertain: commonly linked to appointed executive systems (council-manager form)	Uncertain: greatest potential in appointed executive systems	Strong political executive systems (mayor-council form)	Parliamentary systems (committee-leader or collective leadership form) or appointed executive systems
Key elected official role and contribution	Elected officials set policy goals and oversee implementation	Elected officials approve policy	Executive drives enactment and implementation of policies	Elected officials make policy and interact with administrators in implementation
Involvement in policy by administrators	Low although active in advice and comment to elected officials	High	Low except as agent of politician	Moderate to high as initiators as well as advisers
Level of influence on policy making	Low	High	Low	Moderate

nated to elected officials but the division of roles is determined by elected officials. There is a deeper dependence of administrators on elected officials and greater deference to political values. Politicians actively seek to orient the governmental process toward achieving their goals. Administrators agree with those goals, or they see their interests as dependent on maintaining the support of politicians or parties. Elected officials may also intervene directly in the administrative process in order to influence specific outcomes. The value orientation of administrators is responsive competence. Although administrators seek to align their actions with political preferences, there is presumably "a line below which criteria associated with expertise win out over loyalty or support" (Aberbach and Rockman 1993, 3). Still, there is the risk that administrators may sacrifice competency for obedience, that is, being compliant to the point that they pay no attention to the ends that are being pursued. The model is logically associated with strong elected executive systems, such as the strong-mayor form in local government. The top administrators in this model have low involvement in policy innovation—except as agents of politicians—and low independent influence in policy making.

In the *autonomous administrator* model, administrators are on the same level or have more influence than elected officials despite formal authority arrangements that give control to politicians. The division of roles is one-sided. Elected officials are excluded from administrative matters, but administrators have a substantial or even predominant role in policy making. The administrators in this model are committed to neutral competence because it reinforces their independence but agency-serving norms may prevail over universalistic norms when administrators perceive the need to protect programs, staff, and budgets. Elected officials are primarily involved in approving policy proposals framed by administrators and in providing general oversight of administrative performance, although they are dependent on top administrators for information about performance. The model could be associated with appointed executive systems, although it could apply to any setting in which resources are tilted in favor of staff. Critics of council-manager government charge that the form produces administrative control of local government. The top administrators in this model have high involvement in policy innovation and high influence in policy making. It is possible that agency or bureaucratic interests will dominate decision making. Administrators may be detached and unresponsive to elected officials, that is, independent to the extent that their obedience is questionable.

In the *overlapping roles* model, there is extensive interaction and reciprocal influence between elected officials and administrators. Administrators temper their commitment to neutral competence with responsiveness to elected officials and the public. By implication, top administrators exercise judgement about how to balance professional criteria with the preferences of politicians and the wishes of the public, as Norton observed (1991). Elected officials promote their policy proposals and interact with administrators over shaping policy decisions, and they may play active roles in certain aspects of administration, particularly in attempting to guide as well as oversee service delivery and as the intermediary or ombudsman of citizens regarding complaints about administrative behavior. The model is logically associated with parliamentary-type systems—committee-leader and collective leadership forms of government. The early descriptions and many empirical studies of the council-manager form of government in the United States also approximate the features of the overlapping roles model. The top administrators in this model have high involvement in policy innovation and moderately high influence in policy making.

The Four Ideal Type Models

The four models are constructs for examining political-administrative interactions. In the conclusions of chapters 5–8, we examine the extent to which the chapter findings are consistent or inconsistent with the models. Overall, we present a substantial amount of evidence that is consistent with the overlapping roles model and little that is clearly compatible with any of the other models. Although they are all appropriate as theoretical ideal types, only one matches well the distribution of characteristics found among local government CEOs. Virtually all CEOs have roles that more or less overlap with elected officials. If the four models as ideal types suggested indicators that identify distinct clusters of administrators, their utility as a framework for research would be substantiated. Our analysis will show, however, that these plausible models with substantial grounding in the literature do not fare well as approximations of the real world.

In chapter 9, a different approach is taken to classifying how top administrators relate to elected officials, and another effort is made to use the conceptual models to generate hypotheses about variations among top administrators. We create a typology in which CEOs are divided into groups based on how much influence they have absolutely and in comparison to their perception of how influential elected officials are in budgetary policy making. CEOs are classified as dependent, interdependent, or independent based on comparison of influence ratings. Furthermore, two types of dependent CEOs are created based on attitudes about the CEO's relationship to the political process. "Political agents" among the dependent CEOs assign themselves much less influence than they assign to elected officials, and they believe that the CEOs should hold the same views as the leading politicians. It is plausible to expect that the influence and attitudinal characteristics of these political agents would correspond with the responsive administrator model. "Professional agents" also have less influence but believe that CEOs should have independent views and/or be primarily responsible to citizens rather than to elected officials. These characteristics would seem to match the separate roles model. The interdependent CEOs have approximately the same amount of influence as elected officials and correspond to the overlapping roles model. Finally, CEOs with more influence than elected officials are classified as independent and may approximate the autonomous administrator.

The four models are used as the basis for hypothesizing the characteristics that each type of administrator would have. These characteristics build on the expectations outlined in table 2.1. For example, professional agents would be expected to have low involvement in policy innovation, as the separate roles model would suggest. The analysis shows that CEOs differ by partnership type. Although most fall into the interdependent category, there are substantial minorities that correspond to each of the other types. However, all the types of CEOs have characteristics (e.g., relatively high policy involvement) that more or less approximate those expected of the overlapping roles model. Although the conventional view (Self 1972, 151) is that a model based on separate roles is the normative and empirical starting point for understanding political-administrative relations and that other models are deviations from that model, the analysis will show that overlapping roles is the norm and that the other models are special cases that deviate from it. The separate roles, responsive administrators, and autonomous administrators models may be nicely constructed conceptual houses, but they have few occupants.

A possible explanation for the findings is offered in the concluding chapter where two themes are emphasized. First, CEOs differ by form of government on many important characteristics, but these differences are not as great as those between the models of political-administrative relations. There is not, as one might expect, clear alignment between the models and forms of government. Second, the similarities between CEOs may be explained by the impact of institutional forces and a new general framework for understanding relationships. There is complementarity between political and administrative officials in modern government that encompasses the assumptions of the overlapping roles model, but that also contains certain elements—differentiation, independence, and responsiveness—from the other models as well.

Regardless of the orientation and preferences of CEOs, they are immersed in an institutional setting, a political environment, and a national culture. These elements are examined in chapter 3 and chapter 4. It is presumed that formal structure, the functions assigned to municipalities, the culture, and the characteristics of the political environment will interact with the personal characteristics of the CEO to shape his or her contribution to the political process.

CHAPTER 3

Institutions, National Cultures, and Political Leadership

I have, both in the charter and by the mayor's order, the powers of the mayor. So, in the mayor's absence I can do whatever he entrusts to me. I have his mandate to carry out his agenda. It is a strong agenda because he is a strong mayor. . . . It would be very difficult to work in this government under a weak political leader.

American City Administrator and Deputy Mayor

You are of course CEO for the whole city council, naturally, but I also believe that the loyalty of the CEO at any given time first and foremost should be towards the mayor in office.

Interview, Danish CEO

It is like a ballet. I constantly have to find the right balance between the mayor and the aldermen on the one hand and the administrative staff on the other.

Interview, Dutch CEO

The mayor—whoever the mayor is in the end—I work with them but not for them.

Interview, U.S. City Manager

THE RELATIONSHIP BETWEEN ELECTED OFFICIALS and top administrators occurs within an institutional context that shapes the attitudes and behavior of both sets of officials. To elaborate Self's (1972) apex of the arch analogy one last time, the arch that represents the governmental process may be sharper or flatter in shape, depending on the number of officials at the apex and how easy it is for influences to flow between the political and the administrative arcs. The shape of the arch reflects institutional characteristics in the locality and the country, thinking of institutions both as specific structural features and also as rules and routines rooted in culture that persist over time.

Looking at structural features, the municipal CEOs in the various countries covered by the study have one thing in common. They are the highest ranking nonelected administrative officials in local government. Still, they operate in quite different political and organizational contexts. Although the elected officials are all mayors and council members or their equivalents, they vary greatly in their duties and authority. Furthermore, the top level of elected officials may or may not include other leadership positions such as committee chairs or a minority leader. A focus on the details of these contexts might lead to the conclusion that the CEOs from the fourteen countries are operating in fourteen different political and organizational settings. Concentrating on the details, however, stands in the way of discovering the broad and important commonalities of local governmental systems in the various countries. A search for the central features of the broader context in which CEOs interact with their political masters yields four dimensions.

First, we look at how political authority is constituted. We distinguish four institutional setups or *forms of government*, which hypothetically may have implications for the relations between political and administrative actors. Second, we focus on the question of how political leadership is exercised. Here we deal with the *nature of mayoral leadership*. There are four separate indicators that are used to measure leadership, all of which are measured by the perceptions of the CEOs.

- Are mayors visionary persons with excellent relations with the public (public leadership)?
- How do they engage in policy making and administration (policy leadership)?
- To what extent do mayors promote the interests of their political party (party leadership)?
- Do they react to circumstances or are they actively trying to foresee future events (proactive leadership)?

Third, we place the constitution and exercise of political leadership in a broader *cultural* context. The way in which authority is constituted in a society and is exercised by those in power reflects certain cultural traits that differ across countries. Two cultural dimensions are intuitively related to official behavior and relationships—power distance and uncertainty avoidance. Finally, we classify city governments in terms of their scope and size. Cities are differentiated on the basis of the range and nature of the services they provide and the size of the municipal workforce.

Three of these factors—form of government, culture, and scope and size —are identified as country characteristics in our conceptual framework in figure 1.1. The exploration of these factors permits us to move from using fourteen countries in our analysis to using variables with a small number of categories. In other words, we replace country names in subsequent chapters with more general variables, a goal for comparative research recommended by Przeworski and Teune (1970, chap. 1). Form of government and national cultural traits are used systematically to explain the role of administrators in the political process, including their relationships to the leading politicians. Information on the scope and size of government is used selectively as an additional factor to help interpret specific findings.

The fourth factor—the nature of mayoral leadership—represents one of the four intervening variables in our conceptual framework (along with administrative values, networks, and political environment examined in chapter 4.) One of the core questions of any political institution is who has power to decide what? The answer to this question has both structural and behav-

Table 3.1 Representation and Electoral System in 14 Countries Studied

	Population per elected official	Average size municipal councils	Electoral turnout	Principle of representation	Constituency	Percent one-party majority	Election/ dismissal of mayor/leading politician
Australia	2500	10	85	Majority preferential	Varies	Not relevant	Varies
Belgium	783	22	80	NA	At large	46	Government appointed
Great Britain	2605	42	40	Majority	Ward	59	Majority leader
Denmark	1084	17	70	Proportional	At large	31	Indirect/full term
Finland	394	28	66	Proportional	At large	53	Indirect/full term
France	116	14	70	Mixed, complex	At large	53	Indirect/full term
The Netherlands	1491	19	54	Proportional	At large	7	Government appointed
Ireland	4013	26	62	Proportional	At large	15	Indirect/varies
Italy	397	18	85	Dual, complex	At large	53	Direct/no confidence vote
Norway	515	29	67	Proportional	At large	10	Indirect/full term
Portugal	1125	29	60	Mixed, complex	At large/ parishes	68	Indirect/full term
Spain	597	8	64	NA	NA	63	Indirect/full term
Sweden	667	45	85	Proportional	At large	30	Indirect/full term
USA	NA	7	25	Majority	At large or ward	NA	Varies

Sources: Clarke et. al (1996), Det Fælleskommunale EF-sekretariat (n.d.), Harloff (1987), Klausen and Magnier (1998). Percent one-party majority from U.Di.T.E. Leadership Study.

NOTE: All information refers to municipal level except electoral turnout, which refers to the regional level.

ioral components. The form of government to a large extent defines the nature of mayoral leadership, but offices are occupied by incumbents with particular strengths and weaknesses. The way the individual mayor fills the office is one of the four factors that may vary within countries and may have potentially strong consequences for what happens at the apex of leadership. In subsequent chapters, we trace the consequences of mayoral leadership for the activities and influence of the CEO.

How Political Authority Is Constituted: Organizing Principles

The governments of the fourteen countries share two important traits and almost all share a third.[1] First, the supreme political body of all the municipalities, the council, is constituted through general elections. These governments are representative democracies. Second, there is a recognized political leader in all but one of the countries. Third (and a criterion for inclusion in the study)[2], there is an appointed chief administrator. Each of these features reflects a principle in the organization of a government that laymen should control the government, that a politician should provide energizing leadership, and that professional contributions should be incorporated. Within the framework of council, political leader, and CEO, dissimilarities immediately come to the surface. In their specific provisions, the political governing structure is different from country to country. Some countries have mayors that are strong, some have weak mayors, and a few countries don't even have the position of mayor (although, as noted above, all but one clearly designate a single political leader). As indicated in table 3.1, mayors may be elected directly by voters, indirectly by and from among the members of the council, or they may be appointed by central government. The size of the city councils varies considerably from an average of seven in the United States to forty-five in Sweden. In some countries there are strong executive committees in the city council; other countries have no executive committee at all. In some countries standing committees have decision-making powers, in some countries they play an advisory role only, and in others standing committees are not necessarily used.

Despite the specific peculiarities found in each country, there are common features that reflect the shared traits and four "forms" of government—clusters of characteristics that structure how political power is obtained, maintained, and exercised in municipal government. The structural features of municipal government in any specific country reflect a balance or compromise among the three organizing principles: layman rule, political leadership, and professionalism. Describing these principles and variation in how they are applied provides background for defining the forms of government.

The Layman Rule

The layman rule means that citizens elected for political office should be involved effectively and intensively in making decisions.[3] Representative democracy by definition entails layman government. Elected representatives also serve as a link between citizens and government and often serve as informal ombudsmen to improve the responsiveness of staff to individual citizens. Given their direct accountability to voters, politicians seek to respond to the demands and preferences of constituents.

Once elected the actual involvement of the layman politicians may, however, be constrained or expanded in scope and intensity by the specific governmental structures established. Among the fourteen countries studied, Ireland is at one extreme: council meetings are rare and tend to focus on general policies. There is neither an executive committee nor empowered standing committees. At the other end of the continuum, Sweden has a council with an executive committee that works closely with the CEO and standing committees that are heavily engaged in the day-to-day execution of policies. Countries also differ in the extent to which council members can intervene with administrative staff directly or through committees in pressing citizens' claims or complaints. In some American and Australian cities, for example, council members are not permitted by charter to communicate with any staff member other than the city manager. Such a provision is an example of the tradeoff between the layman principle and professionalism in government.

In the American political tradition, there is a distinction between Madisonian and Hamiltonian values for organizing government (Kettl 2000) that is relevant to the tradeoffs with another of our principles. The Madisonian perspective emphasizes the importance of a wide range of actors in the political process and values competition and political checks and balances. Making greater provision for the layman principle incorporates Madisonian features into government and encourages a higher level of pluralism in the governmental process. The contrasting Hamiltonian perspective emphasizes focused and centralized leadership, that is, the contributions of the political leader.

Political Leadership

The role of politicians in government has been described as that of promoting value choices and feeding energy and passion into the policy system (Aberbach, Putnam, and Rockman 1981, 9ff). In chapter 2, the observation was made that elected officials are not the only source of values and innovation. Still, politicians make a distinctive contribution by raising controversial issues, proposing innovative plans and projects, setting direction, generating resources, making compromises, and mobilizing citizens—in short, making things move. This is what *political leadership* is about: potentially political leaders give direction to government. The Hamiltonian perspective promotes this principle of political leadership by stressing the importance of power in the executive for well-functioning government. Political leadership is organized and emphasized quite differently among the fourteen countries. In French local politics the mayor is the central figure who effectively controls the political body, the council, as well as the administrative organization. In Finland it is not obvious who is actually the political leader. In some municipalities, the chairman of the city council is the key political leader; in others, it is the chairman of the executive committee. In many American localities, mayors do not have executive powers but citizens recognize them as the central figure. If they are effective chairpersons of the council who promote cohesiveness and direction, they can provide facilitative leadership to council members and the city manager and staff (Svara and Associates 1994). In Ireland, on the other hand, where the mayor also lacks executive power, the "power-lessness" of the mayor has been described as "an embarrassment" in certain situations (Asquith and O'Halpin 1998, 69).

Professionalism

Layman politicians could be effective and active representatives who promote responsiveness to demands to solve specific complaints but ignore general, long-term problems that citizens as well fail to recognize. Politicians—including most full-time mayors—are amateurs who lack specialized knowledge about the work that government does. The local government system may also be organized with an eye to expertise, rationality—in the sense of goal-directed activity—and efficiency. The policy system may need energy and passion, but it also needs an infusion of problem analysis and strategic thinking, well-framed proposals that draw on the experiences of other municipalities, consistency and fairness in service delivery, continuity and sustained commitment, and productive use of resources. To be focused and efficient, governments need *professionals* who bring a distinct perspective and background to government. As politicians respond to demands, professionals respond to and seek to address needs (Svara 1990a).

Some small municipalities have no expert administration at all but rather rely on the efforts of elected officials and citizen board members, and other cities have administrative directors at the departmental level but no chief administrator. Most cities of any size (all those included in this study) provide for some combination of political leadership and centralized administrative expertise. The generalist administrator may be the choice of the political leader, as in France and some U.S. cities, and contribute to the work of the government through channeling ideas to the mayor and carrying out assignments from the mayor. Alternatively, the expert may be a city manager selected by the council as a whole and given broad responsibility not only to direct the administrative organization but also to serve as a professional leader who identifies problems and offers recommendations for policies to the council. Such is the case in council-manager type governments in Australia, Ireland, and the United States. Still others, depending on the nature of political leadership, have a more complex set of interrelationships between a mayor, executive committee, and CEO. There are also countries with administrators appointed from outside the city.

Issues in Applying the Principles

Of these three principles regarding the elements of government, political leadership is the starting point for the development of a typology of government forms. The key issue is how political power is obtained, maintained, exercised, and shared. These aspects of political leadership are assumed to be the decisive ones for the nature of interactions between the CEO and elected officials. Political power is a function of the degree of control a political actor—a person or a collective body—has in two arenas. First, to what extent is the city council controlled by one or more political actors? The second arena is the executive, and the question is to what extent does control over executive functions rest with one or more governmental actors? Formal structure is important to answering these questions, but so are informal institutional rules and norms.

Control over the city council is to a large degree a function of the electoral system. In most of the fourteen countries there is one central political figure, the mayor, who is elected by and among the members of the city council.

Some electoral systems are deliberately set up to produce effective majorities. This is true for arrangements in which the largest party or party coalition obtains seats in the council in addition to what they are entitled to according to the proportionality principle. Simple majority, ward based systems also promote one-party majorities. In contrast, at-large based elections where council seats are distributed according to the principle of proportionality tend to lead to a situation where a coalition of parties must agree on the distribution of political positions after the election. As indicated in table 3.1, in only six countries do over half of the cities have a one-party majority. A combination of indirect election (where the mayor is drawn from the majority) and one-party dominance is likely to lead to a situation where one political figure is in effective control over the council. In most cities, however, one-party dominance is not present.[4]

The concept of "the executive" is multifaceted. At the most general level the executive function implies organizational authority: the direction of the municipal bureaucracy and service delivery institutions, the implementation of policies decided by the city council, and horizontal coordination between departments. It also involves vertical coordination, that is, acting as a link between the political and administrative level. Other aspects of the executive function are control over budget formulation, oversight of budget implementation, hiring of staff, appointment of members of boards and commissions, ex officio membership on boards and committees, certain veto powers and the right to fill vacancies in elected offices (Svara 1990a, chap. 4).

The key question is whether control over some executive functions is assigned to political actors and, if so, whether there is one or more politicians who exert executive authority. Probably no mayor or other local political actor has total control over all the facets of executive power. Powers are shared by constitution and by delegation. In some cities, even though general executive responsibility may rest with one person—typically labeled the mayor— some or many specific functions are handled by other persons or political bodies. The city council may be decisive when it comes to hiring the highest ranking administrators, budget preparation may rest with an executive committee, or the actual decision-making authority which is necessary to implement policies established by the council may rest with standing committees. Who has the authority to appoint the CEO is another critical variable. The appointment may be handled by the mayor, the city council, or be shared.

Finally, the CEO exercises authority over at least some executive functions. The authority may be shared with one or more political actors. The appointed administrator has constitutional authority to exercise certain executive powers. The appointing official may exercise the option of removing the CEO at any time or, except for serious misconduct, at the end of a fixed-term contract, but may not reduce the authority of the office without constitutional change.

The legal distribution of executive powers may say a lot about who controls the executive; however, it does not tell us anything about the ability to effectively use powers given to a person or a collective body by constitution. Local governments in most countries are dominated by laymen working as part-time politicians. The actual control that laymen can exercise over a large bureaucracy is a function of the resources available to them, like time, knowledge, experience, and perseverance (as well as the values and behavior of administrators). Categorizing different types of forms will therefore take into account not only formal distribution of powers but also the actual ability of leading politicians to work full-time as political leaders. For example, is the job of mayor considered to be a full-time position, and is the mayor paid enough to devote his or her work life to politics?

Four Ideal Types of Governmental Form

The challenge of categorizing forms is that some structures in certain countries are clearly based on an extant governmental model labeled as a particular form. This is particularly true of the council-manager form in Australia, Ireland, and the United States. In most countries, however, structures have evolved that reflect national conditions and preferences but have not been explicitly labeled. Based on the variations in how the three principles are incorporated into the governmental structure in the fourteen countries, four ideal types of governmental structure can be identified. These types are not an attempt to summarize the varying characteristics within each of four distinguishable clusters, but rather a specification of a "pure" type. The form of government in each of the fourteen countries may be described by its proximity to or distance from one of four ideal types:

• *The strong-mayor form:* The elected mayor controls the majority of the city council and is legally and in actuality in full charge of all executive functions. The CEO serves at the mayor's will and can be hired and fired without the consent of any other politicians or political bodies. The mayor can hire political appointees to help with any function. This form gives primary emphasis to the political leadership principle. The layman rule and professionalism are accommodated to strong political leadership.

- *The committee-leader form:* One person is clearly "the political leader" of the municipality—with or without the title of mayor. He or she may or may not control the council. Executive powers are shared. The political leader may have responsibility for some executive functions but others will rest with collegiate bodies, that is, standing committees composed of elected politicians, and with the CEO. In this form, there is a more even blending of the three principles than in the other forms.

- *The collective form:* The decision center is one collegiate body, the executive committee that is responsible for all executive functions. The executive committee consists of locally elected politicians and the mayor, who presides. In this form, greater emphasis is given to the layman principle (albeit a select body of laymen), and political leadership and professionalism are accommodated to it.

- *The council-manager form:* All executive functions are in the hands of a professional administrator—the city manager—who is appointed by the city council, which has general authority over policy but is restricted from involvement in administrative matters. The council is a relatively small body, headed by a mayor who formally has presiding and ceremonial functions only. In this form, emphasis is given to professionalism with constricted layman rule and limited political leadership.

Not all of the fourteen countries can be described precisely by one of the four ideal types. In all cases (except Norway for reasons explained below) it is relatively clear, however, which of the four ideal types best matches the way local political power is constituted in a country. Each of the fourteen countries is discussed in detail. There is no reference to the CEO unless the method of appointment or the functions assigned to the office are central to defining the form of government in a particular country.

The Strong-Mayor Form

France

The municipal council in France elects from among its members the mayor, who is by any standard the leading political figure in the municipality. The electoral system ensures, through a complicated set of rules, that an effective majority is created: the party or the coalition of parties that gets the most votes will be "overrepresented" in the council. Since the mayor comes from that party/coalition, he or she is usually in effective control of the council. Thoenig (1995) even suggests that municipal council members obtain their legitimacy from the visibility of the mayor. Sometimes ad hoc committees are established by the council, but typically they have limited authority and are tightly controlled by the mayor's office.

With few exceptions, French mayors hold in their hands all executive powers. They must implement council decisions, submit the budget for council approval, and control the municipal organization and personnel. They are, in the performance of these tasks, supported by a number of deputy mayors elected by and from the council. "Supplementary" deputy mayors may be chosen upon the recommendation of the mayor. The mayor is also more or less in control of the deputy mayors as he or she decides what executive powers to delegate to them. As a rule, the deputy mayors have less rather than more autonomy delegated to them (Thoenig and Burlen 1998, 190). In large municipalities the mayor appoints on a partisan basis his or her own staff—the cabinet—the members of which will join the mayor in the event he or she is expelled by the electorate. The French form of government very closely resembles the strong-mayor type.

Spain

Spanish mayors, who are elected indirectly by the city council from among its members, have extensive powers. They preside over the council, draw up the agenda of the council, prepare the budget, implement council decisions, supervise the daily administration, and are generally the visible representatives of the municipalities to the outside world. In municipalities with more than 5,000 inhabitants the mayor is obliged to appoint an executive committee and may delegate particular responsibilities to the individual members of the committee. Also the mayor may decide to establish subcommittees, but such bodies will have no decision-making or executive powers. Although Spanish city councils are elected on a proportional basis, the mayor typically exerts strong control over the council. In almost two-thirds of the municipalities, the mayor will come out of a party which has a majority of the seats (see table 3.1). The form of government found in Spanish municipalities, which has been labeled a "semi-presidential model" (Delgago et al. 1998, 240), comes very close to the strong-mayor type.

Portugal

The council in Portuguese municipalities consists of two groups of politicians. A slight majority is elected directly by popular vote on a proportional basis while a little less than half of the members are the chairmen of the district (or parish) councils within the municipality. The council is the legislative body of the municipality. At the same time as the council is chosen, an election is held for the executive committee on a proportional basis. The executive committee is responsible for the implementation of the council's decisions, prepares the budget, and supervises services and staff. The members may individually be delegated specific responsibilities from the executive committee or from the mayor. The latter is the chairman of the committee.

Most of the executive committees' authorities may be delegated to the mayor, who to an increasing extent (through legislation as well as local practices) has become de facto in charge of the municipal organization (da Silva e Costa 1998, 226). The mayor comes from the party that obtains the most votes in the election. Because one party usually holds a majority (see table 3.1), the typical Portuguese mayor is effectively in control of the political bodies. The form of government found in Portugal is consequently categorized as a strong-mayor system.

Italy

Until a few years ago Italian mayors were elected by and from among the members of the city council. They were, together with the members of the executive committee, responsible for the execution of decisions made by the council. In 1993—as a reaction to the widespread corruption in Italian local politics as well as the inability of many cities to form effective governments— a completely new system was created. Today the mayor is directly elected by the voters at the same time as the city councilors. Through a complicated voting system, the party or the coalition of parties that supports the mayor will always control a majority of seats in the council. In most cases the mayor will therefore be in effective control of the council, although the latter can pass a vote of no confidence with a subsequent extraordinary election to follow. The mayor is in charge of the day-to-day administration together with the executive committee, la giunta. In contrast to the former system, the members of this committee are chosen exclusively by the mayor, cannot be members of the council, and can be fired by the mayor at any time. Although the council may set up subcommittees, such bodies normally do not play an important role in the day-to-day execution of policies. The form of government found in Italian municipalities can best be described as the strong-mayor form.

The United States: Mayor-Council Governments

The political officials in mayor-council[5] governments in the United States occupy the executive and legislative branches as the name of the form suggests. The mayor is directly elected and has separate powers from those of the city council. The latter is a moderate sized body—usually ten to twenty members—commonly elected from electoral districts in partisan elections. The strong mayor in pure form has extensive powers over budget, appointments, and departmental organization, and exerts integrated administrative control over staff. The mayor can veto actions of the city council and is responsible for implementation of decisions taken by the council. The council has legislative authority to pass laws, approve the budget, and, with an extraordinary majority, override vetoes by the mayor. It exercises oversight of administrative performance but it does not have any direct control over administrative staff. Most cities of this type have council committees that review proposals to be submitted to the council and oversee administrative performance.

In practice, any of the powers held exclusively by the strongest of the strong mayors may be shared with the council, for example, the council may have authority to approve department head appointments. In addition, the executive authority of the mayor is often limited by the presence of a civil service personnel system that is responsible for hiring, review, promotion, and removal of middle and lower levels of management (and in some cities certain department heads). Still, mayors are the leading political figures in their government. They are full-time—except in small cities—with personal staff. Informally, they can use media exposure and popular recognition to overshadow the council.

The status of CEO (usually called a city administrator or a chief administrative officer) reflects the overlapping as well as the distinct powers of the mayor and council. The scope of the position and the duties depend on what responsibilities are assigned by the officials who appoint the CEO. These usually include authority over implementation of programs, day-to-day administrative concerns, and budget formulation, as well as playing an advisory role in developing other policy recommendations. Among participants in this study, approximately half of the CEOs are appointed by the mayor with the approval of the city council. Another 38 percent are nominated by the city council, making this official as much responsible to the council as to the mayor, although the mayor would still have general or specific supervisory authority over the CEO. Only 11 percent are appointed by the mayor alone, although direct mayoral appointment is found in half of the cities over 30,000 in population. These American mayor-council cities can best be assigned to the strong-mayor form of government even though the mayors vary in the formal strength of their position.

The Committee-Leader Form

Denmark

The political bodies in a Danish municipality are the city council, the executive committee, and various standing committees. Committee members are elected by and among city council members on a proportional basis. Executive powers are shared among the committees and the mayor. The standing committees are responsible for the "immediate administration" of affairs. The finance committee supervises all financial and administrative matters and prepares the budget.

The position of mayor is considered a full-time position and is paid accordingly. The mayor is the chairman of the city council and the finance committee. He or she convenes the council, establishes the agenda, is responsible for the minutes, and—most importantly—is "superior, daily leader of the municipal administration." The mayor is thus the formal head of the total municipal administration. The mayor may supervise all parts of the administration, demand any information from municipal employees, and look through any cases that are being considered by the committees or the administrative organization. The mayor is responsible for the implementation of decisions taken not only by the council, but by any political body or administrative unit (le Maire and Preisler 1996, 178). However, the mayor cannot interfere with or block decisions taken by the committees. Thus when it comes to specific, day-to-day administrative matters, the standing committees are fully in charge. The form of government found in Danish municipalities may accordingly be characterized as the committee-leader type.[6]

Sweden

City councils in Sweden are large, between 31 and 101 members. Among its members, the council elects the executive committee, most often on a proportional basis. The executive committee, which meets once a month, is in charge of finances, prepares the budget for the council, and oversees general administrative matters. The chairmanship of the executive committee is a full-time position with a full-time salary. As a special Swedish feature, an additional politician is paid on a full-time basis. He or she is elected from the most important opposition party. In large municipalities additional politicians may be engaged full-time (Haglund 1998, 142). The political power center in a Swedish municipality is the so-called working committee composed of full-time politicians only. This group prepares matters for consideration by the executive committee and the council. The working committee also may act in matters that have been delegated from the executive committee.

The Swedish system is clearly one which stresses the protection of minorities, a consensual style of decision making, and broad involvement of laymen through a plethora of committees and boards. On the other hand, the chairman of the executive committee is a full-time politician and is, in many but not all respects, considered on par with the Danish counterpart, the mayor. For these reasons we label the Swedish form of government as committee-leader.

Great Britain

British local government is highly partisan in nature. Council members are elected on a ward basis through majority vote. In most localities one party holds an effective majority, although the so-called hung-councils with no one-party majority have become more common. The mayor is normally a symbolic figure.[7] The locus of political power rests with the so-called council leader or majority leader. This person will most often be in effective control of the council, and he or she chairs the executive (or policy) committee and works closely with the administrative leaders. In many respects, the council leader is the de facto day-to-day political executive. Standing committees oversee departments, although these committees tend to be less important than they once were. When the work of service departments is crucial to the policies of the majority party, the council leader may engage in the details of its work. Although the council leader does not receive a salary, he or she does receive an allowance and a payment for each meeting attended, which in most cases allows the council leader to work full-time in this position.

From a formal point of view, the British form of government is dominated by committees. The majority leader, however, plays a crucial de facto role. We consequently label the British form of government committee-leader government.

The Collective Form

Belgium

The power center in most Belgian municipalities is the executive committee, a collective body consisting of the mayor and two to nine aldermen elected by and from the city council. Each member is elected by majority vote, that is, the majority party or party coalition effectively controls the executive. The executive committee implements council decisions, supervises municipal personnel, and is generally in charge of the day-to-day administration of the municipality. In some areas the executive committee acts on behalf of the provincial or central government. In practice the committee members are often individually responsible for one or more departments, and often they interfere directly in administrative matters. Formally, however, all decisions have to be taken collectively.

The mayor is formally appointed by central government (The Crown) after recommendation by the city council. In practice he or she is the leader of the majority group (Plees and Laurent 1998, 175). The mayor chairs the city council as well as the executive committee, is the ceremonial head of the municipality, and acts in certain areas on behalf of central government. The position of mayor is in salary terms considered to be a part-time job, as are the positions of aldermen. In reality some mayors work more or less as full-time politicians. The form of government in Belgian municipalities is collective government.

The Netherlands

The mayor of a Dutch municipality is appointed by central government. He is not—like his Belgian counterpart—an elected member of the city council. In fact, he is chosen from outside the municipality. Mayors are career people. Although they are often party members, they act like professionals in that they will often strive for career advancement in larger municipalities. Although mayors cannot be removed by the council, there has been a tendency in recent years for mayors to run into serious political problems when they lose the confidence of the council. There have been widely published cases of mayors stepping down from their position under such circumstances, and in reality it becomes less feasible not to step down when the mayor loses the trust of the elected politicians.

Dutch city councils elect two to six aldermen who together with the mayor constitute the executive committee, which is responsible for the daily administration, financial matters, and the implementation of decisions made by the council (Berveling et al. 1998, 161f). In practice each alderman is responsible to the council for a particular policy area. Formally, however, the executive committee acts collectively. The council may withdraw its trust in one or more aldermen, leading to their dismissal. The mayor chairs the council and the executive committee and acts on behalf of central government in certain areas. His or her term is six years, whereas the city council members are elected to a four-year term. Although municipalities may establish committees, they will always act in an advisory role only. The Dutch form of government is a relatively clear case of collective government.

Council-Manager Form

The United States: Council-Manager Governments

The political officials in council-manager governments in the United States have undivided authority to determine the policy of the municipality. The city charter confers authority to the city manager for execution of policy and organizational direction, and the council members rely on the city manager and staff to provide strategic advice and policy recommendations. The council is a small body—usually five to nine members—often elected at-large from a single constituency of all the voters, although election of at least some council positions from districts is becoming more common. The elections are usually nonpartisan, that is, the party affiliation of candidates is not indicated on the ballot. Only in a minority of cities do political parties play an important informal role in elections.

The mayor is usually directly elected but has no independent powers except for those pertaining to the position of presiding officer of the council. He or she can be important as a facilitative leader who supports the actions of other officials and offers broad policy guidance, and the mayor has a closer relationship with the city manager than do the other council members. The mayor does not, however, have any direct supervisory authority over the city manager. In general, the mayor is paid as if he or she were a part-time official, even though in medium-sized and large cities the amount of time spent amounts to a full-time job. The council has legislative authority to pass laws (ordinances) and approve the budget, and the council is responsible for hiring and removing the city manager. The council can dismiss the city manager at any time "without cause."

The city manager is granted executive authority in the city charter. His or her responsibilities include formulating and administering the budget, making staff appointments without council approval, and determining departmental organization. The city manager is responsible for implementation of decisions taken by the council and exerts integrated administrative control over staff.

Australia

All Australian local governments (except the 100 or so community councils organized for indigenous communities) are governed by elected representatives who have undivided authority to determine the policy of the municipality. The city manager has full executive authority over the administrative organization. Within the last decade all the states have codified a distinction between the roles of councilors and managers. Now councilors are supposed to make policy and managers are to implement policy, although practices vary widely. The typical council has ten to fifteen members. Mayors/council presidents are selected by the council or else by election at large, although practices vary within states as well as between them. Generally mayors elected at large are more powerful than those selected by their fellow councilors. Council membership tends to be stable with high rates of long-term incumbency, although this has declined in recent years with an increasing proportion of single-term councilors. Many elections are not contested; 70 percent of seats in rural governments and up to 40 percent of the seats in urban areas have candidates who are unopposed.

The council selects the city manager, who is appointed with a contract of three to seven years. The city manager may be removed during the term of the contract for misdemeanors following formal procedures in the human resource management policies of individual cities and states. If a council feels that the CEO's performance is inadequate for some reason, most states allow the council to remove the CEO (and pay out his or her contract). This is, however, relatively unusual.

Ireland

Elected local politicians in Ireland have no executive powers. The council decides on overall principles and on the budget, approves certain decisions taken by the city manager, and generally supervises the city manager's work. The mayor presides over the council and performs ceremonial functions. In many cases the mayoralty rotates between the members of the council on a yearly basis. There is no executive committee and a number of obligatory standing committees merely have an advisory role. The CEO—the city manager—is in almost total charge of the administration and has "general powers" in the sense that he or she acts in all matters not specifically reserved for the council. Ireland is a clear-cut case of a council-manager system.

Finland

In some ways Finland resembles Denmark and Sweden in its local government. Most municipalities are governed by a coalition of parties in a fairly consensual climate, and minorities are involved in policy making because the committees are constituted according to a proportional principle. In Finland, however, there is no position comparable to the Danish and Swedish mayors.

Decisions are made by collective bodies, particularly the executive committee which is in charge of preparation and implementation of the decisions made by the city council. The formal structure leaves open who is the leading politician. In about half of the municipalities the CEO considers the chairman of the executive council to be the leading politician; in about 40 percent it is the chairman of the city council. In the remaining 10 percent of the cases it is a third politician who is regarded as the leading politician. Personal and partisan factors are more important than formal structure in Finland. In any case, no single politician normally exerts effective control over the council and the administration.

The CEO is normally hired for a fixed period of five to seven years. His or her powers are written into the local government act. The CEO is the daily leader of the municipal administration and the city finances subject to the decisions made by the executive board. In practice the CEO often acts as the leading spokesperson for the municipality. The position is highly visible. The Finnish system is accordingly characterized as a council-manager form of government.

Norway

Features from all the forms of government other than the strong-mayor form are present in Norwegian municipalities. Previously the CEO was responsible for preparing and submitting recommendations to the city council. Accordingly, the budget proposal was prepared by the CEO. These powers were taken away by a new local government act in 1993. At the same time, however, the act strengthened the position of the CEO vis-à-vis departments. The CEO is now by law the formal leader of the municipal administration and can be delegated other powers by the council. So in terms of the CEO's relations downward in the organization, Norway resembles the council-manager form of government, although the Norwegian CEO does not have the same authority as found in council-manager systems vis-à-vis the political level.

One of the objectives of the 1993 reform was to strengthen the overall coordination at the political level and weaken the traditional sectoral mechanisms that followed from the traditional principal standing committee model. Committee government, however, remains a major aspect of municipal governance. In that sense (and in the use of the proportional principle), Norway resembles Denmark and Sweden. The major difference from the other Scandinavian countries is the rather weak role ascribed to the Norwegian mayor, who may more appropriately be labeled "leader of the council." He or she is chairman of the city council as well as the executive committee but exercises his or her powers in close cooperation with other party leaders, acting as the "first among equals." The position has been described as one of mostly symbolic character rather than the source of strong and active leadership (Baldersheim 1990; Larsen 1990; Baldersheim and Øgaard 1998, 130). The CEO's direction of the various service departments is not in any formal sense dependent on the mayor.

All important political parties are represented in the executive committee, which is responsible for preparing all matters to be decided by the council and for overseeing the implementation of decisions. The council can decide to delegate authority over specific matters to the executive council. In this respect Norway's government is similar to the collective form. However, members of the executive council are not (formally or de facto) responsible for a department or a specific policy area, which is the case in Holland and Belgium, and the executive committee does not have a role in directing the work of the departments. Relations between departments are conducted through the CEO. The Norwegian form of government seems to come closest to the council-manager type.

The local governmental systems described for these fourteen countries are categorized by four ideal types: strong-mayor, committee-leader, collective, and council-manager. These four institutional setups will, as a measure of *form of government*, be used as the major explanatory variable in this and subsequent chapters.

How Political Authority Is Exercised: The Strength and Nature of Mayoral Leadership as Reported by CEOs

Implied in the four ideal types of governmental systems are certain norms for political leadership. One would expect a strong mayor to be exactly what the label implies—a politically powerful leader. He or she leads the majority group in the council, establishes policy guidelines for the administration, and handles the details of the daily administration (if not personally, then through political appointees). Due to the importance of the electoral process in generating leadership, strong mayors normally have a strong partisan orientation and seek to promote their party's interest. The strong mayor is the "driving force" in this form of government (Svara 1990a, 82). At the other extreme, the pure version of the council-manager form of government might imply having mayors who are ribbon cutters. They have ceremonial functions only and often the position of mayor is shifted among the councilors on a yearly basis.[8]

These labels, however, are stereotypes that do not allow for strong mayors to be "weak," that is, ineffective, or the ribbon cutter mayors to be "strong." Any experienced local government CEO knows that mayors differ in their approach to leadership and their effectiveness depends on a number of circumstances. As one Norwegian CEO in a government classified as council-manager form stated, "The political climate is very much a function of the mayor. Should the previous mayor return to office after the next election we get a politician who will enter my turf. He will control the details and reduce my influence."[9] So, although one would expect that the mayor's behavior in office will be related to structure, the type of leadership provided by mayors may differ greatly within the same form of government. Formal structure defines the overall parameters of the office, but offices are filled in particular ways, in some instances to the extent that the structure seems to be transformed by leadership.

For examples to support this point, one can consider the case of Denmark, a country characterized by the committee-leader form of government. There are examples of mayors who have been in office since the mid-sixties and have effectively shaped the socioeconomic nature of their community and thereby the power structure of local government.[10] These mayors (mostly Social Democrats), who have enjoyed an effective one-party majority over decades, are in a position that may be described as similar to that of Mayor Daley in Chicago (Banfield 1961) or Chaban Delmas of Bordeaux—both well-known in their countries as examples of powerful political leaders. At the other extreme we find lame-duck mayors who serve at the mercy of the dominant parties that were deadlocked during the government formation negotiations. Such a mayor is—at best—first among equals like some of his Irish colleagues.

Mayors can provide leadership in three areas.[11] First, mayors can be public leaders who help determine the direction that citizens want their city to take. In this area, they vary in the extent to which they are visionary persons who initiate change in the community and have positive relations with citizens. Second, mayors can be party leaders who promote the interests of their political organization. Third, mayors can be policy leaders who shape the content of programs and projects. Policy leaders differ in the extent to which they focus on policy making and are engaged in the detailed work of government.[12] They can be

- innovators whose engagement in policy making as well as in administrative details is high,

- administrators with great attention to detail but low engagement in policy making,
- designers who are highly engaged in policy making with little attention to details,
- caretakers with low engagement in policy making as well as in administrative details.

Beyond these areas of leadership, mayors can differ in the style of leadership they provide. Some mayors react to circumstances as they arise. Others proactively anticipate and help to shape change.

It is plausible to expect that form of government will have the strongest association with the likelihood of being a policy leader, since the structural features of government specify which officials will have the authority to exert executive powers. It seems likely that public leadership may be enhanced by form but is not primarily a product of form. In addition, party promotion may be related to form because of the importance of creating a majority to secure the top political position in strong-mayor and committee-leader cities. Finally, the tendency to be reactive or proactive is likely to be an individual characteristic rather than a style shaped by formal structure.

Mayors as Public Leaders

When CEOs identify the traits of the ideal politician (a topic examined in chapter 7) two activities are on the top of their list. Leading politicians should have a vision of the way in which the municipality will develop in the long run, and they should be informed about citizens' views. No role is more important to CEOs than the one measured by the items that make up the public leadership dimension. In the eyes of the CEOs, however, mayors do not unconditionally live up to these expectations. They come closest to the ideal with respect to knowing what citizens want. Mayors generally have excellent relations with the public. Close to six out of ten CEOs find that their mayor to a very high or high extent has excellent relations with the public and knows what concerns citizens. However, when it comes to having a vision, a little more than a quarter of the CEOs report that their mayor is a highly visionary person who constantly initiates new projects and policies in the locality. Nearly four out of ten CEOs characterize their political master as a visionary person to a little extent or not at all.[13]

Table 3.2 illustrates the distribution on the four leadership indicators across the four forms of government. The distribution across countries is lo-

Table 3.2 CEOs' Perceptions of Mayors as Leaders by Form of
Government (percent)

	Strong-mayor	Committee-leader	Collective	Council-manager
PUBLIC LEADERSHIP				
High	38	29	40	26
Moderate	34	46	40	47
Low	28	26	20	27
Total	100	100	100	100
POLICY LEADERSHIP				
Innovator	19	11	8	3
Administrator	25	22	18	7
Designer	31	40	42	46
Caretaker	25	27	32	45
Total	100	100	100	100
PARTISAN LEADERSHIP				
High	30	35	9	8
Moderate	31	36	18	21
Low	38	29	73	71
Total	100	100	100	100
PROACTIVE LEADERSHIP				
Proactive	42	47	53	41
Mixed	36	32	31	34
Reactive	22	21	16	25
Total	100	100	100	100

NOTE: All four relationships are significant at the .00 level. See the technical appendix for exact levels of significance and distributions by country.

cated in the technical appendix. It is used in some of the interpretations that follow.[14]

There are great differences in the strength of public leadership across countries (see technical appendix). The strongest mayors are found in Italy, followed by Belgium and the U.S. mayor-council cities. Few effective public leaders are found in two of the council-manager countries, Finland and Ireland. However, the share of "weak" mayors ("low" in the table) is by far the largest in a country that comes very close to the strong-mayor ideal type—France.

These observations seem to indicate a nonexistent or at least weak relationship between form of government and strength of public leadership. Although we find a significant difference across forms of government with more effective mayors in the strong-mayor and collective systems, the difference is negligible, particularly when between 20 and 30 percent of mayors are found to be weak under all forms of government. There is large variation across countries within the same form, and in almost all cases one finds outliers that account for the differences between the four forms of government. Finland and Ireland pull down the share of effective mayors drastically in the council-manager cities, while the relatively large share of highly effective mayors in strong-mayor cities would be nonexistent without the high Italian score. Of particular interest is the difference within the United States. There is a significant difference in the expected direction, with the strong-mayor cities producing more effective mayors than the council-manager cities.[15] Still, the difference is in no way as dramatic as one would expect from the American literature on types of mayors (Svara 1990a, chap. 4). Obviously, individual characteristics of the incumbent mayors as well as formal position shape the level of public leadership.

Mayors as Policy Leaders

Mayors in the study governments are generally perceived by their top administrators as policy makers who are not heavily engaged in the details of the administration. CEOs identify nearly half of the mayors as primarily politicians who are engaged in policy making to a high or very high extent. If the point of departure is an expectation that policies are established by leading politicians, it is a surprise that one out of four CEOs characterize their political master as being engaged in policy making only to a little extent or not at all. Obviously, many mayors are not attentive to policy matters. One alternative to a focus on policy is attentiveness to administrative details. Here there is greater variation in the perceptions of the CEOs. About one out of four mayors is described as engaged in details to a very high or high extent, the same proportion is found to be focused on detail to some extent, and one out of four also is described as engaged in administrative details to a little extent and not at all.

The nature of a mayor's policy leadership can be divided into a four-part classification combining the level of involvement in policy making and in daily administrative details. In the second part of table 3.2 we find a clear relationship between form of government and policy leadership. In the collective and council-manager cities with the least formal resources in the mayor's office, 74 percent and 91 percent, respectively, confine themselves to policy making, that is, they are "designers," or are detached "caretakers." Still, even in strong-mayor cities, 56 percent stay out of details as do two-thirds of the committee-leader mayors. Again, there is variation between countries within the four forms of government (see technical appendix), but the variation seems to be lower than was the case for public leadership. All the strong-mayor countries have a score above the overall mean when it comes to concentration on detail (combining innovator and administrator types), and all the council-manager countries have a score below the mean. Looking at particular countries, the Finnish mayors stand out as being skewed toward the caretaker type, while a relatively large share of the Italians are classified as administrators. Designer mayors constitute a majority in three council-manager countries—Norway, Ireland, and United States council manager. Although relatively few mayors are characterized as innovators overall, we find relatively large shares in Spain, Italy, United States mayor-council, and Denmark. Again the difference produced by the two forms of government in the United States stands out. The council-manager mayors are the more focused on policy design, whereas the strong mayors are more engaged in administrative details.[16] Thus, form of government makes a difference in the distribution of policy leadership types, but it does not tell the whole story.

Mayors as Partisan Leaders

Relatively few mayors emphasize the promotion of the party program and the interests of the party members in the view of CEOs. One out of five is characterized as a strong partisan leader and one out of four as moderate; 55 percent are found to be weak in this aspect of leadership (see table 3.2.). Party promotion is the leadership dimension that is most closely related to form of government. Seven out of ten council-manager mayors are described as weak partisan leaders by their CEOs, whereas this is true for only 38 percent of the strong mayors and 29 percent of the mayors from committee-leader cities. Most mayors from strong-mayor and committee-leader cities bring a moderate or strong commitment to promoting their political party to the position. Most mayors in collective and council-manager cities do not. The former are likely to be recognized as party leaders, whereas the latter are individual leaders not strongly associated with a political party. Within the different forms of government there are certain variations across countries (see technical appendix). Most notably there is a large difference in mayoral leadership within the two collective countries—Belgium and the Netherlands. This difference corresponds to divergence in traditions. Although the mayor is formally appointed by the Crown or the central government in both countries, the position is in actuality always filled by the leader of the majority group in Belgium. In the Netherlands, on the other hand, the mayor is considered a professional position. The mayor typically comes from outside the municipality.

The introduction of the council-manager form in the United States had the explicit aim of getting rid of politics, in particular party politics, in favor of professional leadership and was usually accompanied by nonpartisan elections. In American cities with reform government, there are fewer partisan oriented mayors than in the mayor-council cities. The difference, however, is not very large. In fact, even in the U.S. mayor-council cities three out of four mayors score low on the partisan leadership dimension, a share only exceeded in Finland and among the U.S. council-manager mayors.

Mayors as Proactive Leaders

Relatively few CEOs consider their mayors to be reactive. (See table 3.2.) A little more than one out of five CEOs characterize their mayor as a person who reacts to the circumstances to a very high or high extent when new policies are formulated, and a little more than two out of five describe their mayor as someone who only to a little extent or not at all reacts to circumstances when formulating new policies. The remaining 34 percent find their mayors to belong to the intermediate category. Comparing the distribution of levels across forms of government, it is clear that proactiveness is only weakly—albeit significantly—related to form. We find relatively many proactive leaders in the Finnish council-manager cities, the French strong-mayor cities, and the British committee-leader form. It is likely that style of leadership (proactive vs. reactive), more than any of the three previous leadership dimensions, is formed by personal traits rather than structure.

In the following analyses, when form of government is used as a variable, it conveys not only structural characteristics but also a tendency of mayors to differ systematically—but not dramatically—in attention to specific administrative details and in their strength as party leaders. In other words, differences related to form of government reflect to a modest extent systematic variations in the performance of mayors as policy and partisan leaders. Form of government is not a proxy for mayoral leadership. This is even more true of public leadership and proactive style. Insofar as these are important in explaining factors such as CEO involvement or influence, they reflect the characteristics of specific cities and the individual incumbents (as described by the CEO) rather than the institutional framework.

The Cultural Context of Leadership

Form of government is important in explaining the role of elected officials and—as we shall see in later chapters—administrators in the political process. Form of government operates within a broader national setting. The way political and administrative authority is structured may be conditioned by or correlate with other basic characteristics of a country. Obviously, there is within the European context a certain geographic pattern as all four countries from Southern Europe have chosen a strong-mayor form. Is this a coincidence, or a matter of historical circumstance where countries within the same region slowly converge toward the same system? Or are there certain underlying factors that foster certain forms of government or may shape behavior within a form of government? In this section we focus upon one such factor—the cultural context in which governments operate.

France and Denmark have chosen two different forms of government in municipalities. In France one person, the mayor, is the visible power wielder and protector of the local interest. The mayor controls the council and has—formally and typically de facto—complete control over the administrative organization. In Denmark executive authority is spread out across a number of collective bodies, which formally as well as in practice give the Danish mayor less freedom than his or her French counterpart. Is this a coincidence? Probably not. Deeply embedded in the members of the two societies are certain cultural norms that for centuries have been transferred from one generation to the next. Certain "mental programs" are learned by the individual and strengthened from early childhood in the family, from educational institutions throughout childhood, and in the workplace throughout adulthood. Obviously, culture alone does not determine the choice of governmental structure. Some countries, such as the United States, use multiple forms. Still, cultural values may shape how governmental institutions operate and which institutions are chosen.

Geert Hofstede has developed a theory of national cultures which, among other aspects, focuses on how members of different societies look upon their relationship to power and authority and how they deal with uncertainty (Hofstede 1980, 1997).[17] In a study of leadership at the apex, the potential payoff from introducing the two dimensions could be high. The apex of leadership is a place where power is exercised in an environment which almost by its nature is characterized by ambiguity and uncertainty. How many officials are found and what happens at the apex could therefore at the outset be expected to depend on cultural traits which differ across countries. The question is whether differences found among private sector staff in IBM international branch offices—the source of Hofstede's research subjects—will contribute to understanding relationships among officials.

Hofstede defines *power distance* as "the extent to which the less powerful members of institutions and organizations within a country expect and accept that power is distributed unequally" (Hofstede 1997, 28). A large power distance in a country indicates that subordinates are dependent on their superiors and accept and expect the upper echelons of the hierarchy to give them direction and control them. Centralization is popular and people generally accept hierarchy as a reflection of the existential inequality between higher-ups and lower-downs. The powerful are expected to have privileges and to look as impressive as possible. The prevailing political ideologies stress and practice power struggle. In small power distance countries, subordinates prefer consultation with their superiors, hierarchies are looked upon as inequalities established for convenience, the ideal boss is a democrat, decentralization is popular, the powerful try to look less powerful than they are, and political ideologies stress and practice power sharing (Hofstede 1997, 28, 37, 43).

Uncertainty avoidance is defined as "the extent to which the members of a culture feel threatened by uncertain, unknown, ambiguous and unstructured situations" (Hofstede 1997, 113; see also Hofstede n.d., 6). In societies marked by high uncertainty avoidance individuals generally exhibit a subjective feeling of anxiety, feel uncomfortable in ambiguous situations, and have an emotional need for rules and a need to be busy. Society is characterized by many and precise laws and rules, administrators are negative toward the political process and citizens have a low trust in institutions. Individuals from low uncertainty avoidance countries generally do not like rules, but they are not afraid of breaking them if it is found necessary. They are positive toward politics and political institutions and exhibit a subjective feeling of well-being (Hofstede 1997, 125, 134).

The national culture scores shown in figure 3.1 are meant to describe differences between countries. Their absolute values have no meaning. The formulae used were constructed in such a way that scores would normally fall within the 0–100 range (in a larger sample of countries that included many Asian countries with extreme scores, for instance, on the power distance index). The absolute values of the scores from this study do not match those in Hofstede's study conducted around 1970 in another context with a somewhat

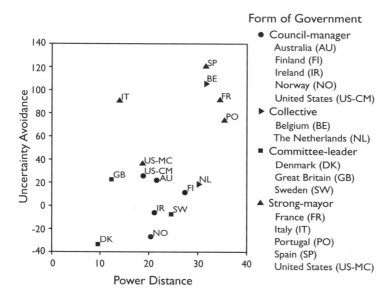

Figure 3.1 Form of government and national cultures

different method for calculating the scores. The relative position of the scores for the fourteen countries in the two studies can be compared, and they are remarkably similar. The simple correlation between the IBM and the U.Di.T.E. measures is .71 for the power distance index and .87 for the uncertainty avoidance index.[18] As a consequence, there is every reason to expect that the two indices measure some deeply embedded cultural differences between countries.

With respect to form of government there are four distinct clusters. Most obviously, countries that have picked the strong-mayor form are characterized by a high degree of uncertainty avoidance and, with the exception of Italy, also by a high power distance. Generally, strong-mayor systems are found in countries where it is accepted that power is distributed unequally, where members are rule oriented and skeptical toward the political process. The U.S. mayor-council cities are a notable exception. Based on these cultural characteristics, one would expect greater emphasis on hierarchy along with concern about clearly specifying the roles and authority of officials. The two countries with the collective form of government exhibit a relatively high score on power distance, but differ on uncertainty avoidance. To the extent that the latter dimension has an effect on the actions of politicians and administrators, we may expect to find differences between the Netherlands and Belgium. For example, adherence to rules will be a matter of greater concern in Belgium than in Holland. The council-manager form of government is found in countries with a low to medium score on uncertainty avoidance and a similar score on the power distance index. The clear difference between politicians and administrators that some have argued should be maintained in this form may not be as important to the participants in the governmental process. These same characteristics should apply to the three committee-leader countries that have similar low to medium scores on uncertainty avoidance, although Sweden seems to be somewhat of an outlier on the power distance index.

In the analysis that follows in subsequent chapters, it is important to bear these clusters in mind. To the extent that the involvement of administrators in the political process varies systematically with form of government, one should consider in what ways the variation may be interpreted as a consequence of cultural differences or a combination of form and culture. It would seem likely that the effects of hierarchy are magnified by greater power distance. Complex arrangements for sharing power are presumably more tolerable when uncertainty avoidance is low. In the analysis performed at the country level, the cultural dimension will be systematically introduced along with form of government.

Additional Contextual Differences

Form of government is related to certain cultural traits. It may also be associated with certain ideas about the role of government in general, and with the role that local government plays in the overall state apparatus. National differences in the size of the public sector and the degree of decentralization of service provision will affect the scale and scope of municipal governments. Countries differ in these respects and in the extent of governmental consolidation that is fostered by policy and practice. These characteristics have a systematic effect on the size of the municipal organization that the CEO directs.

The Scandinavian countries are not only characterized by a large public sector but also by the role assigned to local governments in providing services. They are, according to Goldsmith (1992, 395), representative of the "welfare state model," where "the value of efficient service delivery, linked to national norms concerning equity and redistribution, has shaped the growth and working of local government, which has acted as the producer and deliverer of welfare-state services." Other countries that have been concerned with

Table 3.3 Indicators of the Size of Municipalities and the Municipal Workforce

| | | The U.Di.T.E. sample | | |
	(national statistics) Average population	Median population[a]	Total workforce in municipality with 10,000 inhabitants [b] (full-time equivalents)	Median workforce [c] (full-time equivalents)
Australia	19,100	8,900	100	80
Belgium	17,000	11,500	80	90
Denmark	18,800	10,700	580	610
Finland	10,900	5,500	380	200
France	1,600	15,000	130	220
Great Britain	120,000	119,500	80	730
Netherlands	24,200	14,400	60	90
Ireland	103,000	90,800	100	800
Italy	7,200	13,000	80	90
Norway	9,000	4,500	380	190
Portugal	32,000	15,500	120	130
Spain	4,800	8,000	60	40
Sweden	30,200	15,500	690	1,040
USA	6,600	15,700	100	130

Sources: Average population figures are from Lidström (1996). For the United States and Australia, information was supplied by national teams.

NOTES: Figures have been rounded to the nearest hundred in the first two columns, and to nearest ten in the last two columns. For Britain and Ireland the figures are based on average of municipalities with between 30,000 and 50,000 inhabitants.

a. Figures for Sweden, Britain, Spain, and Australia were interpolated based on population categories (for all countries based on weighted analyses). The calculated median from the sample is close to the median calculated from official statistics in countries where we had access to this (Finland, Norway, Sweden, Denmark, and Belgium). The sample-based median of 2,300 for Italy, however, is much lower than one based on official sources (13,000), because the Italian sample does not draw on the total population of municipalities in Italy. The same is true for the Spanish, French, and American cases. See the technical appendix for sampling information in the fourteen countries.

b. Total workforce in a municipality with 10,000 inhabitants is based on survey data. In order to get to this hypothetical figure we calculated the average number of full-time employees per 10,000 inhabitants in municipalities with population between 5,000 and 15,000. There was little evidence of economies or diseconomies of scale (with the exception of Portugal where some economies of scale were evident) or large differences in the number of functions performed by municipalities in this population range. The Swedish, Spanish, and Australian figures have been interpolated.

c. Swedish figures have been interpolated.

the provision of a wide range of collective consumption goods are, according to Goldsmith, the Netherlands and Britain.

The Southern European countries are based on a second model, a "clientelistic" system of relations between leaders and citizens. Local governments are small, and the primary duty of politicians is to deliver specific public goods to their constituents and make sure the interests of the community are represented at higher levels of government (Goldsmith 1992, 395). As Goldsmith points out, however, the Southern European countries have moved closer and closer to the welfare state model over decades.

A third model is labeled "urban support systems." The governments using this model emphasize the services that are necessary to support the distinctive needs of their residents and that promote the development of the city it-self (Svara 1998b). These governments, although they vary widely in size, have an incentive to limit their size and range of services in order to be com-petitive with other cities in the service/tax combination they provide (Peter-son 1981). Cities in Australia and the United States approximate this model.

It has become customary to compare the size of municipalities across countries by simply dividing the total urban population in a country by the number of municipalities. This is done in the first column of table 3.3. The second column shows the median population size of municipalities in the samples of cities included in this study. The difference between the two columns is attributable to two factors. First, the mean population often ob-scures what is the typical size of municipalities in a country. Second, the dif-ference reflects the fact that the U.Di.T.E. Leadership Study left out the small-est municipalities in countries with many small localities (for a detailed description of the sampling procedure, see the technical appendix). This was done for Spain, Italy, France, and the United States. In the samples for the study, the typical municipality as reflected by the median population in the fourteen countries varies but lies within a range which makes comparisons reasonable. With the obvious exceptions of Britain and Ireland where gov-ernments have been consolidated into large units, the population size of the typical municipality lies within a range of 4,500 to 15,800.

The third column of table 3.3 shows the average number of employees (full-time equivalents) in a typical municipality with 10,000 inhabitants across the fourteen countries. This figure may be interpreted as an indicator of the range of functions performed by municipalities as well as the organiza-tion of service delivery; that is, services are produced within the municipal or-ganization, provided by a higher level or different local government, or con-tracted out.[19]

The more than 4,000 local government CEOs who have participated in the U.Di.T.E. Leadership Study sit on top of very different organizations ranging from those that nearly match the size of Europe's most valuable business en-terprise, Nokia, to those with only a handful of people employed. The median workforce in each country in the U.Di.T.E. sample is indicated in the last column of table 3.3. Unlike column three which attempts to measure a gov-ernment of typical and standard size, this figure is a function of three major factors—population size, range of local government functions, and the or-ganization of service delivery.[20]

In relative terms the Swedish and Danish CEOs direct the largest workforces with 690 and 580 persons, respectively, employed in a municipality with 10,000 inhabitants. The Swedish CEO with the median workforce oversees some 1,000 employees, whereas his or her Danish counterpart heads an organization with about 610 employees. British and Irish cities also have large median municipal workforces. The number of their employees results from large populations rather than a broad scope of services provided by a high number of employees per capita.

To illustrate the variation, the largest organization among the sample cities is found in the City of Copenhagen with a population of around 475,000 inhabitants. The city employs some 43,000 persons (with a budget of 40,000 million Kroner or almost $6 billion, the size of the gross domestic product of countries like Latvia or Honduras).[21] At the other end of the extreme we have in our sample two Spanish CEOs who sit on top of an organization employing four persons! Clearly such differences may have important consequences for the involvement of the CEO in political processes.

The system models suggested by Goldsmith do not correspond completely to the four forms of government, but there is some overlap. The strong-mayor form is found in countries with a relatively small local public sector and relatively small organizations. The committee-leader form of government is found in two countries where local governments play a very important role—Sweden and Denmark—and also in Britain where local governments play a more moderate role but serve very large populations. As a consequence the CEOs in these countries head large organizations. Collective systems are characterized by relatively small organizations. Finally, council-manager systems are found in countries with a small to moderate local public sector. The typical organization in these countries employs between 100–200 persons albeit with one exception, Ireland.

In the analyses to follow it is important to bear these patterns in mind. To the extent that the involvement in the political process of administrators varies systematically with form of government, one should consider whether the variation may be related to differences in scope of government and size of the municipal organization. The latter factor will be applied systematically in several analyses where the unit of analysis is the individual locality or CEO.

Conclusion

The institutions that frame how political power is constituted in local government are quite different. In this chapter, four models of governmental structure have been established as ideal types. The local government systems in the fourteen countries are categorized in terms of their closeness to these ideal types. In almost all cases, there is a close match between countries and one of the forms. Norway in particular has features associated with three of the forms, but the council-manager form seems to better capture its essence than the others.

CEOs operate in a context shaped by the institutional setup and mayoral leadership. The key elected official is the mayor, although mayors vary greatly. Within the framework provided by the form of government, incumbent mayors fill the office in different ways depending on their personal characteristics and political forces and other conditions within specific cities. Mayors can provide leadership in three areas. They can be policy leaders who shape the content of programs and projects. They can be public leaders who help determine the direction that citizens want their city to take. They can be party leaders who promote the interests of their political organization. Furthermore, they can differ in the style of leadership they provide with some mayors reacting to circumstances as they arise and others proactively anticipating and helping to shape change. Although leadership positions are shaped by form of government, the actual behavior of leaders is not determined by form. The relationship between structure and behavior is strongest along the partisan dimension, less strong when it comes to policy leadership, and weakest as far as public and proactive leadership are concerned. Thus, form of government conveys not only structural characteristics but also a tendency of mayors to differ systematically in attention to specific administrative details and in their strength as party leaders. It tells us nothing, however, about the strength of public leadership or manifestation of a proactive style.

Form of government also conveys certain cultural attributes that vary by country. The countries with strong mayors and collective cities tend to score highest on power distance where it is accepted that power is distributed unequally, where members are rule oriented and skeptical toward the political process. The committee-leader countries have the lowest power distance scores (other than Sweden), and the council-manager countries are in between. The countries with council-manager and committee-leader forms are intermixed with low to moderate uncertainty avoidance scores. In these countries, there is a tolerance for ambiguity, less structured roles and relationships, and acceptance of differences. The strong-mayor countries, with the exception of the United States, have high scores. This indicates that hierarchy, fixed roles, and higher levels of conflict over differences are common. The collective cities are split between high (Belgium) and moderate (Holland) levels. To the extent that the involvement in the political process of administrators varies systematically with form of government, this variation reflects in part cultural differences.

Two special situations illustrate the interaction of form and culture. The lack of substantial differences found in the United States between cities that use different forms of government may be attributed to common cultural characteristics. The CEOs in the Netherlands and Belgium share many characteristics, as would be expected in view of their common form of government. Still, they differ in some particular areas such as willingness to get involved in the somewhat risky activity of giving political advice to politicians. The Dutch CEOs are more inclined to do so and the Belgian CEOs less, as one would expect from their differing orientation to uncertainty avoidance.

There is some systematic difference between countries with different forms of government in the size of the municipal organization. The committee-leader cities in countries that have had a tradition of extensive social welfare services stand out from the rest in the size of their governments because of a large public sector and broad range of services assigned to local government and—in the case of Great Britain, or—because of large city size. The strong-mayor governments, on the other hand, tend to provide fewer services and serve smaller populations.

Form of government will constitute a major explanatory theme in the chapters which follow. Does form of government make a difference when it comes to the involvement of administrators in the political process, the development of norms concerning the "ideal" politicians, and the distribution of influence between different political and administrative actors? How much explanatory power do individual and community characteristics provide when the effects of form of government have been removed? To what extent are political-administrative phenomena, including what happens at the apex of leadership, a reflection of deeply embedded cultural traits which cannot be altered by institutional design? It will also be important to bear in mind the differences in the size and scope of the governments clustered by form of government.

In the next chapter, the ways that CEOs relate to the political process are examined. The analysis probes whether administrative values, environmental impacts, and networking by CEOs are shaped by structural and cultural factors.

CHAPTER 4

CEOs' Interactions with Their Political Environment

with Marcel van Dam and Geert Neelen

THE BEHAVIOR OF LOCAL GOVERNMENT CEOs at the apex of leadership is affected by the formal position in the government as described in chapter 3. The CEO brings to the position a complex array of attitudes and experiences that condition, constrain, and enable the CEO to act. It is not possible to know all factors that affect how CEOs fit into their context. We are able, however, to survey a number of salient factors, including their attitudes about government and political responsibility, their assessment of the pressures that they experience from inside and outside of government, and their interactions with other officials and actors in the community and beyond. These factors are described in this chapter and will be used as independent variables in subsequent chapters.

Underlying the discussion are two issues. First, as noted, the position occupied by the CEO is defined by both formal and informal factors. But is there a connection between them? It will be important to determine to what extent there is systematic variation between these attitudinal and contextual factors. Do CEOs who work in different forms of government have different attitudes about their role or responsibilities? If form of government is based on differing models of political-administrative relations, it is possible that CEOs will view the political process and their role in it differently as well. Furthermore, are CEOs subject to a distinctive mix of supportive and restraining internal and external forces depending on their form of government?

The second issue is whether CEOs can at least partially determine their circumstances by the kind of linkages they establish with other actors. We presume that to some extent, CEOs are self-directed actors who shape their environment, not just agents who are acted on by factors in their environment. CEOs have preferences for how they will relate to politicians and the public.

They combine interactions that are automatic or unavoidable in the sense that they are dictated by structure with others that are individually chosen to create a network of relationships. We shall seek to determine whether CEOs who work in cities with different forms of government have distinctive interactional patterns and form different kinds of networks with other actors. Making these determinations is important to knowing what other characteristics if any are "bundled" with institutional structures.

The discussion devotes considerable attention to the values of CEOs concerning their relationship to the political process and their networking behavior. In both areas, variation by both country and form of government is examined. There also is a review of forces in the governmental and community context that support or constrain the CEO. These factors—uncertainty about roles, party conflict, pressures from the community and from relations with other governments—receive briefer coverage with emphasis on variation by form of government. In the conclusion, we will consider the extent to which there is overlap in tendencies across all these factors.

CEOs' Attitudes about Their Relationship to the Political Process

The way that administrators think about their relationship to the political process is presumably shaped by a bundle of value preferences. It is possible to measure attitudes about nonpartisanship, administrative activism, the nature of accountability, and the desirability of having administrators who share the policy goals of politicians. The first two sets of measures suggest ways that administrators view their role in society. The second two indicate how they define political responsibility. Each is considered in turn.

Administrator's Role in Society: Nonpartisanship and Administrative Activism

As discussed in chapter 2, a commitment to neutrality is fundamental to the way we think about the administrative role. Many observers diminish the idea of neutrality to such an extent that it loses any aspect of serving or protecting the public interest (Dunn 1997, 161–62), but broader and more active definitions of neutrality are widely supported. An alternative view is that neutral competence means that administrators take independent stands drawing on "expertise," that is, knowledge and values that are grounded in their practice and their profession, as well as being dedicated to partisan neutrality. The question of whether CEOs are public-serving in their orientation or simply concerned with being detached from politicians can be answered by examining indicators in the U.Di.T.E. survey. The study included the following items that probe the value preferences of CEOs on their role in society.

CEOs may have different opinions about the way in which their relations with elected officials ought to be organized. Below are some statements, which touch upon this subject in different ways. Please indicate whether you agree or disagree with them:

a. The administration should be nonpartisan and only base its recommendations on expert opinion.

b. The administration must be a prime mover in adapting the municipality to changes in society.

c. Certain groups in society are so weak that it is the duty of the administration to speak for them.

In the responses to these items, strong support for the traditional commitment to neutrality and the importance of expertise is found among CEOs. (For a complete summary of responses, see the technical appendix.) Over four out of five believe that CEOs should be nonpartisan and base their recommendations on professional considerations only, and half strongly agree with this position. The support for nonpartisanship varies little across countries; only in Great Britain do less than 70 percent of CEOs agree that it is important. These attitudes are fairly uniform in cities that use different forms of government, although the level of support is slightly lower in committee-leader cities.[1] There is no less support for nonpartisanship in strong-mayor cities. The supposition that CEOs who work with powerful political executives might have a lower level of support for nonpartisanship, that is, are more likely to be committed to responsiveness than neutrality, is not supported by the data. CEOs generally see themselves as expert practitioners who are set apart from political parties and partisan considerations.

The emphasis on nonpartisanship, however, does not mean that CEOs are disengaged from their communities or disinclined to offer leadership. Over 80 percent agree that administration should be a prime mover in adapting the municipality to changes in society. The range by country is 100 percent in Ireland to 69 percent in Sweden who agree with this position. There is somewhat greater variation between cities that use different forms of government than there is in support for nonpartisanship. The council-manager CEOs are the most supportive of administrators playing an active role (91 percent agree), and the collective CEOs are the least (71 percent agree).

A smaller share, but still a majority, of CEOs also support the idea of work-

ing to promote the interests of lower social and economic strata in society, although support is lower. Overall, 57 percent of CEOs agree that certain
groups in society are so weak that it is the duty of the administration to be a
spokesperson for them. The level of agreement ranges from a high of 72 percent in Great Britain to a low of 26 percent in Sweden, with less than a majority agreeing in the United States, Belgium, and the Netherlands. The overall
differences between cities that use different forms of government is not
great, but the average figures mask some of the lower levels of support just
noted in selected countries.

There is a modest positive relationship between favoring an active role for
administrators in local government and protecting the interests of the poor.[2]
There has been a lively discussion in the public administration literature
about a commitment to activism and equity among administrators. The responses of CEOs indicate that there is general support for an activist role and
substantial support for promoting equity, although there is also variation at
the country and individual level. There is no association between these measures of activism and support for nonpartisanship.

In subsequent analyses, the two measures of activism are combined to create an index of advocacy measured on a 100-point scale.[3] The average values
of the advocacy scale for countries grouped by form of government is as follows: strong-mayor, 70; committee-leader, 68; collective, 62; and council-
manager, 72.[4]

Thus, the typical CEO is a politically neutral professional committed to offering leadership in dealing with community problems. The dominant value
preferences of CEOs are consistent with models that stress an active stance
for administrators. Their support for guiding community change suggests
that CEOs will be engaged in shaping and resolving policy issues even
though they operate from a base in the administrative realm. The views of the
minority on neutrality could be consistent with the responsive administrator
model, and the minority views on the leadership role for administrators
could be consistent with the separate roles model.

Nature of Political Responsibility: Accountability and Policy Congruence

Two indicators provide insights regarding how CEOs view their responsibility to the political process. The first examines attitudes regarding policy
congruence:

*It is an advantage if the CEO is of the same political opinion as the majority of the
local council.*

Agreeing with this statement does not necessarily mean that the CEO agrees with his or her council majority, and the opinion may be based on practicality rather than conviction that administrators should match the views of politicians. "There is little doubt," Aberbach and Rockman (2000, 172) observe, "that congruence in the goals of top career and noncareer executives helps to ease relations between them." Still, agreement suggests that one considers it to be desirable that CEOs have congruent views with politicians, whereas disagreement suggests preference for some degree of independence in policy views.

The second indicator examines attitudes regarding accountability. The statement is as follows:

The CEO should be primarily responsible to the political leadership and only secondarily to the local population.[5]

Agreement indicates that CEOs believe that primary responsibility is given to elected officials, that is, accountability internal to government. These CEOs could be viewed as "political servants" primarily serving elected officials and only indirectly the public. Those who disagree with the statement, on the other hand, express a preference for giving substantial responsibility to citizens who are external to government. Because of the wording of the questionnaire item, CEOs who disagree with the statement do not necessarily consider the public to be more important than elected officials. Still, their view of accountability is diffuse and ambiguous in comparison to the CEOs who stress direct accountability to elected officials and could provide the basis for justifying actions that reflect their view of the public interest rather than the preferences of elected officials.

In view of the difficulty in interpreting certain responses to these two statements, it is risky to construct a typology based on them. Cluster analysis reveals four clear groupings with scores that are uniformly high, uniformly low, and with one high and one low score from each dimension.[6] Still, the only category that has values that can be clearly interpreted is the group that favors policy congruency and prefers being primarily responsible to elected officials. These CEOs, who represent about one-quarter of the respondents, seem to approximate the attitudes that one would expect to find among administrators who correspond to the responsive administrator model of political-administrative relations. The other combinations all have some degree of attitudinal support for independence in policy views, orientation to citizens as well as (or instead of) elected officials, or both. Those who combine low

Table 4.1 Variation by Country in CEO Preferences Regarding Policy Congruency and Responsibility

Advantage if CEO has same political opinion as the majority of the council (average agreement = 27%)	*CEO should be primarily responsible to the political leadership (average agreement = 54%)*	
	Majority in country agrees	Less than majority agrees
Majority in country agrees	SM[a] France 56/81[b] SM Portugal 55/71	
Less than majority agrees	CL Sweden 9/89 CL Denmark 5/74 CL Great Britain 20/52 COL Belgium 33/73 COL The Netherlands 15/53 CM Norway 3/50	SM Italy 27/33 SM Spain 30/46 SM U.S. mayor-council 30/23 CM Australia 29/45 CM Finland 49/33 CM Ireland 10/20 CM U.S. council-manager 27/31

NOTES: a. Form of government: SM, Strong-mayor; CL, Committee-leader; COL, Collective; CM, Council-manager

b. The first number after the country name indicates the percentage of the CEOs who agree on the item shown to the left of the row. The second number indicates the percentage of CEOs who agree on the item at the top of the column.

support for policy congruence with direct accountability to elected officials approximate the characteristics of the administrators in the separate roles model. CEOs who disagree that policy congruence is an advantage and consider themselves to be responsible to the public have a mindset that might support the autonomous administrator model. The final combination—responsibility to the public and support for the advantage of congruence—does not clearly match the models of political-administrative relations.

It is apparent that as CEOs operate in the political context, they blend their preferences for accountability and congruency in a wide variety of ways. This variety is reflected at the country level as well, as indicated in table 4.1. In only two countries does a majority of CEOs agree that they should have the same opinion as the council majority and that they are primarily responsible to the council. These countries are France and Portugal—both strong-mayor countries. In six countries, a majority agrees with being directly accountable to elected officials, but generally reject the idea that it is an advantage to share the views of the council. All the countries with this combination use the committee-leader and the collective forms of government, with the exception of Norway which joins two other Scandinavian countries in overwhelmingly supporting policy congruency. In this group, Swedish CEOs manifest a very high level of consistency in their opinions with virtually all taking the same position. In the remaining countries, less than half of the CEOs agree with either statement. Most believe that agreeing with the council is not necessarily an advantage and that responsibility should be directed to citizens at least as much as to elected officials. Three of the five countries that use the strong-mayor form are in this category as are four of the five council-manager countries. Of these, the Irish CEOs demonstrate a high degree of uniformity in their thinking, decisively rejecting both policy congruency and direct accountability. Still, in most countries (with the exception of Sweden and Ireland), CEOs vary considerably in their attitudes about appropriate relationships.

In view of the division in opinion within countries and clusters of countries that use the same form of government, there is the potential for an ongoing dialogue, and in some countries debate, between CEOs about the nature of political responsiveness and accountability. Overall, they are fairly evenly divided in their opinions about the focus of responsibility. Almost half take the position that they should be as strongly oriented to citizens as they are to politicians. Approximately three in ten feel that it is better if CEOs have views that are in line with the majority opinion of their council; the remainder value independence in political views. CEOs are generally agreed that they should be nonpartisan and use expertise and that government led by administrators should be a driving force for change in society. Most also feel they should promote equity in society. CEOs come to the ongoing political relationship as professional activists who differ in their views about policy responsiveness and primary accountability to elected officials.

Supportive and Constraining Forces in the Governmental and Community Context

In order to understand relationships and behavior of CEOs at the apex of the local governmental process, it is important to know more about how smoothly they work with elected officials and what forces impinge upon them from within government and from the external environment. There could be many such forces given the proximity of city government to the citizens it serves and the complex intergovernmental arena in which cities operate. In the U.Di.T.E. questionnaire, CEOs were asked to estimate how their ability to perform the job of CEO had been affected negatively by a wide range of factors during recent years. This section assesses the importance of several sources of adverse impact developed from these factors. The sources are uncertainty, conflicts between political parties, and other external pressures.

Uncertainty

In order to work together effectively, politicians and administrators need to agree on the ends they are pursuing and apportion tasks in a constructive way. In the absence of these qualities, there is uncertainty in the relationship.[7]

When assessments of the clarity of goals and the degree of cooperation in the division of tasks are combined, an index of uncertainty can be created. The lack of clear political goals and unclear division of labor between elected officials and staff create high uncertainty for the administrator. Among the countries included in the study, uncertainty tends to be fairly low. A majority of CEOs considers uncertainty to be low in three countries—Finland, Ireland, and Australia—and rates it as low or moderate in all the remaining countries with the exception of Italy and Spain.

When countries are divided by form of government, uncertainty is lowest in council-manager cities in which there is a clear division of function between the council and the city manager. Almost half of the CEOs consider uncertainty to be low, and another quarter perceive only moderate uncertainty. The council is the governing board of the city, and the manager has undivided executive authority and is head of the administrative organization. Together they set goals, and the city manager is responsible for carrying out those goals. Compared to the three-quarters of the council-manager cities that have low to moderate uncertainty, slightly less than two-thirds of the committee leader and collective leadership cities have low to moderate uncertainty. In strong-mayor cities, on the other hand, almost half of the CEOs report moderately high to high uncertainty. The mayor's substantial executive authority creates more overlap in roles between the mayor and the top administrator than found in other forms of government.[8] Thus, confusion over ends and lack of clear division of tasks represent the exception rather than the rule across all countries, although they are more common in strong-mayor cities.[9]

Uncertainty and the level and type of mayoral leadership, described in chapter 3, are linked. According to the logic of each form of government, the mayor would play the largest role in policy innovation and administration—the two elements of the dimension of policy leadership—in strong-mayor cities and committee-leader cities. The contribution would be lower in collective cities and least in council-manager cities where the ideal mayor would help to design policy but not carry it out. In strong-mayor cities, uncertainty is fairly high regardless of the mayor's approach to policy leadership. Still, high uncertainty is most common when the mayor is a caretaker, that is, neither develops policy ideas nor pays attention to administrative details, in a form in which he or she is supposed to be a strong leader. Uncertainty is least common when the mayor is a designer of policies rather than an implementer.[10] In the committee-leader cities, almost half of the CEOs report high uncertainty when the mayor gets involved in administrative details but does not pay attention to policy development. When there is an innovator type mayor who combines these elements of policy leadership, uncertainty is least common, reported by less than one CEO in five.[11] In the council-manager and collective cities, involvement in day-to-day administration is linked to greater uncertainty.[12] These mayors are "intruding" in the details of implementation and service delivery. From the perspective of the CEO, performance that deviates from norms about proper policy involvement for the mayor produces confusion about who should be doing what.

The other dimensions of mayoral leadership are also related to uncertainty. Variation in the mayor's strength as a public leader is related to the level of uncertainty in committee-leader and collective cities. Certainty about goals and coordination of roles is much more common when public leadership is high, and high uncertainty is much more common when public leadership is low.[13] Furthermore, in strong-mayor, committee-leader, and council-manager cities, higher proactive leadership from the mayor is linked to lower uncertainty.[14]

There are two possible interpretations of the link between mayoral behavior and uncertainty, but it is difficult to determine which is more appropriate. It is not possible to clearly establish whether "problems" with leadership—behavior that is not consistent with structural norms or lower levels of leadership—cause uncertainty or, alternatively, whether a low level of certainty forces the mayor to handle administrative details and undercuts the capacity for leadership. Anecdotal evidence and observation would argue for the former interpretation. There is greater confusion when the mayor is "inappropriately" involved based on the norms for the system. It is not the level of attention to administrative detail per se that lowers uncertainty in committee-leader cities, but this kind of engagement in the absence of attention to policy formation. The mayor's inability to develop policy initiatives and reactive rather than proactive responses create a lack of direction that naturally would leave officials wondering what their goals are and how tasks will be accomplished. Effective political leaders shape goals and organize action when they encounter a policy vacuum and the lack of coordination. Effective leaders are not immobilized by these conditions. It seems justifiable, therefore, to take the leap of faith that uncertainty is produced by conditions in the political environment, including the mayor's capacity to lead. Furthermore, uncertainty is related to structure. There is greater uncertainty in mayor-council cities than in cities with other forms across all types of mayoral leadership.

Conflicts between Political Parties

Another aspect of the political environment is the degree of conflict between political parties. In the measure of factors that impede performance, party conflict was one of the options.[15] It can be a very important factor determining the ability of CEOs to perform their job, just as uncertainty is. On one occasion, a Danish CEO claimed that impossible working conditions created by the party battles in the council had led to the death of a department head. Another Danish CEO described the impact of party conflict in this way in a personal interview:

In this municipality, what decides the agenda and what therefore affects the whole administrative system is the political climate, which is indescribably tense, probably to a degree found nowhere else. And of course it affects what we—the administration—can get through. It affects us because when the administration proposes new initiatives and formulates new ideas then we better be well guarded against any possible attack. We know that we will be subjected to all sorts of attacks and will become part of the political game.

A Norwegian CEO was more direct about the "bad manners" of the politicians caused by intense partisan battles, and how they affected the working conditions of the administration. The following remarkable statement, normally not put in print for public view, appeared in the CEO's annual report.

Over the course of the year we have seen a number of political initiatives with very strong criticisms directed against the city manager and the administration for their weak implementation of decisions made by the council, bad management and defective financial control. "Healthy and deserved criticism" say some, "smear campaign and bullying" say others. I want to mention that this has been a liability, not the least vis-à-vis the executive committee. Many issues have first been presented through the media before they have been known by the executive committee and the city manager, and people have exposed each other and have questioned each other's motives in several connections. This has made life a burden for the administration and the municipal employees and has hurt the relationship of trust vis-à-vis the elected politicians.[16]

The negative impact is undeniable, but this kind of intense partisan battling is not the norm. Only one in eight of the CEOs reported many party conflicts, and one in three reported some conflicts over municipal affairs.

There is variation in the frequency of party conflict in cities with different forms of government. Whereas approximately half of the strong-mayor, committee-leader, and collective cities report a substantial level of conflict (many or some conflicts), only a third of the council-manager cities have this level of conflict.[17]

In all cities, the more common the party battles, the more likely they were to be an obstacle that hindered the CEO from performing his or her job. Although over half of CEOs in the fourteen countries studied reported that conflicts between the political parties had little or no effect on their ability to perform their job, when the level of conflict was high in a city, three-quarters of the CEOs felt that the negative impact on performance was high. Not only does party conflict directly affect the ability of CEOs to perform their job, it also has an indirect impact by increasing uncertainty. This linkage is found in all forms of government. The incidence of the negative impact of party conflict is lower in council-manager cities, but when it occurs, there is a strong connection between party conflict and uncertainty in the governmental process in council-manager cities as well as in cities with other forms of government.[18]

The nature of party competition has a formative effect on the dynamics of official relationships and the generation of political leadership. When party conflicts are common and their impact is great, goal setting and coordination are weak. As in the case of mayoral leadership, it is presumed that party conflicts produce uncertainty rather than uncertainty leading to disputes between the parties.

Other External Pressures

City governments confront a wide range of challenges that arise within their own boundaries and flow from other governments. CEOs rated the extent to which a number of factors besides uncertainty and partisan conflicts negatively affected their ability to function. The factors are divided into pressures from the community itself and intergovernmental pressures. For each set of factors, an index was created by adding and averaging the separate ratings. The community pressures index is formed from the following factors:

- demands for better service
- demographic changes
- pressures from local organized interests
- unemployment and social problems

The problems in dealings with other governments—the intergovernmental pressures index—is based on the following factors:

- financial problems
- new regulations from upper-level governments
- upper-level government control of local finances
- cuts in grants from upper-level governments

The level of intergovernmental pressures is higher than that of the community pressures. The average measure for community pressures is 29, or moderately low, whereas the index score for intergovernmental pressures is 46, or moderate. Both sources of external stress are related somewhat to the level of internal uncertainty, although the impact does not come close to matching that of party conflict.[19]

The circumstances faced by cities with different forms of government differ to some extent. The strong-mayor, committee-leader, and council-manager cities have similar mean ratings for indices of community and intergovernmental pressures. All are close to the overall mean values. The collective cities are different from the rest, with a substantially lower level of external pressures that impact city government. The variations among cities of different forms add another dimension to the contextual factors discussed in chapter 3. When one assesses the factors that test the capacity of a city government to function well, size and scope of services are important. Committee-leader cities stand out from the rest in organizational size and the range of services provided. Here we see that these governments also experience a moderately high level of pressures from higher level governments, although council-manager governments have virtually the same level of stress from this source.

Another key factor is the level of challenge emanating from the community that the government serves. Council-manager cities, although smaller than the committee-leader cities, have a slightly higher level of stress from the local environment. As noted in the previous section, strong-mayor cities experience the highest level of party conflict, although they have relatively lower levels of community and intergovernmental pressure. The collective cities stand out as governments that operate with low levels of external pressure. These conditions together with the moderately low scope and size of collective cities would produce a more stable, predictable environment than that experienced by officials in other types of cities.

Networking by CEOs

By the nature of their position, CEOs have extensive interaction with elected officials and other administrators.[20] They are also likely to communicate with a variety of other actors in their community and with officials in other governments. Despite the likelihood of contact, however, CEOs are free to determine how much communication they have with most actors and to decide how much importance they will assign to these relationships. Thus, variation in the extent, range, and significance of their interactions may reveal important insights about the role and position of CEOs. Presumably, CEOs who create larger networks and assign more importance to network members are more strongly connected to the political process and augment their resources as actors in that process.

In earlier empirical research on the network structure of local political and bureaucratic elites, several typologies are used to describe the different network behavior of elites. Aberbach, Putnam, and Rockman (1981), for instance, use the distinction made by Merton between the "cosmopolitan" and the "local." The differences between the two types of actors pertain to their pattern of communication, interpersonal relationships, organizational activities, and commitments to the local community. Eldersveld, Strömberg, and Derksen (1995) make a similar distinction between the "cosmopolitan" and the "specialist." These views of the differences among administrators suggest a broad differentiation between those with an internal and external orientation in their interactions and between a narrow and broad range of contacts. In the analysis of networking, we will look for evidence of a tendency to focus on the "standard" relationships structured into the position—largely internal and focusing on political superiors and administrative subordinates—contrasted to a choice by the CEO to expand the scope and intensity of relationships. The latter approach could include higher levels of importance given to standard relationships as well as cultivating a wider range of relationships.

The interactions of CEOs could be ad hoc or reactionary, for example, looking for allies when faced with adversity, or they could represent proactive network building. If the latter, CEOs may act as "brokers" or "facilitators" who seek to make the process work better by linking network members to each other and to the political process. They may also act as "entrepreneurs" (Doig and Hargrove 1990) who use the interactional base for achieving their own and/or the city's goals.[21] Although the available measures do not make it possible to separate facilitators and entrepreneurs, it is possible to distinguish between defensive uses of networking and positive efforts that could be related to bringing people together and/or to advancing goals.

Measuring Interactions

The CEOs were asked to characterize their relationship with eleven categories of actors (see table 4.2). The characterization involved three aspects of the relationship: frequency—how often the CEO had contact with an actor; cooperation—rating the nature of the interaction on a scale that ranged from cooperation through neutrality to conflict; and importance—how much the actor contributed to the success of the CEO. There are strong intercorrelations between the three aspects. When measuring the nature of interaction, the midpoint value of 50 on the scale indicates a neutral relationship. The ratings reported in table 4.2 range from very positive to approaching neutral; there are no actors with whom CEOs have a relationship that tends to be negative. The degree of cooperation is related to importance. Likewise, frequency of contact is also related to importance. CEOs do not avoid actors with whom they have conflicts because conflicts are so rare. They have less interaction with actors they consider to be unimportant to their success and have more neutral relations with those actors who are not perceived to be helpful to the CEO. The determination of importance appears to indicate variation in inclusiveness as CEOs think about their networks. Those in-

Table 4.2 Importance, Frequency of Contact, and Cooperation with Actors in City Politics (*index*)

	Importance	Frequency of contact	Cooperation	Correlation: importance & cooperation	Correlation: importance & frequency
Mayor	91	87	85	0.23*	0.36*
Opposition	49	34	68	0.39*	0.58*
Council	57	47	74	0.31*	0.45*
Department heads	87	87	87	0.26*	0.27*
Other CEOs	50	38	76	0.36*	0.39*
State officials	39	23	66	0.42*	0.45*
National officials	36	18	63	0.42*	0.45*
Citizens	55	64	67	0.41*	0.45*
Journalists	34	33	62	0.37*	0.52*
Business	44	30	67	0.48*	0.62*
Other actors	37	24	65	0.40*	0.49*

NOTE: *All correlations are significant at the .00 level.

cluded in the coalition of actors with whom the CEO interacts more extensively are likely to be perceived as helpful and cooperative. The CEO who views actors as less important or considers fewer actors to be important is operating within a smaller network than those who see more actors as making a greater contribution to their success.

The major exceptions to the interconnection of importance, frequency of contact, and degree of cooperation are the relationships with the mayor and department heads. The correlation between frequency and importance is the weakest for one of the most important referents—the mayor. The correlation between importance and cooperation is lowest for the other key referent—the department heads. This suggests that the importance of interactions with these two sets of actors is mainly determined by structure. Structurally and politically, the importance of the mayor is a given. The CEO assigns high importance to the mayor whether or not he or she interacts more extensively with the mayor, and the CEO must work with the mayor whether or not they have a cooperative relationship. Similarly, the department heads have a formal reporting relationship with the CEO, and thus importance and interaction are very high. It should be noted, however, that the levels of cooperation are the highest for these two most important referents. The most intense relationships are also on average the most positive.

In the further analysis of interactions, attention is focused on assessments of importance. Higher importance ratings appear to be shaped by the degree to which an actor is viewed as a partner, that is, one who can help the CEO accomplish his or her objectives, or as an ally who can help to deal with difficulties. Assigning higher importance to others and considering more actors to be important is an active form of outreach and support building by the CEO. These measures are indicators of the extent to which CEOs link themselves to others as a means of succeeding in office. CEOs who rely on formal position to perform their job would presumably not see themselves as depending on as many other actors as would those who seek to augment their authority by establishing linkages with others. The importance of the mayor and department heads is a given—although exact ratings still vary—but the importance of other actors is a matter of circumstances and choice by CEOs and reflects the breadth of their network building.

Interactions with Elected Officials

Potentially, the main political referents of CEOs are the mayor, leaders of the opposition, and other municipal politicians—the other members of the city council. As we have seen, the mayor is by far considered to be the most important actor. The mean ratings of the importance of interactions with opposition leaders and with other politicians are both much lower and more variable.[22]

When the ratings of importance are considered at the country level, the French CEOs almost without exception give the highest possible importance rating to the mayor (a mean score of 98), whereas their Irish colleagues attach the lowest importance score to the mayor (69). These scores reflect the assessment of the formal and informal political leadership offered by the mayors presented in chapter 3. Still, for almost every country the contacts with the mayor are seen as being the most important—the U.S. council-manager cities being the exception with a slightly higher rating for the other members of the council than for the mayor. Much larger differences between countries can be seen in the degree of importance they place on contacts with the other two groups of political actors. The importance of the two other sets of politicians tends to move together with higher importance for one associated with higher importance for the other. (The correlation between these two ratings is .44.) CEOs in U.S. cities are a dramatic exception to this generalization, as are those in Australian and French cities. In these exceptions, the importance of the opposition is much lower that that of other politicians.

Analysis of importance ratings by form of government expands our understanding of the dynamics of internal relationships in each form. The relationship with the mayor is the most important, regardless of the form of government, with an average rating of 91. Although the differences are slight, they vary as one would expect between a high score in the strong-mayor cities (93) and the lowest score in the council-manager form (86). The centrality of the mayor in the committee-leader cities is notable. The mayor's importance is not diminished by being the head of the executive committee. In fact, it is slightly enhanced; the rating of the mayor's importance is highest is the committee-leader cities (96).

CEOs in strong-mayor and in council-manager type cities rate their contacts with other municipal politicians as substantially more important than their contacts with opposition leaders. The ratings of the other two groups of politicians are similar in the committee-leader and cabinet cities, but the level of importance of both groups is much lower in the latter. In committee-leader cities, CEOs evaluate their contacts with opposition leaders as more important than those with other politicians (68 versus 61). It is common for proportional representation to be required in selecting members of the executive and the standing committees. Thus, the political role of the opposition is crucial for the functioning of a CEO, even if there is little prospect for turnover in party control. These CEOs are also likely to view other council members who are part of the majority, but presumably not members of the executive committee, as being highly significant. All elected officials are more or less key referents in committee-leader cities. The questionnaire does not include a rating of the importance of the executive committee itself.

The two collective form countries also view the importance of these two groups of politicians at roughly the same level, but the ratings are much lower. Especially noteworthy is the low rating these CEOs attach to the importance of other politicians in the municipality (43) compared to an average score of 60 for CEOs in other countries. The board of aldermen—the executive committee or cabinet in these cities—plays a crucial role in this form of government, but the importance of the board is covered only in the Dutch questionnaire. Dutch CEOs assign as much importance to the contacts with aldermen as with the mayor. Since the importance scores for the two other groups of politicians in Belgium closely resemble the Dutch pattern (see Berveling, van Dam, Neelen 1997, 115), it is likely that the same result would have been found in Belgium. CEOs in the collective form countries are less likely to include elected officials outside the aldermen as a key part of their network, unlike their counterparts in committee-leader cities who look beyond the executive committee for additional key political referents.

Interactions with External Actors

The importance of external actors is lower than that of elected officials and department heads, as we saw in table 4.2. Among the external actors, the ratings are highest for citizens in community groups and for other local government executives among the intergovernmental actors. It is hard to know, however, how much weight to give to these groups in analyzing networking behavior. The citizen category is amorphous since it could refer to the citizenry collectively or to individual citizens with whom the CEO has contact. Assigning greater emphasis to leaders in the community—journalists, business leaders, and the heads of other community organizations—seems more indicative of coalition building than giving emphasis to citizens.[23]

Similarly, the importance of other local executives may be attributable to the need of neighboring jurisdictions to coordinate services or the nearby CEOs may simply be the closest referents when it comes to the development and implementation of policies. In response to a question about sources of inspiration for developing leadership skills, one CEO summarized the nature of these interactions as follows:

In this area, . . . the nine CEOs meet three to four times a year to discuss professional matters. Out of this network we create smaller groups where those who live closer together meet more often and discuss new initiatives, how to tackle initiatives from ministries and how to strengthen cooperation across the municipal borderlines.[24]

Viewing officials in higher level governments as important seems more likely to reflect entrepreneurial tendencies among CEOs than does stressing the importance of other CEOs. To a modest extent, stressing the importance of community leaders and higher government officials reflects a response to external pressures either from the community or from other governments.[25] With pressures from the local community, CEOs are more likely to network with both community leaders and, to a lesser extent, higher level governments. Pressures from other governments are linked with more importance for higher government officials and linked only slightly with greater interchange with community leaders.[26] Thus, a CEO's external network building is in part a response to factors in the jurisdiction or to pressures from higher level governments that impede the CEO's ability to perform his or her job effectively.

There is also some variation in the importance of community leaders and higher level governments in the four forms of government, although these differences are not very pronounced. CEOs in commitee-leader and council-manager cities give greater emphasis to community leaders. The council-manager and strong-mayor CEOs give the greatest emphasis to relations with higher level governments.

The Types of Networks Created by CEOs

In order to synthesize the discussion of CEOs' interactions, it is helpful to identify what kinds of networks they form among the many actors inside and outside of government. A network is viewed as a set of relationships that is created to enhance an individual's effectiveness and resources. The greatest attention is given to those relationships that are voluntary and strategic. The mayor and department heads certainly form the CEO's most important relationships, but the importance of these relationships is a natural consequence of the structure of local government. These officials are important regardless of variations in the extent of interaction (which is necessarily high) or in the degree of cooperation (although the relationships tend to be the most positive). Thus, these officials are automatically part of the CEO's network and importance varies little with form of government.

There is, on the other hand, considerable variation in the extent to which CEOs emphasize their interactions with other elected officials. There is a striking difference between the CEOs in commitee-leader form cities and those in others with regard to rating the importance of opposition leaders. These CEOs are much more likely to view the opposition as important, whereas strong-mayor and council-manager CEOs emphasize the other members of the council but not the opposition. The CEOs in collective cities pay less attention to either group of politicians.[27] For them, the board of aldermen—like the mayor in cities with other forms of government—is the structurally important set of officials. In measuring the importance of elected officials other than the mayor, whichever officials receive the higher rating—opposition or other members of the council—will be used as the measure of the emphasis on council members in network building.[28]

Two other groups also appear to be less relevant to the network as a set of strategic relationships. Citizens and other CEOs receive the highest ratings among community actors and officials of other governments, respectively. These ratings, however, inflate the overall scores for the category of actors of which they are a part without necessarily indicating a greater inclination to build alliances in order to improve effectiveness. Citizens is a particularly diffuse term that could refer to members of the public encountered by the CEO in a variety of ways, voters who elect city officials and decide referenda, or "the man in the street" whose opinion about city government contributes to a positive or negative climate. To say that citizens are important does not necessarily mean that the CEO interacts directly with any identifiable group. The limited usefulness of "other CEOs" as an indicator is that the interactions may be a consequence of the need to coordinate policy formation or service delivery with neighboring jurisdictions rather than strategic choice. Contacts may reflect the associations among peers maintained for social and professional development reasons. Analysis of networks that excludes the citizens and other CEOs will be more discriminating.

Based on these considerations, a search for variations in networking will concentrate on other elected officials, an index of community leaders, and an index of officials in higher level governments. Cluster analysis identifies four groupings of similar size.[29] One group of CEOs is relatively self-contained. They isolate themselves from the three sets of actors by assigning only moderate importance to council members and relatively little importance to the external actors. A second group that is slightly smaller than the others gives above average emphasis only to higher government officials. A third group that is internally oriented assigns high importance to council members but relatively little to the external actors. The final group is inclusive in its networking. All three sets of actors are much more important to these CEOs than is typical. Obviously, the breadth of their network is also distinctive.[30]

The analysis suggests revision in the way we have normally thought about networking by local administrators. Rather than finding simple insider-outsider or passive-active divisions, there are overlays of the two. Passiveness is manifested in the isolated CEO who operates with relatively weaker connections and fewer partners. The isolated CEO is likely to view any specific actor as less important to his or her success in office than the other types. The CEOs who base their network on internal actors and on other governments are moderately active with one stressing internal and the other certain external actors. CEOs with inclusive networks span the internal/external divide as well as being highly active.

There is considerable variation across countries in the distribution of networking types, as indicated in table 4.3. The proportion of CEOs who are inclusive networkers ranges from under ten in Belgium and the Netherlands to almost three-quarters in Finland. Two-thirds of the CEOs are isolated in the Netherlands, and one-third or more also have this type of network in Belgium, Norway, and Australia. In Ireland, Portugal, and Italy, one-third or more have networks based on other governments. The internal actor network is most often found in Denmark, Sweden, Great Britain, and both types of U.S. cities. Finally, over one-third of the CEOs have inclusive networks in Great Britain, Ireland, the U.S. cities, and Finland.

The distribution of network types by country indicates that there will be considerable variation by form of government. The two countries with the highest proportion of isolated CEOs are collective cities, and three of the top four countries with inclusive CEOs are council-manager cities. It is common, however, for specific countries to deviate widely from the typical pattern among cities of the same form. Consequently, the differences will be muted. Such is the case in the tabulations presented in table 4.3. The collective cities do stand out with the most isolated CEOs. The committee-leader cities are notable for the high proportion of networks based on internal actors and the low proportion based on other governments. With governments that have a complex political structure and tend to be large in size, these CEOs focus on relations with officials within their governments. CEOs in the strong-mayor

Table 4.3 Distribution of Network Types by Country and by Form of Government (percent)

	Isolated	Other governments	Internal actors	Inclusive	Total
France	28	24	26	22	100
Italy	32	36	16	17	100
Portugal	11	45	19	25	100
Spain	18	18	37	27	100
US-MC	3	3	53	41	100
Denmark	31	6	46	17	100
Great Britain	12	10	44	34	100
Sweden	19	2	51	28	100
Belgium	42	37	16	5	100
The Netherlands	67	10	16	7	100
Australia	33	28	13	26	100
Finland	4	14	9	73	100
Ireland	5	49	10	35	100
Norway	33	20	25	22	100
US-CM	2	0	55	42	100
Strong-mayor	21	29	26	24	100
Committee-leader	21	6	47	26	100
Collective	55	23	16	6	100
City manager	16	24	21	40	100
Total	24	21	27	27	100

NOTES: N = 3902, chi-square for form of government = 716.9, significance <.00

cities are fairly evenly balanced across the four types. The council-manager CEOs are most likely to be inclusive in their networking.

Summary of Networking Patterns

The CEO networks of the fourteen countries in our study reveal some similarities and some differences. The similarities pertain to the mayor and department heads being the most important referents across all countries and all four forms of government. These relationships are structured into the CEO's position. The high importance of the mayor and the department heads underscores the role of the CEO as a linking pin between the political and administrative spheres at the local level. The differences pertain to other elected officials, actors in the community, and intergovernmental actors. The interactions with these actors are related to the form of government but also to national differences and the preferences of individual CEOs. The networking behavior of CEOs varies along two overlapping dimensions: internal versus external and passive versus active. The isolated CEOs have relatively low levels of attachment and fewer partners in their networks. Their only important referents are the automatic ones. Higher activity is demonstrated by CEOs who have networks in which the greatest importance is assigned to internal actors, on the one hand, and officials in other governments, on the other. Finally, the inclusive CEOs are active, cosmopolitan, and comprehensive in their linkages.

Conclusion

There are various indicators of how CEOs operate in their political environment. CEOs generally are committed to nonpartisanship and the use of expertise and are also likely to be advocates of an active leadership role for administration in society. Contrary to the traditional expectation that administrative leaders value being independent in their policy views and directly accountable to elected officials, we found that CEOs can be divided into four groups, only one of which incorporates this value orientation. There are also CEO groups who stress official accountability and congruent views, public accountability and congruent views, and public accountability with independent views of policy. The attitudinal profile suggests that many CEOs operate with a substantial degree of independence vis-à-vis elected officials. In their networking, about half of the CEOs fall into contrasting groups of isolates and inclusive networkers, and the remainder are actively linked to either internal actors or officials in other governments.

There are no broad overlapping tendencies among these various characteristics of CEOs. The strength of commitment to advocacy is not related to networking behavior. It might be plausible to expect some overlap between the type of network assembled and attitudes about the political process, for example, a disproportionate share of isolated CEOs who are dependent in their attitudes toward politicians. There is a modest connection between CEOs who make the choice to be accountable to officials or to the public and the network types. Among the isolates, there is more support for being responsible to elected officials (63% agree) compared to the internal (56%) or intergovernmental networkers (52%). The inclusive networkers are least strongly inclined (45%) to be oriented primarily to elected officials. For these officials who have active connections with a range of actors, the definition of accountability is most likely to be broad, encompassing citizens as well as elected officials. Thus, networking helps to shape or may be a reflection of attitudes about the scope of accountability. Still, we will expect in later analysis that attitudes about the importance of other actors and attitudes about accountability and congruency will have independent impacts on other aspects of CEO behavior and influence, if any at all.

The other measures of the political environment also can be summarized in general and distinctive patterns. Most CEOs experience low to moderate uncertainty about goals and how the responsibilities of elected officials and administrators should be divided. Still, uncertainty is at least moderately high in almost half of the strong-mayor cities and over a third of the committee-leader and collective cities. In contrast, only one in four council-manager cities has this level of uncertainty. The nature of the mayor's leadership is related to the level of certainty and, we presume, affects it. Extensive involvement by the mayor in administrative details tends to contribute to confusion about roles and decrease the clarity of goals, as do lower levels of public and proactive leadership. Party conflict is not a factor that impedes the CEO's performance in approximately half of the cities that use strong-mayor, committee-leader, and collective forms of government; the negative impact is moderate in three cities in five and high in two cities in five. In the council-manager cities, on the other hand, two-thirds of the CEOs are not adversely affected by this factor and only one in ten has high negative impact. When conflicts are extensive and their impact is great, the level of political certainty goes down as well. Pressures from problems in the community are a minor concern in cities generally, and intergovernmental pressures are a moderate factor affecting performance, although both sources of external stress are low in the collective cities.

The findings from this discussion of how CEOs relate to the political environment offer some initial guidance in assessing the models of political-administrative relations introduced in chapter 2. These are the separate roles, politically responsive administrator, autonomous administrator, and overlapping roles models. The support for nonpartisanship and expertise might be viewed as consistent with the separate roles model, although we argued in chapter 2 that this neutral competence is a general characteristic of professional administrators and is expected to be associated with all of the models. The four clusters of attitudes about the CEO's relationship to the political process are particularly germane, and the network types may add some additional insights. The CEOs who value being directly accountable to elected officials and having policy views congruent with the majority of the city council seem to match the norms of the responsive administrator. These administrators help politicians accomplish their goals by aligning their own views with the preferences of elected officials. The CEOs who favor direct accountability but noncongruent views presumably correspond to the separate roles model; they are accountable to elected officials but offer independent views in their communications with the mayor and council. Finally, the CEOs who feel that they should be as accountable to the public as to elected officials and favor noncongruent views may have the values of the autonomous administrator. They would be able to justify setting a course based on their own assessment of the public interest, although they would not necessarily have the influence to carry out this approach (an issue addressed in chapters 8 and 9). CEOs who correspond to the overlapping roles model could probably be found in three of four value combinations (the exception is the congruent directly accountable group).

In addition, three of the networking types may suggest what model a CEO does not match rather than being clearly linked to a specific model. Presumably, the isolates would not be consistent with overlapping roles types or autonomous administrators because they lack the broad network to support extensive policy involvement. Those who stress an internal network are not likely to be autonomous administrators because of those close ties with politicians that the internal network indicates. Finally, the inclusive CEOs with active and wide networks are not likely to fit the separate roles or responsive administrator models since these models imply restricted activities and/or a primary orientation to elected officials.

The differences among cities shaped by political culture and form of government are magnified somewhat by moderately systematic variation in the characteristics of the political environment and in the ways that CEOs relate to their environment.

- Strong-mayor cities have higher levels of uncertainty than other types of cities and moderate levels of conflict between political parties. They are less likely to experience high levels of external stress than committee-leader or council-manager cities. In addition to being formally subordinate to the mayor, the CEOs are slightly more likely to be congruent in policy and directly accountable. They are evenly divided among network types.
- The committee-leader cities have moderate levels of uncertainty and party conflict. The CEOs tend to stress independent policy views while being accountable to politicians. Consistent with this orientation, they are most likely to have networks based on internal actors.
- The collective cities also have moderate levels of uncertainly and party conflict. In contrast to the other types of cities, these CEOs report low levels of external pressures. The CEOs are slightly more likely to be congruent and

directly responsible rather than choosing other roles in their orientation to politicians. They tend to be isolates in their networking style.

• The council-manager cities have the lowest levels of uncertainty and party conflict. The CEOs tend to favor independent policy views and being as responsible to citizens as to elected officials. They are most likely to have inclusive networks.

When considering the effect of form of government in future chapters, it is important to keep in mind not only the formal differences and the political position of the mayor. It is also important to factor in the other characteristics just summarized that tend to be bundled with form of government. For example, in strong-mayor cities, not only is there a powerful mayor with centralized formal authority, but there is also greater uncertainty. This condition could create even greater likelihood that top administrators will look to the mayor for direction. In council-manager cities, not only do city managers possess formal executive powers, but there is less uncertainty and CEOs tend to have broad networks. In subsequent analyses, efforts will be made to distinguish between differences based on country or form and also to determine the impact of these other attitudinal and environmental factors that vary with individuals and specific communities when the effects of country and form of government are removed.

CHAPTER 5

The CEO's Activities and Role in Policy Making

The manager has a very important and finite role to play, the bottom line of which is effective administration. You can't have effective administration in today's turbulent times if you don't attend to issues such as securing different revenue sources, achieving political leadership, and forging alliances with other community resources.

U.S. *City Manager*

SO FAR IN OUR CONSIDERATION OF LEADERSHIP AT THE APEX, we have presumed that the top administrators can hold up their side of the relationship. The term apex has been used to suggest the point in the governmental process at which the perspectives and contributions of top politicians and administrators are blended. There has been no demonstration, however, of the kind of contributions that administrators make. Models of political-administrative relations that stress separate roles or administrators who are responsive to politicians imply an image of a pyramid in which there is an exchange that occurs between the administrative base and the political pinnacle. This is not a blending of contributions so much as a hand-off between a superior and a subordinate. Models based on overlapping roles or autonomous administrators, on the other hand, have administrators coming together with elected officials at least in shaping policy. Although the debate over the policy role of the CEO has been won repeatedly by those who take the affirmative side,[1] there has been remarkably little examination of the nature and extent of policy activities or other contributions of top administrators. In order to determine the role of the CEOs in the political process, it is necessary to examine in depth what they do.

There are many activities that would have political consequences if CEOs engaged in them. Beyond making recommendations about options for elected officials to consider and then implementing policy decisions in an impartial way, they could propose goals, initiate projects, and offer reports to shape the identification of problems and the framing issues. Furthermore, CEOs could advise elected officials about the process by which policy is made and how they should fill their roles, that is, they could help shape the process by which decisions are made as well as the content of decisions. In the administrative realm, the criteria for administrative decisions themselves have political implications, even if the criteria stress fair application of rationally determined rules by administrative staff. Administrative staff must evaluate the facts of a particular case, make judgments about which rules pertain to it and how they should be applied, and exercise discretion when the circumstances are not adequately met by the standard rules. Even if they do not consider their actions to be explicitly political, or if their actions have no direct bearing on the electoral fortunes of politicians, administrators can still be contributors to the political process. In the broadest sense, they could be political actors—not the same as becoming politicians—when their actions affect the allocation of resources and values by government, as political scientists define politics (Easton 1965). As political actors they would be full participants at the apex of leadership.

It is obvious from the existing literature and observation of local affairs that CEOs interact extensively with elected officials. They are more than just the providers of information and recipients of instructions from elected officials. CEOs bring certain values and norms with clear political significance to their position. They are committed to neutrality between parties and candidates, but they are committed to acting on the basis of expertise. Rather than barring them from taking policy stands, "expertise" viewed as a bundle of specialized knowledge, experience and familiarity with governmental practices, and professional values may support distinct perspectives on policy. CEOs are commonly advocates for solving community problems and addressing socioeconomic inequities. Most CEOs do not feel it is necessarily advantageous to have policy views that match the majority of the council. They generally do not consider the mayor to be very effective at initiating policies or shaping the city's agenda. Furthermore, they are more or less extensively involved in communications with community groups and officials in other governments and are, therefore, potentially community leaders and "representatives" of citizens as well as administrative directors.

The next step is to extend the inquiry into the policy-making process. Administrators have been identified as "entrepreneurs" (Schneider and Teske

1992), and there are a number of ways that CEOs can be innovators in the policy making. Furthermore, the local government CEO in particular among public administrators is in a position vis-à-vis elected officials to affect the process of making policy and how the spheres of action of elected officials and administrators are divided. As noted here and examined in depth in the next chapter, they also contribute advice about political problems confronting elected officials. Of course, top administrators also handle a wide range of administrative activities. To understand the contributions to the policy-making process, the question is how administrative functions are combined with activities that have an impact on policy making.

The contributions of top administrators reflect what kinds of activities CEOs emphasize in their work, including those through which CEOs could affect the political process. The typical CEO is likely to proclaim, "What I do is not political!" This may be true in the sense that the values and motives behind the actions are intended to promote the public interest rather than partisan or particularistic interests. Still, top administrators potentially affect both the content and process of policy making either by being involved or failing to be involved (Svara 1998a). This chapter provides an in-depth examination of the extent to which CEOs are involved in three dimensions of activities: policy innovation, advice to elected officials, and classical administrative functions. The level of involvement in each dimension and variation among CEOs in how they balance the three dimensions are both considered. The models of political-administrative relations in chapter 2 lead to contrasting expectations about the level and nature of involvement. The separate roles model would be clearly associated with low involvement in policy and high emphasis on administrative functions. The same could be true of the responsive administrators, except that they would presumably be more active in providing advice to elected officials. The overlapping roles model would be consistent with high activity in policy innovation and advice to politicians, whereas the autonomous administrators would be active in policy but less engaged in providing advice of a political nature.

This chapter presents the dimensions and the activities on which they are based. The variation in the level of involvement of CEOs by country and form of government is examined, followed by analysis of the individual and environmental factors that explain the level of involvement. In the conclusion, we consider the implications of the findings for the four models of interaction.

Classifying the Activities of CEOs

The total contribution of CEOs is shaped by their involvement in various aspects of the position. This involvement is measured by the ratings CEOs give of how much emphasis they place on sixteen activities.[2] It is assumed that the ratings of emphasis on each of the varied tasks provides a way of determining what CEOs do and how they assign relative priority to different aspects of their job. After carefully analyzing the conceptual and statistical interrelationships among these tasks, a classification based on three dimensions has been developed.[3] The dimensions are (1) policy innovator, (2) adviser to elected officials, and (3) classical administrator.

The first and second are primary indicators of the political role of the CEO. The level of involvement in administrative activities per se is not a focus of the inquiry. None of the existing models of political-administrative interaction suggests that administrators who are active in filling political roles will not be actively involved in administrative functions. A primary emphasis on the classical administrative dimension in contrast to policy innovation would, however, indicate CEOs who have distinctive priorities. An American city manager identified why the allocation of time can be an issue for administrators: "It is not the job of the city manager anymore to make sure the streets get paved. The streets have to get paved, but if you have to be the one to make sure it happens, it is a misuse of your resources."[4] Thus, it is important to examine the relative emphasis on administrative functions as well as the simple administrative involvement score.

The components of each dimension are summarized in brief. The policy innovator dimension refers to emphasis by the CEO on fostering change through new ideas along with acquiring resources needed to support change. It consists of these activities:

- formulating ideas and visions
- promoting new projects in the community
- attracting resources from external sources
- keeping informed about citizen viewpoints
- making sure that resources are used efficiently

Factor analysis of the importance assigned to sixteen activities listed in the questionnaire identified this dimension and the others (see the technical appendix). The first three components in the policy innovator dimension all involve initiative, and the fourth links innovation to an external referent—the citizens in the community. The strong connection of promoting efficiency with the other activities revealed by the factor analysis was somewhat surprising, since it is often perceived to be an administrative task. Promoting efficiency is also related to activities in other dimensions, but the strongest relationship is to attracting resources and the third highest is to promoting new projects.[5] Promoting efficiency is apparently perceived by CEOs to be an initiative to improve productivity or overall efficiency (i.e., deciding on the relative priorities of the various local government programs) rather than a narrow administrative activity.

The *adviser to elected officials dimension* refers to a dual emphasis on supporting elected officials through recommendations and information and on encouraging cooperation and positive decision-making practices. It consists of these activities:

• giving the mayor legal, fiscal, and other kinds of professional and technical advice
• giving the mayor political advice
• influencing decision-making processes in order to secure sensible and efficient solutions
• developing and implementing norms for the proper roles of elected officials vis-à-vis administrators

There is no presumption that the CEO advises only the mayor, but only the mayor was specifically mentioned in these questionnaire items. The term "political advice" was not defined in the questionnaire. We presume—and additional in-depth studies reported in the next chapter appear to confirm—that it involves assistance in dealing with the "political" aspect of decisions, for example, promoting electoral interests, securing support, and gauging partisan or public response. Thus, the CEO as adviser guides elected officials in handling the content of decisions, the implications of decisions, and the process of making decisions and dividing tasks.

Finally, the *classical administrator dimension* refers to emphasis on generic organizational administrative tasks. It consists of these activities:

• guiding subordinate staff in handling specific tasks
• developing and implementing new routines and work methods
• managing fiscal affairs and accounts and maintaining budgetary control
• ensuring that rules and regulations are followed

These activities are the concern of administrators in any organization and at all levels of supervision. This dimension is relevant to the current discussion in the way that it is combined with the other dimensions. Thus, in addition to the administrative dimension score itself, a separate measure based on the rating for administration minus the rating for policy innovation will also be calculated to determine the relative emphasis on administration.

For each dimension, an index was created by adding the separate activity scores and dividing the total by the number of activities to create a composite index with values that range from 0 to 100. The importance given to each dimension reflects individual values and characteristics and the circumstances in which they work, including the characteristics and activities of other officials, governmental structure and process, and the work context defined broadly. The premise underlying this analysis is that administrators partially shape their roles by their intentions and that CEOs in particular are in a position to choose among tasks in ways that create an individual profile of priorities. One presumes that they are not completely free to choose any combination of activities if they care about their continued employment, but they have freedom to give differing amounts of emphasis to the activities. It is not presumed that the fact that all the respondents are CEOs occupying the top appointed administrative position in a local government will produce the same emphases, although holding essentially the same position should promote some uniformity across cities and countries.

The three dimensions are not mutually exclusive, and the ratings on the three dimensions are interrelated to some extent.[6] It is especially common for variation in the policy innovation dimension to be mirrored in the dimension of advice to elected officials. Emphasis on classical administration is also modestly related to innovation but only weakly related to political advice. CEOs may be strong—or weak—on more than one dimension.

Involvement of CEOs: Overall Levels and Variation by Country

CEOs emphasize policy innovation more than the other dimensions, and this emphasis is fairly uniform across all countries, as indicated in table 5.1. The index score of 72 on a 100-point scale indicates that, on average, CEOs place great importance on the activities that make up this dimension. Even in the countries with the lowest average scores—Belgium, Netherlands, and Spain—the level reflects a score between moderate and great importance. The specific activity in this dimension with the clearest policy content—for-

Table 5.1 CEO Involvement in Policy Innovation, Advise, and Administration by Country and Form of Government *(index)*

Country	Policy innovator	Adviser to politicians	Classical administrator	Administration minus policy
France	70	57	68	–2
Italy	70	57	74	4
Portugal	74	61	77	3
Spain	65	57	71	7
US-MC	71	57	63	–8
Denmark	72	78	42	–30
Great Britain	75	68	47	–28
Sweden	70	63	43	–27
Belgium	64	56	59	–5
Netherlands	64	56	51	–13
Australia	80	64	58	–22
Finland	77	50	48	–29
Ireland	86	60	71	–14
Norway	70	59	59	–12
US-CM	74	56	63	–11
Strong-mayor	70	58	72	2
Committee-leader	72	70	44	–28
Collective	64	56	55	–9
City manager	77	58	60	–18
F score (form of government)	154.2	147.1	575.7	648.3
Significance	<.00	<.00	<.00	<.00
Overall mean	72	60	59	–13
N	3933	3756	3946	3842

mulating ideas and visions—has an average rating that is higher than that for the overall index.[7] CEOs are extensively involved in promoting innovation and expanding support for their governments. They are engaged in seeking additional resources from external sources. They are also concerned about being attuned to citizen opinions, presumably to be responsive to citizen preferences and to gauge how to secure support from residents of the community. CEOs also heavily emphasize innovation to improve productivity.

These results are very important. There has been much debate in discussions among officials, citizens, and scholars of governmental structure and official roles about whether administrators should be involved in policy (as noted in chapter 2). In practice, CEOs generally are actively engaged in this area. In this sense, the results of this survey are not a surprise. An American city manager expressed in one of the intensive interviews the opinion that elected officials need help with policy making and that CEOs should provide it.

As strongly as I respect elected officials and representative government, they simply do not have the tools themselves to set policy and set the strategy for the city, and it is not enough for the manager to give a report or say, "Here is the information, let me know what you decide." The way I do my job, it is my job to help them decide, and candidly it is often my job to decide what I think is good for the city, to test that, not to be arrogant about that decision, and then to help the elected officials to reach that conclusion, and if I am wrong, we readjust. But I don't think the manager can sit by passively.

These views are probably commonly held among local government officials and generally recognized by savvy observers. Still, the extensive policy contributions of CEOs have neither been demonstrated so clearly nor found to be so uniform—despite important variation—in previous research. Top administrators generally are active in shaping the vision for their cities, promoting new projects in the community, seeking external resources, keeping in touch with citizen viewpoints, and linking innovation to the efficient use of resources. Put differently, the CEO attempts to generate resources externally and internally to support initiatives that are grounded in public support. The implications of this finding will be explored further in this chapter and in other parts of the book.

The adviser to elected officials and classical administrator dimensions are emphasized at essentially the same level overall. In both, CEOs generally place more than moderate importance on the activities covered by the dimensions. The CEOs who place greatest emphasis on advising politicians are in Denmark and Great Britain. The classical administrator scores are the most dispersed, with high scores in Portugal, Italy, Spain, Ireland, and France, and relatively low scores in Britain and the Scandinavian countries other than Norway.

Overall, despite the common perception that administrators are preoccupied with administrative functions and only occasionally and exceptionally involved in policy matters, the emphasis of CEOs is the opposite. The typical CEO seeks to shape policy and promote innovation, whereas he or she gives less attention to the classical administrator activities. In addition, CEOs attach as much importance to offering advice to elected officials as they do to internal administration. Thus, our findings regarding CEOs do not support the common distinction between "classical" and "political" bureaucrats (Putnam 1975) or the presumption that the former is typical.

The CEOs of some countries, particularly Italy, Spain, Portugal, France, Ireland, and both types of cities in the United States, are highly to moderately involved in classical administrative activities as well as being active in policy.

These CEOs are not necessarily "classical bureaucrats" with low involvement in policy. Indeed, as indicated in the final column in table 5.1, only in Italy, Spain, and Portugal do the scores on the administrative dimension exceed the policy innovation score, and in France they are virtually the same. At the other end of the scale, the CEOs in Denmark, Great Britain, Sweden, and Finland place much less emphasis on administration than policy innovation. The contrasting groups of countries reflect a southern versus northern European pattern. They also are the most different in the size of municipal government and the level of services provided (as discussed in chapter 3). Another key factor in explaining the pattern of scores on this and the other measures of involvement in countries is form of government.

Involvement of CEOs by Form of Government

The relative emphasis that CEOs place on activities is shaped by their form of government. The influence of these structures, developed in chapter 3, is clearly evident in the comparison of mean scores for activity dimensions in table 5.1.

In the strong-mayor cities—France, Portugal, Italy, and Spain, and some of the U.S. cities—CEOs generally place greater emphasis on the classical administration dimension than on policy innovation. The CEOs in these countries—particularly Portugal but also France and Italy—give substantial emphasis to policy innovation, as shown in the country results in table 5.1. Overall in these countries, CEOs still give slightly greater emphasis to administration. Despite the formal resources in the mayor's office, the CEO provides a fairly high level of policy leadership. It appears that the mayor expects the CEO to take care of internal administrative tasks, but there is no specialization of function with the mayor handling policy innovation and the CEO handling administration.[8]

In the collective leadership type cities, the scores are lower than in cities with the other forms for two of the three dimensions and next to lowest on the third. The relative emphasis is the most even. The CEOs tend to assign moderately high importance to all aspects of their job. Observers of the CEO in these cities, therefore, would probably be unlikely to perceive that the CEO stands out as a policy innovator, adviser, or administrator because activity levels are fairly balanced across the three dimensions.

CEOs in countries with the committee-leader structure—Denmark, Sweden, and Great Britain—give the most emphasis to advising politicians and have the second highest score on policy innovation. On the other hand, they give the least emphasis to administrative activities overall and in comparison to policy innovation.

CEOs in cities with the council-manager form have the highest scores on policy innovation. This form more than others puts the CEO in the position of taking the lead in offering policy guidance to elected officials. These CEOs are also responsible for handling the executive functions in their cities, and they give moderately strong emphasis to administrative tasks.

Differences in Individual Components by Form of Government

The differences in the overall scores for each major dimension of involvement indicate distinctive orientations across the forms of government. There are also many similar scores in three of the four forms in both the policy innovation scale and the advice to politicians scale. A similar average score for the dimension may, however, mask differences in the importance of specific activities. Examination of the components that make up the policy innovation dimension in table 5.2 indicates other important characteristics. The CEOs in the council-manager cities not only have the top overall score, but the highest score on each component as well. The CEOs in the committee-leader cities have the second highest score on three of the components—formulating vision, promoting new projects, and being informed about citizen viewpoints—and were virtually tied for second on improving efficiency. The strong-mayor CEOs give relatively greater emphasis to attracting external resources and promoting efficiency. Presumably the strong mayor wants the CEO to focus more on getting the resources the mayor needs and running the organization efficiently than on the policy- and citizen-oriented components. Finally, the CEOs in the collective leadership cities are relatively restrained in their level of activity across the board, although it should be remembered that these results reflect the difference between assigning moderately great versus great (or very great) importance to these activities.

The CEOs in the committee-leader type cities have the highest score on the adviser to politicians dimension. The components of the advice to elected officials dimension are examined separately in table 5.2. CEOs in the committee-leader cities have higher scores on three of the four components than CEOs in the cities with other structures. They are much more involved in offering political advice than their counterparts in other countries. Several factors may account for this high rating. In these cities, there is somewhat greater importance assigned by the CEO to all internal political actors—mayors, council members, and opposition leaders (as discussed in chapter 4).

Table 5.2 CEO Involvement in Individual Tasks by Form of Government

	Strong-mayor	Committee-leader	Collective	Council-manager	Total
POLICY INNOVATION					
Formulate vision	74	82	71	83	78
Promote new projects	66	74	62	75	70
Informed about citizens	61	68	62	71	66
Attract external resources	69	60	55	76	67
Improve efficiency	79	78	70	84	79
ADVICE TO ELECTED OFFICIALS					
Technical advice	80	75	59	63	70
Political advice to mayor	21	52	38	30	33
Norms for relationships	60	70	58	63	63
Influence decision making	70	81	70	77	75
CLASSICAL ADMINISTRATIVE FUNCTIONS					
Guide subordinates	69	37	54	51	54
Establish new routines	71	56	64	61	63
Fiscal management	72	46	48	73	63
Enforce rules	77	39	55	54	58

Proportional representation provides for the formal inclusion of all politicians, even opposition leaders. Based on the characteristics of the form, one would presume that a number of political leaders have considerable influence in policy making in these cities (a presumption confirmed in chapter 8). Consequently, both they and the CEO are significant actors who must interact extensively regarding their respective roles to maintain balance. As we shall see in the next chapter, these CEOs are also more inclined to offer advice to the political leader on politically sensitive matters.

When the mayor is the leader of a one-party majority government, the level of advice to the mayor is even higher.[9] In the committee-leader form of government, the CEO does not shy away from dealing with political issues when the mayor is a politically dominant figure, but rather gets more engaged in offering advice about such matters. The committee-leader CEOs generally are also more active in developing and implementing norms for the proper roles of elected officials and administrators and in seeking to influence the decision-making process to secure sensible and efficient solutions. These CEOs do not neglect offering technical advice. They have the second highest score on this activity.

The highest score for technical advice is in strong-mayor cities. In view of the supposition that the CEO is a political ally of the mayor in strong-mayor cities, it is striking that the CEOs in these cities are least involved in providing political advice to their mayors.[10] Either these mayors prefer to receive technical advice from the CEOs, or the CEOs are uncomfortable offering advice on political matters to the mayor. In either case, the top administrators in strong-mayor cities do not see themselves as partners with the mayor in addressing political issues. CEOs may be concerned about maintaining their distance from a mayor who is fairly likely to be a strong partisan leader, even though this is not a deterring factor for the CEOs in committee-leader cities who often offer political advice to a strong partisan leader in the mayor's office. Neither strong-mayor nor committee-leader CEOs are the political assistant to the mayor, but the former offers the most political advice and the latter offers the least.

The CEOs in council-manager cities have the second highest ranking on suggesting norms for the relationships among officials and influencing the process of decision making, and they have the second lowest score on giving political advice. Their overall score on the dimension of giving advice to politicians is the same as in the strong-mayor cities, but the profile of their activity across the four components is somewhat different.

Finally, the component scores for the classical administrative dimension are presented in table 5.2. The CEOs in strong-mayor cities are very attentive to all these activities and assign them more importance than do the CEOs in other forms. City managers match their emphasis on fiscal administration, but like the CEOs in the collective leadership cities they are less involved in the other areas. The CEOs in the committee-leader cities place much less emphasis on these activities than those in other dimensions. Presumably, these CEOs delegate administrative tasks to subordinates to a greater extent than in the other cities.

Activity Clusters

The discussion to this point has emphasized the common tendencies of CEOs in each form of government by focusing on the mean for an activity or dimension. Obviously, individual CEOs differ from the mean, and this variation has not yet been examined. Another approach is to use cluster analysis to identify patterns in the combinations of scores on each of the three dimensions for individual CEOs and then see how the individual characteristics are distributed across the forms of government. Although the overall tendencies should be the same as those already discussed, this method can also identify groupings that include tendencies that are different from the average charac-

Table 5.3 Four CEO Activity Clusters: Mean Values on Each Component Variable

Dimension	Underactive	Administrator/ policy innovator	Adviser/ policy innovator	Highly active	Overall average
Policy innovation	58	70	75	85	72
Advice to elected officials	45	52	71	74	60
Classical administration	44	68	42	77	59
Percentage CEOs in each cluster	18%	33%	26%	23%	—
N	661	1187	940	820	3610

teristics. Four clusters of combinations have been identified. The average scores for the dimensions in each cluster are provided in table 5.3.

The first cluster includes CEOs whose involvement levels are below the mean on each dimension; 18% of CEOs are in this group. They are underactive in comparison to their peers, giving only moderately great importance to policy and moderate importance to the activities in the advice and administration dimensions. This cluster is at odds with the generalization that CEOs are actively involved in policy innovation, although even this group is far from being uninvolved. The mean policy innovation score for this group is above the mid-point on the scale, indicating that these activities are more than moderately important. The second and third groups emphasize administration and policy innovation (33% of the CEOs) and advice and policy innovation (26%), but have below average involvement in the third dimension, which they do not emphasize as much. The CEOs in both groups are approximately as active in policy innovation as the average for all CEOs—a rating that indicates great importance is placed on these activities. What stands out is the other component in the combination, which is well above the overall average level for that dimension. In the adviser/policy innovator cluster, CEOs are active in providing advice to politicians, active in policy, and less than moderately involved in administration. In the administrator/policy innovator cluster, CEOs are active in handling administrative tasks and policy, but only moderately involved in providing advice. The final group of highly active CEOs represents almost one-quarter of the CEOs. They are above the average in the rating for all three dimensions. They are very active in policy innovation and active in the other two areas as well.

When we examine how these individual activity clusters are divided across the four groups of cities, the picture is slightly different than when we focused on average levels of activity in each of the three dimensions separately. As indicated in figure 5.1, over half of the CEOs in the strong-mayor group are in the administration/policy cluster and another 30 percent are in the

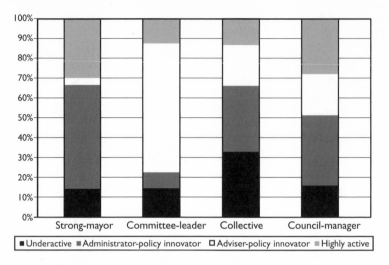

Figure 5.1   CEO activity clusters by form of government

highly active group. The lowest proportion of underactive CEOs are found in cities with this structure. Less than four percent are in the advice/policy cluster. In the collective form cities, on the other hand, four out of ten CEOs are in the underactive group, and another three in ten stress the administration/policy cluster. Within the committee-leader cities, as would be expected from the previous discussion, almost two-thirds of the CEOs are in the advice/policy cluster. The CEOs in council-manager cities are closest to the overall distribution of CEOs across the clusters, although with slight overrepresentation in the administration/policy and highly active clusters and slight underrepresentation in the other two clusters.

A more complete summary view of the differences in activities across forms of government will be offered after a brief discussion of how cultural factors may interact with form of government in shaping the activity level of CEOs.

Structure, Culture, and Activities

The findings indicate that form of government is strongly associated with the relative emphasis on the three dimensions of activities. Since form of government is uniform within each separate country in this study except the United States, it is possible that other country characteristics may also be related to activity level, in particular, the characteristics associated with national culture. It is expected that the high uncertainty avoidance—the tendency to avoid unstructured situations and a preference for order and certainty (Hofstede 1997)—would be related to emphasis on classical administration. This tendency would be reinforced by a cultural preference for ordering of relationships based on power, that is, high scores on the power distance index. In contrast, greater equality in power relationships would be favorable to innovative behavior, and greater tolerance for uncertainty and unstructured situations would correspond to the ambiguities surrounding the activity of giving advice to elected officials on matters other than technical issues.

These possible associations may have an effect that is independent from the effect of form of government or that reinforces the effect of form of government. It is also possible that there will be no direct relationship with activity level once the effects of structure have been taken into account. Analysis of the direct and indirect effects of structure, cultural characteristics, and activities using national-level data helps to sort out these interrelationships. The expected relationships between cultural characteristics and level of emphasis on dimensions are found.[11] Policy innovation is negatively associated with the tendency to avoid uncertainty, whereas classical administration is positively related. The greater the preference for order and predictability as a national characteristic, the more the CEOs from each country stress internal administration and the less they emphasize policy innovation. The level of emphasis on advising elected officials, which brings the CEO close to the political leader with extensive interchange across a wide range of topics, is inversely related to relative power distance and to uncertainty avoidance. The more support there is for hierarchical authority structures, the less emphasis is placed on this dimension.

Of these relationships, the strongest is between the score on the administrative dimension and the uncertainty avoidance index (UAI). The level of association is even higher if the measure of relative emphasis on administration is used instead of the simple administrative involvement score.[12] As noted in the discussion of table 5.1, some CEOs are actively involved in administrative functions as well as being highly involved in policy innovation. The role of the CEO in the political process seems to be better indicated not by the administrative score per se but by whether administrative activities are more important than policy, about the same level of importance, or less important. The array of relative administrative emphasis scores and uncertainty avoidance scores are presented in figure 5.2.

When comparing the impact of these cultural characteristics with that of

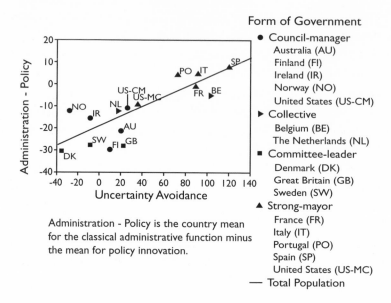

Figure 5.2 Uncertainty avoidance and relative emphasis on administration over policy

governmental structure, however, structure has a greater impact with one exception. When the effects of the two sets of characteristics are considered together, the cultural characteristics drop out of the explanation of policy innovation, and add very little to the explanatory power of structure with regard to advice and administration. A large part of the variation across countries in the emphasis on each of the dimensions can be explained by form of government. There is little additional variation explained by uncertainty avoidance or power distance. Uncertainty avoidance is, however, the most important factor along with dummy variables for strong-mayor and committee-leader forms to explain the relative emphasis on administration compared to policy, the relationship displayed in figure 5.2. The interaction of the two factors can be observed in that figure. Five of the top six scores for relative emphasis on administration are in strong-mayor countries. The one exception is Belgium with the collective leadership form of government, which has the second highest level of uncertainty avoidance. Finally, three of the four countries with lowest relative emphasis on administration use the committee-leader form of government. Within the groups of countries divided by form, the uncertainty avoidance score is related to the level of attention to administration in the strong-mayor, collective, and committee-leader countries.

Form of government is primarily responsible for the variation in policy innovation at the national level. The emphasis on advice to elected officials, on the other hand, is affected both by structure and modestly by power distance. Both uncertainty avoidance and structure affect classical administration forms and the relative emphasis on administrative functions. Obviously, these observations are based on analysis of direct effects only. In chapter 3, we discussed how the cultural values are related to or may shape what form of government is chosen in the various countries. For instance, the strong-mayor system was found in countries where there is a general acceptance and expectation of power inequalities, that is, power distance is high. When it is postulated that form of government rather than culture is the decisive factor when it comes to understanding how CEOs make priorities among the three sets of activities, it is important to emphasize that culture may play a strong "background role." In other words, we underestimate the indirect effects of cultural traits.

Summary of Differences in Involvement across Forms of Government

The activity profiles of CEOs divided by form of government are shaped by the structure of political authority in which they work and also by other systematic differences associated with country or form that have been identified in previous chapters. Before turning to analysis of differences at the individual level removing the effects of country differences, it is useful to briefly summarize the general features of each form of government relating differences in activity levels with national and cross-national environmental factors.

Strong-mayor cities

The CEOs in strong-mayor cities attend to the administrative tasks of their government, thus reducing the time that the executive mayor needs to devote to these areas. They are also active as policy innovators, but with particular emphasis on securing resources and improving productivity. These CEOs have the highest proportion—three in ten—who are highly active across the board. Still, the remainder shy away from giving political advice to their political boss and emphasize providing technical information and recommendations.

The cultural traits found in most countries with strong-mayor cities help to explain these characteristics. Uncertainty avoidance and power distance found at higher levels in mayor-council cities make it less likely that the CEOs will get mixed up in the complex and unstructured area of advising their strong political masters about political issues. On the other hand, the power difference between mayor and CEO presumably reinforces the latter's concentration on the administrative tasks of the city. The relatively smaller size and scope of these cities, as described in chapter 3, also make it more likely that the CEO will take a direct part in handling administrative tasks.

Committee-leader cities

The CEOs in committee-leader cities are active in all components of policy innovation with the exception of securing outside resources. The explanation for this moderately great emphasis (compared to great or very great emphasis on other aspects of innovation) may be that the countries with this form transfer large amounts of money from the national government to cities based on objective formulae, although this generalization is now less applicable in Great Britain.[13] The CEOs devote the most attention overall to offering advice to elected officials and politicians, including a much higher level of political advice than in the cities with other forms. They also provide a relatively high level of technical advice. Most committee-leader CEOs are in the adviser-policy innovator activity cluster (fig. 5.1). As noted in chapter 3, they place the most reliance on internal actors in their networking behavior.

Giving relatively greater attention to these activities seems appropriate in view of the complexity of the official interpersonal relations and the ambiguities of authority in cities with the committee-leader structure. The low level of uncertainty avoidance, that is, high tolerance for ambiguity, and low power distance in these cities enable officials to engage in a good deal of give-and-take. In contrast to the political advice dimension, they are the least involved in traditional administrative activities. The large size of these organizations, based on scope of services provided, population size, or both, increase the likelihood that the CEOs will be managers of managers rather than hands-on administrators. The contrast between the relatively low levels of emphasis on administrative tasks in these cities and the importance assigned to improving efficiency in these cities further reinforces the interpretation of efficiency improvement as a strategic rather than basic administrative activity.

Collective leadership cities

These CEOs report relatively lower levels of emphasis on activities across the board, and collective leadership cities have the largest proportion—almost two-fifths—of CEOs in the underactive cluster of involvement scores. In policy innovation their activity is slightly lower than that of other CEOs but generally of moderately great importance. In the other dimensions, they achieve a second rank in offering political advice and in three of the four administrative activities. The activity levels suggest that each set of officials—mayor, executive committee, and CEO—makes contributions to all the dimensions. CEOs do not have to provide as much policy innovation, and they share administrative tasks with the mayor and executive committee. All these officials jointly can attend to issues about which CEOs advise elected officials in cities with other structures.

The two collective leadership countries have similar and relatively high power distance scores but very different levels of uncertainty avoidance. Extending the generalizations about the differences between the strong-mayor and the committee-leader CEOs, a difference between the two countries in this category may be understandable. The involvement levels in both countries are virtually the same in policy innovation and advice to politicians. In Belgium, with the lower level of tolerance for ambiguity, CEOs have a higher score on the classical administrator dimension than do the Dutch CEOs. Although the total advice scale scores are the same, the Belgian CEOs stress technical advice much more than the Dutch, whereas the order is reversed with regard to political advice.[14] Like their counterparts in strong-mayor cities, the Belgian CEOs shy away from political advice. In the collective leadership countries, the highest proportion of isolates in networking style is found.

Council-manager cities

These CEOs are very active in policy innovation and somewhat active in administration because they are the clear policy advisers to the city council and have undivided authority over organizational direction. These cities have the second highest proportion of CEOs who are highly active in all dimensions. They seek to shape the decision-making process and the coordination of work with elected officials, but steer clear of offering political advice. Although the cultural traits in the countries that use the council-manager form are similar to the committee-leadership cities, the characteristics of the form appear to reinforce a separation between officials when it comes to offering advice on political matters. In all other respects, the CEOs in these cities are highly involved as policy innovators, advisers in areas other than politics, and administrators. Supporting their high activity level, these CEOs are also most likely to have inclusive networks that include the community, other governments, and internal actors.

Individual and Contextual Factors That Affect Activity Level

The analysis to this point has established the importance of governmental structure and national characteristics in affecting how CEOs fill their position. These are the major determinants of the CEO's behavior identified in figure 1.1, which summarizes the conceptual framework for the study. In addition, the conceptual framework provided for measuring the effects of four other possible sources of variation in the activities and other attributes of the CEOs that are relevant to the political process. These factors—administrative attitudes and values, networking behavior, environmental conditions both inside and outside the municipal organization, and the characteristics of mayoral leadership—are all attributes of individual CEOs or their specific community. Attitudes and choices about which actors are important are unique to the individual CEO, and the features of the governmental and organizational process and the positive or negative forces emanating from the environment are different from one city to the next. The mayor's formal authority is built into form of government and is generally uniform within a country, but the behavior and effectiveness of the mayor will reflect the perceptions of the individual CEO and vary within countries.

In order to analyze the effect of the characteristics of individual CEOs or their communities on involvement in activities, it is necessary to examine an individual respondent's relative level of emphasis on a dimension removing country differences.[15] Because tendencies differ by country, it will not be clear whether an association discovered between involvement level and another variable is actually a relationship between the variables being analyzed or between the independent variable and both involvement level and country. For example, the score on the advice to politicians dimension is very high in Denmark and the extent of networking with opposition party members of the council is also very high. An apparent relationship between advise and networking with the opposition may actually reflect in part a relationship between being Danish—with a particular form of government and national culture—and high advice. By removing the country effect from the Danish score, that is, identifying those who are high or low relative to their national peers, it is possible to determine whether there is a direct relationship between the independent variable of networking with the opposition and the dependent variable of policy innovation. In this analysis, the score of each individual CEO is subtracted from the average level for the individual's country. This measurement identifies those who are "high" in an involvement dimension in the sense they are above the mean for their country, regardless of how the mean compares with other countries. For all independent variables other than dummy variables, the same procedure is used. In the example, the level of networking with the opposition is also converted to the difference from the mean score for all Danish CEOs. Since this "difference from country mean" analysis eliminates the extraneous impact of country characteristics, the levels of association are likely to be weaker than would be found in individual level analysis.[16] The same type of analysis will also be used in chapter 8 when examining the influence of CEOs.

The policy innovation and adviser to elected officials dimensions of CEO involvement are analyzed and will be discussed separately.[17] The independent variables have been identified and their potential effects have been discussed in chapters 2–4. The plan for analysis is to select indicators for each of the major factors in the conceptual framework. These are administrative values, networking, internal and external environmental conditions, and mayoral leadership. These indicators are used in regression analysis to identify which are related to the CEO's activity level, their relative weight, and the amount of variation in activity level that the indicators explain. The indicators and their expected relationship to the policy innovation or the advice to politicians dimensions, respectively, follow.

	Expected relationship to—	
Factors in conceptual framework	Policy innovation	Advice to politicians
Administrative attitudes and values:		
Advocacy	+	+
Primarily responsible to politicians	−	+
Advantage to have same opinions	n.a.*	+
Networking by CEO with		
Political opposition	n.a.	+
Other council members	n.a.	+
Leaders of community groups	+	n.a.
Provincial/state government officials	+	n.a.
Internal conditions		
Uncertainty	−	+
Organizational conflict	−	−
Party conflict	−	+
Cooperation with politicians	+	+
External conditions		
Pressures from community	+	+
Intergovernmental pressures	+	+
Mayor's policy leadership	?	*n.a.*

*Not expected to be applicable to this relationship.

In general, we ask the question whether there are individual or community level factors that add to the explanation based on form of government and national culture. In some respects, the analysis of factors that explain variation from the country mean turns out to be disappointing in the amount of explanatory power it offers. The fact that this analysis produces only modest findings reinforces the importance of the themes presented to this point. It appears that once variations associated with country and form are removed, the impact of individual and community characteristics is limited. Still, this part of the analysis produces new insights about why CEOs behave as they do at the apex of leadership in their cities.

Policy Innovation

The policy innovation dimension of activity reflects a commitment to develop and carry out efforts to improve the city. It is to be expected, therefore, that innovation will be related to other indicators of activism, in particular, a commitment to advocacy and extensive networking with community leaders and officials in state government. CEOs who value responsibility to elected officials rather than to citizens are expected to be less involved in policy innovation, indicating a greater deference to the policy initiation of politicians. It is expected that positive internal conditions, for example, low uncertainty, would support higher policy activity because increased security is likely to offset the risk taking associated with innovation. On the other hand, it is likely that innovation is in part a response to problems in the external environment and, therefore, that pressures from the community or other governments would increase involvement in policy. It is not clear what to expect the relationship between mayoral leadership and CEO policy innovation to be because the issue has not been explored in previous research. Contributions from the CEO might increase in the absence of innovative policy leadership from the mayor, that is, the CEO may do more to fill a void in policy leadership. On the other hand, strong leadership from the top politician may expand the opportunities for the CEO to initiate activities within the policy goals established by the mayor (as illustrated in a case by Nalbandian 2000).

When we examine how the indicators are related to the level of policy innovation, setting aside country and form of government as explanatory factors, the results are modest and only a small amount of the variation is explained. Still, most of the expectations are confirmed and the question about the impact of mayoral leadership is clarified, as indicated in table 5.4. CEOs are more likely to be active in policy innovation based on their networking be-

Table 5.4 Regression Analyses of Factors Related to CEOs' Level of Policy Innovation and Advice to Politicians *(beta coefficients)*

	Policy innovation	Advice to politicians
ADMINISTRATIVE ATTITUDES AND VALUES:		
Advocacy	.13	.14
Primarily responsible to politicians	−.05	.09
Advantage for CEO to have same opinions as majority of council	n.i.[a]	.10
NETWORKING BY CEO WITH		
Political opposition	n.i.	.08
Other council members	n.i.	.06
Leaders of community groups	.15	n.i.
Provincial/state government officials	.10	n.i.
INTERNAL CONDITIONS		
Low uncertainty (dummy)	.05	−.07
No organizational conflict (dummy)	.10	.06
Party conflict	n.s.[b]	−.10
Cooperation with politicians	.08	.07
EXTERNAL CONDITIONS		
Pressures from community	.07	.07
Intergovernmental pressures	.05	n.s.
MAYORAL LEADERSHIP		
Mayor innovative policy leadership (dummy)	.05	n.s.
Mayor caretaker policy leadership (dummy)	n.s.	n.s.
Regression results	$R = .317$	$R = .303$
	$Adj. R^2 = .098$	$Adj. R^2 = .089$
	$p < .00$	$p < .00$
	$n = 3449$	$n = 3268$

NOTES: All betas significance $< .01$
    a. n.i.: not included in the analysis
    b. n.s.: not significantly related to the dependent variable

havior and values and the presence of internal cohesion and external pressures in their environment. CEOs who assign more importance to their interaction with community leaders—the strongest single explanatory variable—and with officials in state government are more active in policy innovation. A commitment to advocacy (support for administration as a leader in solving social problem and for assisting the disadvantaged) is linked to higher innovation, as expected. Valuing the norm of accountability to political leaders rather than to citizens is negatively associated with policy activity. The more CEOs feel they should be accountable to politicians, the less active they are as policy innovators. Positive conditions in the organizational and governmental process, that is, cooperation with politicians, low organizational conflict, and low uncertainty, are linked with greater policy innovation, as expected, as is the link with higher environmental pressures. Finally, the analysis provided for the possibility that either high or low policy leadership from the mayor—either demonstrating the characteristics of the innovator or the caretaker as defined in chapter 3—could affect the CEO's policy activity. It turns out that effective mayoral leadership has a positive impact on the CEO's policy innovation rather than the reverse and that CEOs are not more actively involved to compensate for a mayor who is a caretaker.

These results indicate that active policy innovators are also more likely to be actively engaged in their communities and committed to taking an active approach to ameliorating social problems in their cities. A setting characterized by internal cohesion and external pressure seems to be the best for bringing forth a high level of initiative from the CEO. Positive internal conditions encourage and sustain innovation. On the other hand, cities with greater pressures from the community also have the need for more emphasis on innovation. Effective mayors are found with more active CEOs. There is not a fixed amount of innovation that is divided between the top officials at the apex of city government. Rather, more innovation from one can lead to more from the other.

The more innovative CEOs in the study are more likely to be engaged, committed professionals who are actively and strategically linked with actors outside and inside of government. They work with mayors who are also policy leaders and they operate from a secure internal base to respond to challenges from the external environment.

Advice to Elected Officials

The advice to elected officials dimension of activity reflects a commitment to assist politicians and strengthen the process of government. It is to be expected that the CEO's advice will be related to a strong orientation to elected officials, reflected both in networking with council members and valuing the direct accountability to and policy congruency with elected officials. A desire to lead and improve society reflected in a commitment to advocacy should correspond to greater involvement to efforts to improve the governmental process as well. Advisory activities involve more smoothing out difficulties than initiating new endeavors, as is the case with policy innovation. It is expected, therefore, that the internal circumstances that contribute to higher advice would be a combination of negative and positive conditions. Advising elected officials is particularly important when uncertainty levels and party conflict are high, but presumably the CEO is reinforced in this activity by a higher level of cooperation with politicians and lower conflict within the organizational structure of the city. External conditions are not expected to play as great a role in advising as in policy innovation.

Once again, the expectations are supported in the analysis, as indicated in table 5.4. A commitment to advocacy emerges as the most important single factor in explaining variation in advice. In both policy innovation and advice to elected officials, CEOs are acting on their own initiative to intervene in the political process. Administrators who are more committed to taking an active role in solving social problems are also more involved in providing advice to politicians and seeking to shape the policy-making process. CEOs provide more advice to elected officials when they view members of the council, and especially the political minority, as an important part of their network of relationships.

As expected, the value that the CEO is primarily accountable to elected officials is positively related to higher involvement in advising politicians, whereas it is negatively related to policy innovation. Being oriented more strongly to politicians as the source of accountability also makes the CEO more likely to relate to them in an advisory role. The same logic applies to policy congruency. Being more supportive of the view that it is advantageous to hold the same political views as a majority of the city council makes the CEO more inclined to emphasize advice to elected officials. These two findings suggest that an important aspect of emphasizing advice to elected officials is a high regard for the legitimacy of political leadership and a view of one's relationship to the political process that stresses direct accountability and holding opinions that match the majority.

The expected mixed internal conditions are found to be conducive to advisory activities. Low uncertainty and low party conflict are negatively related to the emphasis on advice.[18] Since two of the activities that make up the advice dimension involve fostering positive decision-making practices and constructive division of tasks between elected officials and administrators, it is not surprising that CEOs would devote less attention to this dimension when the level of uncertainty and party conflict are low. There is less need for the activity. CEOs are, however, more involved in advising elected officials when they have positive relationships with them and when the interactions between the departments in the municipal organization are positive. Good relationships with elected officials and a secure administrative base reinforce advisory activities. When there are greater strains from citizen demands for services and social and economic divisions in the city, CEOs are also more likely to be active in this dimension.

When the effects of country and form of government have been removed, CEOs who are more likely to offer advice to elected officials have a strong commitment to advocacy and to the values of primary accountability to political leadership and policy congruency with majority politicians. They are more active in networking with council members, and they are less likely to work in settings that are free of uncertainty and party conflict.

Conclusion

CEOs in local government handle a wide range of activities. By choosing which of these they will emphasize, they create a profile of their priorities. These choices manifest the collective orientation of public administrators as a professional group and reflect their structural and cultural setting as well as their individual characteristics and circumstances. In general, CEOs tend to emphasize efforts to shape the future and guide the course of their government. Most CEOs are central to the strategic process of determining the direction for their governments and to securing the resources to move forward. Many are also involved in making recommendations to elected officials regarding the substantive choices and, to some extent, the political problems with which elected officials must deal. They help to shape the criteria by which decisions are made and the process of dividing the work of government between elected officials and administrators. Overall, they devote approximately the same amount of attention to these advisory matters as they do to handling the traditional administrative tasks of controlling staff, resources, and the work process. The emphasis on the latter activities, however, varies somewhat more greatly both in the overall level and in the relative emphasis assigned to them compared to policy innovation. Some CEOs devote more of their attention to administration than others, but that variation does not necessarily correspond to how much emphasis they place on policy related activities. Most CEOs do not choose policy or administrative involvement but rather are highly involved in policy innovation and choose their level of administrative activity.

The form of government in the city where each CEO works has a strong impact on which activities CEOs emphasize. In strong-mayor cities, CEOs attend to the administrative tasks of their government and are also active as policy innovators but with particular emphasis on securing resources and improving productivity. They emphasize providing technical information and recommendations. In committee-leader cities, the CEOs are active in policy innovation, and they devote the most attention overall to offering advice to elected officials and politicians. On the other hand, they are the least involved in most traditional administrative activities and give the lowest relative emphasis to administration. CEOs in collective leadership cities have relatively lower levels of emphasis on activities across the board. The level of their contribution is the most consistent across all the activities. In council-manager cities, CEOs are very active in policy innovation and somewhat active in administration. Their emphasis on advice to elected officials is comparable to that of CEOs in strong-mayor and collective leadership cities, but with a strong relative emphasis on influencing the process of decision making and shaping norms for dividing tasks rather than on political advice.

The national cultural traits of power distance and uncertainty avoidance are related to activity level with particularly strong relationships between advice to politicians and power distance and between administration and the relative emphasis on administration and uncertainty avoidance. As power distance goes down, the amount of advice increases, and as uncertainty avoidance goes up, the emphasis on administration increases. In a statistical sense, power distance does not hold up as an explanatory factor for the level of advice when controlling for form of government, although the relationship between uncertainty avoidance and relative emphasis on administration is found even with controls. The tight linkage between form of government, cultural traits, and activity level suggests that structure and national characteristics reinforce each other in shaping the extent of involvement in the two areas for which there is greatest variation across countries. Involvement in policy innovation is generally higher than the other dimensions and varies with form of government rather than cultural traits. As noted above, policy innovation is highest in council-manager and committee-leader cities.

In addition, a number of individual and contextual factors are related to emphasis on activities. A commitment to advocacy by CEOs, a sense of responsibility to the larger citizenry, and active networking reinforce policy innovation. Furthermore, policy innovation is higher when the CEO operates in a secure and harmonious setting in which mayoral leadership is clear. Many of these same factors—in particular advocacy and active networking—relate to the emphasis on advice to elected officials as well, but there is an important shift in the way the CEO defines to whom he or she is responsible between the two dimensions. The adviser is more likely to feel that the political leaders in government should be the key referent rather than the larger population of citizens. The adviser is reinforced by a positive relationship with elected officials and harmony among his or her subordinates, although CEOs offer less advice if there is less need as indicated by low uncertainty and the absence of party conflict. Both innovators and advisers also respond to external challenges from their communities to develop new policy approaches, secure new resources, and promote ways to strengthen coordination in the governmental process.

The analysis of involvement contributes to sorting out the models of political-administrative relations introduced in chapter 2. These are the separate roles, responsive administrator, autonomous administrator, and overlapping roles models. It is evident that the CEOs in these fifteen country/institutional settings do not all behave in ways that correspond to one model. The typical CEO appears to approximate the autonomous administrator or overlapping roles model with extensive involvement in policy innovation. The top administrative official devotes a great deal of attention to shaping a vision for his or her community, developing proposals, securing resources and support, and improving the performance of government. Furthermore, and more in line with the overlapping roles model, most CEOs advise politicians about technical matters and in the process have further opportunity to shape the perceptions of elected officials about community needs and the options for action. A similar number of CEOs are involved in extensive interchange with elected officials regarding the process of policy making and the division of tasks between them. Rather than being simply the recipient of instructions from elected officials, CEOs contribute to the content of the "instructions" through policy recommendations and technical advice, and they help to shape the process by which they are developed. Some CEOs even offer advice about political matters to the mayor—an activity that could also indicate overlapping roles.

Considering the four clusters of CEOs derived from the characteristics of their involvement, it would seem likely that the comprehensively highly active CEOs and those who combine a high level of advice and policy innovation are most consistent with the overlapping roles model. Their extensive interaction with elected officials through advisory activities would seem to preclude their acting as aloof, autonomous administrators. Those who combine policy innovation with emphasis on administrative functions might match the autonomous profile if they are relatively free to set the course for their governments and run their organizations. The underactive group might match the separate roles model, although one would have expected the representatives of this model to be more involved in administrative functions even though they are appropriately uninvolved in policy and unengaged with elected officials. Although in chapter 4 we identified a cluster of attitudes regarding the political process that is consistent with the responsive administrator model—those who value direct accountability and policy congruency—the characteristics of involvement examined in this chapter are not clearly consistent with this model. The responsive administrators, presumably low in policy involvement but highly involved in advice to political leaders as well as attentive to administrative functions, do not emerge from the analysis. It is possible that other characteristics examined in subsequent chapters will identify additional characteristics that approximate this model, just as additional analysis will help to clarify the other models.

CEOs commonly manifest extensive involvement in policy formation and initiation. These activities suggest extensive interdependency between officials in local government. In addition, they also consider it as important to be involved in an advisory relationship with elected officials as they do to handle classical administrative tasks. For both policy and advisory activities, harmony is a precondition to strong emphasis. There is suggestive evidence that strong elected political leaders work with strong CEOs and that weak political leadership and internal disharmony depress the leadership from the top appointed administrator. The CEOs who place greater emphasis on administration than policy are the minority—less than three in ten of our sample. The typical CEO places great emphasis on policy innovation and seeks to shape the process by which the government operates while paying some but often not a great deal of attention to the traditional tasks of administration. Based on the findings from this chapter, it is even more evident that no one model of political-administrative relations is applicable to all CEOs. Still, most would appear to correspond to the overlapping roles model based on assessment of involvement alone.

CEOs as Political Advisors to Elected Officials

An American city manager described with confidence and vigor how he had transformed the economic development policies and fiscal philosophy of a medium-sized city. The city council that hired him knew they had a problem but had no idea how to deal with it. He had shaped their thinking and led the community into a period of sustained growth. When he was asked about the situations involving politically sensitive and electoral matters, however, he visibly shrank. He was uncomfortable and hesitant. He appeared to want to get out of the room.

Commentary on interview with American City Manager

A Danish CEO had endured a period of narrow block politics that had been extremely detrimental to the working conditions for administrative staff. On election night, the voting results indicated that the block rule could be continued. The CEO on his own initiative approached the mayor and the other party leaders to urge them to form a broad coalition. He had entered the inner sanctum where governments are formed.

Commentary on interview with Danish CEO

THIS CHAPTER EXAMINES HOW CEOS affect the governmental process through involvement in the "politics" of city government. This is an important but essentially unexplored topic. Policy involvement of CEOs has not received the attention it should, even though it comes as no surprise based on the previous literature. Even traditional views of the roles of administrators include the expectation that CEOs offer extensive technical advice. How top administrators initiate or get drawn into providing assistance to officials as politicians or assist officials in dealing with politically sensitive situations has not been examined, however. This issue will be explored using personal interviews and the results of a special study in three countries—Denmark, Netherlands, and United States—to supplement the survey data from the fourteen countries in the U.Di.T.E. Leadership Study.

The results presented in chapter 5 indicate a wide degree of variation in the emphasis on "political advice" from the CEO to the mayor. It is not obvious, however, what the officials had in mind when they indicated that such advice was offered. Getting a better grasp of the meaning of this activity prompted the special studies, and intensive interviews had already been conducted in these countries as well as several other countries included in the overall project. These sources provide a rich and intensive source of information that sheds light for the first time on a hidden (but not necessarily dark) aspect of the work of local government CEOs. Thus, we explore what has commonly been viewed as a contradiction, at least in theory—the involvement of professional administrators in the political as opposed to the policy aspects of the political sphere. This inquiry considers the possibility that the exchange of views among leaders at the apex of the governmental process spans a wider range of topics than previously recognized.

The discussion begins with a review of what it means for CEOs to be involved in this way as a historical and conceptual issue. In view of the extensive but widely varying levels of political advice, the final section defines what such interaction entails and why it is undertaken. We propose a new conceptual framework for classifying the kinds of interactions that occur between elected officials. Pictures are sketched of the relationship between elected officials and CEOs in the three countries based on the special survey responses and focus group discussions. They differ in detail but all present the intimate relationship and blurred boundaries between the top political and administrative leaders of the city. CEOs at times and to differing degrees enter the political space of elected officials.

Historical and Conceptual Background

A basic value in modern public administration is political neutrality. It is the companion value, if you will, to that of political insulation. Administrators should not be partial in the political process, and elected officials should not interfere in administrative decisions. Although often equated with a complete separation of political and administrative spheres, neutrality and insulation have importance even if one rejects a model of political-administrative relations based on separate spheres. Indeed, this pair of values is the core of differentiation that is part of all models for the relationship, with the possible exception of the model of responsive administrators (chapter 2). These values, along with the argument that each set of officials should fill different roles and bring its own unique perspectives to decision making, serve to preserve the distinctness and protect the integrity of the two elements that come together in the governmental process.

From the perspective of administrative behavior, the key value is neutrality. As a basic restriction, it means that administrators should not participate actively in party politics and should not mix political and civil service careers. It may also mean that administrators are impartial (Green 1998); they should not take sides and provide information in a way that gives advantage to one set of politicians over another. Administrators have an awesome opportunity to affect the fortunes of politicians if they are not bound by the value of neutrality. Administrators serve changing masters, and there is substantial turnover in elective office and politically appointed positions even if the control of the same party is maintained. Administrators have continuity, they have mastery over the information of the organization, and they have institutional memory of the practices, debates and decisions, and discussions with political leaders from the past. Furthermore, they control the work of government. For these reasons, they could use their knowledge, experience, and memory to help some politicians and harm others. They could make some governments look positive by enthusiastic implementation and make others look inept by obstructing the implementation process.[1] Their commitment to neutrality is central to protecting society from such abuses of bureaucratic power. It is closely linked to the value of political accountability of administrators. The essence of accountability and its purpose to protect democratic control of government are undermined if administrators choose their masters and determine their decisions.

Practices and the implicit meaning of neutrality vary across countries, as you might expect. In the British administrative tradition, there has been strong emphasis on both the fusion of policy and administration and the value of neutrality (Thomas 1978, 6–8). In fact, one could argue that the close interaction of elected officials and administrators in policy making and the administrators' potential influence make administrative neutrality particularly important. For ministers to do well, they must develop proposals that reflect the party philosophy and are also "technically" sound, and their ministries must perform effectively. In both policy making and administration, they depend heavily on administrators who in turn depend on the ability of the minister and the government as a whole to set a clear course and secure the resources necessary to carry out the work of government. Administrators are also drawn into the relations between ministers and the parliament. Since ministers face questions about the administrative work of their departments, administrators must "conduct their work with caution so as to avoid sensitive problem areas that might provoke embarrassing Parliamentary questions" (Thomas 1978, 9). According to Price (1985), it is important that administrators are members of Her Majesty's Civil Service. Civil servants have a degree of independence that derives from their overarching responsibility to the state as embodied in the monarch as opposed to their loyalty to the government in power. British administrators must be neutral both in the sense of being impartial custodians of knowledge and standards and in the sense of serving politicians from all parties with equal loyalty.

The Danish tradition has similarities, but the loyalty of the top administrator to the politician is stronger than in Britain, and neutrality appears to have a more limited meaning. The CEO is more the helping hand of the politician rather than the independent civil servant as in Britain. Danish administrators appear to have "limit" standards—a line they will not cross (Dobel 1984). They will not lie on behalf of their minister, but they may not always tell the whole truth. They will help the party in power advance its position and offer information to be used against the government's opponents. Thus, taking sides is not precluded, but permanent loyalty to a particular party is. Furthermore, administrators distance themselves from politicians once an election is called. Neutrality seems to mean staying out of election campaigns and being willing to provide the same assistance to the winner that the previous government had received.

Despite the importance of neutrality, the meaning and implications of it have not been examined carefully. It has been viewed as general prohibition without specifying what is being proscribed. The Danish view is a narrow interpretation of neutrality: provide the same loyalty to whomever is in power, do not establish loyalties to politicians that extend across elections, and do not affect the outcome of elections. The British tradition extends neutrality to include norms regarding the impartial—but not politically naive—use of information.

The simplest interpretation of neutrality, often articulated in the United States, has been to equate neutrality with no involvement of any kind in politics. This view, however, is a substantial extension of the concept of neutrality beyond its core meaning. It also exceeds what is necessary to secure equal service and comparable accountability to changing elected officials. As we have noted, policy advice and discretionary choices that impact the content of policy are extensive, and these activities do not violate the value of neutrality as long as the advice and discretion are guided by professional and technical considerations rather than "political" preferences. Furthermore, such a narrow definition ignores the interpersonal dynamics of relationships between officials. Caiden (1996, 37) suggests that, given that there are closer ties and greater similarities between politicians and administrators than we often recognize, they may "warn each other about possible violations and abuses, . . . watch for excesses and mistakes, . . . rectify one another's errors and make up for one another's deficiencies." One can imagine instances in which administrators do or are asked to violate neutrality or to narrow the scope of neutrality, and later we examine such situations. After considering similarity and variation in the responses to comparable situations in three countries—Denmark, the Netherlands, and the United States—a more clear definition of neutrality will emerge.

It is not possible to go further in the discussion without offering better definitions of the troublesome concept of "politics." The term is used in two different senses. The first, common in the late nineteenth century as public administration was assuming its modern form, stresses the electoral aspect of government and related activities such as patronage. Thus, the emphasis on getting politics out of administration referred to shielding administration from these kinds of activities. The current social science definition of politics, noted in chapter 5, stresses the process by which a society authoritatively allocates resources and values. Thus, one could argue that administrators should not be involved in the first kind of politics if they observe the value of neutrality, but they cannot avoid being involved in the second kind of politics. These perspectives serve as the basis for two definitions. To differentiate them, it is useful to distinguish between the politics of securing office and the politics of governing society—a distinction similar to March and Olsen's (1995) "exchange" and "institutionalist" perspectives.

The *politics of power* describes the actions taken to secure, maintain, and wield authoritative governmental power. Power politics is centered in but extends beyond elections. It is essentially a contest of opposing agents as individuals and as collectivities and entails conflict in the focused sense of actions to advance one's own goals and to block others from attaining their goals (Axelrod 1884; Svara 1990a). Ultimately, there is a winner and a loser in the struggle for the decisive last vote in an election or a legislative dispute. The conflict of power politics is moderated by bargaining and trading and temporarily resolved by compromise, but the underlying conditions that divide the actors remain. A coalition government results not from a cessation of political conflict, but from the failure of a single party to win a majority. To secure advantage over opponents in power politics, there is exchange of benefits for support. Here, we shall examine how administrators may affect the outcome of political contests among politicians by lending support in a variety of ways to one side or the other.[2]

The *politics of governing* includes and is affected by the politics of power but is much broader. It involves the full range of actions taken to define social problems, develop approaches to deal with those problems, and implement those approaches, that is, the process of governing society (Meier 1998). It includes rational and nonrational elements, deliberation and expediency, and conflict and cooperation. There is extensive interaction between elected officials and administrators in this process, and each can make a distinctive contribution to identifying problems and solutions. Administrators do not have to play a power political game in order to have influence over governance. Good analysis can positively shape perception of a problem, and good proposals can raise the quality of policy choices, even in the absence of power over authoritative policy makers who secure office through power politics.

Much of the discussion throughout this book deals with the involvement of administrators in the politics of governing. The remaining discussion in this chapter, however, will explore involvement of administrators in the politics of power.

Variations in Level of Political Advice

Over two-fifths of the CEOs devote at least a fair amount of attention to giving political advice.[3] Such widespread emphasis on an aspect of professional management that has not been recognized as part of the job description of appointed CEOs warrants further investigation. The amount of political advice varies widely across the fourteen study countries, as indicated in table 6.1. In four countries, over half—indeed two-thirds or more—of the CEOs consider political advice to be at least moderately important. These are Denmark, Britain, Netherlands, and Australia. In six countries, over a quarter but less than half attach this level of importance to political advice—Ireland, Sweden, Portugal, U.S. mayor-council, Belgium, and Norway. Finally, in four countries, less than a quarter consider political advice to be moderately or more important—U.S. council-manager, Italy, France, and Spain. Most of the strong-mayor countries are found together with low emphasis on political advice. CEOs in council-manager cities are slightly more involved, although Australia has a much higher level than the rest. The collective leadership cities deviate from each other with a moderately low level of political advice in Bel-

Table 6.1 CEOs Rating of Importance of Giving Political Advice to the Mayor by Country and Form of Government *(percent)*

	Very little or no importance	Little	Moderate	Very important	Utmost importance	Total
France	44	35	15	6	0	100
Italy	53	25	17	2	2	99
Portugal	32	32	32	5	0	101
Spain	61	23	10	3	3	100
US-MC	33	33	22	9	3	100
Denmark	2	8	30	36	24	100
Great Britain	13	16	21	33	17	100
Sweden	30	26	30	12	1	99
Belgium	32	38	22	6	1	99
Netherlands	9	24	37	26	3	99
Australia	12	20	36	24	8	100
Finland	48	38	11	2	1	100
Ireland	36	14	31	13	5	99
Norway	36	37	22	4	1	100
US-CM	40	35	20	3	1	100
Strong-mayor	46.	29	19	4	1	99
Committee-leader	15	17	27	27	14	100
Collective	20	31	30	17	2	100
Council-manager	34	29	24	10	3	100
Total	31	27	24	13	5	100

NOTES: $N = 3942$
   Chi-square for form of government = 652.5, significance <.00

gium and a moderate level in the Netherlands. The committee-leader countries offer more political advice, with Sweden lagging a bit behind.

Three of the four countries with the lowest importance assigned to political advice are countries with strong-mayor cities, and the other two countries with this form are moderately low. Although it might have been supposed that strong mayors politicize their top lieutenant, the impact appears to be the opposite. The generally low engagement in political advice for these CEOs—together with other evidence presented in chapter 5 concerning higher relative emphasis on administrative functions—suggests that strong mayors "managerialize" CEOs rather than absorbing them into the mayor's political orbit. These CEOs are more likely to specialize in the management aspects of the city and less likely to have interactions with political content.

Additional elements can be added to the explanation of differences. Analysis of variation of political advice at the country level helps to clarify the relative importance of form of government. Structural characteristics by themselves are highly related to advice and explain much of the variation. Certain cultural variables are also strongly related. The greater the tolerance of CEOs for uncertainty and the more they accept ambiguity, the greater is the level of political advice across countries. Any interchange with the mayor over matters the CEO perceives to be political places him or her in unpredictable situations. The implications of the advice may be unclear, and the knowledge base the CEO draws upon is not the one normally used. Professional and technical expertise is not sufficient to respond to these issues. The interchange does not follow established rules; indeed it may deviate from them.

Furthermore, the degree of power difference between people as a cultural norm may affect this kind of advice. The greater the sense of hierarchy and control, the less likely it is that CEOs will offer political advice. Discussions about such topics that may be considered off-limits are more likely to occur when the CEO feels "closer" and more equal to the mayor. As power distance increases, the level of advice declines.[4] Form of government and these cultural factors each add to our understanding of why this activity varies, and the combined effects account for a large amount of the variation in political advice across countries.[5] These two sets of factors interact in complex ways but the cultural features and the dynamics of the structures of the political authority reinforce each other. CEOs most likely to engage in advice are found in countries in which the avoidance of uncertainty is lower and equality is more common and in which the form of government divides executive authority among many officials, necessitating particularly close interaction between the CEO and elected officials. The nature of that "closeness" will be examined later in the chapter.

Aspects of Political Advice

Responses to the U.Di.T.E. Survey indicate substantial levels of political advice, but can we trust these responses? This question is relevant in any social science survey research, but it is more urgent when there are unexpected findings in response to a sensitive issue. In most countries, to engage in political matters deviates from generally accepted norms about the role of administrators. The unexpected results prompted an effort to dig deeper into political advice methodologically, conceptually, and empirically.

There are three methodological problems that may have produced results that deviate from reality with respect to the overall level of advice as well as variation across countries. First, the term *political advice* may have different connotations across countries. In some countries the term *political* may be interpreted as *partisan*, that is, party-political, whereas in other countries CEOs may associate the term with the *political process*. In the latter case, one should expect CEOs to be more willing to advise politicians. Second, the norms about political involvement may differ across countries. If political advice is more illegitimate in some contexts, CEOs could underreport their own involvement even when they are asked about it anonymously in a mail questionnaire. In this respect it is interesting to note that the Danish CEOs who seem to be highly involved in political advice were not anonymous vis-à-vis the researchers.[6] A third and similar methodological problem is that political involvement may be fashionable in some contexts. Involvement in political games is considered cool and something one should brag about, if not in public then in small peer groups or to researchers. Obviously, we do not know anything about the strength of these sources of potential methodological distortion.

Before we discuss the different dimensions of political advice to be used in the special in-depth study, a conceptual clarification is needed. In most of the countries involved in the U.Di.T.E. Leadership Study, local governments have one political leader who stands above all other politicians, and in many countries this official has more or less full authority over the municipal administration. Mayors or other political leaders fill a governmental role and a party/political role. The CEO may give advice to the political leader in his or her capacity as the formal or de facto leader of city government. Although such advice may spill over into the political realm and give the political leader an advantage vis-à-vis other local politicians (or if the advice was bad, make the leader stand out as incompetent), the effects are normally indirect. The examples are legion. When a mayor gets involved in negotiations with a union concerning a labor conflict, he or she is acting as the head of the municipal administration responsible for the smooth operation of the organization. Clearly such a conflict may have political overtones and the way it is handled may have large consequences in the electoral arena. Advising the mayor in such situations, however, is probably considered as a natural part of the responsibilities of the CEO in most countries. There are few if any limits to the extent and content of the advice given. Furthermore, it is probably considered to be completely legitimate that the mayor will handle the situation in close cooperation with the highest ranking appointed official. Similarly, when the mayor acts as a representative of the municipality to the outside world, for instance, interacting with regional or central government officials, it may have electoral consequences. The advice given by the CEO in such situations, however, will not be considered problematic; it is part of the job of most CEOs.

Beyond overseeing administration and representing the city to the outside world, mayors act in other capacities. Mayors are politicians—in most countries party politicians—and as such they are constantly engaged in a power struggle with competing politicians and parties. Similarly, incumbent politicians are not only involved in competition with each other, but their seats are challenged by outsiders. Politicians and political parties constantly try to position themselves in such a way that they will have advantages over their competitors. This is a struggle that goes on all the time but gets increasingly more intense the closer it gets to the next election. Involvement in this struggle normally is not considered part of the CEO's job. When things become too politically sensitive, CEOs are expected to back off. Power struggles are for politicians, not professional administrators. These are the situations that we want to examine to determine whether and under what circumstances the CEO might provide advice or service to politicians.

To construct a model for examining these political situations, it is necessary first to define the terms. *Political advice* refers to information, recommendations, and opinions that are offered as background for or a guide to action by the recipient in handling situations in which the interests of elected officials, politicians, or political parties are involved. The advice may potentially give the recipient or the recipient's party a direct or indirect advantage over other political actors or, if the advice is not given or is bad advice, will give the competitors an advantage. Political leaders may gain advantages in other ways than through direct recommendations or opinions of the CEO. Overlapping with political advice is *political service*, which we define as a tangible product or action that may potentially give the recipient or the recipient's party a direct or indirect advantage over other political actors. The fact that these products or actions are tangible implies that they may be detected or known by actors other than the recipient. The other actors may know that the service has been given and may even know the content of the service.

Advice may be given orally in a face-to-face meeting involving only the advisor and the recipient. Service could involve a product—a report, a memo, a talking paper, or even a campaign speech—or behavior by the CEOs that rightly or wrongly may be interpreted as an effort to help some actors to the disadvantage of others. Generally, we hypothesize that because of the open (or potentially observable) nature of political service, CEOs are more likely to engage in political advice than in political service.

A second major aspect of political advice and service has to do with the arena in which they are offered. Politicians may gain advantages over others in three related arenas: the policy-making arena, the electoral arena, and the government formation arena. The three arenas are presented here in a kind of "chronological" order. Events in the policy-making arena precede what will happen in the two other arenas and only indirectly or remotely affect the other two. Events in the electoral arena similarly may affect what happens in the government formation arena where political leaders form working majorities. Government formation is decisive for the ability of political leaders to gain, maintain, and enhance their political power.

Two contrasting expectations may be formulated concerning the arenas. We can hypothesize that CEOs run a higher risk as they move from the policy-making arena to the electoral arena and to the government formation arena in involving themselves in the business of helping certain politicians to gain advantages over others. The likelihood of their involvement would decline as risk increases. CEOs, however, can be expected not to base their actions only on the risks or costs. Their actions may also generate benefits, which are greater in certain arenas than in others. The most important decision is the way governments are formed, that is, which persons and which parties will combine to form a ruling coalition. It shapes the political environment (level of conflict between political parties, ambiguity about roles, and uncertainty about goals discussed in chapter 4) in which the CEO and the whole municipal organization will have to work in the period until the next election—in most countries the next four to five years. CEOs are keen observers and they often carry with them experiences from other municipalities or from previous periods in their present locality that may produce preferences for certain coalitions as against others. Some persons may be preferred to others for key positions. CEOs are human beings who exhibit sympathies and antipathies. The stakes are high, particularly in situations where the CEO can foresee a total stalemate that would obstruct any progress and innovation as a consequence of certain coalitions. So, it may well be that the risks are increased when it comes to involvement in the government formation process, but so are the stakes in certain situations. The incentive to engage oneself politically in the government formation arena, therefore, may be under certain circumstances as high or higher than the incentive to become involved in the other two arenas.

A third major dimension of political advice and service provided to political leaders is what we term the "intent" of the action. We would expect that CEOs exhibit a psychological inclination to "protect" rather than "harm." In situations where political leaders are threatened by outside forces such as political opponents, interest groups, the media, or individual citizens, CEOs may be inclined to step in and support the leader in question with advice as well as service. One of our Danish interviewees was very clear about his obligations here, but also about the dangers: "When there are some of the very unfair attacks on the mayor, I do of course frequently help protect the mayor, and then you do not become particularly popular with his opponents." The contrasting situation is when one elected official asks the CEO to help him or her take advantage of opportunities which are likely to advance his or her own interests and/or hurt one or more opponents. In this situation, we would expect the CEO to be more inclined to back off. In the policy-making and electoral arenas we identify "threats" as situations in which the position of a political leader is being threatened by other actors, and "opportunities" as situations where a political leader may exploit a situation or an event because it will harm other political actors. In the government formation arena, the meaning of threats is broadened to include perceived threats to the CEO. The CEO may see threats in the form of deterioration in the working relationship between elected officials and staff or the continuation of negative relationships between council members that undermine effective communication. In addition, opportunities may arise for the CEO to be able to influence the future political environment to improve the prospects of achieving his or her goals. In this situation we hypothesize that CEOs are more willing to be involved in the government formation process to offset a threat rather than to take advantage of an opportunity to create a more favorable condition such as a governmental coalition that supports addressing major city problems.

The final important aspect is initiative. Is political advice or service supplied at the initiative of the political leader, or is it initiated by the CEO? Since professional norms do not support involvement in politically sensitive situations, we expect that CEOs will be more willing to get involved when invited. Conversely, they are expected to be much more reluctant to engage in political advice and service at their own initiative.

Methodology

In order to study the phenomenon of political involvement of CEOs, two sources of qualitative information are tapped. First, in nine of the fourteen countries involved in The U.Di.T.E. Leadership Study, a number of intensive interviews were conducted based on a common question guide developed in cooperation between the national teams.[7] Excerpts from these interviews are used in the following discussion. Second, to probe the complexities of advice, a special study was conducted in Denmark, the Netherlands, and U.S. council-manager cities. These three countries represent three of the four structures of political authority developed in chapter 3: committee-leader, collective, and council-manager. As a consequence the relationship between the mayor and CEO varies across the three countries. Although the CEO is chosen by and accountable to the entire council in both the United States and Denmark, the Danish mayor has some executive authority and political support based in the party that controls or is part of the controlling majority of the council. In the United States, the mayor has no administrative authority and is not necessarily the "real" political leader of the council even though he or she nominally occupies this role. Since the mayor is usually elected separately from the rest of the council, there is no certainty that a majority of the council will support the policy positions of the mayor. In the Netherlands, the mayor is an impartial presiding officer appointed by the central government who has administrative authority only over public safety and will not be the source of requests to support particular policy or political initiatives. In fact, the CEO might consult with the mayor as a source of disinterested advice about how to handle a delicate situation. Thus, the CEO is politically dependent on the mayor, and their administrative responsibilities are intermixed in Denmark. The CEO is politically and administratively independent of the mayor in the United States, but can be affected by the nature of their relationship. In the Netherlands the CEO and mayor occupy analogous roles as objective guides to elected officials.

In addition to variation in the mayor's position, there are a few other major characteristics of city government in these countries that help to interpret the findings. In Denmark, the mayor chairs a finance committee (approximating an executive committee) elected on a proportional basis from the city council. American city councils are small—seven to nine members are common—and function as a whole, using committees in some cities only to give preliminary review to matters that will be decided by the entire council. Council members are usually elected on a nonpartisan basis, and parties are not important in organizing the council in most cities. Dutch city councils elect from their members a board of alderman chaired by the mayor that acts as an executive committee responsible for daily administration, financial matters, and the implementation of decisions made by the council. CEOs may see themselves more as agents of the board rather than of the city council as a whole.

The three countries differ with respect to the extent of political advice as reported by the CEO (see table 6.1). Denmark is clearly at the top among the fourteen countries studied with nine out of ten CEOs who consider political advice to be at least somewhat important. In the Netherlands, two out of three express this opinion (a level similar to that of Great Britain and Australia). In the U.S. council-manager cities, only one in four view political advice as being moderately or more important in their daily work.

The special study in the three countries was based on a combination of survey research and a variant of the focus group method. In the first step a series of brief cases describing hypothetical situations were constructed in order to cover the different dimensions discussed in the previous section. The various combinations of the four dimensions that were covered by cases are indicated in table 6.2. (The numbers in parentheses are the numbers that identify the questions in the survey.)

It is important to note that table 6.2 refers to "mayor initiative." This is the term that the original Danish questionnaire used. Subsequently the questions were adapted to the particular Dutch and American structure of political authority. In the Netherlands the focus was on the executive committee, and in the United States the focus was usually on the council rather than the mayor. This shift in focus from country to country is important to keep in mind when the results are interpreted. Not all possible combinations were covered. In the shaded boxes in table 6.2, no attempt was made to develop cases covering hypothetical situations. It was assumed that only under extreme situations would CEOs render political service on their own initiative and that they would rarely be invited to participate in negotiations about government formation.

In the second step a group of CEOs was asked to complete the questionnaire anonymously. In Denmark, CEOs from one particular county were selected and twenty responded. In the Netherlands, the CEOs were selected from a list prepared in cooperation with a group of CEOs. The selected respondents came from municipalities throughout the Netherlands, and sixteen CEOs participated. In the United States, twenty-one out of thirty-one selected CEOs in a metropolitan area in North Carolina responded. Subsequently the questionnaires were analyzed.

In the third step the respondents were invited to a half-day seminar in which the ideas behind the survey were presented briefly and the results were discussed. Particular emphasis was placed on the question of why the CEOs had responded the way they did, and under what circumstances they might

Table 6.2 The Four Dimensions of Involvement in Political Advice and Service

Arena	Nature of situation	Political advice		Political service	
		Mayor initiative	CEO initiative	Mayor initiative	CEO initiative
Policy-making arena	Threats	Avoid position that will be harmful to party in the council (2D)	Identify expected problems with proposal (2E)		
	Opportunities			Supply arguments for possible illegal proposal (1D) Oppose reform proposal from opposition (1E) Attend meeting of mayor's supporters (2I)	
Electoral arena	Threats	Advise on conflict of interest (2F) Impact of closing facility (2G)	Warn mayor of revolt (2H)	Help deal with scandal (1C)	
	Opportunities	Advise on leaking information (2B)		Summarize political achievements (1A) Summarize problems facing city (1B)	
Government formation arena	Threats		Broaden coalition (2J)		
	Opportunities	Choose political successor (2A) Composition of majority (2C)	Encourage incumbent mayor to run for re-election [U.S. only] (2K)		

change their responses.[8] In the following sections, the findings are reported item by item and then in terms of general patterns in the responses. We compare responses from the surveys and focus groups with our expectations regarding involvement.

Political Advice and Political Service in Different Arenas and Situations

The situations presented to CEOs in three countries were created to examine many possible combinations of the dimensions summarized in table 6.2.

Some of the original Danish cases were adapted from real incidents, but all were transformed to some extent to focus on particular issues. The "translation" to the other two countries required altering the type of officials included in the situation to match the structure of political authority in each country, making the appropriate reference to subgroups on the council—parties in Denmark and the Netherlands and majorities and minorities in nonpartisan U.S. city councils. Sometimes we changed the nature of a policy issue to match the functional responsibilities assigned to the cities included in the study, for example, closing a fire station in the United States versus closing a school because the cities included in the special study do not have functional responsibility for schools. A review of each of the situations and a summary of the questionnaire findings and focus group discussion for each follow. The discussion is ordered according to the conceptual scheme, starting with an account of the political advice items pertaining to the policy arena, the electoral arena, and the government formation arena. The results are summarized in figure 6.1. This is followed by a discussion of the political service items.

Political advice

How to obtain largest possible support on the council for a proposal (item 2D)

In this situation, the mayor or the board in the Netherlands asks for advice about how to secure the greatest possible support from the entire council for a policy that is potentially controversial or unpopular. Most CEOs in Denmark and the Netherlands feel that they can advise the mayor or the board on this matter. In Denmark, the advice would be an example of the fairly free and broadscale interchange—presuming there is a normal working relationship—that occurs between mayors and CEOs. The term *sparring partner* is sometimes used in job notices to describe one of the roles to be filled by the CEO. It is not uncommon in the interchange that occurs for the mayor to ask, "How can I sell this to the council?" The CEO will respond and may well ask in return, "Do you have the votes to get this passed?" An excerpt from one of the Danish interviews illustrates this point.

Interviewer: So political sparring is to challenge [the politician]. . . ?

CEO: Yes. And obviously there is also a bit of party strategic thinking involved here, where I become involved by saying, "How do your opponents think and react here?" . . . (later) . . . "You might meet opposition here, so it would be tactically wise to do such and such."

This free exchange will be evident in other situations as well. In the Netherlands, advice on a matter such as this is a part of the support that the

CEO should provide to the board, particularly because the scenario in the Dutch questionnaire referred to the policy as part of the board's agreed-upon policy goals. It is not controversial or professionally suspect for the CEO to help the board accomplish its program. In the United States, CEOs are more reserved about what could be perceived as helping the mayor as one member of the council win support from the rest. Still, on balance, the U.S. CEOs would provide the advice and their counterparts in the other two countries would overwhelmingly do so.

*Helping politicians recognize negative reactions to a
proposal (item 2E)*

In this situation, the CEO feels that the mayor or the board is preparing to make a decision that will be used by the opposition against the mayor or will generate major political problems for the mayor or the board (vis-à-vis the entire council). Most CEOs in all three countries would advise the political leaders that they anticipate problems with the decision. The Danish CEOs appear to be acting out of loyalty to the mayor and the Dutch CEOs out of loyalty to the board. A U.S. CEO indicated that he would be inclined to offer the mayor "friendly advice" in order to prevent the potential negative response to his proposal. Describing the action in this way suggests that the extent to which the CEO likes the mayor will influence his willingness to offer the advice. This situation is in the policy arena, which makes it easier for the CEO to get involved. Even though the CEO is taking the initiative, it is an action that can be taken without taking sides or choosing to support the mayor or board over another side. Thus, it is different from the first situation. It prevents harm rather than promoting the position of the leader.

*Advising a politician how to handle a conflict-of-interest
charge (item 2F)*

During an election campaign, the mayor or a board member wants the CEO's advice about whether he should go to the media and defend himself against a conflict-of-interest charge or ignore the accusation. The primary issue here is not the nature of the advice but whether the CEO would enter a conversation with a politician about such a matter. Most CEOs would do so, with the Danish the most inclined to offer advice without reservation. The others are also inclined to do so, although somewhat more likely to take the circumstances into account before acting. One CEO indicated that his advice would be that the mayor should fully discuss the accusation so as not to appear to be covering up his actions. In this situation, as in the last one, the political figure did not ask the CEO to support his position but only what he

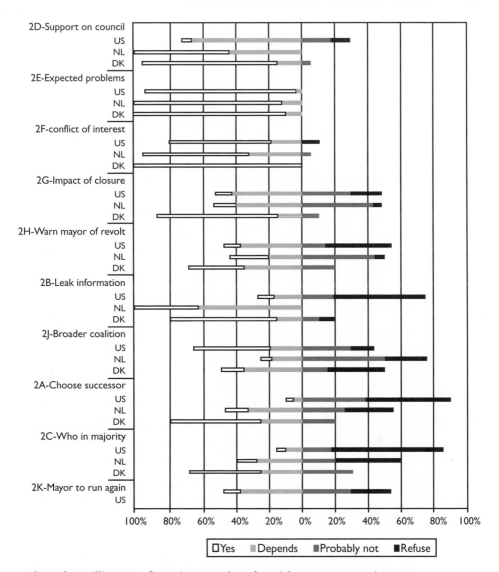

Figure 6.1 Willingness of American, Dutch, and Danish CEOs to engage in political advice   / Collective Committee Leader
nonpartisan

should do. Without needing to defend the official or take his side, most CEOs would offer advice.

Advising officials on the electoral impact of a decision (item 2G)

In this situation, elected officials want advice about whether making the highly controversial decision to close a facility (a school in Denmark and the

Netherlands, a fire station in the United States) will be damaging to them in the next election. Opinion is evenly divided in the Netherlands and United States with only a few CEOs being clearly willing to advise the officials. Most felt that this is the kind of deliberation a politician should make and, therefore, the CEO should not get involved. Elected officials must decide whether they are going to make tough decisions. Put differently, CEOs should stay out of a matter when it involves a pure political choice. In Denmark, most were willing to get involved in this matter. Presumably they saw the situation as a threat to the mayor and felt that they should offer advice, particularly since they would be simply estimating what the impact would be, not advising the mayor about what he should do or supporting his position. Assessing support for and political implications of actions appears to be part of the legitimate conversation that can take place between a Danish mayor and CEO if they have a sound working relationship.

Warning political leaders about being dumped (item 2H)

Should the CEO warn the leader of political "danger?" There are a number of factors that lead to the prediction that the CEO would not do so. This is an electoral matter involving the action of parties or other political factions, and it requires that the CEO take the initiative rather than being asked for advice. Reflecting these factors, the CEOs were much more cautious about intervening. Most Danish CEOs would warn the mayor, showing the loyalty to the mayor observed in other situations. The Dutch and American CEOs are fairly evenly divided, although more of the former definitely would approach and fewer definitely would not approach the elected official who was threatened. Thus, the Dutch overall were modestly inclined to act and the Americans inclined not to act. Here again, an element of pragmatism and personal feelings enters into the calculation. One U.S. CEO asked about this case, "Do I like the mayor or not?"

Advising political leaders on leaking damaging information about
an opponent (item 2B)

This situation involves not a threat to the political leaders but rather the opportunity for them to undermine an opponent. As in the case of handling the conflict-of-interest charge, the question is not what advice would be given but whether the CEO would offer advice at all. This situation produces one of the strongest splits between the Danish and Dutch CEOs on the one hand and the American on the other. Most of the former would advise the political leaders, although many of the Dutch CEOs were tentative in their willingness to do so. If they were asked for their advice, then they would give it.

Most of the Americans definitely would refuse to get involved, although one in five would advise the mayor under some circumstances. They feel it is wrong and dangerous to get involved at all. One suggested that he would refer the mayor to the city attorney and remind him or her of the potential negative personal consequences of disclosing confidential information.

Advising elected officials on selection of candidates and government formation (item 2A, C, J)

Three situations used in all the countries plus one used only in the United States deal with the question of whether the CEO will get involved in ways that could affect who sits on the governing board and how it is organized. Two of the common situations involve offering advice about successors to the mayor's or leader's position and about who should be included in a new majority coalition. The American CEOs are very reluctant to get involved in these matters or the one situation used in the United States alone. The International City Management Association code of ethics prohibits taking part in elections, and these government formation situations are apparently perceived to be a forbidden area. Even when asked (the situation used only in the United States) whether they would encourage their incumbent mayor to run for one more term when several important projects might be jeopardized by the mayor's departure, the CEOs were evenly split, and those opposed to acting were more intense in their feelings. The CEOs in the Netherlands were mildly opposed overall to getting involved in picking a successor and deciding who should be included in the majority. The Danish CEOs, on the other hand, were generally willing to get involved in both areas. They interpreted these situations as ones that affected the strength of the governmental system, and they would act out of loyalty to the "system." They are willing to get involved in these areas as a kind of process engineering that will contribute to the smoother operation of government and improve interaction with administrators.

The third situation presents the CEO with the choice of whether to initiate efforts to end "block rule" with a narrow majority. The conflict between those inside and outside the majority has been detrimental to the working conditions of the CEO and staff. In view of the negative consequences of the current block rule and the interest that CEOs have in improving the process of decision making, it might be expected that they would make the overture to the mayor or, in the Netherlands, to the leaders of all the parties to form a broad coalition. On the other hand, there are factors that would be expected to produce caution. The CEO has to initiate the action. He or she would be entering an arena that is highly political, involving as it does the results of elections, the fortunes of candidates and parties, and the formation of the body to whom that CEO is accountable. For ethical reasons, the CEO should not try to manipulate the membership of the majority. Reflecting a preference to see the council achieve consensus rather than having a majority maintain narrow control, the American CEOs tended by a small margin to be willing to intervene. The CEOs in the Netherlands and Denmark opposed approaching the political leaders by similarly narrow margins.[9] Even those who agreed to act viewed this as "dangerous business." The difference in perspective may be that the American CEOs would have been arguing for inclusiveness as a principle applying to the relatively small number of individuals on their councils, whereas the Danish and Dutch CEOs would have been urging that certain parties be included in a broader coalition, and they were less willing to do that. Thus, despite the potential advantages of a broader coalition, this situation produced the least willingness to get involved.

Political service

The following discussion and figure 6.2 summarize the responses to the political service items that appeared in the questionnaire.

Provide note raising objections to proposal from minority (item 1e)

The opposition has developed a major proposal, and the mayor or the board wants the CEO to submit a note that provides arguments against it even though there are no technical problems with the proposal. The Danish CEOs generally feel that they can provide the note, although they make a distinction between an opinion shared only with the mayor and a formal position paper that would be officially attributed to the CEO. The Dutch CEOs are more reserved and make a similar distinction between a personal memo from the CEO to an elected official that is private and a report that is open to public inspection. In the United States, only information provided orally can be private because of open records requirements. Since providing a paper would amount to publicly taking sides with a faction on the council, the American CEOs are generally unwilling to comply with this request.

Attend a meeting of the leaders' supporters to explain a proposal (item 2i)

The mayor or a board member asks the CEO to attend a meeting and answer questions about a proposal from the finance committee in Denmark

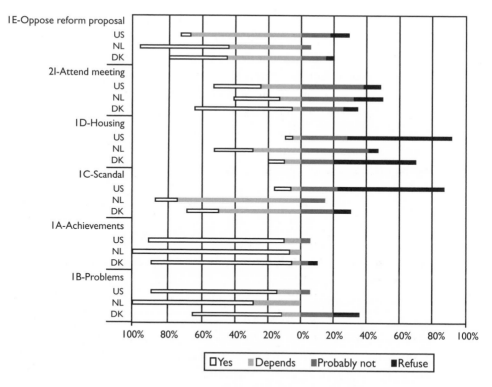

Figure 6.2 Willingness of American, Dutch, and Danish CEOs to engage in political service

and from the board in the Netherlands. In the United States, it is a proposal which the CEO supports and has been working on, although the mayor is also a strong proponent. What makes the meeting problematic is that it will be a gathering of the mayor's supporters or a meeting of the board member's party group in the Netherlands and Denmark. As a consequence, the CEOs are cautious about agreeing to go. The meeting is presumptively political because of who is present. On the other hand, this request simply entails an explanation of a proposal and answering questions about it, as opposed to endorsing a proposal. The CEO's contribution will neither promote new policy nor directly endorse anything the mayor is doing in an electoral sense. Realistically, supporters of the mayor could well be important supporters of this project. On balance, the CEOs in all three countries agree to attend, although those opposed are almost as numerous as those who would attend in the Netherlands and the United States.

Support political leaders in a proposal that may be illegal (item 1d)

In this situation, the mayor or the board member responsible for housing wants to change the housing policies in ways that may illegally affect the placement of immigrants (in Europe) or the location of low-income housing (in the United States). The political leaders ask for a note supporting their position, and CEOs in Denmark and the United States overwhelmingly refuse. On the surface, this situation might be seen as one in which the leader was potentially at risk of taking a position that could be damaging, and the CEO might advise the leader in order to prevent this harm. As presented, however, the CEO sees a number of warning signs that indicate that he or she should not get involved: this is public support of one politician, it benefits this politician over others, and it violates the professional norm of supporting the law. The Dutch CEOs by a narrow margin agree to provide the note, although they emphasize that the note would include an objective presentation of the legal arguments. Generally, CEOs will not enter this situation unless they carry the protective shield of legality. For a larger group, the questionable legality and the way they would have to contribute, that is, support a position rather than provide advice about what position might be taken, keeps them from getting involved in the first place.

Support political leaders in defending a supporter against a charge of scandal (item 1c)

The leaders are trying to defend a member of the majority on the board from charges of scandal and ask the CEO to prepare arguments that can be used in this effort. The U.S. scenario added two specific elements: the critics who are demanding removal include members of the minority on the council, and the local newspaper is supporting their effort. The prospect of supporting one side over the other in a controversial matter with no policy content caused the American CEOs to overwhelmingly refuse to accept the request. The Dutch and Danish CEOs on balance agreed to comply, even though the Danish CEOs were asked to prepare a press release explaining why the mayor supports the council member from his party.

Provide reports to political leaders on achievements or city problems that will be used in an election campaign (items 1a and 1b)

In two separate situations, political leaders ask for reports that can be used in connection with elections. In the first, the leaders want a report of the greatest achievements in the past electoral period (or the last five years in the United States) for which they can take credit. In the second, they want a report on current problems in the city, and it is clear that this will be used in the election campaign. Even though these reports provide general support to politicians and might be interpreted as giving incumbents an advantage over nonincumbents, most CEOs in all three countries agreed to provide the reports. Their willingness stems in part from the similarity between these reports and others that CEOs commonly provide to the council on the work of council and the state of the city. Some CEOs in the Netherlands even suggested that the second paper provided an opportunity to help create awareness of problems the city should be addressing from the administration's perspective. CEOs are regularly involved in policy innovation aimed at focusing attention on problems and goals.

The CEOs can also justify filling this request because the information would be made generally available and not provided to incumbents alone. Although this was not explicit in the situation, it is an important norm. CEOs promote equal access to information and a level playing field for all candidates in local campaigns. One American CEO routinely sends copies of information requested by any single candidate, whether an incumbent or challenger, to all other candidates during the electoral period. Another holds an orientation meeting for all candidates and up until the election distributes to challengers exactly the same information that is sent to council members, for example, meeting agenda packets with items to be considered and background information. Presumably if these situations had involved special assistance to some candidates not available to others, the CEOs overwhelmingly would have refused to provide it.[10]

General Observations about the Situations

The responses given within each country exhibited certain patterns. In the Danish case there seem to be two underlying dimensions. The first dimension covered three items in which the mayor was exposed to external threats in the policy-making and the electoral arena (items 2D, 2H, and 2G). There was a clear tendency that CEOs who were willing to advise the mayor on how to maximize the majority on an issue dangerous for his or her party would also not hesitate to offer advice on a potentially damaging election issue (school closure) and would warn the mayor about opposition within his or her own party. This "loyal to the mayor" dimension was discussed during the focus group session. There seems to exist a general agreement that high loyalty toward the mayor exists in municipalities where the mayor has a strong and secure position. Other research has supported this view: the CEO "depends upon the mayor's ability to handle turbulence and conflicts in the political system" (Hansen 1997).

In the Netherlands, there is a similar tendency. In general, the CEO is very loyal to the Board of Mayor and Aldermen. If they ask the CEO to prepare a note, her or she regards it as a duty to do so unless there are reasons why it should not be done. Generally, the Dutch CEOs display higher support for and less opposition to preparing reports than do the Danish or American CEOs. In this sense, they are more responsive to board direction.

The American CEOs display no sense of loyalty to the individuals who occupy elected positions. In fact, they are extremely sensitive to the appearance of taking sides between council members, and they offer no special support to the mayor. The American city managers are not inclined to offer assistance that might be interpreted as political service. If information that is potentially useful to incumbents is provided, it is transmitted publicly and shared with all candidates. Supporting the position of the mayor over the rest of the council or the majority over the minority are opposed for reasons of ethics and survival. The CEO quoted at the beginning of chapter 3 who worked with, not for, the mayor was very clear about the responsibility to not take sides:

Part of what can go wrong is the manager gets sucked into taking sides. You have an eleven-member council, seven of them have this opinion, four of them have this opinion. You devote all your energy to the seven. That is a fatal mistake. I have an absolute responsibility to deal with all eleven of them, and to listen and try to sometimes serve as the interpreter between the minority and the majority and go back and forth, and say to the majority, "This is what the minority is feeling like, this is what is troubling them." And then go back to the minority and say, "Here is what they are trying to do," and serve as a mediator and a facilitator in that communication, and then as a collaborator in terms of helping them.

In the small fluid American city councils, today's dominant faction can fracture or be replaced. The mayor does not have any independent control over the city manager's position, nor can the mayor protect the manager if the council is opposed to him or her. Maintaining positive relations with the mayor is important in part because friction between the mayor and manager can undermine support among other council members. This does not mean supporting the policy stands of the mayor, but neither does it mean remaining silent if the mayor is unknowingly about to alienate the council nor refusing to help the mayor (under the right circumstances) to identify ways to broaden support on the council.

The second dimension in Denmark involved the three items on government formation. It can be argued that involvement in the government formation process is probably motivated by concerns of the CEO about the future functioning of the political-administrative system. Who leads the government (the person) and who participates in the governing coalition (the persons and parties) are major concerns for Danish CEOs. The Dutch CEOs are less involved in offering advice on electoral matters than the Danish CEOs, that is, they do not see themselves as partners in managing the politics of the board. They will offer advice, however, if it can be justified by a desire to make the process work smoothly. This contribution might be viewed as "process engineering." The CEOs in the United States do not feel it is appropriate to actively intervene in shaping the composition of the board majority. They shy away from involvement in campaigns and identifying candidates, and by a small majority do not even feel it is appropriate to encourage a mayor with whom they work well to seek another term.

What circumstances foster involvement in politics by administrators? The Danish CEOs offered several circumstances that would lead to more intense involvement. First, it was maintained that it is the political leader who defines the "space" for or the "limits" of advice. How the mayor sets the limits will, among other things, depend on the CEO's ability to meet the mayor's need for support. If the personal chemistry between the two persons is optimal and if the CEO can trust the mayor he will be more inclined to engage in political advice and service. Trust refers to the extent to which the mayor can be expected to know and adhere to the unwritten rules of the game under which the advice is offered. One such rule is that politicians should never involve the CEOs in political battles by referring to their opinions and recommendations given in face-to-face meetings with the mayor.

In the United States, the city manager appears to be more assertive in setting the limits. Trust and regard for the mayor will increase the likelihood that the manager is willing to offer "friendly advice" that is intended to be helpful to the mayor. The manager, however, must be able to justify doing so for public-serving reasons, not just to help the mayor and certainly not simply because the mayor has requested the assistance. In the Netherlands, the limits issue appears to be less central to what kind of advice is provided and more relevant to the content of the advice. Some CEOs stress that they will provide a report but will include in it the considerations that they feel are important and relevant even if this counters the political intentions of the officials requesting information. Others feel that it is their responsibility to help the board communicate its arguments as clearly as possible and will help frame the arguments. The resulting product would be a statement from the board, however, and not a separate supporting note from the CEO.

Political involvement is also a function of characteristics that lie outside the immediate relations between the CEO and the mayor. The Danish CEOs suggested that their dependency on the political opposition has an impact. The more important the opposition is to their success, the more likely the CEOs are to advise the mayor on politically sensitive issues.[11] The causal relationship, however, could go either way. When a CEO becomes involved in political advice, the opposition will focus attention on the CEO, and he or she will become dependent on the reactions of the opposition leaders. On the other hand, if a CEO views the opposition as important, he or she becomes more sensitive to the political implications of actions and advises the mayor more on political matters. In the former explanation, the advice comes first and causes the opposition to scrutinize the CEO; in the latter, the importance of the opposition is the prior condition that affects the CEO's efforts to minimize uncertainty by offering political advice to the mayor, including matters that will affect the relationship to the opposition. In the Netherlands, CEOs appear to interact more with the board as a whole without concerning themselves with the relative balance of forces. In the United States, as already noted, the small size and potentially shifting division of the board make it very important for the CEO to treat all councilors equally.

When it comes to political service the Danish CEOs were very careful to make a distinction between what could be termed "supporting notes" issued to the mayor and "public notes" which were issued by the "Office of the CEO." Supporting notes like a talking (or cue) paper for the mayor are less risky than memos and reports issued in their own name. The latter can be used and misused by the mayor as well as the opposition, increasing the chances that the CEO becomes engaged in political battles. A similar distinction is made in the Netherlands but does not apply to the United States where both types of written communication could be accessible to the public. Furthermore, all meetings attended by a majority of council or committee members (or even a smaller proportion in some states) are required by law to be announced in advance and open to the public. These conditions reinforce a tendency in the United States to look for reasons to not provide political advice rather than for justifications to do so.

Entering the Political Room

As implied in the stories at the beginning of the chapter, it is helpful in understanding the political advice or service to think of engaging in these activities as entering a special space. From the CEO's perspective, the space lies beyond a threshold and within barriers. To make the image even more concrete, we can think of the space as a room—an image that matches the way CEOs talk about political advice. They say that they do not want to "get close to" certain topics as if they had a spatial as well as content dimension. They think of these matters as being "off-limits," that is, outside the area they normally occupy. It is a place where they are not in control. It is a place where they can feel trapped and from which they want to escape, although it is also a place where they may be able to say things they could not say in a public place. The image also seems appropriate because it implies an entrance—and what it takes to enter—walls or limits, and inner chambers.

The threshold or passageway to the room is a set of conditions that must be fulfilled before the CEO will enter or even consider entering the room. These include trust in the politicians to follow the unwritten rules noted above, for example, they will not expose the CEO's contribution even though they will not necessarily protect the CEO if his or her contribution is revealed. In addition, the relations among political groups are sufficiently regularized that the CEO can know the contending factions and their positions. In a chaotic free-for-all conflict between individuals and groups, CEOs will not consider approaching the room because it is too risky.

The walls that make up the room block admission unless one goes through the door. Once inside, there are additional walls and doors to inner chambers that the CEO may refuse to enter. The areas represent the arenas of policy making in the outer area with elections and government formation as the inner chambers.

The CEO is cautious about entering the room because of the nature of the interactions within it. Politicians are in control of what happens and what is considered. In this room, the discussion concerns the politics of power. The participants emphasize the exchange of favors for support, gaining advantage, weakening opponents, and securing victory. The topical area being discussed also affects how willing the CEO is to enter the room or its inner chambers. Policy making is discussed in the outer area. CEOs commonly discuss policy as a normal part of their job, but in the room the additional elements of political power are added. The discussion turns to questions such as what will it take to sell this policy, will it hurt us, or will it give us an advantage over the opposition? When the discussion moves into the electoral chamber—how will the policy affect us in the next elections?—CEOs are less willing to go along. When it shifts to government formation, they are even less likely to participate unless invited to serve as a source of technical information.

Whether or not the CEO will enter the room (or stay in it) is affected by a number of factors. Entry is more likely if the CEO is invited rather than taking the initiative to appear. The risks must be acceptable, although greater risk may be accepted if there is the possibility of greater benefit or the prevention of greater harm. It is probably easier to go into a room without windows or with the curtains drawn, but some discussions are so sensitive that the CEO would not want to be seen going behind closed doors to take part in them.

Norms and characteristics of the structure and dynamics of political authority in each country affect how difficult it is for CEOs to enter the room and how they will rationalize doing so. In the United States, there has been a historical tendency to define political neutrality in the broadest way. Therefore, the room is normally off-limits. American CEOs have sensitive antennae to detect and steer clear of power politics. Furthermore, they also do not want to be present when politically sensitive matters are being discussed because their presence could imply that they are taking sides even if it were possible to contribute to the discussion in a neutral way. One way to rationalize entering the room is to offer "friendly advice." The term implies that it is not official advice but guidance couched in terms of "If I were you, I would consider. . . ." The term also implies that the advice will be given differentially depending on how the CEO feels about the politician. If there is no positive regard, the advice is not given. Generally, the American CEOs were most likely to agree to offer advice if it would prevent harm. The other two ways that U.S. CEOs can rationalize entering the room are if the action promotes fairness, as in providing information to incumbents since it will be provided to challengers as well, or if it promotes values important to the CEO. Paradoxically, more U.S. CEOs were willing to enter the most inner chamber of government formation, but it was to tell the mayor to be inclusive, "include everyone in your governing team."

The Dutch CEOs appear to be invited into discussions with the board of aldermen—their key referent—on a regular basis. These CEOs can justify entering on the basis of being the loyal counselors to the board. They are present at sensitive discussions and they offer advice on matters that may confer advantage to the board members over others, but the content of the advice is technical or offered as part of their duty to help the board communicate as effectively as possible. They also seek to maintain effective working relationships between the board and staff, and this includes finding ways to do what is asked if possible. Thus, these CEOs were willing to be involved in a wider range of situations than the CEOs in the United States. The advice they offer, however, often extends beyond the scope of what is requested, as when their report on a proposal of questionable legality included factual references to the law. They seek to balance their professional standards with their desire for positive relations with the board and their loyalty to it.

The Danish CEOs have a close advisory relationship with the mayor and engage in broad-ranging exchange. They are expected to fill the role of sparring partner, which implies that the interaction is both frank and hard to confine. In filling this role, the Danish CEO will enter the room regularly to discuss policy matters and administrative arrangements as they pertain to the mayor's dual role as politician and executive. Presumably the CEOs need to be there because the sparring takes place in the outer area of the room. They are engaged in an exchange of ideas in which there is probing and testing that can lead each to ask about the other's sphere. The mayor will ask the CEO whether he or she can develop a proposal that will advance the mayor's party program, and the CEO will ask whether the mayor can get it passed. As one CEO explained, he and the mayor do not discuss the internal dynamics of his party, but still, "I may perhaps be able to ask, 'Do you have your party behind you in this.' He would perhaps say, 'I will have to work on it.'" The CEOs who enter the room have met the threshold conditions of a sound working relationship with the mayor, and they commonly engage in this frank exchange about the political aspects of policy choices. It is not difficult to move into the electoral chamber out of a sense of loyalty to the mayor and if the mayor asks you to do so, because the mayor sets the limits of advice. One Danish interview revealed an extreme version of the general phenomenon:

Interviewer: We talk a lot about political advice and sparring. Where do you set the limit?

CEO: There are no limits. Actually there is not. . . . I do not set any limits when it comes to supporting the mayor, I don't.

Interviewer: If the mayor has a question about party political tactics, do you go into this?

CEO: You bet I do.

Another interviewee in Denmark was more cautious than most of his colleagues, however. Referring implicitly to the many firings of CEOs in the early 1990s, he stated the following:

I believe the idea of being a sparring partner with the mayor has to be taken with a grain of salt. Really, sometimes I think that the idea of being a sparring partner is the wishful thinking by city managers. They want to believe that they are at the right hand of the politicians. I believe you have to be careful. The longer I am here the easier it becomes to use the particular jargon of the profession and also try to make yourself out to be wise about party politics. I do have a good deal of knowledge about it, but I want to try to avoid it if I can, because I believe it will be the death of many colleagues.[12]

The various rationalizations for entering the political room have a common element. CEOs view politicians as acting out of narrow interests or being concerned about helping themselves or their party. In a sense this is correct, since power politics ultimately involves one's own success or the success of one's faction or party in order to secure the positions they must occupy to accomplish their goals. The goals of politicians may be broad and inclusive but the pursuit of power is ultimately narrow and exclusive. CEOs, on the other hand, believe that they are serving the public interest. They are motivated by a desire for fairness, equity, and meeting needs rather than responding to demands in exchange for voting support. Their public service ethos leads CEOs to take what appear to be contradictory positions. On the one hand, they will generally take the position that they should not get involved in matters affecting the narrow interests of politicians, and, therefore, they do not want to enter the political room. On the other hand, because their motives are pure, they are justified in entering the room if doing so will advance the public interest directly or indirectly.

Conclusion: The Meaning of Political Advice and Neutrality

Political advice has been defined as information that helps the recipients handle situations in which political interests are involved and that may give the recipients or their party a direct or indirect advantage over other political actors. Political service provides the same kind of advantage through tangible products that may be detected or known by actors other than the recipient. The exploration of the situations in which political advice and service may be provided and the reasons why it is or is not offered help us to understand their importance and their consequences.

Although CEOs have great impact on the policy-making process and the politics of governing generally, they are also contributors to the politics of power among elected officials and contenders for office. Over two-thirds of CEOs in the fourteen countries attach at least modest importance to the vague activity of political advice, that is, less than one-third reject the activity completely as having little or no importance to them, and two out of five give moderate or greater emphasis to it. The special studies in the three countries indicate that at a minimum, most CEOs are willing to accommodate requests for information as long as it does not give some politicians an unfair advantage over others. Such actions may be justified by converting the request for a political service into a general service, although a large majority of the CEOs were willing at least under some circumstances to help leaders increase support and promote their accomplishments. Most would let political leaders know that they think that the leader is moving into difficulty. There are more misgivings about helping the leader secure support for a proposal on the council, particularly in the United States, but most would at least under some circumstances provide this kind of advice. Over half would attend a meeting of the leader's supporters to answer questions about a proposal, and—with more misgivings—would help politicians understand the impact of a controversial decision. Just under half in the United States and over half in the other countries would help to construct arguments against a major proposal from the political minority.

Most CEOs would be willing to come into the political room under certain circumstances to address matters like this. They are in the room to accommodate political leaders on whom they depend, without compromising their ideals. In fact, they can rationalize their actions by the beneficial impact of the advice or service they provide. They elevate the level of discourse and give politicians a stronger legal or factual foundation for their arguments, they moderate the attacks on opponents or level the playing field among contenders, and they help politicians avoid problems that could have negative repercussions for working relationships. Regarding this last benefit, they help keep political leaders from appearing to be inept, bumbling, self-serving, and excessively contentious, thereby helping to strengthen the image of politicians and of government itself. Even CEOs who attach only modest importance to political advice—a level that is commonly found in the United States and six other countries—are involved in helping elected officials handle certain politically sensitive situations.

Overall, in these matters in which most feel they can get involved, they enter the political room to help their partner in governance. Because of the caution with which they enter and the professional shield they carry, they are not demeaned or corrupted by the interchange that takes place there. These CEOs come from countries in which the tolerance of uncertainty ranges from fairly high to very high, and this could help account for the results. They are professionals in an unprofessional place acting more or less as professionals. For structural as well as cultural reasons, the American CEOs are the most anxious about being in the political room, the Danish are the least anxious, and the Dutch fall in between. The CEOs in the Netherlands are the most willing to be loyal counselors to the board and help it do its work, even the work that carries political overtones. The Danish CEOs are most inclined to be not only sparring partners in policy matters but also junior partners in the political management of the city council, in part because the two are hard to separate. The American CEOs will generally not go into the inner chambers of electoral advantage or government formation except to argue for broad, apolitical inclusiveness.

Based on their overall scores on the political advice index and their proximity in cultural values regarding power, one could infer that the British CEOs are similar to the Danish in their approach to political advice; the Australian and, to a lessor extent, the Irish and Swedish are similar to the Dutch, and the Norwegian and Italian are similar to the American CEOs. Because of relatively high power distance scores in the remaining countries, their CEOs are likely to be even more cautious about offering political advice. In Finland, the practice might be rejected because of rigid adherence to professional standards. In the remaining countries with politically powerful mayors and cultural values that reinforce hierarchy—France, Portugal, Spain, and Belgium—the CEOs prefer to avoid the political room to prevent being captured by the mayor but they are sometimes forced to enter it.[13]

The discussion adds new richness to the understanding of neutrality. If we start with the presumption that the CEOs in our study are professionals who are trying to live up to an ideal of neutrality, then we can examine their attitudes and behavior for a definition of neutrality in action. This definition will accept an extensive but varying amount of political advice and service. The minimal level of neutrality, that is, the behavior that minimally constitutes neutrality, is equal service without favoritism over time to all leaders in authoritative policy-making positions. CEOs will offer their best advice and service to whomever is in charge regardless of party or other political characteristic. They will help any incumbents but not actively oppose or disadvantage challengers. They will serve new political masters as they did their predecessors. Neutrality requires that actions do not undermine accountability. If administrators seek to determine who is in charge, their accountability is questionable and they have created a conflict of interest that casts doubt on neutrality. Since they could enhance their interests by making elected officials beholden to them, they could not be relied upon to act neutrally between more and less preferred candidates. Normatively, it is appropriate for CEOs to enter into the government formation arena, but only to the extent that their impartial actions affect the size of the coalition, not who controls the coalition.

The second level of neutrality incorporates the first but adds limitations on providing advantage to one political actor over others. The minimal level is potentially troublesome because of the advantage conferred to incumbents by the type of political advice and service that is provided. A crucial additional factor in making this assessment may well be how electoral campaigning is structured. If parties are present and effective as a continuing source of support for individual candidates, then it may be presumed that contributions by the CEOs of the kind we have considered here do not substantially affect electoral outcomes. When candidates run essentially as individuals, however, the impact of supporting incumbents could be much greater. In the United States where this condition is commonly found, the emphasis on not taking sides, not helping incumbents against challengers, and insisting on equal distribution of information to all candidates is particularly important. Without extending the meaning of neutrality to include fair treatment for all, CEOs could enhance the already strong position of incumbents over challengers.

A possible third level of neutrality would proscribe any kind of political advice or service. Although a small minority of CEOs appears to take this position in their outright rejection of political advice, such a prohibition seems both unrealistic and unnecessary to insure fair competition and administrative accountability. The notion that CEOs are essentially apolitical and turn away from any situation with political overtones assigns them a position on the sidelines, detached from the close interaction with elected officials that the position requires if the CEO is to realize the potential inherent in the position.

It is partly through political advice and service that the major components of the local government system are knitted together. In the political room, the political and professional leaders come to terms with their distinct perspectives, looking for ways to reconcile them without abandoning them. Through political advice, CEOs acknowledge, deal with, and perhaps constructively contribute to the politics of power without being absorbed by it.

The discussion sheds some additional light on certain aspects of the four models of political-administrative relations. Some CEOs do not provide political advice or service. These CEOs could be acting in ways that are consistent with the separate roles model in which CEOs do not engage in political advice and presumably do not want to do so. Some of those who steer clear of political advice could also be autonomous administrators who remain aloof from the political concerns of elected officials. There is little evidence that matches the responsive administrator model in which administrators are converted into the partisan or electoral supporters of leading politicians. The CEOs in strong-mayor cities who might be considered the most susceptible (or vulnerable) to being cast in this role maintain the greatest distance from political advice. Indeed, the potential to be totally absorbed in the mayor's sphere of activity may lead these CEOs to eschew the political adviser role. The findings are generally consistent with the overlapping roles model, and they help illuminate the subtleties and complexities of the overlap.

The conclusion is not that top administrators become politicians when they offer political advice and service but that administrators get more involved in the political life of elected officials than we have realized. Some CEOs do not engage in this kind of interaction at all, but they are a minority. Some do so willingly as a natural part of the complex relationship they have with their political masters. The largest segment of the CEOs offers political advice and service sparingly and reluctantly, but it is given nonetheless and there are professional arguments to justify it. Advice to politicians can also be based on empathy and personal regard that can develop between administrators and politicians. For most local government CEOs, the political and administrative spheres overlap, and the political room is always nearby. The dialogue that occurs there is a critically important part of the broader fusion of perspectives that occurs at the apex of government.

CHAPTER 7

The Ideal Politician

One of the most persistent Danish traditions is the Christmas lunch. At these events families, good friends, or colleagues at work gather to celebrate the coming of Christmas at a huge smorgasbord. With the large selection of food comes plenty of beer and schnapps, the Danish vodka. It was at one of these events that a newly elected politician was given an important lesson: Mind your own business! A year before he had run for mayor. He did not get the job, but entered into a coalition with the old mayor. As part of the deal he became chairman of one of the standing committees. Following the old traditions, the council members and the highest-ranking civil servants—all with their spouses—were celebrating the coming of Christmas. The politician was seated next to the wife of his department head. After the introductory small talk, and after the consumption of several beers and schnappses, she began to turn hostile. Why could he not leave her husband alone? Why was he making things hot for him all the time? Why was he interfering in his affairs? Why didn't he stick to his own affairs, the affairs of true politicians, and let the bureaucrats do their jobs? In short, her husband's life had been turned into a hell in less than a year.

THIS INCIDENT DRAMATIZES AN ASPECT OF LEADERSHIP at the apex of local government not considered up to this point: What are the roles and behavior of elected officials as perceived by top administrators? Answering this question is part of the larger task of defining a proper division of functions between elected and appointed officials. We have examined how the CEOs define their own values and priorities for action. It would be helpful to have parallel information from elected officials, but such information is not available for all the study countries. Still, the attitudes of CEOs about what roles elected officials should fill are also important for two reasons. First, they are an indirect indicator of how CEOs view their respective roles. Implicitly, the profile of the ideal politician is also a profile of the ideal administrator. Second, as the incident reveals, the close interaction between politicians and administrators makes it likely that the norms of CEOs shape to some extent the attitudes of elected officials about what they should do. Just as the civil servant's wife intemperately tried to socialize the politician, administrators subtly shape the behavior of politicians as they communicate their expectations. They cannot dictate to politicians what role to play, but they offer cues about what is and is not acceptable.

Two of the components in the dimension of activities labeled *advisor to elected officials* introduced in chapter 5 are developing and implementing norms for the proper roles of elected officials vis-à-vis administrators and influencing decision-making processes in order to secure sensible and efficient solutions. More than half (55 percent) of the CEOs found the former activity to be very important or of utmost importance, and 77 percent attached the same level of importance to shaping the decision-making process. As for advice to politicians on sensitive political matters examined in the previous chapter, CEOs often try to inject professional perspectives into how the elected officials resolve political challenges and conflicts. Top administrators are thus involved in efforts to influence how elected officials define their roles and how they fill them, and administrators help to shape the norms in city government.

This chapter focuses on the normative ideals of CEOs regarding the proper role of politicians. Put simply, how do top administrators define the ideal politician? Are politicians expected to set broad goals and decide on policies as representatives of certain interests and/or the citizenry at large? Or are they expected to participate in the daily decision-making process of government, maybe even in this capacity acting as ombudsmen for citizens or local groups? To what extent is the definition of the ideal politician a function of the form of government? In the second part of the chapter we investigate how the CEOs assess the performance of politicians: To what extent do elected officials actually live up to the roles defined by the bureaucrats, and what can account for possible differences in the role perceptions among politicians and bureaucrats? In the third part of the chapter we focus on the politicians themselves: How do they see their own role in government, and to what extent does their own role definition correspond to that of the CEOs? Although the first part is based on the full U.Di.T.E. survey, the data for the last two sections are drawn from special studies carried out in Denmark and the United States.

A role can be defined as the norms and behavior that determine how one fills a position. An important source of the norms is the expectations concerning the proper behavior of persons in a particular position. Such expectations arise from many different actors when it comes to politicians: voters, attentive constituents, the party organization, the media, politicians themselves, and administrators. Here we concentrate on the expectations of the top administrators of municipalities. At least four separate mechanisms can be at work at the same time in forming the expectation of CEOs vis-à-vis council members.

One such mechanism is the underlying basis and organizing principles for the governments covered by this study developed in chapter 3. According to the structural feature of representative democracy and the principles of layman rule and political leadership, politicians are the main link between citizens and the governmental system. They are expected to set the direction and ultimately be in charge of the government. With the incorporation of the principle of professionalism, politicians have at their disposal an appointed chief administrator and other full-time officials who help them formulate and implement public policy. The presence of the two sets of officials implies a division of function and distinct roles. Such basic commonalties can be expected to create certain similarities across countries, cultures, and forms of government in the way bureaucrats look at politicians.

Secondly, norms about the proper role of politicians may be conceived as a subset of ideas about "proper governance and management" that are invented, developed, and spread in a larger organizational field and interpreted and adapted by individual municipalities. Historical traditions shape widely shared assumptions about the appropriate contributions of officials. Management consultants, training institutions for administrators and politicians, professional associations and associations of local governments, and universities disseminate and refine these norms of appropriateness (Berg 1999). Following this line of thinking, the outlook of administrators within a country could be similar and independent of the specific situation shaped (for example, by the city's political environment). Administrators from different countries could have quite different ideas as to how an ideal politician should act.

One must allow for the possibility, however, of a cross-national organizational field. Indeed, there is evidence that a cross-national perspective on proper roles is emerging. Associations of professional administrators are strengthening interchange of members and exchange of information across national boundaries. U.Di.T.E. as a European organization of local chief executives and the International City Management Association with strong ties to Great Britain, Canada, Australia, and New Zealand, and expanding contact with continental Europe and the Orient, are examples. Universities share ideas about model education programs for preparing local government administrators, and there is a large body of comparative scholarly work with a shared normative dimension. Among practitioners and management trainers and consultants, the "new public management" is a global movement espousing similar norms for public-sector management and, implicitly, for elected officials.

Thirdly, CEOs' expectations of politicians are likely to be a product of their experience based on the conditions in which they work. Politicians compete for power against each other. As such, politicians are always a source of uncertainty and unpredictability for top-level administrators. But not all administrators have the same experience with and the same perceptions of the political level. As discussed in chapter 4, forms of government are likely to produce different loci and different levels of uncertainty, and experience may vary within countries as a function of the political environment of the individual CEO.

Finally, national culture may contribute to shaping norms. Members of different societies may feel differently about threats arising from the uncertain and ambiguous situations that are inevitable given the complex sharing of functions between politicians and bureaucrats. National culture has been included in the discussion at many points, but one cultural trait—uncertainty avoidance—is expected to be especially important in explaining CEOs' views about the characteristics of the ideal politician.

The four approaches represent alternative and potentially complementary explanations of the following findings or as frames of reference that can help interpret the findings. We can measure directly the three approaches based on form of government, cultural traits, and the CEO's environmental conditions using the data collected in the survey. The fourth approach, which stresses similar roles across countries and cities, is supported by the absence of differences based on community characteristics or national culture. In view of the strong potential for the cultural trait of uncertainty avoidance to override form of government as a factor that explains attitudes that CEOs have about their superiors, the analysis of role preferences will consistently examine both form of government and cultural traits separately and simultaneously.

A Typology of Roles

Politicians are perceived as performing two main roles, the linkage role and the governmental role. They act as a link between government and environment, and they make decisions about what government should do.[1] In contrast to previous studies we conceive the linkage role as involving a two-way process. Traditionally, the role as representative has been stressed, that is, elected officials are expected to channel the wishes and interests of the electorate at-large, social classes, parties, and other specific groups and individuals into the governmental process. What has not been studied systematically, however, is politicians' acting as channels for information running in the opposite direction, from government to citizens. One American city manager pinpointed this two-way communication in the following way:

I would always prefer the council members be the primary point of contact with constituents, and that I help them get the information back and forth that they need. I don't personally like spending a lot of time at neighborhood meetings and things like that, but I do when I need to. And what I will do with an elected official, if we have a meeting coming up, I'll sit down with them and say: "I think you are getting at these kinds of questions, here are the answers . . ."

In this capacity politicians act as ambassadors of government vis-à-vis the environment or as "salesmen" seeking to legitimize the actions of government.

The governmental role involves the actions of politicians to direct the work of the executive and the municipal bureaucracy. Such direction can take the very general form of overall principles and broad goals set by politicians acting as governors. There can also be specific directions in the form of "instructions" established by rules and routines or the decisions made in specific cases. In these actions, politicians are acting as administrators. In between we find a separate role, labeled the stabilizer role, through which politicians are expected to create stability and establish specific and precise goals for the administration.

What Do Administrators Expect from Their Political Masters?

The following question was posed to measure the values of CEOs concerning the proper role of politicians.:

Politicians must give priority to different tasks in their daily work. As a local government official, to which tasks do you think the leading politicians ought to attach

Table 7.1 Importance of different roles of politicians according to CEOs *(index values)*

	Total sample	Strong-mayor	Committee-leader	Collective	Council-manager
GOVERNMENTAL ROLES					
GOVERNOR	**81**	**79**	**85***	**79**	**80**
Decide on major policy principles	77	73	84*	74	77
Have a vision of the way in which the municipality will develop in the long run†	85	86	87	83	83
STABILIZER	**69**	**75***	**61**	**60**	**66**
Create stability for the administration	67	72	59*	66	69
Formulate exact and unambiguous goals for the administration	70	78*	62	75	63
ADMINISTRATOR	**39**	**53***	**25**	**39**	**33**
Lay down rules and routines for the administration	31	45*	20	25	25
Making decisions concerning specific cases	37	61*	31*	53	41
LINKAGE ROLES					
AMBASSADOR	**67**	**65**	**73***	**62**	**63**
Represent the municipality to the outside world	71	70	76*	63*	70
Defend the authorities' decisions and policies externally	74	73	76	76	72
Be a spokesperson vis-à-vis the press.	55	53	67*	48	49
REPRESENTATIVE	—				
Be informed about citizens' views	82	80	85	78	82
Implement the program on which he/she has been elected	60	71*	62	59	47
Be a spokesperson for local groups or individuals who have issues pending decision by the authority	40	49*	30	37	38
Be a spokesperson for their political party	40	28	65*	46	30

NOTES: *Score significantly different from other forms at the .10 level based on correlations between country mean scores and dummies for form of government and without control for uncertainty avoidance index. (*N* = 15 because of the U.S. split between strong-mayor and council-manager categories.)

† Italics indicates that differences across form of government are *not* significant.

particular importance? Please make your entry on a scale from 1 (very little or no importance) to 5 (of utmost importance).

The responses for all CEOs in the fifteen countries are presented in table 7.1 as indices, which convert the original scores to a 0 to 100 scale. (See chapter 1 on the calculation of indices.) The tasks are organized by roles. For four of the five roles, the items are sufficiently strongly linked to justify calculating a composite score, which appears in bold type in the table. The exception is the representative role for which a composite score would be misleading.[2]

In the examination of CEOs' preferences for elected officials' roles, close attention is given to the relationship between the CEOs' attitudes and cultural characteristics. The cultural traits must be measured at the country rather than the individual level (see chapter 3 and the discussion of the Hofstede cultural variables in the technical appendix at the back of the book). Consequently, tables and figures will report the aggregated country average scores. The total number of "units" in this type of analysis is fifteen, with the U.S. respondents split by form of government. The method and standard for assessing the statistical significance of differences between countries and groups of countries is adjusted from the approach used in other chapters because of the small number of units in the analysis.[3]

In table 7.1, the main tendencies in the preferences of CEOs are clear from the three items with index scores over 75. The scores indicate nearly unanimous support for the item. First, politicians are expected to define the mission and establish major policy principles for city government. Thus, the ideal politician is a governor. Second, the politician should be informed about citizens' views in order to link citizens to government. In addition to these roles, there are others that receive wide support or are typically rejected. The ideal politician is a stabilizer and an ambassador to the outside world. Almost as many CEOs agree what the elected official should not be, that is, the average index scores are moderately low. The ideal politician should generally keep off the administrators' turf. The general view is that elected officials should not be administrators, the view expressed by the administrator's wife at the Danish Christmas lunch. With respect to separate items in the representative role, the expectations are mixed. As noted, virtually all agree that politicians should be informed about and represent citizens' views, but there is less support for politicians to implement their electoral program. There is overall opposition to having them act as spokespersons for political parties or as ombudsmen for groups and individuals. Thus, there is nearly unanimous support for the role of the politician as governor and for linking

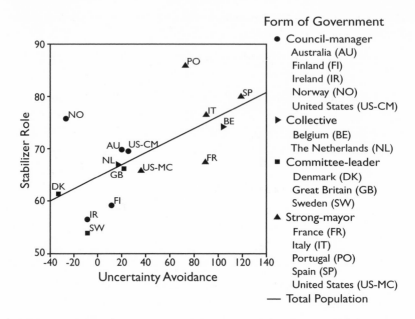

Figure 7.1 Uncertainty avoidance and the importance of the stabilizer role to CEOs

the citizens and their views to government. Most CEOs also agree that elected officials should be ambassadors and stabilizers and should not be administrators. There are mixed preferences for other representative roles, with general acceptance of promoting campaign promises and general rejection of being party spokespersons or ombudsmen for constituents.

Form of Government, National Culture, and the Ideal Politician as Perceived by CEOs

Across forms of government, CEOs have varied opinions on most items, as reflected in the remaining columns in table 7.1. In this section, we analyze each of the five main role dimensions one-by-one in order to investigate the importance of form of government. In the analysis of patterns across countries, we also include uncertainty avoidance as well as form and assess their relative weight in explaining preferences for the ideal politician.[4]

The Governor Role

The ideal politician emphasizes the governor role. On the average, CEOs find this role to be "very important" to "utmost important." The scores do not vary much across countries. The highest score is 87 for Sweden; the lowest, 72 for Spain. The scores across forms of government are listed in table 7.1. The governor role is, on the average, valued the same way in strong-mayor, collective, and council-manager governments. In the committee-leader form of government, it is only slightly more important, although the difference is significant. Cultural differences do not play a role in the assessment of the governor role.[5] Overall, the governor role is a major part of the definition of the ideal politician independent of form of government, and the difference across form of government is almost negligible.

The Stabilizer Role

The stabilizer role is defined as very important by the average CEO. The two subroles, on which the composite index is based, are found to be equally important. On this dimension scores vary across countries. Swedish CEOs tend to favor the stabilizer role least (index score of 54), and the Portuguese CEOs value it the most (86). The value attached to the stabilizer role varies considerably across form of government, as indicated in table 7.1. In strong-mayor systems it is valued more than in countries that use other forms. More extensive analysis, however, suggests that this preference for elected officials to be stabilizers can be explained by national culture rather than form of government. The contribution of each factor is illustrated in figure 7.1.

Uncertainty avoidance is a reliable predictor of the extent to which administrators want politicians to create stability for them and establish "exact and unambiguous" goals. In countries marked by a high degree of uncertainty avoidance, there is a tendency for the stabilizer role to be ranked higher than in countries with a low level of uncertainty avoidance. A look at figure 7.1 indicates that form of government hardly plays an independent role after control for the uncertainty avoidance index, and this is confirmed by statistical analysis.[6] CEOs generally feel it is important that politicians act as stabilizers for the administrative organization. How strongly CEOs feel this varies, however, because they live in different cultural settings, not because they work in different forms of government.

The Administrator Role

The administrator role for elected officials involves activities that come closest to the administrators' turf—decision making in specific cases and establishing rules and routines for administrators to follow. In table 7.1 it is clear that CEOs generally do not want politicians to engage in administrative matters (the mean score across all countries is 39). However, the score for the

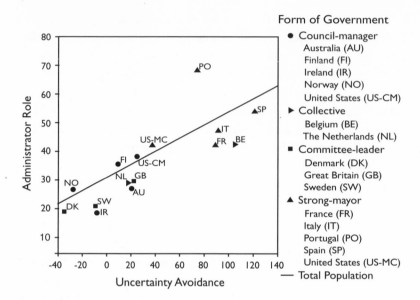

Figure 7.2 Uncertainty avoidance and the importance of the administrator role to CEOs

administrator role varies quite substantially from country to country, with the lowest score (18) found in Denmark and the highest in Portugal (69). The CEO's ideal politician in Denmark would keep his or her distance from administrative affairs, whereas the ideal politician in Portugal is expected to lay down rules and routines for the administration and be involved in making specific decisions.

The two countries are extreme representatives of the two forms of government that diverge more widely on this dimension than the others—strong-mayor and committee-leader (see table 7.1). The administrator role is much more valued in strong-mayor systems than in committee-leader systems.

Some CEOs prefer that elected officials make a significant contribution in the administrative sphere, which has implications for the models of political-administrative interaction introduced in chapter 2. Consequently, it is important to do an in-depth analysis of this finding. In view of the conclusion regarding the stabilizer role that culture rather than form explains national variations, this cultural trait is included in the analysis to explain preferences for the administrative role.

Figure 7.2 illustrates national cultural differences with respect to uncertainty avoidance. Almost two-thirds of the variation in the administrator index is attributable to this cultural variable. In a multivariate analysis, form of government comes close to playing an independent role, although the statistical significance of the finding is weak, and the correlation could be attributable to the extreme Portuguese score, which is widely divergent from other countries in figure 7.2. Thus, it appears that on this particular dimension the important difference between the fourteen countries is not form of government but rather a cultural phenomenon—uncertainty avoidance. The finding strongly supports Hofstede's contention that individuals living in societies marked by high uncertainty avoidance need guidance for action in the form of rules or decisions from their superiors.[7]

When politicians are engaged in establishing rules and routines and making specific decisions, they approximate the classical administrator role of CEOs (chapter 5). These include telling subordinates how to handle specific tasks, developing new routines, and ensuring that rules are followed. The variation in the importance of the classical administrator role can mostly be ascribed to form of government, although the relative emphasis on administration compared to policy innovation is more strongly related to uncertainty avoidance. The classical administrator is most commonly found in strong-mayor systems and is rarely seen in the committee-leader form. Such a pattern might imply a clear demarcation of responsibilities under the strong-mayor form between politicians and top bureaucrats. The latter take care of administration while the former are involved in politics. We know, however, that the strong mayors are more extensively involved in the details of administration than mayors in cities with other forms (chapter 3). Thus, there is no clear separation of roles with regard to administration.[8]

A second interpretation is possible. The importance of administrative functions for both politicians and administrators is due to a combination of structural and cultural factors. Although the analysis in chapter 5 concluded that cultural traits were generally less important than structure, examining the issues from the perspective of norms for politicians indicates that both factors affect behavior and attitudes. The correlation between the classical administrator scale and the administrator role ascribed to the ideal politician by the CEOs is very strong—.71 at the country level of analysis.[9] In other words, when CEOs from different countries see themselves as classical administrators, they strongly tend to value the administrator role for politicians as well. And in countries where CEOs put relatively little emphasis on their administrative activities, they also want politicians to stay away from those activities.

The differences in the analyses here and in chapter 5 call for interpretation. On the one hand, involvement by CEOs in classical administrative functions is related to form but not culture when controlling for form. On the other hand, the CEOs' preference for the administrator role for politicians is related to culture but not form when controlling for culture. If the two component items—establishing rules and making specific decisions—that make up the administrator role for council members are examined separately, however, the order of importance between the variables reverses.[10] For the contribution of politicians to establishing rules and routines, there is a similar sorting of countries to that for the relative emphasis on the classical administrator role as presented in figure 5.2, and form is more important. The strong-mayor cities all score higher than cities with other forms. For the preferred level of politician involvement in making specific decisions, on the other hand, there is much more intermixture. The U.S. council-manager cities are next to France, and two of the top five scores are found in Finland and Belgium— countries without strong-mayor cities but with high scores on uncertainty avoidance. For CEO preferences regarding politicians making specific decisions, it is uncertainty avoidance that sorts out the scores rather than form.

One might argue that attitudes regarding sharing tasks with one's superior will be more strongly affected by uncertainty avoidance than attitudes about the division of functions. There are countless cases when city officials must make specific decisions. Administrators know that in some of these cases when citizens or organizations are dissatisfied with the outcome, they are likely to appeal the decision to a politician. CEOs acknowledge and accept this review by elected officials at a moderate level, as reflected in the overall score for this activity. Indeed, administrators themselves may refer controversial close calls to the politicians. Depending on attitudes regarding uncertainty, there will presumably be national differences in the extent to which administrators prefer to have politicians make the specific decisions or not. Put simply, the more uncomfortable you are with the possibility that your superior will override your decision or second-guess you, the more likely you are to prefer that the superior make the decision in the first place.

When it comes to assigning functions in the governmental structure, on the other hand, the norms (and political realities) of form of government are relatively more important. CEOs in all forms of government except strong-mayor resist the idea that politicians should tell administrators how to perform their administrative tasks by establishing the rules and routines for organizing activities and handling specific cases. In the strong-mayor cities, there is a higher level of acceptance of politicians having this kind of involvement in the administrative arena, although only in Portugal is there majority sentiment in favor. The strong mayor who exercises executive functions is partially accepted as a player in specifying how administrators will do their job.

The overall linkage between the two measures—structure and culture—is important. Structure does not uniformly affect the preferred roles for politicians, but structure does have a modest impact on the CEO's involvement level. Looking at the U.S. sample, there is no difference in preferred roles between council-manager and mayor-council cities and no difference among the mayor-council respondents based on who appoints them to office—mayor or council. There is a very slight difference, however, in the mean scores for involvement in classical administrative tasks based on who appoints the CEO.[11] On the other hand, cultural traits can have a powerful effect as well. The Dutch and Belgian CEOs operate in a very similar governmental structure and share many attributes, although they differ substantially in uncertainty avoidance. As noted in chapter 5, the Dutch CEOs resemble their counterparts in committee-leader cities in their involvement in political and technical advice, whereas the Belgian CEOs approximate the strong-mayor administrators in these areas. They also differ greatly in their preferences regarding the ideal politician when it comes to the administrator role, as shown in figure 7.2.

Thus, the degree of emphasis on classical administrative tasks by the CEOs reflects the impact of structure, but cultural traits reinforce the tendencies. With strong mayors, the CEO is more active in management, not as a consequence of a specialization of effort but rather as a kind of comanagement arrangement. When the mayor gets involved in administration and has the authority to override the CEO, the CEO is more active as well and also willing to defer to the mayor in administrative matters. A preference induced by structure to look to the mayor for direction in establishing rules and routines is combined with an inclination induced by culture to defer to the mayor on specific decisions. On the other hand, in committee-leader cities, which have the second most involved and powerful mayor as well as an important executive committee, the CEO is not highly involved in classical administrative tasks and wants politicians to stay out of administrative matters (although we will see that they do not do so). These CEOs are much more involved in managing their complex interaction with politicians and less involved in day-to-day management. Their relatively large organizations could also contribute to being detached from administrative tasks. They want to direct their own organization rather than look to politicians for direction in administrative affairs. They are also culturally inclined to make their own decisions rather than defer to elected officials. These CEOs do not feel as much discomfort as CEOs in other governmental forms about mixing it up with politicians, often acting as their sparring partners (see chapter 6).

The Ambassador Role

The ambassador role involves representing the municipality to the outside world, defending decisions and policies, and speaking to the press. This role was emphasized by the CEOs as on par with the stabilizer role, less important than the governor role, but significantly more important than the administrator role. Responses on the ambassador index vary somewhat across countries with a high in Sweden of 78 and a low in the U.S. strong-mayor cities of 57 (and 59 in U.S. council-manager cities).

The variation across forms of government is due to two of the individual items—"represent municipality" and "press spokesperson." The source of the difference is the contrast between the committee-leader systems where support for these roles is strong on the one side, and the other forms of government with somewhat lower scores on the other. National culture is not related to the assessment of the CEOs on this particular dimension.

The Role as Representative

According to Eulau and Prewitt (1973, 438), "the core issue in representation is not how leaders are chosen or petitioned, but whether they are responsive." Electoral processes and pressure from external groups are part of a multitude of activities through which responsiveness may emerge. Once selected, politicians face different clienteles who expect services from them. It is likely that the legitimacy of different clienteles varies across countries, forms of government, and national cultures. For example, several times in the previous chapters we have described how the council-manager system of government was conceived as a reaction to the dominance of political parties and the favoring of party supporters in awarding jobs and contracts.[12] Parties are not likely under these circumstances to be viewed as a legitimate participant or "petitioner"; they are not a desirable focus of representation (Wahlke et al. 1962, 270). To the extent that such a role orientation exists in a political system, it is unlikely—ceteris paribus—that city councils will be responsive to pressures from the political parties.

The preferences of CEOs regarding the representational role of elected officials can be viewed as a product of the political environment and professional values. Their preferences may reflect the prevailing attitudes in a country or a city about the legitimacy of a group as well as the views of professional administrators generally about which groups make constructive contributions to the political process or what kinds of representational activities by politicians are appropriate. The impact of administrators' attitudes on council members' behavior is difficult to assess. The attitudes of CEOs do not determine the behavior of elected officials, but they presumably contribute to the definition of norms of appropriate behavior that elected officials seek to meet. For example, if administrators feel that it is inappropriate for a council member to seek redress for a citizen who claims to have been treated badly, the council member may still act on the citizen's behalf but will feel constrained in doing do. The constraints may affect the council member's view of how serious the problem must be to warrant intervention or may cause the council member to feel obliged to "compensate" the administrators for violating the norms. One Irish CEO described how "the anticipated reaction" played an important restraining role for the council members in his city:

Unlike some city managers, he took pains to consult them (the councilors) about likely decisions affecting their locality, which were his legal responsibility—before taking a final decision. He said that no [administrative] official could match the intimate knowledge of a good councilor, for example, concerning someone who might have jumped the housing queue by deliberately making themselves homeless, and he found that councilors did not abuse the influence which he gave them because they knew that if they did there would be murder, and all such decisions would be taken on a work-to-rule basis by the officials alone.[13]

In other words, if the council member interferes in the CEO's realm, every administrative task affecting that council member and his or her constituents will slow to a crawl. Presumably, council members do not ignore this risk. As this quotation clearly shows, the attitudes of the CEO are also important as an indicator of how top administrators view the democratic process. For example, if the CEO does not feel that council members should actively promote their party programs as policy makers, the CEO may "discount" certain proposals as "merely" an attempt to advance the party rather than addressing the public interest. If a council member perceives that his ideas are not taken as seriously by the CEO if the partisan connection is explicit, he may even couch the proposal differently. Differences in the ideals for politicians reflect views about how citizens and groups are connected to government through the democratic process.

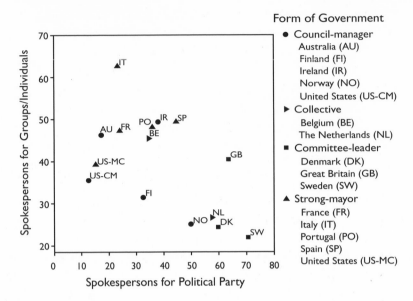

Figure 7.3 The importance of politicians as spokespersons for party or community groups to CEOs

There are many potential "publics" that may represent important foci for elected officials. In the U.Di.T.E. Study we included four focal points for politicians that were initially expected to vary across countries and forms of government. They include being knowledgeable about the views of citizens at-large, acting on promises made to the electorate, being spokespersons for political parties, and being spokespersons for individuals and groups who have decisions pending before the municipal government. This last item approximates acting as an ombudsman for citizens.[14] Whereas the previous four role dimensions taken separately were based on items that were correlated, the four representation items do not form a single underlying dimension. Also, the mean scores for all CEOs vary quite substantially from 82 (be informed about citizens' views) to 40 for each of the two "spokesperson" items, as indicated in table 7.1. For this reason we have not calculated a composite score for the representative role. Almost all CEOs across the four forms of government prefer that elected officials be informed about citizen views. At the country level of analysis, the four items are uncorrelated except for "spokesperson for party" and "spokesperson for individuals and groups," which are negatively correlated.[15] These two items strongly discriminate the different forms of government from each other, in particular the wide differ-

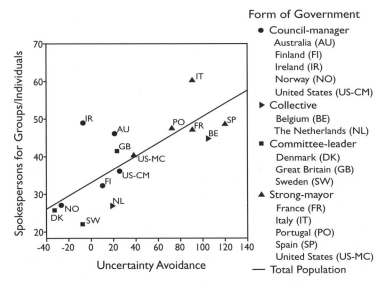

Figure 7.4 Uncertainty avoidance and the importance of the ombudsman role to CEOs

ences found between the strong-mayor and the committee-leader systems that were indicated in table 7.1. The variation by form is also clear in figure 7.3.

In the strong-mayor systems the top administrators tend to prefer elected officials who implement their electoral program and stay away from the party spokesperson role. In cities with the committee-leader form, the opposite view is common. CEOs prefer that politicians stick to their partisan affiliation and stay away from being a spokesperson for groups and individuals.

The council-manager form is associated with still another constellation of values concerning the ideal politician. Here the CEOs generally do not want politicians to represent a political party (Norway is an exception, as indicated in fig. 7.3) and they do not want politicians to act as spokespersons for groups and individuals. They also put less emphasis on the electoral program as a guideline for action. The council-manager form of government reflects the opposition to partisanship and particularism in reform circles in the United States. More coherent governance and more effective and efficient administration were the positive goals of the reform movement, but reducing the influence of parties and groups who would make special claims on government were perceived deficiencies the reform movement sought to combat. Furthermore, the historical role prescribed for council members was to act as trustees who would balance the specific promises made in an election campaign with the actions necessary to advance the good of the city as a whole. These sentiments may have colored the expectations of officials in countries like Australia and Ireland that sought to introduce council-manager government in fairly pure form. Presumably, there would be less impact of these values on a country like Norway that has come to approximate the council-manager form through adapting its own long-standing institutions and where there is extensive support for party involvement in the political process among administrators, as is the case among their Scandinavian counterparts. Beyond the origin of these values or their relationship to the logic of the form, CEOs in council-manager governments are poorly suited to deal with partisan battles. We observed in chapter 6 that the American city managers are the most uncomfortable (compared to CEOs in collective and committee-leader countries) about offering political advice and assistance. They require the most elaborate justifications, grounded in professional and public service concerns, before they will enter the "political room," and they prefer that elected officials not be partisan politicians.

For three of the four individual items there is no relationship with national cultural traits; but the spokesperson-for-groups-or-individuals correlates strongly with the uncertainty avoidance index.[16] This is also clear from figure 7.4. The figure indicates that form of government plays a role here, in particular the somewhat large differences between strong-mayor systems and committee-leader systems, but also that uncertainty avoidance plays an even more important role. The impact of this trait accounts for some of the differences within the different forms of government; for instance, the score for the U.S. mayor-council CEOs compared to the other strong-mayor cities, the difference between Denmark and Britain, and particularly the difference between the Netherlands and Belgium.

The reason for the link between national scores for uncertainty avoidance and the preference for being a spokesperson for individuals and groups is not obvious. The fact that the indicator refers to speaking for persons who have a decision pending in the municipal government, however, and the similarity between these results and those observed with regard to preference for decision-making by the council offer some clues. The clientelistic style of governance in most of the countries that use the strong-mayor form (Goldsmith 1992; chapter 3) brings citizens and elected officials together in a service-requesting and service-dispensing relationship. In the process, elected officials make specific decisions involving particular persons and cases. A preference for both activities may reflect this distinct orientation to defining the purpose of government, one that overrides the typical professional opposition to both activities. Furthermore, the low tolerance for ambiguity that is linked to these preferences could make CEOs highly averse to interfering with the close service relationship between constituent and politician. Put simply, if council members are acting as ombudsmen for citizens, it is better for them to make the decisions about requests than for the CEO to be caught in the middle. In contrast, greater tolerance for ambiguity and acceptance of risk enables a CEO both to discourage elected officials acting as ombudsmen and to resist the council taking over specific decisions.

The multivariate analysis shows that the cultural factors and form of government can explain 67 percent of the variation in the value ascribed by the CEOs to the role as spokesperson for groups and individuals. Form of government affects the assessment of this role merely through a low value in the committee-leader cities.[17] From this analysis it follows that different representation norms, corresponding to the form of government, exist in different countries, and one of the items is also strongly related to cultural differences.

If we shift from the country level of analysis and turn our attention to the individual CEOs, we find clusters of attitudes about representation that reflect some of the differences associated with form of government already discussed. This method of analysis also adds some new elements to the picture of preferred representational roles. We find a distinct constellation of preferences not previously identified as well as variation among CEOs who work within the same form of government. The responses of the CEOs to the three items about which preferences differ (omitting the item "being informed about citizens' views") divide into four clusters. These clusters can be interpreted as alternative normative ideals about representation. The four clusters are the following:[18]

• Trustee: A trustee ideal for representation is indicated by a low score on all three items, that is, minor emphasis on implementation of electoral program, on being a spokesperson for groups or individuals (ombudsman), and on being a party spokesperson. By implication, politicians, unswayed by party or interest group, should base their political stands on their own independent judgment formed outside the electoral arena. (24% of the CEOs)

• Delegate: A delegate ideal is indicated by a high score on all three items. Politicians should, accordingly, base their actions on what they have promised during the election and what their party stands for (or what the party

Table 7.2 Ideal Representation Roles of the CEOs by Form of Government *(percent)*

	Trustee	Delegate	Partisan representative	Nonpartisan representative	Total
Strong-mayor	12	31	6	52	101 (1169)
Committee-leader	10	33	53	3	99 (849)
Collective	22	30	29	19	100 (576)
Council-manager	44	21	14	22	101 (1354)
	24%	28%	22%	26%	
	(950)	(1093)	(874)	(1031)	

NOTES: N = 3948, chi-square = 1463.7, significance <.00

leadership or members want them to do), and they should act as spokespersons for groups and citizens. (28% of the CEOs)

• Partisan representative: Indicates a high score on the party spokesperson item and the electoral platform item but a low score on the ombudsman index. (22% of the CEOs)

• Nonpartisan representative: This ideal politician would keep electoral promises and be an ombudsman for citizens, that is, act as spokesperson for groups and individuals but not be active as a representative of a political party. (26% of the CEOs)

It is important to note that all CEOs regardless of their preferred type of representation prefer politicians who know what citizens want. This aspect of representation, however, does not entail any action on the part of the elected official; what he or she does with this knowledge of public opinion is not specified. The CEOs who want council members to be trustees prefer that council members incorporate their knowledge of citizen views into the independent judgment they exercise. The delegates act on citizen views and demands. The partisan representatives blend party programs and citizen views, whereas the nonpartisan representatives seek to balance the particular demands of individuals and groups with the broad needs of the citizenry as whole.

As indicated in table 7.2, in committee-leader cities CEOs have a strong idea about what role the politicians should play, which includes acceptance of the legitimacy of political party linkage as well as other kinds of representational roles. The two combinations that involve council members representing political parties—partisan representative and delegate—have 86 percent of these CEOs. On the other hand, CEOs in these cities offer the least support for roles that involve representing individuals and groups, 36 percent in the delegate and nonpartisan representative roles.

In contrast, the mayor-council cities also have a strong preference for the role as spokesperson for groups and individuals without party linkage (52 percent). Almost half the CEOs in council-manager cities prefer the trustee who is detached from citizens. But if the ideal council member is not a trustee, there is a divergence in preference about what he or she should be. They have the lowest support for a combination that includes the role as spokesperson for parties—35 percent. Finally, the collective form CEOs are widely dispersed in their preferences, although they are the second highest in their acceptance of party representation (59 percent).

The importance of the delegate role should be noted. Although it is the most preferred role only in cities with collective form (and only by one percentage point over the partisan representative role), it is by a slight margin the most preferred role overall—28 percent are in this cluster—and the second-ranking role in committee-leader and strong-mayor cities, and almost tied for second in council-manager cities. A substantial minority of CEOs supports broad and active representation across all forms of government.

An individual level analysis based on item scores corrected for the country means show very few important relationships between the environmental variables and the definitions of the ideal politicians (see chapter 4). The highest correlation found among the more than 4,000 respondents is .13 between uncertainty about goals and roles and the inclination to support the stabilizer role. In other words, among the four perspectives introduced in the start of the chapter, the third one (i.e., that role expectations are formed by the political environment) cannot be substantiated by the data.

How Do Administrators Perceive the Behavior of Their Political Masters?

The common elements in political roles in all countries and the differences that one would expect for countries representative of committee-leader and council-manager cities are evident in the comparison of Denmark and the United States. In both countries, CEOs want politicians to be governors and to be informed about citizens' views. In Denmark there is strong support for council members being spokespersons for parties, and in the United States somewhat greater support for council members being spokespersons for groups and individuals. The council should play a larger role in stabilizing city government and directing administrators, according to U.S. city managers.

Additional questions asked in the surveys used in these two countries

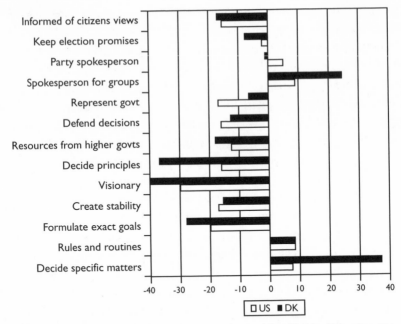

Level of perceived performance is subtracted from ideal level. Negative score
indicates that rating for actual behavior is lower than rating for ideal.
There is no difference in either country for role of spokesperson to press.

Figure 7.5 Difference between ideal and perceived performance of elected officials in
Denmark and United States

make it possible to determine how well council members measure up to the
CEO's preferences in their actual behavior. Immediately after the question
about the ideal traits, the Danish and American CEOs were asked to assess to
what extent the politicians actually live up to the ideal.

In some instances administrators may experience a gap between what they think the
leading politicians ought to emphasize and what the politicians actually do. To what
extent do you find that the leading politicians engage in the following tasks: (with five
response categories from 1 (to a very high extent) to 5 (not at all).[19]

The CEOs were then presented the same list of tasks as in the previous question.

Although the degree of deviation varies, the politicians tend to fall far
short of the ideal in the same roles in both countries, as illustrated in figure
7.5. The gap particularly occurs in the governance, stabilizer, and ambassador roles, and in the representational role most strongly favored by CEOs—
being informed about citizens' views. Thus, the roles in which CEOs would

like to see the greatest commitment from politicians are the ones in which the shortfall is greatest. On the other hand, the actual emphasis as perceived by the CEOs exceeds the ideal in the roles that CEOs support less—being a spokesperson for groups and deciding specific matters. In both cases, the departure is much greater in Denmark, with its low ideal scores for these areas, than in the United States, with more moderate scores. In both countries, politicians are moderately more involved in laying down rules and routines than CEOs prefer that they be. Politicians are less governors and more administrators and spokespersons for groups and individuals than CEOs would prefer.

Indeed, the differences in CEO role preferences for politicians in the administrator and ombudsman roles between committee-leader and council-manager governments do not carry over to the actual behavior of the politicians in these two countries. Stated differently, there is more uniformity among politicians in practice than in the ideal views about them held by administrators. Pronounced differences still emerge in party representation, acting as press spokesperson, and representing the municipality, but in many other areas, elected officials behave similarly despite the differences in form of government and the differing preferences of CEOs.

Although measures of performance are not available for city councils in other countries, it is possible to make a crude comparison of the ideals and the actual behavior for the whole sample of CEOs in all countries by examining the mayoral leadership introduced in chapter 3. CEOs emphasize the public leader traits to a very high degree. The top politicians—and by extrapolation all elected officials—should know what citizens want, and they should have a vision for the long-run development of their municipality. These are the two most important characteristics of the ideal politician, but mayors generally do not live up to this ideal. About one in four CEOs characterizes her or his mayor as a weak public leader (low on the public leadership dimension). In none of the countries except Italy does a majority of the CEOs find the mayor to be a strong public leader (see table 3.2 and the technical appendix).

It is not surprising that discrepancies exist between the role expectations of the CEOs and the actual behavior of the politicians. CEOs are only one, and maybe not the most important, "significant other" for politicians. Within this line of reasoning, additional studies in Denmark and the United States give several clues about why the discrepancy exists and suggest that the gap may be wider now than in the past.

First and foremost, politicians have their own perceptions as to what they ought to do. At the time of the Danish CEO survey, a parallel survey was conducted with 211 mayors and 859 ordinary councilors in 72 municipalities (response rate about 75 percent for both groups). Both groups of politicians were asked the question about "the ideal politician" (Mouritzen 1996). In general, the dual role of the mayor as chairman of the council elected from and among its members and as the daily leader of the administrative organization is reflected in the mayors' definition of the ideal politician. On some items the mayors' ideal comes close to that of the CEOs; on others the mayors' view is between that of the council members and the administrators (spokesperson for groups and individuals and deciding in specific cases). On yet others the mayors respond like council members (implement program and party spokesperson). However, the overall response pattern of the mayors and the ordinary politicians in comparison with that of the CEOs exhibits a striking characteristic. While administrators expect that politicians will differentiate among roles and give some more emphasis than others, politicians themselves seem to look at their different tasks in a much more uniform way—all tasks are more or less of great importance. In that respect the actual behavior of the politicians as assessed by the CEOs is not that surprising, because it reflects to some extent the politicians' own role definition. This is particularly true for two of the tasks where CEOs seem to exhibit the largest frustration with politicians: making decisions in specific cases and acting as spokespersons for groups and individuals.

Outside the formal machinery of government, additional "significant others" have expectations vis-à-vis elected officials. Such actors include their party, local voters, private business, voluntary associations, municipal employees, labor unions, and the like. These outside forces will almost always represent particularistic interests that pressure politicians to intervene in specific cases no matter how much the politicians emphasize a generalist style. One Danish CEO gave a vivid description of these mechanisms and also tended to accept them.

You [a council member] are always so close to the citizens that time and again a single case will turn up, which you will fight for . . . and the moment these cases turn up, you set aside your policy priorities. You couldn't care less. You fight for your specific case. And you use it to create your political identity.

He observed that the mayor is the only politician who works full-time in his governmental job and continued his commentary.

The attempt to introduce the "ideal politician" in the City of Odense [20]

One of the first and most ambitious attempts to push politicians into a new role was carried out in the City of Odense in the early 1990s. This city of nearly 200,000 inhabitants had a form of government that closely resembled the Belgian and Dutch collective form, the so-called magistratstyre that existed only in four of the largest cities of Denmark. The twenty-nine Odense council members decided to decentralize authority to the service-producing institutions, and at the same time reduced the format of the budget to less than twenty appropriations items. Politicians were expected to stay away from details and concentrate exclusively on their roles as governors. The system did not function as planned. Council members quickly became frustrated, particularly because they were unable to respond effectively when they were approached by citizens, their constituent organizations, unions, the local business community, or the media.

In 1995, as part of the study of mayors and councilors, all members of the city council were asked to indicate how often they were approached by various groups. The average share of Odense councilors who were approached monthly or more often by various groups follows:

Party organizations	76%	Unions	25%
Local associations	52%	Street-level bureaucrats	29%
User boards	50%	Business	32%
Individual citizens	59%		

Partly as a consequence of the politicians' frustrations, a new form of government was implemented in 1998 introducing standing committees with executive authority over service departments.

I cannot understand how our local politicians, who also work full-time [in nongovernmental jobs], how they really should have the energy to say, "Now we must decide on policy priorities." What I mean is, [policy] becomes more or less diffused for a number of our politicians, in contrast to these single cases about whether some teacher at a school is paid too little, or whether there are too many potholes in a bad-looking road at the other end of the municipality, or whether this or that road which used to be asphalted now is going to be a dirt road, etc. It is in these tangible specific cases they involve themselves, and I can well understand it. In reality it is very understandable, and from the bottom of my heart I don't believe that it will ever be any different.

Even if politicians did agree with the top administrators about what they ought to do and not do, the situation may require them to behave otherwise. Berg (1999) characterizes politicians as "multi-standard actors," who may exhibit several different identities, each of which involves a set of "logics for appropriate behavior." The individual politician chooses what stimuli to react to in any given situation, thereby also choosing which one of the multiple identities to make operational in the specific instance.

Local voters in Denmark have shown a remarkable change in attitudes over the 20-year period from the mid-seventies to the mid-nineties. In the mid-seventies they generally expected politicians to make decisions based on their own convictions—to act as trustees. This was the response of six out of ten voters in 1978. In 1993 almost two-thirds of the voters wanted local council members to act more like delegates, that is, to follow the wishes of their constituents in case of a conflict between voters and politicians (Berg and Kjær 1997, 328 f). Over the same period one can detect a reduction in trust in local politicians (Urban 1999). There is no doubt that such changes in the political environment have made it much more difficult and painful for politicians to live up to the norms for "good political leadership" formulated by the top administrative leadership.

Independent studies in the United States reveal similar characteristics in the attitudes of elected officials to those found in Denmark and also some evidence of change over time. Studies in the late sixties indicated that the trustee role was most common among council members (Eulau and Prewitt 1973; Zisk 1973, 99–100) and that the typical elected official in council-manager cities was a "volunteer" who ran for office as a form of community service rather than as part of a political career (Prewitt 1970). In a study conducted in the mid-eighties, council members in six moderately large council-manager cities indicated a preferred profile of involvement for themselves that stressed the governor role and rejected extensive involvement in administrative matters—views that reflected the preferences of administrators in these cities as well (Svara 1990a). A 1998 study using a similar methodology in the thirty largest council-manager cities identified a shift in attitudes (Svara 1999b). Although the top administrators would still prefer that elected officials focus on setting goals and avoid involvement in administrative matters, the council members now have an ideal for themselves that reflects an activist orientation including much more emphasis on helping citizens resolve their complaints with city government. Like their Danish counterparts, council members now want to be active across all roles, although they recognize that they are not.

More council members now intend to run for higher office than before. The councils have become more boards of electoral activists than boards of governors, although administrators would still prefer that councils be the latter rather than the former (Svara 2000).

Conclusion

The local top administrators generally want politicians to concentrate on the establishment of overall principles and the formulation of vision and to possess a thorough knowledge of the wishes and needs of citizens. They generally want politicians to stay out of the traditional administrative turf of establishing rules and routines and deciding specific cases. So as a general rule, administrators have a somewhat clear conception about the distinction between policy and administration for elected officials. These basic characteristics do not vary greatly across countries and forms of government and as such they can be attributed to the commonalties of the position that a CEO fills as the highest-ranking appointed officer in a politically controlled decision-making system.[21] However, administrators from different countries, forms of government, and cultural settings also disagree on other aspects of ideal politicians.

In strong-mayor cities, politicians are expected to have substantial involvement in administration and create stability for the administration. They should implement their programs and act as spokespersons for groups and individuals who have decisions pending with the local authority. Politicians should act as non-partisan representatives. The national culture of those countries marked by a high degree of uncertainty avoidance reinforces a tendency to defer to the mayor and elected officials in areas in which the CEOs and the politicians are both engaged. Since the mayor has executive authority, the CEO prefers that the mayor give direction to administrators. Furthermore, since leading politicians are speaking for citizens who have decisions pending in city government, the CEO is more likely to feel that elected officials should be active in making specific decisions. These preferences may save the CEO from getting caught in the middle in disagreements involving citizens and politicians. Furthermore, they may reflect acceptance of the clientelistic orientation to the purpose of government.

Administrative affairs belong to the sphere of professional administrators, not of politicians, according to the committee-leader CEOs. Politicians should act as a board of governors, as ambassadors of the municipal organization vis-à-vis the outside world, and as partisan representatives. The idea that it is legitimate for elected officials to speak for parties is much more widely accepted in these countries than in the others. Indeed, there is a preference for representatives to speak for parties rather than for other kinds of groups or for individual citizens. In these countries, there tends to be a low degree of uncertainty avoidance and presumably a greater willingness of administrators to counter the inclination of politicians to act as ombudsmen. These cultural traits may enable CEOs to interact more comfortably with elected officials as partisan politicians than CEOs in other countries. Rather than leaving their partisanship at the council chamber door, they are expected to bring it in. Furthermore, these CEOs are also more inclined to go into the political room of the elected officials, as we observed in chapter 6.

Council-manager CEOs represent a mixture of the two previous forms. They show a general distaste for partisan representation (as do CEOs in strong-mayor cities), but they also want politicians to stay out of administrative matters. The ideal elected official in these cities tends to be the detached trustee. Among the four forms of government, CEOs in council-manager cities have the highest level of direct contact with key groups in the community. Thus, although they expect council members to be knowledgeable about citizen views, the CEOs themselves are also capable of representing citizens. These officials accept a higher level of ombudsman activity from council members as well as a moderate level of involvement in making specific decisions. Appropriate to the mix of restrictive and permissive attitudes about the role of politicians, uncertainty avoidance scores are generally low.

The collective form of government presents a less clear picture. A close examination reveals that the Netherlands and Belgium are divided on the issue of preferences for electoral roles. Belgium, with high uncertainty avoidance as a national trait and a mayor nominated by the dominant local party or coalition and designated by the crown, resembles the Southern European strong-mayor systems with their emphasis on administration and stabilization. The Netherlands, on the other hand, with moderate uncertainty avoidance and a quasi-professional mayor chosen by the crown, is much closer to the response pattern found in the Northern European committee-leader countries with their emphasis on partisan representation and distaste for group representation.

The analysis has shown that the distaste for party politics often ascribed to administrators is not shared uniformly across all forms of government. This antipartisan orientation may be traced to two divergent political traditions. The problem facing reformers in the United States at the start of the century was how to increase the centralization of fragmented governmental forms and keep partisan influence out of the daily administration. The response was structural reform based on a nonpartisan council and a strong appointed executive who would be divorced from parties. In the council-manager cities, the preferred mode of behavior for council members is to be detached from all referent groups in the community—individual citizens, the electorate, and parties—while being strongly committed to promoting the interests of the city as a whole. The elected officials blend a general view of citizen preferences with their own judgment and the CEO's recommendations to establish goals and policies.

In European strong-mayor systems, centralization is achieved through the strength of the political leader. Since the executive branch is in the hands of a politician usually commanding a majority in the city council (and thereby maybe weakening the influence of the CEO), and since spokespersons for groups as well as individuals are likely to address their concerns to the political power center—the mayor's office—the obvious reaction for CEOs in these systems is a wish to keep partisan considerations out of the decision-making process. CEOs want the mayor to rise above party. In these cities, it is not possible (or even desirable according to CEOs) to separate the mayor from administration, but CEOs hope to separate parties from administration.

The line of reasoning may be the opposite in committee-leader cities. A number of politicians are engaged in the daily details of the administration. Since a dominant strong political leader cannot control all these politicians and since parties do play an important role, administrators do not want politicians to become spokespersons for groups and individuals. The direct connection between parties and individuals in the administrative process, as opposed to the electoral process, could bypass administrators and overload the system with direct representation of groups and individuals as well as representation of party interests. Parties absorb and aggregate citizen demands and regularize the contacts between citizens and government. Thus, most CEOs hope that council members acting as agents of political parties will be a buffer that reduces individual and group demands on government.

Despite these tendencies, there is a sizeable minority of CEOs who prefer that elected officials fill the delegate role and actively link citizens to government through helping individuals, acting on campaign promises, and speaking for their party. Some CEOs support broad and active representation across all forms of government.

Preferences for the ideal politician offer some new perspectives on the four models of political-administrative interaction. The prevailing views among CEOs could be consistent with the separate roles or the autonomous administrator models. Elected officials should stick to their sphere, link citizens to government, focus on broad policy, and support the administrative structure. These preferences are sufficiently strong that even CEOs who might match the overlapping roles models may generally prefer that administrators overlap with the roles of elected officials rather than vice versa. Whereas chapters 5 and 6 generated few findings that were consistent with the responsive administrator model, the support among a minority of administrators for active involvement of elected officials in certain administrative decisions might be consistent with this model, as is support for the delegate and partisan types of representation. These findings would suggest that the responsive administrators, in addition to actively promoting the goals of politicians, may prefer that politicians make certain administrative decisions. They may also be supportive of elected officials including party perspectives, electoral promises, and/or constituency concerns in their legislative behavior.

At several points in this chapter, the question has been raised whether the views of CEOs about the ideal politician will have any impact on the elected officials. A critical factor in determining impact would presumably be the amount of influence the CEO has. The more influence the CEO has relative to elected officials, the more his or her views about acceptable behavior may constrain politicians. The measurement of influence is the topic of chapter 8.

CHAPTER 8

The Influence of Local Government Officials

*In a special section of the local newspaper commemorating the opening of a new civic fa-
cility in Raleigh, North Carolina, the key players were identified: "From the time the
idea was conceived to the time the halls were built, dozens of people had a hand in shaping the . . . Center for the Performing Arts. [Among] some of the most influential" [was]
Dempsey Benton, Raleigh city manager, 1983–2000. He conceived the idea for an af-
fordable performing arts center and sold it to other city leaders."*

Raleigh News & Observer, February 18, 2001, 3I.

THE FINAL, AND SOME MIGHT ARGUE THE ULTIMATE, question
about the relationship of officials at the apex of government is how much influence they have over policy decisions. It is presumed that elected officials
convert their formal authority over policy making into influence, although reality may not match potential. The extent to which CEOs shape decisions—as
opposed to participating in decisions—is the unknown in the political-
administrative equation. Exploration of the contributions of appointed administrators in local government has been preoccupied with the nature of the
role and the kinds of activities in which CEOs are involved. Research has focused on whether top administrators are policy makers, as discussed in chapter 5. Relatively little attention has been given to the impact these officials
have on the governmental process, although it has been assumed to be substantial (Banfield and Wilson 1963; Downs 1967).

Some expectations about influence are obvious. On the one hand, expertise, organizational resources, and professional values should translate into
considerable influence for all top administrators (Gruber 1987; Stillman
1977; Yates 1982, chap. 2.). On the other hand, it is expected that influence
will vary with the structure of local government, including the form of government. When new mayors are elected, there is greater change in policies in

cities with the strong mayor form of government than in council-manager cities in the United States (Wolman, Strate, and Melchior 1996). Lineberry and Sharkansky (1978, 164) argue that "municipal bureaucracies have more power and autonomy in reformed systems, and elected decision makers have corresponding smaller bases of power." It appears that the stronger political leaders are in formal terms, the more influence they will exert, and the less influence the appointed officials will have and vice versa. Implicit in this approach is the assumption that the amount of influence is fixed and that the increase in the influence of one actor comes from a loss of influence by another; that is, this is a zero-sum situation. To use a different analogy that makes the same point, some view the relationship between the mayor and the city manager as a "hydraulic system" in which a "decrease in the manager's power would result in increased mayoral power," as Sparrow (1984, 6) has noted. Thus, form of government and the assignment of authority within it are assumed to be a major determinant of influence, and the influence of politicians and administrators is expected to be inversely related. Furthermore, a number of individual and community characteristics could increase or decrease the influence of key officials within the overall pattern determined by form of government.

In view of the substantial interaction between elected officials and administrators, CEOs are likely to be able to affect the content of political leaders' decisions and make some policy decisions themselves. Despite the importance of administrative influence to democratic theory and an understanding of the urban political process, the existing literature has not systematically measured this phenomenon. This chapter seeks to answer the question: How much influence do top administrators and other officials including the mayor, members of the council, and committee chairs have? After reviewing the general patterns of influence among all official actors, in-depth analysis of the mayor and the CEO will determine the extent to which they share or compete for influence. The inquiry will search for explanations of the differing levels of influence between mayors and CEOs.

Two kinds of decisions can be examined based on the U.Di.T.E. data, budget and economic development. Virtually all cities make decisions in these two areas, as opposed to other functions that may not be municipal responsibilities in some countries. Budgetary decisions reflect control over the key organizational resource of money, and influence over these decisions indicates political power over the allocation of resources for the city. Economic development decisions affect the way a city grows and changes as a center for economic activity. These decisions impact the growth of the community as a whole as well as the way that city government contributes to the process. Thus, officials who influence this area of policy have an impact on both the amount and kind of economic development activity.

It is expected that the characteristics of influence will differ between the two types of policies. The budgetary process is oriented to the internal operation as well as the public outputs of government, and CEOs have intimate knowledge of the budget as a policy tool (Meltsner 1971, 51–60). There are some who argue that administrators are powerful actors capable of protecting their budgetary base and expanding their resources (Niskanen 1971). Considering these factors, it is likely that the influence of the CEO will be higher in budgeting than in economic development. All cities are involved in economic development, but the extent of activity and the division between direct and indirect methods of affecting development produce wide variation in the scope of economic development activity. The influence of elected officials is likely to be relatively greater in this policy area than in budgeting.

In three of the study countries, the question about influence in economic development was not included in the questionnaire. Thus, there are no data for Belgium, Italy, and Portugal regarding this activity.

The measure of influence is the CEO's ratings of his or her own influence and separate ratings for each of the other actors on a scale that ranges from zero for no influence to 100 for high influence.[1] This approach allows for the possibility that decisions may have a small or large number of contributors. It does not presume that the influence of one actor necessarily precludes or decreases the influence of another.

An important limitation of this measure is that the assessments of all officials are made by the CEO alone. There is no independent confirmation of actual levels of influence. The choice of this measure, however, was informed by a previous Danish study. Forty CEOs were asked to indicate the influence on the budget of eight different actors or groups of actors. The patterns in their responses were identified and used in analyses of budget growth in the following four-year period. The study showed that the budget grew at a slower rate in municipalities where the guardians (mayor and executive committee) had been rated as most influential, whereas the budget grew at a faster rate in municipalities where advocates (department heads) were influential (Mouritzen 1991, chap. 11). These results can be interpreted as an external validation of this method of measuring influence. Ratings by the CEO are associated with differing outcomes that reflect the interests and perspectives of the most influential actors.

Another objection to this measure is that responses might be consistently biased, although the direction of bias could vary. On the one hand, top administrators might tend to exaggerate their own influence and downplay that of other officials. This would reflect a human tendency to make oneself seem important. On the other hand, the norm of political control of local government has been so strong that CEOs might be inclined to understate their impact. It is not possible to directly assess the validity of these counterarguments. It may be that the effects of one tendency would cancel those of the other. We will presume that distortions are common across all countries. Comparisons of influence ratings between countries, therefore, may be more valid than the absolute level of influence.

Variations in Influence by Country

A complete breakdown of variation by country is provided in the technical appendix (table A.7). Regarding the budget, mayoral influence is 79 on the 100-point index and ranges from a low of 42 in Ireland—where the mayor's office is formally very weak—to a high of 96 in Portugal. The influence of the majority group on the city council is lower than the mayor's at 71, but varies somewhat less. The CEO's influence score is 72—slightly higher than the council's influence rating overall—and ranges from a low of 52 in Portugal to 92 in council-manager cities in the United States. Regarding economic development, once again mayors have the most influence (an average rating of 67), with ratings that range from a low of 47 in Ireland to a high of 87 in France. The CEO's influence is 64 and ranges from a low of 41 in Spain to 90 in Ireland. Both the mayor and CEO are more influential than the council, which has an average rating of 58 for economic development decisions.

The relative position of the mayor compared to other politicians is measured more precisely when the influence of elected officials is compared in each city. Although mayors are usually the leading politician, this is not always the case. In over one-fifth of the cities, either the council as a whole or the committee chairs are more influential than the mayor in budgeting, and this situation is found in 18 percent of the cities with regard to economic development decisions. Cities are not included in this category if the mayor and the other officials have the same influence rating.

In order to assess the influence of the CEO, it is useful to examine it in

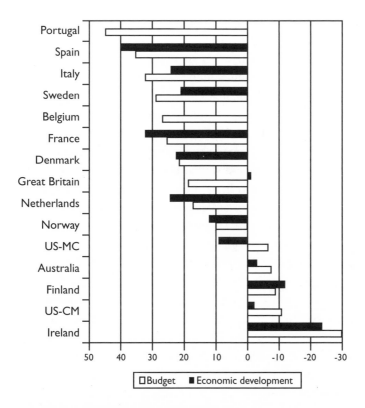

Influence rating of elected officials *minus* CEO rating. In Great Britain, CEO
has one point greater influence in economic development. No data available
for economic development in Belgium and Portugal.

Figure 8.1 Relative influence of most influential elected official and CEO

both absolute and relative terms. Overall, the CEO has the second highest
level of influence among officials in both areas of policy, but this finding
masks substantial variation. The CEO is less influential in budgeting than
any of the elected officials in two countries, than two of the sets of elected officials in six countries, and than one set of officials in two countries. The
CEO is the most influential official in budgeting in five countries. In economic development, the CEO has somewhat greater clout in comparison to
the council and committee chairs and is the most influential official in five
countries. The range of variation is highlighted by subtracting the influence
score for the CEO from that of the most influential elected official or set of
officials. The results are displayed in Figure 8.1.

Elected officials have the greatest influence advantage over the CEO in Portugal, Spain, Italy, Sweden, Belgium, and France, and more modest but still substantial influence differences are found in Denmark and the Netherlands. The difference is even more modest in Norway but elected officials are somewhat more influential than administrators in both areas of policy. In Great Britain and the U.S. mayor-council cities, there is a split result. The CEO is more influential than the most influential elected official in economic development in Great Britain and in budgeting in the United States. In the remaining countries—Finland, Australia, Ireland, and U.S. council-manager cities—the CEO has higher influence than either set of elected officials in both areas of decision making, and the advantage is substantial in Ireland.

In sum, mayors tend to be the most influential political figures in city government, followed by the majority group on the council. Among elected officials, the council in five countries is more influential than the mayor in budgeting, and in three countries the council has greater influence in economic development. In only two cases are committee chairs more influential than the council—both in budgetary decision making—and in no countries are the chairs more influential than the mayor. CEOs also have an important impact on decisions. Even at the lowest level, CEOs are more than moderately influential in budgeting and somewhat influential in economic development. In four countries, they are the most influential actors in both spheres of policy, and in two additional countries the CEO is the most influential in one but not the other area of policy. Thus, not only are CEOs highly involved in policy innovation and active advisers of politicians (as we have seen in previous chapters), but they also have considerable influence in policy making.

Variations in Influence by Form of Government

The variations among countries can be explained in part by the use of different forms of government. There are important differences and also similarities across cities divided by structure of political authority. The average levels of influence for each set of officials in budget and economic development decisions are presented in the technical appendix.

The distribution of influence generally corresponds, as one would expect, to the assignment of authority to officials in each form. In the strong-mayor cities, the mayor overshadows the council and the CEO, who are each in turn more influential than council committee chairs and department heads, respectively. In the committee-leader cities, on the other hand, committee chairs are intermediaries between the council and the operating departments of city government. They have considerable separate influence. Likewise, the department heads have the same amount of influence in budgeting as the CEO. In the collective cities, the mayor is not as influential as the powerful political leaders in the executive committee—the board of alderman (not included in appendix table A.7). Still, the mayor has a higher rating than the remaining officials, all of whom have approximately the same amount of influence.[2] In the council-manager cities, the CEO has more influence than the elected officials in both budgeting and economic development. The council is slightly more influential than the mayor in budgeting and only slightly less influential in economic development. The department heads are substantially less influential than the CEO, although their ratings are higher than in other types of cities.

Within individual cities, three patterns of influence among officials can be identified using cluster analysis. Two separate analyses were done for each area of policy making with similar results, although one of the clusters differs in an important way. In both budgetary and economic development decisions, one consistent pattern is high influence by all officials with the mayor displaying the highest influence. The inconsistency appears in the second cluster. Although the mayor and, to a lesser extent, the council are the most influential (hence the name mayor-centered cluster) the mayor's influence is only moderately high in this cluster in economic development. In the third cluster found in both budgeting and economic development, administrators—CEOs and department heads—have much more influence than elected officials.[3] The most common combination is relatively high influence exerted by all officials found in half of the cities in budgetary decisions and in 45 percent in economic development. The mayor-centered pattern is more common in economic development decision making (35%) than in budgeting (23%), although it should be noted again that in the former no official has very high influence. The mayor has the highest influence in economic development in this cluster, but it is only moderately high. The reverse is found regarding the administrator-led pattern. It is more common in budgeting (27%) than economic development (20%).

Table 8.1 presents the distribution of these patterns across the forms of government. The pattern with all officials having high influence is very common in committee-leader cities, especially in budgetary decisions. Four-fifths of these cities have widely dispersed, high-level influence among all officials. The mayor-centered pattern is most common for economic development decisions in collective cities and for budgetary decisions in strong-mayor cities.

Table 8.1 Clusters of Influence among Officials by Form of Government *(percent)*

	Mayor centered	All officials highly influential	Administrator centered	Total
Budget				
Strong-mayor	46	39	15	100
Committee-leader	15	79	6	100
Collective	35	42	23	100
Council-manager	4	45	51	100
Total	23	50	27	100
Economic Development				
Strong-mayor	47	48	5	100
Committee-leader	30	62	8	100
Collective	61	29	10	100
Council-manager	26	37	37	100
Total	35	45	20	100

The administrator-centered pattern is most often found in budgetary decisions in council-manager cities. Thus, there is a tendency for the mayor to play a leading role in strong-mayor cities and for the CEO to do so in council-manager cities, but deviations from this rule are common. Decision making reflects the combined impacts of a wide array of actors. There is extensive sharing of influence among elected officials and administrators. Although the form of government has the effect of tilting the strong-mayor cities (and collective cities in economic development) toward the mayor-centered pattern and the council-manager cities toward the administrator-centered pattern, wide sharing of influence is commonly found in all forms of government. Without diminishing the importance of other actors, it is important to examine more closely the variations in influence of the two key officials in the apex of local government—the mayor and the CEO.

Influence of Mayor

Leadership, Form of Government, and Mayor's Influence

Mayors can provide leadership in three areas (see chapter 3). They can be public leaders who help determine the direction that citizens want their city to take. They can be policy innovators who shape the content of programs and projects. Finally, they can be party leaders who promote the interests of their political organization. One would expect that these types of leadership would be related to the mayor's influence, although the relationship is presumably constrained by the advantages that form of government gives to some mayors over others. In addition, the longer the mayor remains in office, the more influential the mayor is likely to be.

The results of the analysis confirm the expectations. The mayor's strength as a public leader, one who is visionary and has positive relations with the public, increases influence. The public leader is effective at developing proposals for the future of the city that are based on awareness of citizen preferences. Presumably, these are the mayors who can bring the public together around shared aspirations for change. In chapter 3, it was noted that there is only a weak relationship between public leadership and form of government. The formal resources built into the mayor's office are not necessarily translated into a high level of effectiveness at mobilizing public support. Table 8.2 displays the influence ratings of mayors at differing levels of public leadership. The results indicate another aspect of how public leadership varies across cities with different structures.

Just as we observed earlier that form does not determine the strength of leadership, the forms differ as a setting for translating public leadership into influence. The strong mayors have a uniformly high level of influence in budgeting regardless of their public leadership. For these mayors, form is associated with a high level of influence in a function for which they have at least some formal authority independently of their leadership. In economic development, however, the extent of emphasis by city government and the tasks to be performed are less clear-cut in the formal structure. There is also modest variation in the mayor's influence in this policy area associated with

Table 8.2 Mayor's Influence by Strength as Public Leader *(index)*

	Strong-mayor	Committee-leader	Collective	Council-manager
Budget				
High	91	93	83	71
Moderate	89	90	73	63
Low	89	80	59	56
F score	0.09	21.1	36.6	22.3
Significance	n.a.	<.00	<.00	<.00
N	875	533	566	1272
Economic Development				
High	85	82	73	69
Moderate	82	77	61	58
Low	80	68	46	48
F score	3.0	15.2	25.9	49.3
Significance	<.05	<.00	<.00	<.00
N	607	528	284	1254

leadership strength. The pattern of results is similar in the committee-leader cities. There is modest variation in influence related to leadership in budgeting and a greater spread in influence between high and low levels of leadership in economic development. Thus, there is fairly uniform influence in a function supported by formal resources, but low public leadership is associated with less, albeit very substantial, influence in the less "structured" decisions regarding economic development.

In the collective and council-manager cities, the relationship between leadership and influence is pronounced. High public leadership partially offsets limited formal resources for the mayor in both budgeting and economic development, although the *most* effective leaders in collective and council-manager cities still rate below or only slightly above the *least* effective leaders in strong-mayor and committee-leader cities in their level of influence. Looking at the bottom end of the leadership ratings, it is apparent that low public leadership magnifies the structural weakness of the position. If the mayor does not bring a high level of creativity and interaction with the public to the office, he or she is a modest player in policy making.

The nature of policy leadership provided by the mayor is also related to his or her level of influence. This measure has two aspects—involvement in the details of the daily work of administration and attention to broad policy matters rather than a focus on specifics. Being highly involved in both aspects approximates the innovator type of leadership that has been identified in American studies of mayoral leadership. The "innovators" have the highest influence ratings overall: 92 in budgeting and 78 in economic development. The "administrator" mayors who focus on detail and ignore policy are close in influence with ratings of 88 and 74 in budgeting and economic development, respectively. In some forms of government in one policy, they exceed the innovator's influence in one policy area or the other.[4] The policy "designers" who are concerned with policy to the exclusion of details have somewhat less influence, although their relative weakness compared to innovators and administrators is less in economic development (rating of 68) than in budgeting (rating of 76). Presumably, the designers' interest in a policy vision make them more adept at impacting decisions about the economic future of the cities than they are at influencing the details of the budget. The "caretaker" mayors who ignore both aspects of policy are detached. They have the lowest ratings overall (70 in budgeting and 62 in economic development) and rank lowest in influence in each form of government.

To summarize the somewhat mixed results, in six of the eight situations, that is, four forms of government and two areas of policy, the innovators are at least tied for the most influential in six of the eight. The administrators also have more influence than the designers in six of the eight situations, although the differences are not always great. Finally, the detached caretaker-type mayors always have the lowest influence. The mayors who have the greatest impact on decisions in their cities pay attention to both the big picture and the day-to-day details. Mayors who get low ratings on both aspects of policy leadership, regardless of the form of city government used, have lower influence than their peers in the same form. Not surprisingly, mayors who are detached from policy concerns have less capacity to have impact on policy decisions in their cities.

Being a party promoter has an inconsistent impact on influence depending on the form of government. In cities with the strong-mayor, committee-leader, and collective forms of government, influence is slightly higher in budgeting when mayors stress party leadership.[5] In council-manager cities, on the other hand, strong party leadership by the mayor is associated with the *lowest* influence (a rating of 48). When there is a medium level of party promotion, the rating is 57. Finally, mayors in council-manager cities who give little or no attention to party promotion receive an influence rating of 66.[6] In these cities, party promotion may be viewed as "putting the party ahead of the city," and the influence of the mayor who adopts this approach is reduced. In this case—unlike the higher influence that goes with involvement in details of administration—violating the norms of the form is associated with less influence.

Tenure, Form of Government, and Mayor's Influence

One other factor that is related both directly and indirectly to the amount of influence in budget and economic development decisions is the length of time the mayor has spent in office. When comparing mayors with four or fewer years and with five or more years tenure, the more experienced group rates three to seven points higher in both areas of decision making in the strong-mayor, committee-leader, and collective cities. In the council-manager cities, the difference is more substantial: shorter term mayors rate 59 and 56 in budget and economic development, respectively. In budgeting, those with five or more years in office have an influence rating of 73. In economic development, it is 65.[7] In addition, mayors in cities with the council-manager form tend to be less experienced overall.[8] Thus, the impact of shorter tenure is greater in council-manager cities, and less experienced mayors are more common in cities with this form.

Shorter tenure in council-manager cities may be explained by two factors. First, there is intentional turnover in the position in Ireland. Second, with no direct control over organizational resources that can strengthen the official's political position, there are fewer opportunities for the political leader in the council-manager form to use the position as the base for a career in public office. Consequently, incumbents are less likely to seek to hold onto the position for a long time. In general, mayors who are less familiar with the office and the running of city government have less impact on the outcome of decisions. The effect is particularly pronounced in council-manager cities in which CEOs with considerable formal authority are more likely to be interacting with relatively inexperienced political leaders.

The most important factor shaping the mayor's influence is form of government. The mayor has the most influence in the strong-mayor form of government and the least influence in the council-manager form. No other factors are associated with large variations when the effects of form of government and other country characteristics are removed. Highly effective public leaders or ones who are attentive to both the broad and detailed aspects of policy in cities where the mayor lacks formal powers do not leapfrog over the ineffective or detached mayors in cities where they do have formal resources to become much more influential. Furthermore, the "behaviorally" strongest mayors in collective leadership (Belgium is an exception) and council-manager cities do not match the behaviorally strong and formally potent mayors in strong-mayor and committee-leader cities at the top of the influence scale. Still, these modest additional factors that affect influence level are of interest. Within the overall pattern produced by form of government, the mayor's influence is enhanced by his or her strength as a public leader, involvement in setting policy goals or the daily details of policy implementation or both, and experience in office. At least at the margins, mayors are individual as well as institutional leaders.

Influence of CEO

Just as the mayor's influence is shaped by form, so too is that of the CEO. The differing distribution of executive authority among the mayor, council executive committee, and the CEO gives the CEO relatively fewer formal resources for influence in collective and particularly strong-mayor cities and relatively more resources in committee-leader and particularly council-manager cities. There are no simple contrasting models in which the mayors are advantaged in one set of cities and disadvantaged in the other with the CEO's formal position being the inverse of the mayor's. Whereas this is the case with the contrasting strong-mayor and council-manager cities, the committee-leader form provides structural advantages to the CEO *and* the mayor. The linkage between structure and influence is also more clearly evident in budgetary than in economic development decisions. Budgeting is a function that all governments must perform and do so in similar ways. The CEO is involved in the formation of budgets and their execution as an organizational leader in all forms, even though this function may be shared to a greater or lesser extent with other officials, depending on the structure.

In policy making regarding economic development, on the other hand, the nature and extent of activities vary widely, and formal duties for officials are less clearly prescribed. Some cities will devote little attention to economic development, and some CEOs may see the function as one that politicians should handle. Thus, greater variation in the level of CEO influence in economic development is expected. Furthermore, because it has more discretionary elements, the personal characteristics of CEOs will have a greater impact on their influence in economic development than budgetary decision making. In other words, we expect that the nature of the office will shape budgetary influence with individual traits having only marginal effects, whereas the behavior of the individual CEO will be more important in shaping the level of influence in economic development.

CEO's Involvement, Form of Government, and Influence

As noted in the previous section, the rank order of the CEO's influence across forms of government from high to low is council-manager, committee-leader, strong-mayor, and collective. Within the constraints of formal structure, the activity level of the CEO is associated with differing levels of influence. In chapter 5, the CEO's involvement in a variety of activities was analyzed in terms of three dimensions: policy innovation, political advice, and classical management. It would seem likely that the more active the CEO in policy innovation, the greater his or her influence would be. Influence could be derived from the number of proposals and the visionary qualities of the CEO, or the freedom and opportunity of the CEO to make policy proposals could be based on his or her influence. Regardless of the direction of causality, however, policy innovation and influence should be linked. Analysis supports this expectation. CEOs who are highly involved in developing a vision for their cities, proposing projects, and seeking outside resources are more influential, particularly in economic development policy making.[9] The relationship is strong in all forms of government, although city managers tend to be influential in budget decisions regardless of their level of policy involvement.

The extent of advice to politicians could be linked to influence for different reasons. Because the CEO is active in offering advice on technical and sensitive political matters and in shaping norms for decision making, the more likely it is that the CEO would be able to influence policy outcomes or be viewed as a potent confidant and adviser when policy choices are made. This linkage is much weaker than is the case for policy innovation. The only strong relationship in budgetary decision making is found in committee-leader cities where active involvement in advice to politicians is found with higher influence.[10] The same phenomenon is observed in strong-mayor cities with regard to economic development influence, where CEOs have more influence as their political advice increases.[11] When working with the highly influential mayors in strong mayor and committee-leader cities, the close relationship signified by active advising appears to pay off in higher influence for the CEO.

In contrast to the expectation of higher influence with more policy and advisory activity, it is not expected that higher involvement in administrative functions would be translated into influence, although it is possible that CEOs would be able to translate high involvement in administrative functions into influence in the formation of the budget. The original expectation is upheld by the analysis with no exceptions. More attention to classical administrative functions does not contribute to higher influence in either area of policy.

To illustrate the combined effects of different levels of involvement in all areas, the influence ratings of the "underactive" and "highly active" CEOs introduced in chapter 5 can be contrasted. The underactive have the lowest influence rating in both budgetary (66) and economic development (55) decision making, and this is true within each form of government. CEOs who are comprehensively active at a high level have the highest influence ratings in both areas with ratings of 77 in budgeting and 75 in economic development. Active CEOs are influential CEOs across forms of government.

Individual and Community Characteristics and
the CEO's Influence

It is clear that influence is affected by the institutional features of local government and country characteristics. The analysis now shifts to the individual influence level compared to other CEOs in the same country. Measuring influence as the difference between the individual score and the country mean removes the effect of differences that are linked to country, including form of government. The characteristics of individual mayors and CEOs and of specific communities refer to the four categories of intervening variables presented in the conceptual framework in chapter 1 and used in the analysis in chapter 5. The elements in the framework are administrative values, networking by the CEO, mayoral leadership, and the political environment. By incorporating the results from other parts of the analysis, it is also possible to examine individual variation in involvement level and attitudes about the ideal politician as factors related to influence. It is expected that the characteristics of CEOs and the cities in which they work have only a modest impact on their influence in budgeting, because behavior in this policy area is shaped by structure, including the formal assignment of authority and the legal specification of the budgetary function. On the other hand, individual and community characteristics are expected to have a considerable impact on influence in economic development.

The results of the analysis summarized in table 8.3 clearly confirm the expectation. Overall, as the formulas at the bottom of the table indicate, there is only a small amount of the variation in relative budgetary influence explained by regression analysis that includes individual and community characteristics. The twelve factors listed in the budget column add to our understanding of the relative differences in the CEO's influence even though none of the factors has a substantial impact. In contrast, the six factors associated with influence in economic development—four of which are common to factors related to budgetary influence—explain over four times more of the variation. Thus, individual and community characteristics are much more important to understanding the impact CEOs have on economic development than on budgetary decisions.

The factors that are significantly related to influence out of a wide range of possible explanatory variables offer a portrait of how the CEOs' values and context relate to their weight as actors in the policy-making process. Major elements that have been explored separately in previous chapters and earlier

Table 8.3 Regression Analysis of Factors Related to Relative Influence of CEOs in Budgeting and Economic Development[a]

	Budget[b] (beta)	Rank of importance	Economic development[c] (beta)	Rank of importance
MAYOR'S LEADERSHIP				
Influence of mayor (v)	.04*	12	.40**	1
Low policy leadership (d)	.05**	10	.04*	6
IDEAL POLITICIANS				
Council should have long-term vision (v)	.06**	3		
Council should formulate exact goals— negative (v)	−05**	7	−.04*	5
CEO ACTIVITIES, VALUES, AND NETWORKING				
Policy innovator (v)	.07**	2	.21**	2
Political advisor (v)	.05**	6		
Advocacy (v)	.06**	4		
Advantage if views of CEO match majority of council (v)			.06**	4
Community communication (v)	.04*	11	.10**	3
GOVERNMENTAL AND COMMUNITY CONTEXT				
Cooperation with politicians (d)	.09**	1		
Low uncertainty (d)	.06**	5		
Population under 5000 (d)	.05**	8		
Intergovernmental pressure (v)	.05**	9		

NOTES: *Significance <.05
  **Significance <.01
  a. Influence is measured by the individual rating minus the mean for the CEO's country.
  b. Budget: $R = .23$; Adjusted $R^2 = .049$ ($n = 3268$)
  c. Economic development: $R = .47$; Adjusted $R^2 = .22$ ($n = 2762$)

in this chapter come together to shape the CEO's influence. These are the leadership of the mayor; characteristics of the ideal politician; CEO activities, values, and networking; governmental context; and community context.

Mayor's Leadership

This first factor is the most important in economic development and is symbolically important in budgeting decisions. The relative level of the mayor's influence is positively related to the CEO's influence. Rather than being competitors with the increasing influence of the mayor decreasing influence of the CEO, the two officials move together up or down in their impact on decisions. The relationship is very weak with regard to budgeting; the mayor's influence is the lowest ranking factor in importance (among twelve factors that explain very little of the variation in the CEO's influence). In economic development, the relationship is very strong and suggests that the mayor and CEO move in tandem in shaping efforts to promote their cities.

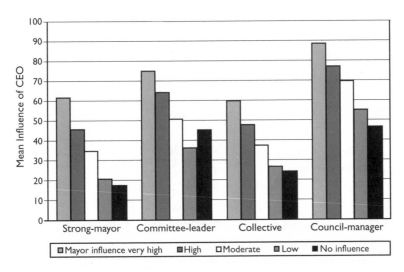

Figure 8.2 Levels of mayoral influence and influence of CEO in economic development

This interaction is displayed in figure 8.2. Within each form of government, the CEO's influence drops dramatically when the mayor's influence declines. Although the CEOs manifest some influence even when the mayor is rather weak, the CEO's potential to impact development decisions is enhanced by being paired with a more influential mayor. This positive relationship in the influence of the two key officials in city government offers additional evidence of a partnership between the mayor and CEO.

With this positive interaction in mind, another feature of mayoral leadership can be considered. As indicated in table 8.3, *low* policy leadership is associated with higher CEO influence. Earlier, we observed that policy leadership was important to the mayor's influence. Here we see that the CEO to a modest extent fills a vacuum, having higher influence when the mayor's policy leadership is weak; that is, the mayor is detached from both the details and the broad framework of policy. Thus, although the CEO's influence increases as the mayor's influence increases, CEOs also expand their influence when the mayor is detached from policy making and implementation.

Ideal Politicians

When CEOs have a greater preference for elected officials to formulate exact and unambiguous goals for administrators, their influence rating is lower in both budgeting and economic development. The causation in this relationship could run in either direction. On the one hand, desiring more direction could accompany a tendency to view one's own influence as more limited than is typical among one's peers. On the other hand, CEOs with more limited influence may need the elected officials to assert direction and impose order. In contrast, CEOs with relatively higher influence are more likely to prefer that elected officials create a long-term vision. The vision establishes a framework within which the CEO's influence over specific decisions can be exercised. CEOs may also hope that elected officials who have a long-term perspective will not get as involved in specific, short-range fiscal matters over which CEOs have responsibility. Insofar as their preference for elected officials to act as governors is realized, the CEO has more space in which to exert leadership without encountering politicians who are focusing on details. As we have seen, this focus on the part of the mayor is linked to higher influence in the elected head of government. The CEOs who have an especially strong preference for visionary elected officials have more influence in budgeting; those who are more likely to look to elected officials for direction have less influence in both functional areas.

CEO Activities, Values, and Networking

As indicated above when considering involvement by the CEO in dimensions of activities, CEOs who are relatively more active in policy innovation are somewhat more influential in budgeting and much more influential in economic development. This is the second strongest factor in both areas of decision making, but the weight of policy innovation is much greater in economic development. Greater emphasis on political advice is also associated with higher influence in budgeting. CEOs who are stronger advocates—supporters of an activist role for administration and of help for the weak in society—are more influential in budgeting. Those who more strongly believe that it is an advantage for the CEO to have the same opinions as the majority on the council have more influence in economic development. The CEOs who feel that it helps to have opinions in line with those of elected officials may be more comfortable acting in economic development decisions because they are in sync with the council's preferences. CEOs who place greater emphasis on communicating with community leaders and citizens have higher influence in economic development. This association between communication and influence reflects a higher activity level by the CEO in the community as well as more extensive networking to maintain a community resource base from which influence can be derived.

Governmental and community context

The last set of factors affects only the CEO's relative influence in budgetary decisions. Internally, cooperation with politicians—the most important factor among all considered in relationship to the budget—and low uncertainty about goals and division of roles are associated with higher influence. Pressures from other levels of government and small city size also reinforce influence. Operating from within a predictable and positive set of relationships while facing external challenges enhances the CEO's weight in decisions, particularly in small cities where the CEO is very likely to have a high level of training and experience in comparison to other officials. The CEO can focus on responding to the pressures emanating from other governments, secure in the positive relationship with politicians and the clear working arrangements with elected officials.

Conclusion

There is great variation in the level of influence for each key set of officials as well as differences in their relative influence in budgeting and economic development. In both areas of policy making, mayoral influence is highest over all. Closer examination at the country level shows that the mayor is a dominant figure in some countries, fairly evenly balanced in influence with other elected officials and the CEO in a second group of countries, and surpassed by the CEO in still other countries. When the influence of elected officials is compared in each city, some other elected official is more influential than the mayor in budgeting in 22 percent of the cities, and this situation is found in 18 percent of the cities with regard to economic development decisions. Although mayors are usually the leading politician, this is not always the case. Similarly, the CEOs rank second in influence overall among officials in both areas of policy, but their relative position varies greatly. Even in the countries in which the level of influence is lowest, the CEO is moderately influential in budgeting and somewhat influential in economic development. At the highest level, the influence of the CEO exceeds that of any other actor in both areas of policy in four countries.

The differences among countries can be explained in part by the use of different forms of government. In the strong-mayor cities, the mayor often overshadows the council and the CEO. There is widespread sharing of high-level influence in committee-leader cities and widespread sharing of moderate-level influence in collective-leadership cities. In the council-manager cities, the CEO typically has more influence than the elected officials, and the council is slightly more influential than the mayor. A mayor-centered pattern is most common for economic development decisions in collective cities and for budgetary decisions in strong-mayor cities. The administrator-centered pattern is most often found in budgetary decisions in council-manager cities. Still, there is extensive sharing of influence between elected officials and administrators in cities of all types. A distribution of influence in which all officials are highly influential in budgeting is found in approximately two-fifths of cities with strong-mayor, collective leadership, and council-manager forms of government. It is found in almost four of five cities with the committee-leader form of government. The shared influence pattern is somewhat less common—and the mayor-centered pattern more common—in economic development policy making, but the shared leadership pattern is still quite pervasive.

In addition to form of government, the mayor's influence is shaped by his or her strength as a public leader, involvement in setting policy goals or in the daily details of policy implementation or both, party leadership, and experience in office. These relationships (except for party leadership) are strongest in collective leadership and council-manager cities. Strong qualities as an individual leader offset to some extent a constitutionally weak office but make less difference when the mayor has a strong formal position.

The CEO's influence is to some extent the reciprocal of the mayor's, but the CEO is also quite influential in committee-leader cities where fairly strong mayors are also found. The linkage between structure and influence is also more clearly evident in budgetary than in economic development decisions. In policy making regarding economic development, the nature and extent of activities a city chooses to undertake vary widely, and formal duties for officials are less clearly prescribed. The personal characteristics of CEOs have a greater impact on their influence in economic development than in budgetary decision making. In budgetary decisions, a wide variety of factors have a modest effect on the CEO's influence. These include the involvement of the CEO in policy innovation and political advice, level of advocacy, and the extent of communication with the community. The mayor's influence level is weakly but positively related to the CEO's influence and also to the type of policy leadership provided by the mayor. The latter factor is "negatively" related, that is, CEOs have more influence when paired with detached mayors. Their influence is also enhanced by a positive internal climate and the need to respond to external stress. In economic development decisions, there is a strong positive relationship between the mayor's influence and the CEO's, and CEOs who are engaged in policy innovation are much more influential. In both types of policy, CEOs who prefer that the council formulate exact goals have less influence. In their attitudes about the ideal politician, CEOs with less influence prefer more focused direction from politicians.

There are three important issues that are illuminated by these findings. Does structure shape the influence of officials? Are elected officials and administrators in competition for influence? Is the influence of administrators a threat to democratic governance?

The direct effect of structure is evident because the variation in the respective influence of the two key officials depends on form of government. In the forms of government that differ most with regard to the authority of politicians and administrators, the mayor's influence is highest in the strong-mayor cities and lowest in the council-manager cities. The CEO's influence, on the other hand, is highest in the council-manager cities and lowest in the collective leadership cities. There is not a simple continuum of respective influence across the four forms. The second highest influence ratings for the mayor and the CEO are found in the committee-leader cities. The mayors in the collective leader cities rank third, and the CEOs in these cities rank fourth in influence. Thus, forms of government empower both politicians and administrators and may do so in various combinations. The indirect effect of structure is evident when we combine results from the present chapter with results from chapter 3 on mayoral leadership. As discussed in this chapter, the influence of mayors is related to their leadership activity; the latter, however, tends to be somehow related to form of government, particularly as mayors differ systematically in attention to specific administrative details and in their strength as party leaders (as discussed in chapter 3). Finally, form of government acts as a conditional factor when it comes to the relation between mayoral leadership and mayoral influence. Leadership activity is more important under some forms of government than under others, as indicated in table 8.2. When the structure of government gives the mayor more formal authority, variations in leadership behavior are less important. The reverse is true in the collective and council-manager cities. More effective and better-focused leadership are important for offsetting the formal weakness of the position.

As for the second issue, it is evident that the mayor and the CEO are not engaged in a zero-sum struggle for influence. There is a modest but positive connection between higher influence by the mayor and greater influence in budgetary decisions by the CEO and a very strong positive relationship between the influence levels of the two officials in economic development decisions. Rather than a contest for control, there is interdependency and reciprocal influence between the mayor and CEO. The form of government shapes the average levels of influence, and the specific level of influence of the political and professional leaders moves up and down together. This is true to a modest extent in budgeting and to a substantial extent in economic development.

Thus, there is an apparent contradiction in the findings of the comparative status of mayors and CEOs depending on whether one examines the institutional or community level. Choice of the institutional powers assigned to the mayor has a direct bearing on the CEO's weight in the political process—the more powerful the mayor, the less influential the CEO. On the community level among cities that use the same form of government, however, the greater the influence of the mayor, the greater the influence of the CEO. The assignment of authority in the design of institutions may be a choice between mayors and CEOs, although the committee-leader and collective forms demonstrate that the choice can be to distribute authority more or less evenly. The way that officials actually work together, however, is typically a cooperative approach in which the efforts of one official positively affect the status of the other.

The comparative influence tradeoff is illustrated by the situation in economic development policy making (displayed in figure 8.2). When mayors have very low influence, CEOs usually have greater influence than the mayor, and when the mayor has very high influence, the CEO has less influence than the mayor. Still, the CEOs who are relatively weaker when paired with a high-influence mayor have substantially more influence than their counterparts who work with less influential mayors in other cities. A Danish CEO captured the essence of the situation: "The best a civil servant can wish for is a strong political leader. . . . A strong CEO can never compensate for a weak mayor." In this positive sum relationship, when the mayor's influence rises, the CEO's influence does as well.

The third issue is the role of the CEO in the democratic process. Given the substantial influence of CEOs revealed by the data—a level that exceeds that of the mayor (or other elected officials who have more influence than the mayor) in some countries and in many individual cities—is the influence of the CEO a threat to democracy? A general answer is derived from the common distribution of influence in cities. In the vast majority of cities, influence is exerted disproportionately by the mayor or widely shared among many officials. One could argue that in these cities, the CEO exercises influence within the democratic process rather than in contradiction of it. The CEO typically exerts extensive influence as part of an array of other influential actors. Still, there are cities in which the CEO has substantial influence and some in which the CEO is the most influential actor. To assess the implications of this situation, it is useful to consider the relative influence more fully and to examine the characteristics of the CEOs grouped by their relative influence vis-à-vis leading politicians: What are the characteristics of CEOs with less, the same, and more influence than elected officials? That is the focus of the next chapter.

The characteristics of the CEOs' influence make a modest contribution to our understanding of the four models of political-administrative interaction, but suggest that a new approach be developed for categorizing CEOs in relationship to elected officials. On the surface, CEOs with low influence approximate either the separate roles or responsive administrator models, those with substantial influence in settings with many other influential actors approximate the overlapping roles model, and those who are found in administrator-centered clusters of influence approximate the autonomous administrator model. Whether these distinct groupings of CEOs match the other characteristics of the CEOs of each of the models, however, is not clear. The models as *ideal* types reflect a theoretically distinct combination of characteristics that may or may not match the real CEOs found in the cities of Western democracies. In chapter 9, the approach taken is to construct a new empirical typology using relative influence as the basis for distinguishing CEOs. The characteristics of these CEO types can then be compared with those that would be expected if the ideal typical models were reflected in the attitudes and circumstances of real-world CEOs.

CHAPTER 9

Partnerships at the Apex of Local Government

THE LEADERS AT THE APEX of local government have a close relationship and extensive interaction. In the aggregate the top administrators have substantial influence in policy making, as do elected officials and other actors in government. Still, there is variation in absolute and relative influence of officials, and these differences may reveal consistent patterns in the characteristics of political-administrative relations. In previous chapters, we have looked for phenomena that are consistent with or illuminated by four models that may be used as ideal types to conceptualize the relationship between elected officials and top administrators. There has been scant correspondence between findings and three of the models—separate roles, responsive administrator, and autonomous administrator—and there are many findings that are consistent with the fourth model—the overlapping roles model. However, before coming to a final conclusion about the relative utility of the four models as guides to inquiry and understanding, a new analytical approach can be taken. A typology based on empirical analysis of differences in influence is constructed that parallels the four models. In this approach, we categorize how CEOs differ as partners with elected officials based on how much influence the administrator has compared to the politician. The four original models are used as the basis for hypothesizing the characteristics that each partnership type would have.

It is possible to identify types of CEOs with the same amount, more, and less influence than elected officials. In this analysis as in chapter 8, the measures of influence are the CEOs' perceptions of their own influence and that of other officials. It is plausible to argue that these types based on relative influence will roughly correspond to the conceptual models. Equally influential

CEOs—a type we will call *interdependent*—may match up with the overlapping roles model. CEOs with more influence than elected officials, that is, *independent* CEOs, may correspond to the autonomous administrator model. Less influential or *dependent* CEOs may have the characteristics associated with the remaining two models. If these dependent CEOs are further divided based on their attitudes about political responsiveness, there are two types that correspond to the separate roles and responsive administrator models. *Political agents* among the dependent CEOs believe that CEOs should hold the same views as the leading politicians and be directly accountable to them. Thus, they resemble the responsive administrator model. *Professional agents* also have less influence but believe that CEOs should have independent views rather than reflect the views of elected officials and/or should be as responsible to citizens as to elected officials. These characteristics would seem to match the separate roles model.

In addition to linking the partnership types to the models, it is possible that they are linked to form of government as well. Since the influence of top politicians and top administrators is affected by the amount of authority they have in the formal structure, the partnership types and models may coalesce in different forms of government. It may be that there is a grand scheme that ties together many of our findings. One would expect that strong-mayor cities will have more dependent CEOs who are politically compliant and have other characteristics that correspond with the responsive administrator model. Collective cities in which influence levels are modest and evenly balanced are likely to have dependent CEOs who maintain professional distance from politicians and therefore could match the separate roles model. Committee-leader cities are likely to have interdependent CEOs who match the overlapping roles model. Finally, council-manager cities are likely to have independent CEOs who could be characterized by the autonomous administrator model.

In this chapter, we start with an explanation of this approach to classifying CEOs that divides them into different types based on relative influence and attitudes about the political process and look at the distribution of the four types. Further analysis examines whether the four types of CEOs differ in other important characteristics associated with the four models of political-administrative relations and whether they are found in cities with different forms of government. In other words, we seek to determine whether the apex of government differs consistently in its shape and internal dynamics.

The Rationale for Partnership Types

In the preceding chapters, many facets of leadership and the relationships that accompany it have been explored. The top administrators in local government vary in their professional values, networking, policy innovation, and advice to politicians. They differ in their attitudes about what kind of contributions should be made by elected officials—an image of politicians that offers a reflection of their own preferred roles. Finally, they differ in the amount of influence they exert in policy making individually and relative to other political actors. In this final data analysis chapter, we will consider the implications of different levels of relative influence for the nature of the CEO partnership with elected officials. The goal is to develop a typology that either builds on or replaces the four models of political-administrative relations from chapter 2 that were drawn from the literature of public administration and political science. Developing a typology requires a reconsideration of the bases for differentiating CEOs and creating an operational measure that can be used to classify CEOs according to the types. It will then be possible to describe the characteristics of each type and assess to what extent they match the standard models viewed as ideal types.

One approach to the task of classifying CEOs is to identify distinctive combinations based on a range of behaviors and attitudes. The clusters presented in previous chapters might overlap to create an overarching typology of clusters. It seems plausible that CEOs could be divided into groups that would differ across a number of dimensions of attitudes and behaviors. Even if not all CEOs were included in the categories, identifying some empirical "pure" types of leadership can be instructive. Various attempts at identifying clusters based on advocacy, orientation to the political process, networking, involvement in policy or advice to politicians, and view of the ideal politician were unsuccessful because each set includes more similarities across clusters than differences. Thus, this search turned out to be a futile one—an interesting finding in itself. The population of local government CEOs is not segmented by multiple overlapping divisions.

The approach chosen for developing a typology is to look at the influence characteristics of the CEO in the political process as the basis for identifying distinctive types of CEOs. This approach serves to focus attention on an issue of great concern to citizens and scholars and a matter that practitioners must confront continuously—how much and in what ways do appointed CEOs impact the political process as they interact with elected officials, and how much do elected officials affect the way that administrators carry out their responsibilities? Based on the discussion to this point, we presume CEOs are partners with elected officials, that is, they are neither the fully controlled clerks of the politicians nor the hidden masters of them. But if they are partners, then what kind of partners are they? How much submission or clout do they bring to the relationship? What are the different types of partnerships?

As discussed in chapter 2, much of the relevant literature has presented CEOs as dependent or independent in their interaction with elected officials. This is the subordination dimension, which along with the distance dimension was used to develop the models of political-administrative interaction. Dependence—clear subordination of administrators to politicians—is commonly viewed as the ideal in the sense that it corresponds to what is perceived to be the original conceptualization of how administration relates to politics. Dependency appears to be the administrative stance "required" by democratic theory. Dependency can be accompanied either by distance and clear differentiation of politicians and administrators—the separate roles model —or close alignment of administrators and politicians and political involvement in the administrative sphere—the responsive administrator model. Independence, on the other hand, reflects a realistic view of how CEOs behave and the substantial impact they have in practice. It is associated with the autonomous administrator model. The independent stance raises the democracy-bureaucracy issue; that is, who is in charge of the governmental process, elected official or administrator? It is unclear the extent to which the traditional literature recognized the reciprocity inherent in the relationship. The choices, according to Heady (1984, 408), are whether administrators are instrumental or usurpative. Viewed in extreme terms, the former characteristic can undermine professionalism, particularly when administrators are politically responsive, and the latter can undermine democracy in the partnership.

An alternative to the dependence-independence choice is a type of leadership characterized by interdependence in the relationship between politicians and administrators. Viewing the relationship in this way is consistent with the overlapping roles model described in chapter 2. Administrators are viewed as instrumental and also as contributors to the policy process. Reciprocity and shared influence between elected officials and administrators are also grounded in basic concepts of democratic public administration and do not necessarily represent usurpation of political leadership.[1] The analysis of data from the U.Di.T.E. survey presented in previous chapters offers many examples that appear to be consistent with the interdependency view. Many CEOs

- have broad and balanced networks that could support their status as independent actors,
- are extensively involved in policy development that is also the central function of elected officials,
- offer advice in dealing with sensitive political choices and in shaping the policy-making process, and
- exercise considerable influence alongside the influence of other internal and external actors.

Still, not all CEOs share these characteristics. Presumably they are not all equally "interdependent."

Thus, the search for a typology begins with three major types loosely drawn from models in the literature: dependent, interdependent, and independent CEOs. The dependent types may be further differentiated into those who are separated from politicians and those who are responsive to them. In the first stage in constructing the typology, the data on the influence of local government officials can be used to construct an operational definition of the three major different views of the role and clout of top administrators. In the second stage, additional variables will be considered to divide the dependent group into two subtypes.

The three major types of CEOs reflect different levels of relative influence between elected officials and CEOs. The operational definitions are as follows: Dependent CEOs have substantially less influence than elected officials, interdependent CEOs have approximately the same amount of influence, and independent CEOs have more influence. The dependent group is divided into two types by considering the CEOs' attitudes regarding accountability and policy congruency with politicians. Building on the conceptual models presented in chapter 2, the expected characteristics of each partnership type is identified. Data analysis will determine the extent to which the expectations are confirmed. To preview our findings, the picture that emerges from the analysis is that the four types are distinct in their orientation in some respects but that they share many characteristics as well. Furthermore, all the types in the aggregate have attitudes and behaviors that are consistent with "norms of appropriateness" for professional administrators in a democratic system. The dependent CEOs do not appear to deviate from appropriate norms of professionalism, and the independent CEOs do not appear to violate norms of democratic accountability.

Having identified the types and examined their characteristics, three sets of questions are examined. First, do the CEO types differ in their deference to political direction and their responsiveness to politicians? In particular, how compliant are dependent CEOs, and how self-directed are interdependent and independent CEOs? Second, although the four types generally fall within appropriate boundaries of accountability and professionalism, are there outliers who go beyond the boundaries because of excessive dependence or independence? Third, how well do the CEO types match up with mayors? Is there a healthy partnership that matches leadership qualities provided by the mayor with the qualities supplied by CEOs of differing types? In the conclusion, the implications of the partnership types for democracy and professionalism in governance are considered.

Defining the Types of CEO Partnerships

The characteristics of the CEO as a partner with elected officials in the political process are determined by the CEO's individual and relative influence. In classifying CEOs as actors in the political process, we presume that CEOs with low to moderate influence have different leadership prospects from those with substantial influence, regardless of their attitudes or activities. Furthermore, those who have substantial influence but interact with elected officials who have essentially the same amount of influence are in a different kind of situation from the CEOs who have more influence than elected officials.

When comparing influence, one issue to be resolved is who the referent will be. Certainly the mayor is the key political figure in most cities, but this may not be the case in certain cities, particularly those that use the council-manager form of government where the council may have more clout than the mayor. In collective and committee-leader cities, committee chairs among the council members may have greater influence. A comparison of the influence of the CEO with sets of elected officials supports this supposition. The CEO is more influential than the mayor in 27 percent of the cities in the study, more influential than the council in 32 percent, and more than the committee chairs in 50 percent, but more influential than the most influential elected official or group of officials in only 16 percent of the cities. The importance of the mayor should not be obscured, but this official is not always the most influential politician. The mayor is the most influential elected official in over three-quarters of the cities, the council in one-fifth, and the committee chairs in only 3 percent.[2] In order to have a fair measure of partnerships based on relative influence, it is important to compare the CEO to the most influential politician (the method used in figure 8.1) rather than comparing the CEO to the mayor alone.

The operational definition of partnership types is based on the amount of influence reported by the CEO and this amount of influence compared to the CEO's perception of the influence of elected officials in making budgetary decisions. Influence ratings for budgeting—instead of economic development—are used in this analysis for four reasons. First, this activity is carried out in a fairly uniform way in all cities. Second, budgeting decisions affect both policy and administration in government. Third, data on influence in budgeting are available in all the study countries, whereas the question about economic development was not included in the survey in three countries. Finally, budgets are the "life blood of government." As Wildavsky (1984, 9) argued, "If politics is regarded as a conflict over whose preferences are to prevail in the determination of policy, the budget records the outcome of this struggle."

The three categories of influence are defined as follows:

• CEOs with low-to-medium (50 or less on a 100-point scale) and inferior influence compared to the most influential elected official (or group of officials) are *dependent*.

• Those with substantial or high influence (75–100) who work with politicians with only slightly more or the same amount of influence, that is, 75–100, are *interdependent*.

• Those with substantial or high influence (75–100) and greater influence than elected officials (+25 or more) are *independent*.

The rationale for this classification is straightforward. It is presumed that CEOs with no more than moderate influence who work with elected officials who have greater influence will have a limited capacity to have impact on the policy-making process alone. Those with substantial influence have the capacity, but it is affected by the influence of the elected officials. A CEO with substantial but slightly less or equal influence has different potential than a CEO who has higher influence than the most influential elected officials. The independent CEOs may have the capability to set their own course, that is, to be autonomous from elected officials. Whether or not they act autonomously is an issue to be examined in the analysis. There are two variants of dependency that have been identified as conceptual possibilities. In the more common version, the administrator is politically neutral and clearly separated in his or her activities from the work of politicians. This person is the *neutral agent* or *classical bureaucrat* type of administrator. Despite the argument in chapter 2 that the concept of neutrality should be given an active and expansive meaning, it is advisable to use a label that does not connote a narrow value orientation. Thus, this type is called the professional agent rather than neutral agent. The other variant stresses that the dependent CEO should be responsive to political leaders and seek to advance their programs. In other words, in this view the CEO would be the political agent of the key elected official. This is the distinction Moe (1985, 239–40) and Aberbach and Rockman (1993) make between "politically neutral" and "politically responsive" competence.

The subtypes that we call the professional agent and the political agent can be distinguished in terms of their orientation to the political process (discussed in chapter 4). The political agent is one who believes it is advantageous for the CEO to have opinions that are congruent with politicians and who believes that he or she should be primarily responsible to them rather than to the public. Thus, the political agents believe they should be responsive and accountable to elected officials. The professional agent, on the other hand, does not consider it to be an advantage to share the political opinions of the majority of the council or feels that the CEO should be at least as responsible to the public as to elected officials. Approximately one out of three dependent CEOs have the characteristics of the political agent. In contrast to this compliant and directly accountable group, the remainder have some basis in their values for distinguishing themselves from politicians. This group either favors holding divergent policy views from the majority (29%), feels broadly accountable to the public rather than directly accountable to politicians (15%), or both (24%). Given their influence limitations, they are appropriately seen as agents of politicians, but they are professional agents rather than politically responsive ones.

Before proceeding to the analysis of the characteristics of the partnership types, one adjustment to the data is required. A review of the breakdown of the types by country revealed an anomaly that needs to be corrected. There are far more high-influence types of CEOs in Ireland than any other country. Over three-fifths have the characteristics of the independent type, and the remainder are interdependent—a far greater skewing of the distribution toward the high-influence types than found in any other country. As a result of the conventions for weighting subjects used in the analysis, distortions can result when the Irish respondents are heavily represented in a category that

Table 9.1 Summary of Characteristics and Distribution of Partnership Types

Leadership types	Amount of CEO influence in budgeting[a]	CEO influence compared to elected officials[b]	Percent of CEOs excluding Ireland	
Dependent: Political agent[c]	Low to moderate	Much less	10%	(344)
Dependent: Professional agent[d]	Low to moderate	Much less	20%	(741)
Interdependent	Fairly high	Slightly less or equal	56%	(2049)
Independent	Fairly high to high	More	13%	(463)
All other combinations	n.a.	n.a.	2%	(72)
Total			100%	(3669)

NOTES: Missing data = 122 and Irish CEOs excluded.
    a. Low to moderate is a rating of 50 or less; fairly high = 75; high = 100.
    b. Less for the dependent category is any rating lower than the most influential elected official's rating; for the interdependent category, influence is slightly less (–25) or equal.
    c. Prefer that CEOs be accountable to elected officials and hold views consistent with opinion of majority.
    d. Prefer that CEOs not necessarily hold views consistent with opinion of majority on the council, be accountable to public, or both.

has a small number of occupants overall.[3] Since respondents were weighted in the analysis to create an equal number of respondents from each country, the actual small number of Irish respondents is inflated greatly. As a consequence, the weighted Irish CEOs in the independent type would represent over one-fourth of all the independent CEOs. Thus, any description of this type is influenced by the characteristics of the Irish CEOs. In order to eliminate this possible source of distortion, the Irish respondents are removed from the general analysis (except for breakdowns by country). The factors that make Ireland a special case are considered in the discussion of the breakdown of the types by country and form of government.

A summary of the four types and their distribution in the sample is presented in table 9.1. Almost 30 percent of the CEOs match the dependent type with modest individual and inferior relative influence; 9% are political agents and 20% are professional agents. A majority of CEOs—56%—are in the interdependent category. All these CEOs have substantial influence but slightly less or the same amount of influence as elected officials. Finally, 13 percent have the influence traits of the independent administrator. Only 2 percent of the CEOs do not fit into one of these combinations.

A superficial answer to the great debate over what role top administrators play in the political process is provided by these results. Most CEOs have substantial impact on their governments and operate essentially on an equal footing with elected officials. They are influential and interact with influential politicians. The majority of interdependent CEOs in the thirteen countries on which this analysis is based approximate the overlapping roles model of political-administrative relations. There is a substantial minority that appears to approximate the separate roles model as professional agents with much less influence than politicians. This model that has figured prominently in the public administration literature corresponds to a partnership type that represents one-fifth of the CEOs. Overall, the independent CEOs are uncommon. Only one in eight CEOs views himself or herself as substantially more influential than elected officials, but this is still a sizable number of CEOs who potentially match the characteristics of the autonomous administrator model. Are these CEOs a challenge to democratic control of administration? Finally, it is also important to discover that one in ten CEOs is a political agent. Do these CEOs sacrifice professionalism in order to be politically responsive administrators?

Having created the types, the next step is to identify the characteristics of officials who represent them. To do so, we form expectations drawing on the literature and then compare these expected traits with the characteristics of the CEOs of each type. The premise underlying the classification is that the four types of CEOs have influence characteristics that give them different prospects for leadership. The analysis seeks to determine whether they are also different kinds of leaders.

Expected Characteristics of the CEO Types

The CEO partnership types—dependent (political and professional agents), interdependent, and independent—have been created using the officials' individual and relative levels of influence. To better understand the types, it is important to know how they differ in other individual characteristics as well as discover how the types are related to the political structure and characteristics of the political environment. In other words, do CEOs of different types have dramatically different characteristics? The discussion of the four models in chapter 2 suggests that they are different kinds of leaders with substantial variation in attitudes and behavior. Using the literature as a guide, characteristics drawn from variables developed in earlier chapters will be attributed to each type on the assumption that personal characteristics are different across the types of partnerships. When these expectations are tested by empirical analysis, we may discover (a) that the types do not differ or differ less substantially than expected, (b) that they differ in ways that depart from expectations drawn from the literature, (c) that the expected differences are present, or (d) parts of all of the above.

The Dependent CEO

The essence of the dependent model is the subordination of administrators to elected officials. As the dependent type has been described in the literature, this subordination goes beyond legal inferiority vis-à-vis elected officials. Elected officials are politically dominant as well. The dependent CEOs have already been divided into subtypes. The political agents prefer accountability to elected officials and holding policy views congruent with the political majority. The professional agents prefer to hold noncongruent views, to be accountable to citizens, or both. It is also expected that the subtypes will differ in their attitudes about the roles of council members (chapter 7). The political agent is more likely than the professional agent to support strong political linkages between representatives and their party and constituents. It is also possible that the political agent is less supportive of the value of nonpartisanship than the professional agent, although the discussion of neutrality in chapter 2 suggested that it is a core value of all administrators, even those committed to responsiveness. This analysis provides the opportunity to test these alternative views.

Alongside these differences, we would expect that both types of dependent CEOs would share certain characteristics. The attributes and the rationale for each characteristic follow. The chapter in which they are discussed is listed in parentheses.

• Low advocacy (chapter 4): Dependent administrators do not promote substantive ends on their own nor do they see themselves as the driving force in government.

• Low community networking and probably low intergovernmental networking as well (chapter 4): These administrators are internally oriented. It seems likely that the political agents will be even less involved in community networking because of their strong orientation to politicians. The low intergovernmental networking expectation is based on the presumption that these administrators are not inclined to be entrepreneurs who seek support and resources from other governments.

• Low involvement in policy innovation and political advice (chapters 5 and 6): These administrators are not policy actors and they stay clear of political matters.

• Accept a high level of specific direction from elected officials (chapter 7): These administrators oppose partisan meddling in administrative matters, but their deference to elected officials produces a preference for the city council to formulate exact goals, decide specific matters, and establish rules and routines.

• In addition to differences and similarities in personal characteristics, it is likely that the stronger the political executive—both in formal structure and political leadership—the greater the likelihood that the dependent CEO in general and the political agent in particular will be found.

Although CEOs generally do not restrict their activities to a separate sphere with little direct involvement in the policy-making process, it seems plausible that the dependent CEOs will be confined to a separate sphere. Furthermore, although most administrators do not strongly emphasize responsiveness to politicians, the political agents among the dependent CEOs will.

The Interdependent CEO

As noted earlier, there is substantial evidence of extensive interaction and reciprocity of influence between politicians and most administrators. Based on the operational definition, almost three CEOs in five have substantial influence on their own and interact with political leaders who also have substantial influence.

The interdependent CEOs are expected to be more active than the dependent ones in their advocacy, networking, policy involvement, and advice to politicians. The interdependents are expected to find congruency less important and are more likely to be public servants than the dependent CEOs, especially the political agents among the dependent CEOs. They are also expected to be less supportive of the idea that council members should represent political parties and adhere to campaign promises, and they prefer less direction from elected officials. The interdependent CEOs are most likely to be found in committee-leader cities in which authority is widely distributed among various elected officials and administrators.

The Independent CEO

The independent CEO operates under political control but has the greatest capability to set his or her own course of action. This CEO has high influence in budgeting and interacts with a political leader who has less influence. These officials could be committed to promoting their own interests, or they could be committed to advancing professional perspectives with less attention to political considerations and a lower regard for the political values of politicians. Our expectations about the characteristics of this type of leader are based on the presumption that professional rather than personal interests are paramount. The characteristics of the independent CEO are expected to be the following:

- high advocacy
- high public servant orientation, putting little emphasis on congruency with the political majority
- high networking level in the community and in higher level governments
- high involvement in policy; moderately low involvement in advice to politicians
- opposition to specific direction from elected officials
- opposition to party representation and strong electoral linkages among council members

Higher advocacy, public servant orientation, networking, and involvement in policy innovation than found among the interdependent CEOs are plausible expectations, because each characteristic reinforces the likelihood of and capability for action that reflect one's professional orientation to addressing public affairs.

Actual Characteristics of the Partnership Types

To determine the characteristics of each type of leader, we examine the mean value of certain variables for each of the types and subtypes and their distribution across categories of certain key attributes, particularly values regarding their relationship to the political process and form of government. Unlike some of the analyses in earlier chapters, no attempt is made to remove the tendencies of CEOs in certain countries to have distinctive qualities. We want to know who the different types of CEOs are and where they are with regard to their form of government and country.

Similarities among Types

Although the types differ in their influence characteristics, they have important similarities that should be kept in mind when examining differences. All CEOs are highly committed to nonpartisanship and evidence moderately high levels of advocacy. The scores (using an index with value of 100) across the four types—political agent, professional agent, interdependent, and independent—are as follows:

- nonpartisanship—82, 81, 78, and 79
- advocacy—69, 65, 69, and 69

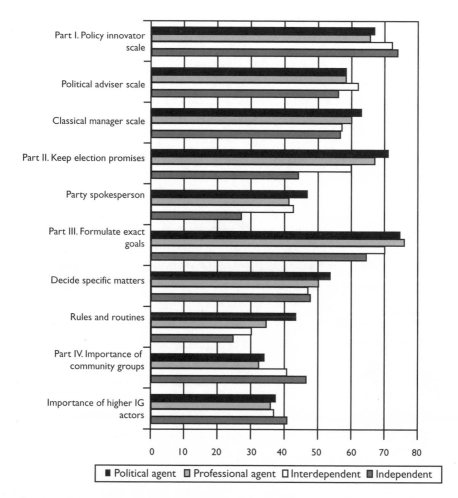

Figure 9.1 Comparison of partnership types

A third area of high uniformity is one aspect of the ideal politician. Unlike some other preferred council roles about which CEOs have differing views, there is uniformly high support for the governor role for elected officials. CEOs of all types want elected officials to create a vision and establish broad principles for the government.[4]

Furthermore, the first three comparisons in part I of figure 9.1 indicate that the differences in involvement level are modest (and this is also true for a number of the measures in other parts of the figure). The interdependent and independent CEOs rank higher than the dependent types in policy involvement, the interdependents are highest in advice to politicians, and the dependent types are highest in the classical administrative functions. Still, none of the functions are absent from the repertoire of any of the types. Our expected characteristics need to be revised to reflect these similarities. Dependent CEOs score as high on advocacy as other types, and they are slightly less but still substantially involved in policy innovation. Dependent CEOs are neither value-free nor uninvolved in policy matters or providing political advice to elected officials. Our view of the independent CEOs also needs to be adjusted. They are not dramatically different from the dependent and interdependent CEOs in advocacy or policy innovation, because the latter two types also score fairly high on these measures and the independents do not manifest extraordinarily high levels of commitment and involvement. All the types of CEOs share the basic characteristics of being nonpartisan, committed, and engaged leaders who look to elected officials to set goals and provide broad direction for their governments.

Political Linkages

As expected, the types differ in their preferences for the kinds of linkages that elected officials have to the public, as indicated in part II of figure 9.1. Political agents are most supportive of politicians keeping election promises (followed by professional agents) and also most supportive of politicians serving as spokespersons for their parties (followed by the interdependents).[5] The independents have distinct views on these matters. They prefer that elected officials act as trustees and rise above electoral and partisan politics. They are especially strong in their disagreement with elected officials acting as spokespersons for their parties. The independent CEOs appear to prefer working with council members as individuals rather than as members of a political collectivity.

Preferred Political Direction

Formulating exact goals is a desirable role in the view of all types of CEOs, as indicated in part III of figure 9.1, although the dependent types are most supportive of this role and the independents are least supportive, as expected. The dependent types also tend to be more supportive of elected officials deciding specific matters, although the difference in level of preference is slight. The political agents are much more supportive of having the council establish rules and routines, and support for this role declines across the other types. The dependent types, especially the political agents, are most supportive of a quasi-administrative role for the council members. The independents are most opposed. The CEOs with the greatest relative influence are the strongest proponents of keeping elected officials out of administration.

These findings are the opposite of the dichotomy concept because this partial separation of functions serves to reinforce the prerogatives and high policy influence of the CEO. The political agents who match most closely the controlled agent aspect of the dichotomy model are also the most willing to have elected officials get involved in administrative tasks—a violation of the logic of dichotomy. Thus, the strongest support for strict separation does not indicate an exclusion of administrators from policy but rather a preference among the most influential administrators to be shielded from political direction. On the other hand, the greatest acceptance of political direction comes from those administrators who are most clearly subordinated and subject to political incursion. The separation supported by the dichotomy provides the basis for—or it accompanies—administrative independence. The subordination supported by the dichotomy increases the acceptance of political involvement in the details of administration. It is ironic that a strict dichotomy may increase the potential for results that are antithetical to the concept itself—administrative autonomy or political interference.

External Networking

The interdependent and independent types have closer ties with the community than the dependent types, as indicated in part IV of figure 9.1. These findings match expectations. The political agents, however, engage in slightly more community networking than the professional agents. The expectation that they would be less involved in networking because of their orientation to politicians is not supported; feeling responsive to politicians does not make the political agents less inclined than the professional agents to have contacts with individuals and key groups in the community. Networking increases with greater influence; the independent CEOs are the most active local network builders. They also have by a modest amount the strongest ties with officials in higher-level governments.

Orientation to the Political Process

A key distinguishing feature between the types is values regarding accountability. Two-thirds of the political agents support being primarily accountable to elected officials, and 89 percent feel that it is advantageous for the CEO to hold views that are the same as the majority on the city council. In contrast, the professional agent has strong tendencies in the opposite direction with only 24 percent and 48 percent sharing the same opinions as the political agents on these matters. The interdependent and the independent CEOs hold the same views and are closer to the professional agents on the necessity of holding views that are the same as the majority. Approximately two-fifths agree. The support for responsibility to citizens, on the other hand, is a characteristic that distinguishes the interdependent and independent types. The former tend to be political servants—60 percent of the interdependents feel that they should be primarily responsible to politicians—whereas 58 percent of the independents are public servants who consider themselves responsible to citizens.

The choice here is between direct and indirect accountability and between secondary and primary identification with professional standards. The independent CEOs prefer the diffuse accountability that comes from being responsible to citizens as much as (or rather than) to politicians. This orientation also provides a rationale for supporting the public interest when, in the opinion of administrators, it conflicts with the preferences of politicians.

Country and Form of Government

Form of government is strongly associated with the partnership type filled by the CEO. The data presented in table 9.2, however, indicate that there are important differences between countries that share the same form. The strong-mayor cities are bunched toward the more controlled end of the scale. Most CEOs in strong-mayor cities are dependent—Portugal and France have high proportions of political agents, whereas Italy and Spain have more professional agents. Interdependent leaders are also common, especially in France. The special case among the strong-mayor countries is the mayor-council cities in the United States. National context and the example of independent city managers contribute to this exceptionalism as does the preponderance of a structural feature that makes these cities very similar to the council-manager form. In most, the CEO is appointed by or confirmed by the city council, and these CEOs assume leadership styles that stress accountability to the council rather than to the mayor.

As indicated in table 9.2, the dependent types are the most common within strong-mayor cities followed by the interdependent CEOs. In the committee-leader and the collective cities where one finds both a formally strong body of elected officials as well as a mayor or equivalent with formal executive authority, the most common are the interdependent type. Dependent

Table 9.2 Partnership Types by Country and Form of Government *(Percent)*

	Political agent	Professional agent	Interdependent	Independent	Total
France	21	11	64	4	100
Italy	9	48	38	5	100
Portugal	27	30	41	1	100
Spain	8	43	44	5	100
US-MC	0	6	60	34	100
Denmark	3	23	72	2	100
Great Britain	5	18	70	7	100
Sweden	17	20	63	0	100
Belgium	18	20	58	4	100
The Netherlands	11	38	43	7	100
Australia	2	5	57	37	100
Finland	1	3	54	42	100
Ireland	0	0	36	64	100
Norway	2	11	74	13	100
US-CM	0	1	58	41	100
Strong-mayor	16	31	48	6	100
Committee-leader	8	20	68	3	100
Collective	15	29	51	5	100
Council-manager (including Ireland)	1	4	56	39	100
Council-manager (excluding Ireland)	1	5	61	33	100
All countries (including Ireland)	9	19	56	16	100
N =	345	742	2144	632	3863
All countries (excluding Ireland)	10	21	57	13	100
N =	344	741	2049	463	3598

NOTE: Table excludes other combinations of CEO and elected official influence from Table 9.1. *N* = 72.

types, particularly the professional agents, are much more common in committee-leader and collective cities than the independent type CEOs. In the council-manager cities, interdependent CEOs are the most common type. Norway has more interdependents and independents than the committee-leader or collective cities, although there are few independents in comparison to the other council-manager countries. There are a substantial proportion of independent CEOs in the council-manager cities in the United States, Australia, and Finland. In Ireland, two-thirds of the CEOs are independent types—a finding that led us to exclude Irish CEOs from the analysis of the characteristics of the various types.

Two comparisons illustrate the difference that form of government makes in the distribution of partnership types. In Scandinavia, there are similarities in structural features particularly among Norway, Sweden, and Denmark. Norway is sufficiently distinct that it was placed in the council-manager group of countries along with Finland that clearly matches the major features of the council-manager form. To some extent, Norway differs from the "pure" council-manager governments in the relatively high proportion of dependent CEOs. In Norway, 13 percent of the CEOs fall into one of the dependent categories compared to 7 percent in Australia—the next highest—and 4 percent in Finland. In contrast to the committee-leader countries in Scandinavia, however, the proportion is low when compared to 37 percent in Sweden and 26 percent in Denmark. Even with similar cultural characteristics and some overlap in institutions, the council-manager characteristics contribute to a much higher proportion of interdependent and independent CEOs in Norway than in Denmark and Sweden. In Finland with a pure council-manager form, the proportion of independent CEOs is much higher and the proportion of dependent CEOs much lower than in Norway.

The United States offers a contrasting illustration. Here, the same cultural and social characteristics virtually eliminate the differences in partnership type between cities with different forms of government. Only 6 percent of the CEOs in the mayor-council cities compared to 1 percent in the council-manger cities are dependent types. There are, however, some structural factors that affect attitudes about the role of the CEO in mayor-council cities (Svara, 2001b.) Most city administrators in mayor-council cities are in fact appointed by or approved by the city council. Only 12 percent have an administrator accountable to the mayor alone. When appointed by the mayor, city administrators tend to see themselves as the agents of the mayor and dependent on the mayor for authority. When the council approves the selection, on the other hand, administrators more often feel accountable to the entire council and believe that they can instill professional values in management. The more the CEO is formally linked to the mayor through the appointment, the more dependent are the attitudes expressed about his or her role. On the other hand, the CEOs who are appointed by the council are similar to city managers in their capacity for independence.

The exceptional country is Ireland, in which 64 percent of the CEOs are independent. A number of factors elaborated by Asquith and O'Halpin (1998) may account for these striking results. First, the formal structure in Ireland gives high organizational authority to the CEO. By law since 1942, policy matters are to be determined by members of the council, but the CEO and staff are responsible for all other aspects of operating local government. This gives CEOs great powers, because it prevents councilors from getting involved in any detailed aspects of administration. As observed in chapter 7, the councilors are dependent on the CEO for getting services for constituents. The formal assignment of policy authority to the council and their exclusion from administration has the paradoxical effect of reducing their influence in policy making. Second, the chairmanship/mayoralty rotates among councilors on a yearly basis so the level of focused political leadership is low. Third, CEOs tend to have long incumbency in contrast to the rotating chairmanship. Fourth, the CEOs are selected by a national body, the Local Appointments Commission. A local authority cannot turn down the candidate selected by this body. Only since 1992 have terms been limited by the introduction of contracts for CEOs, although an incumbent is eligible to compete for reappointment at the end of the term. Finally, governmental affairs are highly centralized, with local government put in the role of delivering services defined and financed at the national level. In this situation, the CEO serves as a key link to higher-level officials and agencies, and the possibilities for policy making by elected officials are limited. Irish city managers are concerned with building close working relationships with elected officials, they are careful not to be too prominent, and they defer to politicians in public. Still, Asquith and O'Halpin (1998, 66) observe that "they are almost entirely free from local political control, and they have a good deal of administrative discretion."

The following paragraphs summarize the major characteristics of each type of CEO, which are reviewed and compared to the expected characteristics.

Dependent Types: Professional and Political Agents

The characteristics of the dependent CEO are consistent with expectations in some respects but deviate in others. Even when the tendencies of the dependent CEOs point in the right direction, however, the profile does not match the stereotype fostered by the literature. Although dependent CEOs are appropriately lower or higher on certain measures than the other types, they are not dramatically different from other CEOs in some important respects. The dependent CEOs score nearly as high on advocacy as CEOs generally. They are less active but still substantially involved in policy innovation. Although they exert only modest influence and operate within the shadow of a more highly influential elected official, they are neither apolitical classical bureaucrats nor unprofessional hired hands. These characteristics add further evidence to the inadequacy of the dichotomy model. Although these CEOs are clearly subordinate to elected officials in terms of influence and support strong political direction in administrative affairs—particularly the political agents—both political and professional agents are more engaged as professionally committed policy innovators than the dichotomy model would have predicted. Furthermore, the political agents are more politically attuned than the model would have allowed. The political agents are most supportive of strong linkages between elected officials and the electoral process and political parties. Despite support for electoral politics in the governmental process, however, there is no less support among the political agents for the concept of nonpartisanship than among the professional agents.

The professional agents approximate the classical bureaucrat who makes a substantial contribution to the political process but operates with more separateness than any of the other types. In comparison to the other types, the professional agent is the least connected to individuals and groups in the community and the second most strongly supportive of being accountable to the public rather than elected officials. This group more than any other type disapproves of the idea that administrators should have the same political opinion as the majority of the council. Thus, the professional agents are detached from elected officials, determinedly independent in their views, and somewhat aloof from the community, but still they are professionally committed and broadly involved.

Interdependent Types

The characteristics of the interdependent CEOs are consistent with expectations in the sense that they usually fall in between those of the dependent and the independent CEOs. The interdependent CEOs have intermediate scores (appropriately higher or lower depending on the measure) compared to the dependent types on the following measures:

- involvement in policy
- support for council members keeping election promises
- support for direction from elected officials in formulating exact goals and setting rules
- support for council members acting as a spokesperson for a political party
- networking with community groups

With regard to responsibility to elected officials, the interdependents evidence higher support for direct accountability than the professional agents but less than the political agents. The outstanding characteristic of the interdependent CEOs is high involvement in providing advice to politicians.

Interdependency is the most common partnership type at the apex of government. About half the CEOs in strong-mayor cities and collective cities belong to this category, as do over three-fifths of the CEOs in council-manager cities. In the committee-leader cities about two out of three CEOs are interdependents.

Independent Types

The expected characteristics of the independent CEOs are generally present. In absolute terms they have pronounced traits, and in comparative terms they are (with only one exception) either highest or lowest in the expected direction among the types of leaders. They display higher scores on community and intergovernmental networking and responsibility to citizens and lower scores on support for elected officials keeping election promises, serving as party spokespersons, formulating exact goals, and establishing rules and routines for administrators. They have the highest, but not dramatically different, scores for policy innovation. They are highly engaged and committed and actively involved in policy formation. They prefer that elected officials act as individual officials rather than as party representatives, as trustees rather than delegates who follow through on campaign promises, and as detached reviewers who do not give specific instructions or intervene in particular administrative matters. This type illustrates the distinct version of separated spheres associated with the autonomous administrator model. Elected officials would be confined to a limited sphere of activity if the CEO's preferences obtained. The elected official would set the broad parameters for the CEO but do so disconnected from party and constituency. The CEO, on the other hand, has a broad scope of policy involvement, an extensive network, and, of course, high influence.

When we look across forms of government, the independent CEOs are disproportionately located in council-manager cities where they represent one-third of the CEOs. It is worth emphasizing, however, that most city managers are not independents. When considering the distribution of the four types of leadership among the council-manager CEOs, the most common is the interdependent type, which accounts for approximately 60 percent of the city managers. Still, if one wants to observe independent CEOs, the most likely place to find them is in council-manager cities.

Issues in Partnerships

The four types of CEOs defined by their influence profile have certain distinct attitudes and behaviors while sharing some basic characteristics as involved, committed professionals. Having identified the types, three issues arise concerning their involvement in the political process. First, how do they differ in the extent of self-direction, especially the interdependent and independent CEOs? Second, although the four types appear to operate within the bounds of professional responsibility, are there outliers who either sacrifice professionalism to political compliance or undercut accountability? Finally, how do mayors match up with each of the types? What kinds of partnerships between political and administrative leaders are found in practice? Each issue will be explored in turn.

How Self-Directed Are the Interdependent and the Independent CEOs?

Variations in types of influence have been identified, but do CEOs of each type behave (or think that they should behave) differently with regard to accountability to elected officials? Two indicators are available to answer this question. First, the CEOs were asked to what extent should administrators undertake major policy reviews without political direction. Second, to what extent should administrative officials make themselves acquainted with the intentions of the elected officials who appoint them and put forward proposals in line with these intentions only? Analysis of responses to these items indicate that the political agents are most likely to accept political direction. Eighty percent would seek guidance from elected officials before reviewing major policies. In contrast, just over half of the independents would look to politicians before starting a review. All the types, with the exception of the independents, demonstrate a similar moderately low inclination to align their recommendations with the preferences of elected officials. Only one in three or fewer of the political agents, professional agents, and interdependents agree that clearance is needed.[6] The independent CEOs stand out from the rest in that they are much less likely to bring recommendations that are consistent with the preferences of elected officials. Only 12 percent of them favor doing so.

An indication of a basic commitment to using professional judgment as the basis for recommendations (as opposed to following political direction) is that all the types tend to oppose following the preferences of politicians in developing proposals, although this tendency is even more pronounced among the independents. An indicator of democratic accountability of CEOs is that most accept the idea of getting political direction before undertaking policy reviews, although there is only a slight majority among the independents who support getting political clearance.

The Eunuchs and the Mandarins: Do They Exist?

The description of the two polar types of CEOs stresses the blend of distinct and similar characteristics. They are different from the interdependent CEOs, but the degree of difference is modest and all CEOs are alike in certain ways. The political agents and the independent CEOs fall within the bounds of professional and responsible administration, although they are closer to the boundaries than the professional agents and the interdependent CEOs. These tendencies do not, however, rule out the possibility that there are outliers that could be differentiated from the others even in the polar groups: clerks or eunuchs at the edge of and perhaps outside the political agent group, and mandarins or autonomous bureaucrats that go beyond the normal characteristics of the independent group in their self-direction. There are sufficient subjects in our sample that it may be possible to identify such outliers and even have enough subjects to safely describe their characteristics despite the fact that they are only a small percentage of the total sample. To identify the outliers, the level of influence in economic development will be considered as well as influence in budgeting in order to find those who are generally low or high in influence.

Among the dependent CEOs, the extreme cases would be administrators who have much less influence (at least 50 points lower) than elected officials in both areas of policy and also are only moderately involved in policy innovation (no higher than 50 on the policy innovation scale). These CEOs might be called "passive servants." Searching the sample determines that such CEOs are quite rare. Only 3 percent meet all these conditions. Examination of their characteristics determines that their attitudes are not extraordinary. Only slightly more than one-third of these administrators agree that their proposals should be consistent with the political intentions of council members compared to one-quarter of the sample as a whole. They have almost as high an advocacy score and are just as committed to nonpartisanship as CEOs generally. Thus, passive-servant CEOs are rare, and even those who have the characteristics of this subtype are reasonably committed professionals. They do not appear to belong in a separate category of officials who are merely clerks to the politicians.

Among the independent CEOs, the extreme cases would be dominant CEOs who have much more influence (at least 50 points higher) than the most influential elected official in both budgeting and economic development decision making. Only 1.5 percent of the CEOs outside of Ireland meet these conditions (compared to 15 percent in Ireland).[7] The attitudes of the dominant CEOs are farther from the mainstream than is the case with the passive servants. They are much less likely to agree that proposals submitted to the council should be in line with political intentions (5% vs. 28% for other CEOs) and that policy reviews should not be undertaken without political direction (34% vs. 66%). Furthermore, they are less likely to agree that CEOs should be primarily responsible to the political leadership rather than the public (29% vs. 57%). Other differences are slight. Compared to other CEOs, they have only slightly higher advocacy scores (73 vs. 68) and policy innovation scores (78 vs. 72). These dominant CEOs have a great influence advantage over elected officials and are more likely than other CEOs to have attitudes that justify using their influence in a self-directed way. These CEOs are a very small proportion of CEOs overall outside of Ireland, but they do represent about one-tenth of the independent CEOs. The presence of potential "autonomous bureaucrats" who run governmental affairs with little control being exerted by politicians is uncommon overall. Still, they are a discernible minority among the independent types.

Mayors and CEO Types: What Is a Healthy Partnership?

In view of the analysis of mayoral influence in chapter 8 and CEO partnership types in this chapter, it is possible to consider how the leadership and CEO types combine. In chapter 8, evidence was presented to demonstrate that mayors who are effective public leaders—visionaries who maintain close ties with the electorate—and innovators who pay attention to both broad policy matters and the details of implementation have the greatest influence over policy making. To simplify consideration of the ideal relationship between mayors and CEOs, the leadership measure can be condensed to combine what appear to be the crucial elements from the two measures: the visionary quality of the mayor and the amount of attention to details. Four clusters of leaders emerge from analysis of the overlap between these two attributes.

These are the *hands-on leader*, the *visionary*, the *checker*, and the *nonleader*.[8] The hands-on leader is active in both areas—developing ideas and paying attention to details—and the visionary focuses on the former. The checker is the detail-oriented official who is not interested in painting the big picture but notices when specific objects are not well drawn. The nonleader is not active in either area.

We shall consider both the hands-on leader and the visionary to qualify as "effective" leaders. It is assumed that all cities are advantaged by having a mayor who provides visionary leadership. If mayors are to be out front of other elected officials in bringing energy to the political process, they should be visionary persons who constantly initiate new projects and policies in the locality. Attention to the details of administration, if combined with visionary leadership, is also useful to help insure that broad goals and plans are being converted into policies and programs that achieve their intended purpose. Some might argue that a mayor who does not attend to specifics cannot be effective because the resolution of detailed choices can undermine the inspiration the mayor offers other officials and the public. Others might contend that getting involved in details interferes with administrative performance and undercuts the ability to remain focused on broad goals. We will, however, accept either as effective styles.

There is a strong association between the type of CEO partnership and the type of mayoral leadership provided, and this relationship holds up regardless of form of government.[9] The proportion of mayors who can be classified as hands-on leaders or visionaries in cities with CEOs of different types is as follows:

CEO type	Percent with "Effective Mayors" as perceived by CEO
Political agent	58%
Professional agent	52%
Interdependent	44%
Independent	27%
Total	44%

Mayors manifest effective leadership behavior in over half the cities with political agent and professional agent type CEOs. Approximately two in five mayors paired with interdependent CEOs are effective, and only a quarter fall into this category when the CEO is independent.

This relationship presents an interesting question about which factor precedes the other. It is not surprising that mayoral leadership—indirectly one of the elements in classifying the CEO types[10]—would be either more or less common when the influence of elected officials is either high or moderate as in the dependent and independent types. When CEOs are interdependent, however, they also interact with influential politicians (although not necessarily the mayor) and consequently they are not filling an influence void as could be the case with independent CEOs. Still, effective mayors are not as common in cities with interdependent CEOs.

Stating the relationship in reverse, there is a higher proportion of interdependent and independent CEOs when mayors are weak in providing visionary leadership and focusing on the details of city government. This same condition is found whether or not the mayor is formally strong. Based on the definitions of CEO types, the dependent CEOs work with an influential mayor. It is likely that they are also working with an effective mayor. On the other hand, independent CEOs, who work with mayors who have less influence than they do, are also likely to be working with ineffective mayors. Although one would not have expected it, interdependent CEOs, who work with elected officials who have at least as much influence as they do, are more likely than not to be working with a mayor who is not an effective leader as we are measuring it. Thus, even in cities where mayors have substantial resources or considerable influence, many are not effective leaders. In cities where they have less influence than the CEO, few are effective leaders.

The weak showing of mayors on these measures of performance means that there is often not a strong focal point of effective political leadership in city government. In the political-administrative partnership, presumably something is lost when the political leadership is not concentrated in the office where one expects to find it. Even if other politicians are more influential than the mayor, there are limitations to the effectiveness of political leadership.[11] Presumably a group of officials, either the council as a whole, an executive committee, or committee chairs, does not operate with clarity or flexibility without an effective individual leader, even if the body of officials has considerable clout.

It is important to consider the implications of these findings regarding the pairing of mayors and CEOs of different types for the nature and quality of policy leadership in the city. Based on the full range of findings in this chapter, it is possible to describe the kind of contribution that the mayor and CEO are likely to make to policy making. This is done in table 9.3, and the table also presents the proportion of cities that match each combination of CEO type and level of mayoral leadership. Overall, more than half of the cities have

Table 9.3 Contributions of Mayors and CEOs to Policy Making under Different Types of Partnerships and Mayoral Effectiveness

CEO v	Mayor: low policy leadership	Mayor: effective policy leadership
Dependent: Political agent	Moderate policy innovation in city government with proposals coming from CEO who seeks to advance the mayor's political interests [4%]	CEO contributes to and helps to shape active policy innovation coming from mayor [5%]
Dependent: Professional agent	Weak policy innovation in city government with professionally grounded (and presumably modest) proposals coming from CEO who must secure the support of influential mayor [10%]	Political leadership from mayor in advancing policy proposals and professional advice and recommendations from CEO [10%]
Interdependent	Give and take with active innovation from CEO and accepting/blocking by influential elected officials [32%]	Mutual reinforcement and extensive interchange between mayor and CEO in developing policy proposals [25%]
Independent	CEO sets agenda for elected officials [11%]	Mayor and council create a framework of goals filled by CEO's policy proposals [4%]
Total	[56%]	[44%]

mayors who do not provide a high level of visionary leadership. Of those who are visionaries, some are also attentive to the details of government and some are not, but the mayor who focuses on details without initiating policies is not considered to be effective. It is known from our analysis in this chapter that CEOs vary in their absolute and relative influence, but all types tend to provide a fairly high level of policy innovation. The descriptions in each cell of the table express how a CEO involved in policy innovation with varying levels of influence interacts in policy matters with a mayor who may vary in both policy innovation and influence. If the CEO is among the minority who are not policy innovators, the policy process is likely to be even more anemic when the mayors leadership is ineffective.[12]

When the leadership of the mayor is low, that is, when the mayor is a checker or nonleader, the political agent may be a better match for creating a somewhat stronger policy process than the professional agent. The political agent is comfortable bringing proposals that are congruent with the preferences of elected officials, even if the mayor is not effective at initiating proposals on his or her own. These CEOs can say, "This is what I suggest that you do in order to accomplish your political goals." This combination is uncommon. In contrast, the professional agent will fill the policy void to some extent with professionally grounded proposals. These proposals may not resonate with the political orientation of the mayor, and they may not promote his or her political program. In the absence of initiative from the influential mayor, the policy agenda may consist of competent but modest proposals from the CEO, who has limited capacity to influence the outcome of decision making. Approximately one city in ten has this combination.

Low leadership by the mayor who interacts with the interdependent CEO —found in one city in three—presumably produces complex dynamics. These CEOs are active innovators, and they have clout. Still, the mayor as an individual or part of a group of politicians has equal or greater clout. Presumably, there is considerable give-and-take between the two. The CEO must win acceptance from the mayor, although the CEO may have other sources of leverage. If the mayor is willing to accept the proposals of the CEO, the policy process can proceed smoothly. In contrast, the independent CEO who works with an ineffective mayor is in the position to shape the political agenda of the council. Although the acceptance of the CEO's proposals cannot be assured, it is likely that the proposals for policy innovation that make it onto the political agenda will have come from the CEO.

Effective mayoral leadership provides for a more active and creative partnership between mayor and CEO. In view of our findings that mayoral and administrative influence move up together rather than being related negatively, it is expected that CEOs regardless of their level of influence and policy involvement will be a positive co-contributor with the mayor in policy innovation rather than seeing the mayor's leadership as threatening. Consequently, the CEOs make contributions to policy making that are appropriate to their absolute and relative influence, that is, appropriate to their type. The political agent contributes to and helps to shape active policy innovation coming from the mayor. The professional agent offers professional advice and recommendations that balance the political initiatives coming from the mayor. The interdependent CEO and the mayor can mutually reinforce each other and engage in extensive interchange in developing policy proposals. Independent CEOs are advantaged by having a policy framework that the council has set with the mayor's leadership, which they can fill with detailed policy proposals.

There is a partnership between the mayor and the CEO in all of the combinations, but substantial variation in the extent to which the CEO is filling gaps in political leadership, on the one hand, and actively joining with capable political leaders, on the other. The interactions suggest, however, that the consequence of low mayoral leadership is not expansion of the CEO's impact beyond what one would expect from their influence level alone. The consequence appears to be a less effective and balanced policy process. CEOs may have a greater share of the responsibility for policy decisions made when political leadership is weak, but presumably fewer decisions are made and the policies adopted have less scope and reach. To use a simplistic metaphor, the CEO may account for a larger piece of a smaller policy pie when political leadership is weak. Of course, the size of the piece is also affected by the CEO's influence. With effective political leadership, the CEO may be responsible for a smaller piece of a much larger pie. The exception to this generalization could be the independent CEO who works with officials who offer low leadership. Although the formal authority to approve policy lies with them, they may become dependent on the CEO to such an extent that the policy process is dominated by the perspective of administrators.

In sum, CEOs differ in how they approach the partnership with elected officials and demonstrate differing degrees of independence. It is also important to consider the characteristics of the elected officials with which they have a partnership. Although in cities with dependent and interdependent CEOs, elected officials have an influence advantage over CEOs or possess the same level of influence, there may be an imbalance between political and administrative leadership when appropriateness of focus and effectiveness of performance on the part of the mayor are taken into consideration. In cities with independent CEOs, the CEOs have an advantage in influence, and the impact of this advantage may be magnified by interacting with mayors who are least likely to be effective leaders.

Conclusion

The underlying issue in the consideration of partnerships is a dual one—the impact of the CEO in the democratic process and the impact of politics in administration. Given the substantial influence of elected officials in some cities, is politics a threat to professionalism? Given the substantial influence of CEOs in other cities—a level that sometimes exceeds that of any elected official—is the influence of the CEO a threat to democracy? Whether CEOs in city governments are dependent or independent is not an either-or question, that is, there are some of both, and there are additional options besides these two choices. In this analysis, relationships are defined in terms of the relative influence of the most influential elected official and the CEO, and among CEOs with less influence by the attitudes of CEOs toward the political process. There are two types of dependent CEOs differentiated by the degree of neutrality or responsiveness displayed by the CEO plus the interdependent and independent types of CEOs. One in ten CEOs is a dependent political agent, and two in ten are dependent professional agents. One in eight is independent. Most CEOs (56%) are interdependent, even though this type of administrative leader has only recently received explicit attention in the literature. These CEOs clearly are consistent with the overlapping roles model of political-administrative interaction: they have a complementary relationship with elected officials.

Further analysis of the partnership types indicates that the characteristics of most administrators—not just the interdependent type—are consistent with the idea of complementarity of politics and administration (Svara 1999a, 2001a). Complementarity is based on the premise that elected officials and administrators join together in the common pursuit of sound governance. Complementarity implies separate parts, but parts that come together in a mutually supportive way. One fills out the other to create a whole. Complementarity stresses interaction and reciprocal influence between types of officials. Dependent CEOs are also in a complementary relationship with elected officials—even the political agents—and bring distinct values and attributes along with considerable policy involvement and moderate influence to the governmental process. They are politically responsive but not politically dominated to the exclusion of professionalism. Nor do they operate in a separate sphere from politicians. Thus, the political and professional agents do not match key characteristics of the responsive administrator and separate roles models. Dependent CEOs represent one variation on the theme of complementarity.

The independent CEOs who report higher influence than any elected officials may also have a complementary relationship with elected officials although they play a larger role and have greater impact on decisions. They operate in a complex pattern of interaction with many actors in a broad network they have helped to create. Before considering to what extent the independent CEOs match the autonomous administrator model, it is important to note some characteristics they share with others. All the types of CEOs are nonpartisan, committed, and engaged leaders who look to elected officials to set goals and provide broad direction for their governments. All types of CEOs exert at least moderately high influence as part of a complex of leadership partnership with political leaders whether they have somewhat less, about the same, or more influence than the elected officials.

The independent CEOs, particularly those with broad influence across multiple policy areas, could become aloof, self-directed leaders—the kind described by the autonomous administrator model. Most of the independent CEOs do not work with a mayor who provides effective leadership. Their attitudes about their own role reinforce a sense of responsibility to maintain professional standards, even if these counter the preferences of politicians, and to be accountable to the public as well as or instead of elected officials. They also prefer that elected officials operate on a high plane of generality setting the direction for staff rather than specifying the details. It should be acknowledged that they support (although less than other types) elected officials specifying exact goals—not just broad policy—and this view presumably provides attitudinal support for accountability to elected officials. Still, they would have the opportunity, if their preferences were realized, to exercise discretion in filling in the details of policy and administration with little political oversight. Their ideal politicians would identify with the governing board rather than functioning in office as a part of a political party or as a delegate closely connected with constituents. The professional agent has similar attitudes but does not have the influence advantage to act on these attitudes to the same extent that the independent CEO does. Professional responsibility as a constraining force—an "inner check" (Friedrich 1940)—is particularly important for these officials who operate in a setting with only weak external checks.

Dependent and independent CEOs have distinct tendencies compared with the interdependent types, but in most respects the CEOs are alike rather than sharply contrasting. The dependent CEOs are not clerks or political hacks; the independent CEOs are not an autonomous elite. The examination of possible outlier types reinforces the main conclusion. There are minorities that may be dominated by politicians or aloof from politicians, but their numbers are very small. Although relationships and CEO characteristics differ, the variation for virtually all CEOs occurs within what would appear to be the limits of complementarity. The boundaries of appropriate behavior are examined further in the concluding chapter. The largest body of administrators is right in the middle of this model of interaction. They are interdependent in their relationship with elected officials—tending toward neither dependence nor independence.

The dependent and independent CEOs share many characteristics with or vary only moderately from the majority of CEOs who are interdependent in influence. According to the tendencies of the distinct types, CEOs are smaller or larger partners in democratic governance with elected officials. They are more or less attuned to political direction and committed to administrative standards, but they operate within the confines of democracy and professionalism. In their partnership with elected officials, a majority of CEOs have the challenge of working with mayors who are incomplete or ineffective as leaders, even when they or other elected officials exert considerable influence. Most mayors fail to offer visionary leadership, including some who are also inattentive to the details of running the city. Because of these characteristics, CEOs cannot necessarily expect to receive creative ideas from the mayors as either a guide or a counterweight to their own innovation. In this situation, the independent CEOs, particularly those who are more influential across several policy areas, may allow their advantage in influence and in innovative ideas to strain the bounds of democratic control. Even though most CEOs are not autonomous bureaucrats, a very small proportion may be or have the potential of becoming self-directing.

Despite this possibility, the more common situation may be one of diminished capacity for city government as a whole rather than administrative autonomy. When leadership is a partnership as it appears to be with CEOs of all types, the weakness of one partner is likely to adversely affect rather than advantage the other. On the other hand, a partnership based on mutual strength can lead to expanded capacity for effective democratic governance.

CHAPTER 10

Conclusion and Implications
of the Study

THE CONCEPT OF THE APEX OF LEADERSHIP builds on Peter Self's visualization of the governmental process as an arch with one arc representing the political process and the other the administrative process. The top of the arch—the apex—represents the junction where politics and administration meet (Self 1972, 150–51). At the apex, political and administrative logics converge and may collide, the legislative function meets the executive function, and the political and administrative levels of government are tied together. The central purpose of the study has been to better understand what happens at the apex.

Conceptually we perceive the apex to be embedded in a broader institutional and cultural context. This context, of which only the structures of government can be changed by deliberate reform, has been shown to be extremely important for political and administrative leadership. Self's image of impulses flowing between spheres is substantiated by this study of city governments in fourteen countries. One does not find separate spheres of politics and administration but rather a "fusion of political and administrative influences." The specifics of what happens at the apex vary, however, and are to a large extent framed by the context. Institutions matter and so does culture. The behavior of individual officials—the nature and level of leadership—matters as well.

The fourteen countries studied have certain institutions in common. Local government is based on the principle of representative democracy. Localities are governed by an elected body that has at its disposal an administrative organization manned by appointed officials. The CEO is the highest ranking appointed official who is the main link between the elected body and the administration. These shared structural features give rise to certain shared behaviors, values, and outlooks that most CEOs share. Most CEOs emphasize nonpartisan community leadership with concern for helping the disadvantaged. Thus, they bring neutral but committed competence to their relationship with elected officials and the public. There is overwhelming support for a robust version of neutrality among CEOs. According to the norms of neutrality, they are not beholden to any political group over the long term (although there are differences in the extent to which they help incumbents) and they are honest and independent in their communications with politicians. Neutrality does not, however, mean a lack of commitment or involvement. Operating from the professional realm, CEOs see themselves as leaders who guide change in their community. The typical CEO is highly engaged in shaping policy. Overall, elected officials and administrators do not divide functions. Rather there is a mutual filling of the policy role and a shared concern for the process of policy making.

CEOs want politicians to define the mission and set the goals for the city regardless of the form of government. Politicians are also expected to defend decisions to the external world and to know what citizens want. There is consensus that politicians should be, first, the "governors" of their cities who set broad direction and defend the municipality and, second, the "representatives" who link the public to government by channeling citizen preferences into the governmental process. Drawing inferences from additional studies in two countries, top administrators independent of the institutional setup rarely find their ideal politician in the real world.[1] The gap between ideal and actual performance is particularly great in the governor roles. Elected officials do not devote as much attention as CEOs think they should to creating the vision and determining the broad policy principles to guide the work of city government. On the other hand, they are more engaged than CEOs would prefer in making specific decisions.

Mayors and CEOs are not involved in a zero-sum contest for control. Although form of government gives either the mayor or the CEO greater influence or reinforces equality of influence, when the effects of structure are removed, the influence of the two officials rises and falls together. Rather than a contest for control, there is interdependency and reciprocal influence between the mayor and CEO.

This description of the typical characteristics of CEOs and their relationships with politicians may be interpreted in two ways. Either it embodies norms about how officials should behave or it reflects ways that the two sets of officials divide up the municipal turf through a process of give-and-take. A combination of the two perspectives is also possible. Some of the findings presumably reflect norms derived from the prescriptions of associations of municipalities and public administration professionals. Nonpartisanship among CEOs and the emphasis on the governor role for elected officials might be viewed as examples of the norms of appropriateness—a concept propounded by the normative institutionalist theories (March and Olsen 1995, 25–27). On the other hand, some characteristics may reflect a balance of roles that emerges from the ongoing interaction of officials, in particular the levels of involvement and respective influence. Professional associations have tended to ignore and not be particularly forthright about the policy role of top administrators and have evaded the issue of administrative influence. Whether the active, influential contribution of CEOs represents an implicit "appropriateness" or the power that self-interested administrators are able to accumulate in deviance of norms is an issue to be explored. Dissecting the issue will illustrate the contrasting perspectives of the normative and the public choice institutionalists.

We begin this concluding chapter by interpreting the findings of the study in terms of alternative modes of institutional analysis. The discussion then turns to a consideration of a general framework of understanding political-administrative relations and implications of the study for local democracy.

Comparison of Structures and Culture

The fourteen countries exhibit different ground rules concerning how political power is obtained, maintained, exercised, and shared. Examining the extent to which there are variations associated with these different structures is consistent with the simple empirical investigation of structural impacts. The founding fathers of local government and subsequent reformers in the various countries have come up with different solutions to finding a balance between layman rule, political leadership, and professionalism. Form of government differs across the fourteen countries. Some countries emphasize strong political leadership, others the sharing of power and the involvement of laypersons in the executive as well as legislative functions of government, and still others have confined politicians to the legislative function and cast their lot with strong professional leaders.

Based on a careful analysis of legal and behavioral factors in the fourteen countries, four forms of local government were identified:

- *Strong-mayor form* with an elected official who is the primary political leader of the governing board and possesses considerable executive authority (France, Italy, Portugal, Spain, United States mayor-council cities)
- *Committee-leader form* with a quasi-parliamentary form with standing committees, an executive (or finance) committee, and a mayor, or majority leader in the case of Britain, drawn from the dominant party or party coalition in the city council (Denmark, Great Britain, Sweden)
- *Collective leadership form* with a cabinet leadership structure in which an executive committee of the council exercises executive authority along with a mayor who has limited authority and a chief executive officer primarily responsible to the executive committee (Belgium and Holland)
- *Council-manager form* with a governing board headed by a nonexecutive leader and an appointed chief executive officer (Australia, Finland, Ireland, Norway, and the United States)

The preference for one or the other is not arbitrary. Form of government tends to reflect deeper dispositional structures among the citizenry of a country. Strong political leadership is preferred in countries where the less powerful expect and accept that power is distributed unequally, in other words, where power distance is high. Layman rule and dispersion of authority is preferred in countries where power distance is low.

Aside from the differences in cultural traits, overlapping with these groups of separate countries (with the exception of the United States) are variations in the scope and function of government and the range of city sizes found within countries. The committee-leader cities in countries that have had a tradition of extensive social welfare services stand out from the rest in the size of their governments because of a large public sector and broad range of services assigned to local government and—in the case of Great Britain—because of large city size. The strong-mayor governments, on the other hand, tend to provide fewer services and serve smaller populations.

In mayor-council cities, the formal powers of the mayor are highest compared to cities with other forms, and this official is clearly the leading politician. These cities tend to be smaller with more limited scope of services and to experience higher levels of uncertainty and conflict between political parties than other types of cities. Greater power distance and greater uncertainty avoidance along with these community characteristics could induce officials to look to the mayor for direction. The CEOs in these cities are actively involved in policy innovation but they are also the most highly involved in classical administrative tasks and the least active in providing political advice to their mayor. The influence level of the CEOs is moderately high but lower than in cities of other types. There are more dependent CEOs than in other forms, and a slightly higher proportion of political agents who feel that they should be responsive to the mayor's policy direction. Still, even in these cities professional agents outnumber political agents among the dependent types, and over half are interdependent. Still, strong-mayor CEOs are virtually indistinguishable from other CEOs in their support for nonpartisanship and advocacy.

The committee-leader cities have the greatest dispersion of authority among the mayor, executive committee, standing committees, CEO, and department heads. Power distance and uncertainty avoidance are moderately low in these countries, and the cities have moderate levels of uncertainty and party conflict. The CEOs tend to adopt the stance of the noncongruent political servant—independently competent but accountable to politicians. Consistent with this orientation, they are most likely to have networks based on internal actors. They are very active as policy innovators and have the highest scores for giving advice to politicians among all CEOs. They are least involved in filling classical administrative functions, perhaps in part as a consequence of serving in large municipal government organizations. They have high influence levels but work with politicians who are also very influential. Consequently, there is a high proportion of interdependent CEOs in the committee-leader cities. If they are in the dependent category, they tend to be professional agents rather than political agents, based on their strong commitment to observing professional norms rather than following the preferences of politicians in their conduct in office.

The collective cities give extensive authority to the executive committee. The CEOs are likely to see themselves as agents of the executive committee, responsive to its views and reliant on the top politicians rather than other actors for their ability to function effectively as the CEO. CEOs tend to be isolates in their choice of networking style. They report the lowest activity level in policy innovation, advice to politicians, and classical administration. In these cities, the CEOs tend to have moderate influence. They are close to strong-mayor cities in the proportion of dependent CEOs and the split between political and professional agents. As in strong-mayor cities, interdependent CEOs make up a slight majority.

The council-manager cities place substantial authority in the office of the

CEO and give no executive authority to elected officials. CEOs from these cities experience the lowest levels of uncertainty and party conflict. This form of government is found in countries marked by moderate levels of uncertainty avoidance and power distance. CEOs view themselves as noncongruent public servants stressing their professional independence and their accountability to citizens as well as elected officials. They are also most likely to have inclusive networks with both strong internal and external linkages. Council-manager CEOs are very active in policy innovation and somewhat active in administration. They seek to shape the decision-making process and coordination of work with elected officials but steer clear of offering political advice. These CEOs have the highest influence in all the forms of government, and their relative influence is also the highest. As a consequence, council-manager cities have the fewest dependent CEOs and the most independent types, although the proportion of interdependent types is essentially the same as in committee-leader countries.

Contrasting Institutional Perspectives

The conceptual framework set forth in the introductory chapter indicates the major categories of variables and the relations between them. We posit that leadership at the apex is directly influenced by certain country characteristics: form of government, scope of government, and national cultures. However, these characteristics also were expected to have an indirect effect on leadership at the apex through four sets of intervening variables: administrative values, mayoral leadership, networks and the nature of the political environment.

As the summary indicates, we have demonstrated that different institutional arrangements lead actors to behave in different ways. As we stated in chapter 1, however, it is one thing to demonstrate empirically—as the so-called empirical institutionalists have done—the impact of institutions. Another is to explain how they affect individuals. Explanations require some behavioral assumptions that connect the individual with the overall institutional setup. The conclusion we draw from our study is that rational as well as normative forces are at work here.

First, we deal with the rational types of explanations, or, in the words of March and Olsen (1989), explanations based on a logic of consequentiality. Rational choice institutionalism builds on three assumptions: preferences are exogenous, actors behave rationally, and they are driven by egoistic motives. We suggest that local government CEOs would seek to advance a broadly defined set of interests, including a preference for stability, autonomy, and personal gain.

Second, we focus on normative types of explanation. Normative institutionalism assumes that behavior is based on premises that are shaped by institutions and cultural characteristics rather than being fundamentally based on a pursuit of self-interest. Action is driven by a logic of appropriateness. Appropriateness is shaped not only by the norms of a particular government but also by the standards of organizations that span governmental boundaries, for example, city administrators as a professional group, and national cultural traits. Expectations about how individuals should relate to each other are affected by values regarding power and rules that are widely held in a society.

Rational Choice Institutionalist Explanations

The basic behavioral postulate is that CEOs will try to optimize their position as defined by degree of autonomy, degree of stability, and personal rewards. Promoting personal gain has been central to rational choice approaches. There is little evidence that CEOs are simple budget maximizers, although there are other interests that top administrators presumably do pursue. It is the contention in rational choice theory that bureaucrats follow their own ends and that politicians—the principals—will have great difficulties controlling the bureaucrats—their agents. Bureaucrats have their own goals and they are able to pursue them because of their superior knowledge, that is, information is distributed asymmetrically to the advantage of administrators.

The analysis in this study does not support the picture drawn by the rational choice theory of bureaucrats as budget maximizers (Niskanen 1971). The argument that administrators seek greater well-being in the form of greater salary, power, and reputation by expanding the budget simply does not hold for the local government CEO. Salaries are often fixed by national pay scales, and even if they are not, few politicians would reward their top administrator for expanding the budget. In fact, the opposite is likely to be the case. The power of the CEO is not connected to the size of the budget— whether it be the total budget or the budget of the mayor's or CEO's office. Rather it is connected primarily to the authority conferred by structure, the CEO's ability to create a strong partnership with the mayor, and the CEO's involvement in policy innovation.

To the extent that an information asymmetry exists, it may even have the effect of "budget minimization" as CEOs often see themselves as the guardians who must control the officials who spend without paying much attention to revenue—the city council (Meltsner 1971). One of the Danish interviewees reported regularly underestimating revenues as a way of holding down spending by the city council. The CEO viewed himself as the "defender of the taxpayer." Similarly, another CEO in the United States commented that he never tells the council the "whole truth" about the city's financial reserves because he fears that they will be inclined to view any extra reserves as a resource that could be used for current expenditures.

The CEO as a top administrator has, according to Dunleavy (1991, 179), potential benefits available to him or her from courses of action other than budget increases. For Dunleavy these actions involve bureau shaping: "Rational officials want to work in small, élite, collegial bureaus close to the political power centres" (Dunleavy 1991, 202). To a large extent, this is what CEOs do. Their work is individually innovative, they exhibit a broad scope of concerns, they normally have a low level of public visibility and work closely with the political power centers. Their position at the apex of leadership as the highest ranking appointed officials gives them considerable leeway when it comes to internal reorganization and the assignment of tasks. Thus, CEOs may be interested in protecting their position at the center of power and expanding their freedom to act, but they do not accomplish these ends by expanding budgets.

We assume that CEOs want to pursue certain goals without being substantially constrained by their political, social, and economic environment. They want autonomy to increase their opportunities and dampen the limitations on their choices. There are many key tasks pursued by CEOs that could be enhanced by autonomy; indeed, they may be a mask for a drive for autonomy. Four of the five most important tasks that CEOs emphasize in their daily work are making sure that resources are used efficiently, formulating ideas and visions, influencing decision-making processes in order to secure sensible and efficient solutions, and promoting and encouraging new projects in the community. Similarly, more than four out of five CEOs agree that the administration "should be a prime mover in adapting the municipality to changes in society." As the key official and the prime mover in the society, the CEO has great potential for self-direction. Although autonomy may be used for constructive ends, the rational choice view is that it can be used for self-serving ends and support shirking, steering, or substituting the CEO's goals for those of elected officials.[2]

Increased autonomy, however, may have its costs. The CEOs we studied all work in a system governed by elected politicians. Politicians and political parties are striving for power and votes. As a consequence the sovereign political body is always potentially a source of uncertainty and instability. More than one-third of our 4,000-plus respondents reported that ambiguity about goals and roles at the political level have affected them negatively during recent years to a high or moderately high extent.[3] Whatever the source of instability, CEOs will normally seek to reduce the likelihood that potential threats develop into catastrophes—they will actively try to control their political environment. More than half the CEOs indicated that the task of developing and implementing norms concerning the proper role of politicians vis-à-vis the bureaucrats was of utmost importance or very important in their daily work. The wider socioeconomic environment—private business, citizens, neighborhood groups, local organizations, and upper level governments—may similarly pose threats to the administrative organization. Many CEOs proactively try to negotiate the environment as indicated in the examination of networking behavior. They also prefer having politicians act as a buffer—an ambassador (chap. 7)—between the system and the wider environment. So politicians are sources of instability but they can also be actors who provide stability.

To create a predictable environment is not always costless. Negotiating the environment is often a give-and-take situation where stability may be obtained only at the cost of autonomy.[4] One obvious example is when a hostile environment is eased through concessions of different sorts, which will reduce the options available for the CEO in the longer run. However, the relationship between autonomy and stability is not always a trade-off where an increase in the former will result in lower stability. For example, being involved in and having influence over policy decisions promotes predictability and lessens the likelihood of elected officials moving into a policy-making vacuum to change policy goals. Thus the pursuits of autonomy and stability are intertwined, and both must be sought in ways that do not damage the reputation of the CEO in his or her city or in other cities that may offer opportunities for a better job.

The rational choice institutionalist perspective offers a general interpretation of our findings. Forms of government differentially permit officials to accumulate influence and pursue the ends they prefer. CEOs are as autonomous as they can be under each structure within the constraints of maintaining stability and reputation. CEOs favor rules and norms that promote their preferences, for example, elected officials should stick to general goals and stay out of the administrative realm. The ideal politician is the one who would make life most pleasant for the CEO, although the nature of the preference is adjusted for structural differences. In strong-mayor forms, life may be more predictable if the mayor is involved in administrative details rather than leaving the CEO with ambiguous responsibility for such decisions.[5] The attitudes toward partisan representation by council members seem to reflect a differential calculation of whether parties contribute to stability or instability. In the former situation in committee-leader cities, party participation is legitimate in the eyes of the CEO; in the latter case in council-manager cities, it is not.

Offering political advice can be partly explained by self-serving motives when the payoff in stability and improved interaction with politicians offsets the natural risk of entering the "political room." Their willingness to help the mayor is affected by their dependence on the mayor as shaped in part by structure. As demonstrated in chapter 9, when CEOs have higher influence relative to political leaders, they demonstrate higher autonomy in undertaking policy reviews and display greater independence in offering proposals that are not in line with the intentions of elected officials. This would be expected with greater asymmetry between principal and agent.

Normative Institutionalist Explanations

The normative perspective holds that institutions tend to have a "logic of appropriateness" that influences behavior more than the effort to promote beneficial payoffs. Appropriate behavior upholds values of the institution and helps the institution to succeed. Individuals will make conscious choices but will operate within the parameters set by institutional norms as interpreted by the individual (Peters 1999a, 29). We consider norm-driven behavior to be consistent with the values of democracy and professionalism and to be directed toward supporting other actors and advancing the public interest rather than simply advancing one's own interests. For example, the International City Management Association affirms in its code of ethics that CEOs should "be dedicated to the concepts of effective and democratic local government by responsible elected officials and believe that professional general management is essential to the achievement of this objective." From a calculus of benefits, this tenet supports the employment opportunities of professional public managers and offers a defense of protecting their prerogatives from those who might infringe on their turf. From a normative perspective, the tenet expresses the "internal goods"—the ultimate public-serving purpose—for which the city management profession is organized (Cooper 1987).

The normative institutionalist perspective adds some important insights and counters some of the rational choice views. To return to the key tasks performed by CEOs listed earlier as possible indicators of the desire for autonomy, these tasks also reflect the orientation of the CEO as a shaper of programs, process, and performance. CEOs value the positive contribution that administration makes to society, and many are committed to speaking for the interests of weak groups in society even though they will typically be excluded from the groups that control city governments. CEOs presumably want to contribute to sound governance and to help elected officials. They seek to connect the goals and energy of politicians to the administrative organization, but seek to do so in ways that will not undercut the effectiveness of administrative performance. A high level of involvement and influence may be irrational since it draws attention to CEOs and makes them vulnerable to political attack. There would be safety in anonymity. Still, CEOs are active because it is expected of them.

The ideal politician conforms to the CEO's concept of the best division of labor between politicians and administrators. With regard to the importance of the governor role, if filled appropriately it would insure that democratic direction and political vision are provided to the governmental process. With regard to involvement in administration decisions, the view of CEOs may be different from that of elected officials, but the difference is based on professionally shaped attitudes about what conditions produce administrative performance that is efficient, effective, and fair.

Political advice is limited by the norms of nonpartisanship. CEOs get involved at some risk and in partial conflict with professional norms because of the expectation that they should help make the governmental process operate more smoothly, more democratically, and more competently. They set limits to the extent that groups out of power can be disadvantaged by assistance to incumbents. Self-interest demands that CEOs not be identified with one party or faction, but public interest promotes the creation of a level playing field between competing political forces.

Consistent with the normative institutionalist perspective is the surprising degree of consistency across countries in policy involvement, nonpartisanship, commitment, and support for democratic ideals. It appears that local government professional management has emerged as an institution that shapes the values of individual CEOs in separate countries.[6] There is variation to be sure—reflecting culture, community circumstances, and individual characteristics—but the difference might be greater if structure or culture alone determined attitudes and behavior. The common characteristics seem to reflect public service norms as much as or more than self-interest.

Blending of Perspectives

There is a fine line between consequentiality and appropriateness. Interpretations of some of the major findings of our study illustrate the blending of incentives and norms in understanding the circumstances and behavior of CEOs.

The Managerialization but not Politicization of the CEO

The involvement of CEOs in administration, policymaking, and advice to politicians is dependent on form of government. It might have been supposed that strong mayors politicize their top lieutenant by drawing this official into the political sphere. The CEO is the right hand of the mayor, expected to handle matters as the mayor would prefer. Concern for job security is relatively greater in strong-mayor cities, and CEOs from strong-mayor cities experience higher levels of uncertainty than those from other types of cities. In view of these characteristics, top administrators in strong-mayor cities might be expected to follow the path of least resistance to become politically responsive. The adherence to professional norms of nonpartisanship and independence, however, is virtually as high in these cities as in others, even among political agents. Managerialization rather than politicization occurs, and these CEOs manifest professional commitment to advocacy and policy innovation.

CEOs in the Political Room

Political advice is most common in the committee-leader cities and least common in strong-mayor cities. In collective, council-manager, and committee-leader systems, the greater perceived distinctness between politicians and administrators makes it possible for the CEO to be more involved in political issues. With a stronger professional image and a formally stronger position, they can operate "in" the political realm with less likelihood of being considered "of" the political realm than the mayor-council CEOs. Ironically, greater distinction in roles permits greater overlap in functions. Does this reflect "calculus" or "culture?"

Case studies in Denmark, Holland, and the United States revealed that most CEOs are willing to come into the political room to be accommodating to political leaders on whom they depend without feeling that they are compromising their ideals. The CEOs may secure benefits from the intervention despite the attendant risks. They help politicians avoid problems, which could have negative repercussions for working relationships with administrators. From a normative perspective, they can also rationalize their actions by the beneficial impact of the advice or service they provide. They feel it is professionally appropriate to help strengthen the image of politicians and government itself. They can justify giving aide to a political leader in order to strengthen government and the governmental process. Overall, in these matters in which most CEOs feel they can appropriately get involved, they enter the political room to help their partner in governance. In the process, they also help themselves.

Politicians in the Administrative Room

In the consideration of CEO views of the ideal politician, two atypical preferences emerged. One was the acceptance of a large role for elected officials in administrative decisions in strong-mayor cities. The second was the high level of support for a party spokesperson role for council members in committee-leader cities. Each offers an interesting situation for examining institutional models.

In strong-mayor cities, CEOs do look to leading politicians for administrative direction in establishing rules for administrators as well as resolving specific decisions, and they accept that politicians fill the ombudsman role. The noninterference norms to which other CEOs are generally committed are weak in these cities. Of course, under the formal arrangement in strong-mayor cities, the mayor is acting in ways that are consistent with legal authority. CEOs accept this involvement. Doing so reflects an not only an acceptance of reality, but also an acceptance of the norm of political supremacy.

Politicians as Partisan Leaders

CEOs in strong-mayor cities may well want the mayor to resolve specific matters but not do so on a partisan basis. In the council-manager cities, CEOs want leading politicians to be governors and trustees for citizens rather than active representatives who stress ombudsman or partisan roles. Elected officials should provide broad direction but not be influenced by party considerations or campaign promises.

This is in contrast to the CEOs in the committee-leader cities who respect the partisan perspective of elected officials but want autonomy for themselves and no interference from politicians in administrative details. They expect that council members will be representatives of parties—articulators of party principles and programs—but do not want them to get involved in specific decisions or serve as ombudsmen for citizens who have complaints. In these cities politicians are heavily engaged in the day-to-day operation of government through the system of standing committees. Free-floating politicians, who seek to advance their own electoral fortunes, could soon screw up the system. Parties based on ideologies and strong party discipline represent a stabilizing mechanism which creates a more stable and predictable environment for the administrator. Long-established corporatist arrangements in many of these countries (Peters and Pierre, 1998, 235) may reinforce the legitimacy of organized collective involvement by outside groups in the governmental process. In a sense, appropriateness and self-interest are interlinked and the distinction is blurred.

Theoretical Models for Understanding Local Democracy

The characteristics of CEOs and interactions of elected officials and the top appointed administrator in local government are best understood in terms of the model of complementarity of politics and administration, which builds on and expands the model of overlapping roles introduced in chapter 2. Complementarity recognizes that there is interdependency and reciprocal influence between elected officials and administrators (Svara 1999a, 2001a). Elected officials and administrators maintain distinct roles based on their unique perspectives and values and the differences in their formal position, but the functions they perform necessarily overlap. As a normative model, complementarity presumes that administrators respect political supremacy and the need for accountability to elected officials, but they also understand their accountability to the public. Administrators support the democratic process and seek to serve the public as well as to serve elected officials. In their role as shapers and implementers of policy, administrators seek to advance professional standards and goals and promote the public interest. In their dealings with elected officials and the public, administrators are independent and honest and act in an ethically principled way.

The findings from this study add substantial new evidence to support the model and the contention that it generally explains political-administrative relations. Administrators are independent with a separate professional identity. They articulate their distinct perspective in the governmental process. CEOs are committed to a high level of advocacy. Most agree that administration should be a prime mover in adapting the municipality to changes in society. A smaller majority supports the idea of working to promote the interests of lower social and economic strata in society. Most believe that they should not limit their recommendations to proposals that are consistent with the intentions of politicians.

Evidence of the deference to elected officials is present as well. Most CEOs feel that they should not initiate policy review without political direction. There is interdependency between elected officials and administrators. CEOs consider the leading politicians to be highly important to their success. One can infer the dependence of elected officials from the administrators' practice of offering advice in dealing with sensitive political choices and their formative role in shaping the policy-making process.

There is also strong evidence of reciprocal influence between elected officials and administrators. Although the relative balance of influence varies, virtually all CEOs have at least moderate levels of influence in policy making. Officials have overlapping functions as elected officials provide political oversight of administration and administrators are involved in policy making. Most CEOs accept a moderate level of elected official involvement in certain management decisions, and politicians tend to be even more involved than administrators prefer. Furthermore, CEOs are extensively involved in policy development that is also the central function of elected officials.

Along with extensive interaction and interdependence, there is simultaneously distinctness in attributes and cooperation in relationships. Elected officials and administrators maintain distinct roles based on their unique perspectives and values and the differences in their formal positions.[7] Almost all CEOs feel that politicians should set policy and not decide routine matters. They see elected officials playing the roles of governors and representatives. For their part, most CEOs believe that they should be nonpartisan and make recommendations based on expertise. Distinction, however, does not mean distance in the relationship. CEOs report high levels of cooperation with elected officials, and most have not been adversely affected by an unclear division of labor between elected officials and administrators. The two sets of officials and the political and administrative functions each provides are intertangled but identifiable as separate parts. Tied together in a cooperative relationship, each complements the other to form the whole of the governmental process.

Coexisting with the norms that shape these attitudes and behaviors are considerations based on self-interest and assessment of consequences. Complementarity assumes that administrators (and politicians) are not selfish, but it does not presume that they are selfless. It does not place primary emphasis on control and compliance, but it does not ignore their importance. Complementarity seeks to accommodate both Finer's (1941) emphasis on external control and Friedrich's (1940) call for administrators to impose the inner check on their behavior based on professional responsibility.

A General Framework of Understanding
Political-Administrative Relations

The objection might be raised that complementarity is generally applicable but can not encompass all the types of CEO partnerships—dependent, interdependent, and independent—despite the arguments in chapter 9. The match between the interdependent CEOs and complementarity is obvious, and a majority of CEOs fall into the interdependent type. Are the other models from chapter 2, however, needed to describe the other types? To sort out what kinds of relationships are and are not compatible with complementarity, a general framework can be used to understand the full range of political-administrative relationships.

The relationship between elected officials and administrators could be seen as simply the interaction between political control and professional independence. Control involves the capacity to set direction and maintain oversight. Independence involves asserting professional perspectives in policy formation and adhering to professional standards in implementation. If one explains relationships only in terms of what March and Olson (1995, 7) have called "exchange perspectives," the interplay of these two forces of control and independence could lead to dominance of one over the other or a balancing of the two (Krause 1999). In the language of public choice institutionalism, we see the actors' exogenous values rooted in self-interest at work. Using relative influence alone to determine the nature of relationships would be consistent with this perspective. The dependent administrator—particularly the political agent—would be dominated, the independent administrator would be self-controlled, and the interdependent administrator would be part of a balanced relationship in which each side impacts the other. To use the models from chapter 2, the responsive administrator, the autonomous administrator, and administrators who maintain separate roles would be outside the boundaries of complementarity.

The analysis of characteristics of the CEO partnership types has shown, however, that other factors are at work. The dependent administrators are not dominated and the independent administrators are not in control. The evidence presented in this study indicates that there are few CEOs who match the characteristics of the models other than the overlapping roles model. The resolution of this contradiction between theoretical expectations and empirical findings comes from a different perspective on relationships. Officials do not simply seek to promote their interests in conflict with other actors. The normative institutionalist perspective would add that officials seek to act in terms of norms of appropriate behavior that will make institutions work—endogenous values shaped by institutions (March and Olson 1995, 25–28). In addition to the value that reflects the primary self-interest of each set of officials vis-à-vis the other, that is, control by politicians and independence for administrators, there is a value that expresses and supports the reciprocal nature of the relationship. The reciprocating values are respect for administrators on the part of politicians and commitment to accountability on the part of administrators. These values add balance and constraint to the relationship.

A case could still be made for the public choice perspective. One might argue that the driving interests of each set of officials are self-limiting. Neither control nor independence can be pushed to the absolute limit without fundamentally altering or destroying the relationship. Miller (2000) transforms the standard principal-agent relationship to argue that it is necessary for the agent to resist the control that principals might seek to exert that would have the result of undermining both democratic purpose and optimal allocation of resources. "To be efficient," Miller (2000, 325) concludes, "governments should and sometimes do devise constitutional checks and balances that constrain rather than unleash popular democratic control over bureaucracy." For bureaucracy to check the particularistic and self-serving interests of politicians, top administrators must be separated from politics and relatively autonomous. The findings of this research, however, show that leaders at the apex of local government interact extensively and manifest reciprocal influence. There is evidence that officials have positive reasons for maintaining the close relationship that go beyond enlightened self-interest. In political-administrative relations, one finds neither top-down control of administrators nor bureaucratic self-control, but rather an integration of the two in a "dialogue" process, as Mayntz and Scharpf (1975, 96–105) argue based on their study of policy making in Germany. The reciprocating values help to explain why officials restrain themselves while engaging in extensive interaction, that is, why politicians do not undermine independence and why administrators do not undercut control.

Thus, a new framework is proposed in which interplay between control and independence may be restrained by the reciprocating values of respect and deference. The reciprocating values are in a sense "contained" within the limits of control or independence, that is, when control is too low, administrative accountability is absent and vice versa. Thus, one could argue that the relationship is essentially the result of relative strength of the actors with respect or accountability abandoned when the other actor is not strong enough to compel it. Another perspective more compatible with complementarity, however, is that the reciprocating value permits the other actor's driving impulse to be effective. The politicians' respect for administrators permits independence, and commitment to accountability by administrators permits control. Regarding the latter, Friedrich (1940, 19) observed that responsible administrative conduct "is not so much enforced as it is elicited." Administrators choose to comply.

Combining all four values produces an array of possible political-administrative relationships. These are displayed in figure 10.1. Any of these combinations is possible if the defining conditions are present. The political dominance that results from high political control and low administrative independence is the condition attacked by the reformers in the United States from the Progressive Era to the present because of concern for loss of administrative competence and the potential for political corruption. Bureaucratic autonomy is feared by the critics of the administrative state who argue that administrators are self-controlling and advance agency interests rather than the public interest. In both these situations, the key reciprocating value is not present: politicians do not respect administrators, or administrators are not committed to accountability. A conceptual possibility is the combination of low control and low independence to produce a live-and-let-live attitude among officials. Presumably a condition of governmental drift would prevail or the limited ability to impact the other officials could produce stalemate.

The largest space in the figure is the zone of complementarity. When elected officials have moderate to high levels of control and administrators have moderate to high levels of independence, the conditions of complementarity can be found. The seemingly incompatible elements of these characteristics are overcome by the reciprocating values. Elected officials have some level of respect for the competence and commitment of administrators; ad-

Elected Officials: Degree of Control

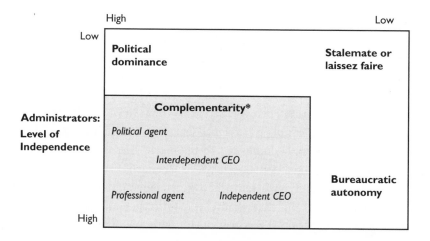

*Within this area, officials have reciprocating values. Politicians respect administrative competence and commitment, and administrators are committed to accountability and responsiveness.

Source: Adapted from Svara (2001a). Reprinted with permission from the American Society for Public Administration, *Public Administration Review*, March/April 2001.

Figure 10.1 Variations in the interaction between politicians and administrators

ministrators have some level of commitment to being accountable to elected officials. The evidence presented in chapter 9 indicates that most interactions among officials most of the time reflect complementarity.

The types of CEO partnerships reflect differences in the nature of complementarity. It is possible to distinguish whether there is relatively more control being exerted by politicians or relatively more independence being exercised by administrators or an even blending of the two. The dependent CEOs are differentiated by the degree of independence they have—the political agents have less independence and the professional agents have more—but both types are subject to high control. The interdependent CEOs have moderate independence but are somewhat less controlled than the dependent types, and the independent CEOs have high independence and are subject to the least control. Still, the same fundamental point applies to all governments characterized by complementarity. Leadership in governmental affairs arises from the blending of political and administrative leadership.

The framework presented in figure 10.1 indicates other possible combinations that would fall outside the bounds of complementarity. Given the large sample size in this study, the existence of "outlier" types can be identified, as noted in chapter 9. There may be CEOs who are controlled so completely that they are politically dominated and their professional standards are threatened. Approximately 3 percent of CEOs have much less influence than elected officials in both areas of policy and also are only moderately involved in policy innovation. These apparent "passive servants," however, have attitudes and values that are indistinct from other dependent CEOs. It does not appear that these CEOs are politically dominated to the extent that their professional standards are undermined by politicians. The dependent CEOs are consistent with complementarity even when they have little relative influence.

At the other end of the scale would be self-directed administrators who have such high influence that they may operate beyond political control, that is, autonomous bureaucrats. As is the case with extremely dependent CEOs, the number of CEOs who have much higher influence than elected officials in both budgetary and economic development decisions is quite small. Less than 2 percent of the CEOs outside of Ireland (but 15 percent in Ireland) have much more influence (at least 50 points higher) than the most influential elected official in both budgeting and economic development decision-making. These CEOs, however, are not extreme in their attitudes about roles and power. The presence of an autonomous bureaucrat who runs governmental affairs with little control being exerted by politicians appears to be even more rare in most countries than the politically dominated type of CEO. Still, those who fall into this small group have attitudes that could make it possible to justify ignoring weak political officials. The key factor that would keep these administrators within the bounds of complementarity would be their respect for political accountability.

This examination of possible outlier types reinforces the main conclusion. Although relationships and CEO characteristics differ, the variation for virtually all CEOs occurs within the boundaries of complementarity. These boundaries indicate strong but not overwhelming control by elected officials who are restrained by respect for administrators, on the one hand, and extensive but not unfettered independence by administrators with the restraint of respect for accountability to politicians. The largest number of administrators is right in the middle of this model of interaction. They are interdependent in their relationships with elected officials—tending toward neither dependence or independence.

In sum, although complementarity is based on a model of overlapping roles between politicians and administrators, it incorporates features from each of the other models. For two elements to complement each other, they must maintain their distinctness, and, therefore, aspects of the separate roles model are found in complementarity. The interaction and sharing that are outstanding features of complementarity do not represent the merger of politics and administration. Clearly CEOs prefer that politicians stay out of administrative matters, and they stress the importance of their own nonpartisanship. These attitudes coexist with complex forms of interaction and overlapping roles. Elected officials do not fully correspond to the administrator's ideal image in their involvement in administrative decisions. Although CEOs may not make the connection in their own minds, the mayors who are rated as more effective by CEOs are also more likely to be involved in administrative details—but not exclusively concerned with specific issues. The boundary between politics and administration is porous but it continues to be important. Negotiating the location of the line and what passes through it—involvement in administrative and management decisions by politicians and policy innovation and political advice and service by CEOs—is a key aspect of the dynamics of leadership at the apex.

Complementarity also entails responsiveness, not only an obligation to implement the policies of elected officials but a commitment to help politicians articulate and accomplish their goals. The emphasis CEOs place on the governor role may be interpreted as an effort to keep elected officials distant from the discretionary choices of administrators, but it also represents a preference for politicians to set the goals for government. Politicians must give directions for administrators to be responsive, and administrators are willing to help politicians specify these directions in ways that are in keeping with their political goals. CEOs at the same time seek to maintain their own perspective and their autonomy. They have their own view of the public interest and are generally inclined to advocate it. They exercise professional judgment rather than basing recommendations on the policy preferences of elected officials. They help politicians express their goals, but they do not feel bound by them in their consideration of alternatives to propose. Many seek to develop networks of supporters inside and outside of government that may enhance their freedom of action. Finally, they have influence over policy as the autonomous model suggests. Some have more, some less, but all have at least moderately great clout in the decisions of their government. But that influence is not exerted unilaterally nor primarily to advance the CEO's own interests, but rather is exerted reciprocally and responsibly.

Complementarity encompasses key aspects of all of the models of political-administrative relations. The models based on separate roles, responsive administrators, and autonomous administrators are useful as ideal types that identify theoretically possible clusters of characteristics. The interplay of control and independence and the extent of respect and deference can produce conditions that would be conducive to the emergence of CEOs that match any of these models. The greatest likelihood, however, is that officials will have a complementary relationship bringing aspects of separation, responsiveness, and autonomy in varying degrees to their fundamental condition of overlapping roles.

Comparison to Other Models

Complementarity has greater conceptual and empirical validity than alternative models. The dichotomy model—in its strict version a caricature of early efforts to differentiate the interconnected roles of politicians and administrators—was never conceptually sound nor has it been empirically verified. The political agents in our model approximate the influence differential that the dichotomy might have required but the support for holding views that match those of politicians and the extensive policy involvement of political agents are not consistent with the dichotomy.

There are two variants on the dichotomy, but they do not fare much better when subjected to empirical examination. First, a modified version featuring "classical bureaucrats" that stresses separateness but impotence for administrators does not match the close interactions found at the local level. The professional agents approximate the classical bureaucrats in their support for public as well as political accountability, but even these CEOs are not highly separated from politicians, simply somewhat more detached than other types. Second, the principal-agent model assumes a hierarchical and one-way relationship. It is a more realistic approach than the dichotomy because it recognizes that political direction may be resisted or undermined. It is deficient, however, because it assumes that a hierarchical relationship is the norm. Principal-agent models are used to analyze the control (or lack thereof) of exogenous political authorities over administrative agencies. A variation presumes clear separation and administrative autonomy, disguised by the myth of dichotomy that helps administrators prevent political subversion of policy commitments (Miller 2000). Both alternatives, however, are based on a degree of separation of spheres and a one-direction flow of inputs from politicians to administrators that are not consistent with our findings.

Aberbach, Putnam, and Rockman (1981) in their images 2 and 3 reflect a complementary view of the relationship and present two different versions of the distinct orientations of each set of officials. The contributions of each set of officials that they identify, however, do not match the attitudes and behavior of local officials. According to image 2, politicians bring value perspectives to the political process and make value choices, whereas administrators stress facts and choice based on objective evidence. This study as well as others shows that administrators are not value-free. For example, CEOs rank fairly high in advocacy. Administrators stress objective evidence, but they are not value-free. Rather, they bring different professionally based values to the political process, and most do not agree that it is necessarily advantageous to have the same views as their political masters.

Nor can politicians and administrators in local government be distinguished based on who brings energy and equilibrium to the political process. Most mayors do not perform well in providing visionary leadership, and the council's performance in setting long-range goals is fairly weak if one can generalize from the assessment of Danish and American council members. On the other hand, CEOs commonly consider it very important to formulate new ideas and visions and to promote new projects in the community. Most feel that it is very important in their work to be able to influence the future development of their community.[8] Thus, CEOs are also a source of energy and innovation in the governmental process, although the nature of their innovations is presumably different from those that politicians can potentially raise. They also use different methods and arguments to promote their initiatives. Furthermore, their creativity and innovation may be directed to conserving an existing mission (Terry 1995). Equilibrium cannot be maintained simply by passively defending the status quo. CEOs contribute to equilibrium as they absorb and incorporate the proposals of politicians for short-term action, but they also energize the governmental process.

Dunn (1997, 162) observes in Australian national government that administrators are commonly invited to the "policy-making table." In an approach that approximates the complementarity model, he does not see this interaction of administrators and elected officials in policy deliberation as a contradiction of neutral competence among administrators. Indeed, it is a condition for being involved. Elected officials feel that administrators can be included without being another partisan with political stakes in the outcome.

Krause (1999) pursues a line of argument that is very similar to the complementary model, although with important differences. He presents a "dynamic systems perspective of governmental institutions." The idea of simple hierarchical control (or deviation from it) is replaced with dynamic feedback and mutual adaptation when politicians and agencies each influence the preferences of the other. Rather than one side controlling the other, "a more temperate, symbiotic relationship transpires among agencies and political overseers" (118). Still, values that affect behavior are largely absent from Krause's model. The interaction between officials is the interplay of "stimuli" (104), and each set of officials is seen as responding "to unanticipated movements in another institution's environment" (110). Krause notes that "professional norms" lead agencies to implement policies "in a manner that is not always consistent with the principal-agent paradigm of control" (125), but he does not consider what these norms are and whether they simply screen out political stimuli or promote public-serving behavior. Krause, in contrast to other empirical studies in political science, begins to identify for agencies "a legitimate role in matters of policy administration" but he does not specify what it is.

In contrast to the dynamic systems model, complementarity assumes reciprocating values, not just constraint of self-interest or mutual adjustment. It assumes that public administration professionalism is a bundle of characteristics including expertise, substantive values, and public service values. Under normal circumstances, control and independence are not alternatives but rather coexist. Support for accountability is not a concession to political power but a norm that is integral to the values of administrators. Independence is not defiance of control but rather adherence to the norms that administrators must observe in order to fill their institutional role.

Politicians also manifest reciprocating values. Administrative independence is both secured through the power of administrators and also allowed by the deference of politicians. Why have administrators if politicians are not going to listen to them and permit them to do what is professionally right? Political control does not necessarily imply the subversion of professionalism. Although political dominance as well as administrative defiance are possible, they both violate the norms of the democratic governmental process. Furthermore, this study shows that the patterns of behavior that deviate from complementarity are extremely rare in western local governments.

Implications for the Study for Local Democracy

The findings of the study raise questions about the nature of the administrator's role. Has the CEO become indistinguishable from politicians? The substantial influence of CEOs and the resources on which they can draw could make the CEO a threat to the democratic process or a non-neutral actor who favors certain political groups or ends. Finally, the findings have implications for our understanding of the characteristics of top politicians and their behavior. One can ask whether potential threats to democracy arise not from the "commissions" of top administrators but rather from the "omissions" of leading politicians. To summarize this section, recommendations regarding the respective contributions of elected officials and top administrators will be considered.

Are Administrators a Threat to Democracy?

In view of simplistic models in which administrators are passive agents who implement the instructions of elected officials, the idea that some CEOs are highly active in policymaking and have greater influence than elected officials may seem antidemocratic. It could appear that bureaucratic mandarins are dominating political outcomes. Even equal influence could put political control at risk in view of the considerable resources CEOs possess to shape policy choices and determine the exact form of policy implementation and their extensive opportunities for exercising discretion in the allocation of resources.

The simple answer is that CEOs do not challenge the authority of elected officials by their own influence. First, they are filling the active role intended for them in the design of governmental forms that combine elected officials and generalist administrators. Second, their activity level does not supplant that of politicians. Indeed, it may enhance it. Third, the influence of the CEO in budgeting is uniformly high; it is the influence of elected officials that varies. Fourth, in economic development policymaking, the influence of the CEO moves up and down together with the influence of the mayor—not against it. Finally, it is important to recognize what equal or greater influence means. CEOs are not able to say "Do it my way!" if they have superior influence or to check the council if they have equal influence. Rather, even CEOs with equal or higher influence must use tact and indirection along with balanced presentations of evidence to win the support of the council.

The more fundamental response draws on the concept of complementarity. Administrators enable politicians in the democratic state. The rise of administration is often presented as if it represented the loss of democratic innocence (e.g., see Long 1965, 117). An alternative view is to see the growth of administration as an essential part of the expansion of governmental functions and the increase in the number of channels through which citizens can communicate with government. It is administration that creates the capacity for collective action in society.[9] Anticipating an argument for complementarity, Long notes that professional administrators "do not replace but they add importantly to the democratic elective model of how to achieve the public interest" (1965, 119).

In addition, CEOs are making the kinds of contributions that elected officials prefer. The data sources used in this study do not offer any additional confirmation of this assertion, but studies of U.S. council members (Svara 1990a, 1991, 1999b) indicate that elected officials recognize that top administrators are highly involved in setting goals and making policy. Indeed, in the most recent of these studies in the United States, the council members give the city manager involvement ratings higher than their own in these areas. When asked separately about their preferred level of activity, council members do not prefer less involvement for the city manager although they would like to see themselves making a greater contribution.

In conclusion, active CEOs do not supplant elected officials. They bring their own distinct perspective, knowledge, and expertise to the relationship. As long as they respect accountability to elected officials and the public, they work with the mayor and council in a complementary relationship.

Are CEOs Neutral?

Even if CEOs do not supplant elected officials, there are two other issues to consider. In this section, we discuss whether top administrators take sides or whether they maintain neutrality in making their substantial contribution. In the next section, the issue considered is whether politicians in general and mayors in particular make such limited contributions that administrators are able to (or forced to) fill a leadership vacuum.

When considering neutrality, it is important to acknowledge the value commitments that administrators have. Rather than consider neutrality to mean a value-free or valueless orientation, it should be defined to emphasize a nonpartisan orientation together with professional norms such as openness, fairness, and objectivity, and professional values such as the importance of offering leadership to solve problems and the desirability of promoting social equity. Neutrality requires that administrators be committed to be honest and independent-minded in their interactions with politicians. Otherwise, administrators become mere instruments who mindlessly carry out instructions from elected officials. They should offer their best judgment equally to all politicians about whether and how their policies can serve the public and accomplish their intended objectives. They should also offer their recommendations about community needs and appropriate policy remedies equally to any political directors. They may take up the cause of a political leader, but they cannot lay down their professional commitment to fairness, honesty, and objectivity in so doing (Nalbandian 2000).

Another dimension of neutrality is the extent to which "neutral" administrators abstain from getting involved in sensitive issues and taking sides in political contests. There appear to be three different levels of neutrality. The behavior that minimally qualifies as neutrality is equal service without favoritism *over time* to *incumbent* leaders in authoritative policy-making positions. CEOs will offer their best advice and service to whomever is in charge regardless of party or other political characteristics. They will help incumbents but not actively or directly oppose or disadvantage challengers. The second level of stricter neutrality incorporates the first but adds limitations on providing advantage to one political actor over others. Administrators should not give advantages to incumbents by the political advice and service that is provided. Rather, they should seek to maintain a level playing field for incumbent and challenger alike. They should also seek to treat in an even-handed way the interests of officeholders and citizens. Still, even these CEOs may get involved in discussions of how to handle difficult situations and to warn elected officials when they are moving into political trouble.

A possible third and even stricter level of neutrality that would proscribe any kind of political advice or service seems both unrealistic and unnecessary to insure fair competition and administrative accountability. CEOs would decline to participate in discussions with any political overtones. Although this level may be the standard that local government CEOs have been expected to follow, it is not the standard they have met. CEOs appear to adopt either standard one or two. The notion that CEOs are not just neutral but thoroughly apolitical assigns them a position on the sidelines, detached from the close interaction with elected officials that the position requires if the CEO is to realize the potential leadership inherent in the position. There are close connections between top administrators and leading politicians at the apex of local government. The neutral professional administrator brings public service values to the political process rather than being swayed by partisan or ideological partiality and does not seek to determine who his or her political master will be. The neutral CEO does not, however, shrink from making active contributions to the political process.

Are Politicians Making the Appropriate Contribution to the Democratic Process?

CEOs may not supplant politicians, but they may still be taking over too much responsibility as a result of shortcomings among political leaders. If the mayor does not provide appropriate leadership, the CEO's role could expand to inappropriate proportions. One might be concerned that independent CEOs and perhaps some interdependent CEOs paired with an ineffective political leader could be taking over the roles of elected officials in policy formation by filling a policy vacuum. Before turning to consideration of the contributions of elected officials, one may observe that it is unlikely that CEOs have become uncontrolled policy mandarins. Administrators do not develop and initiate projects in the same way that politicians do, nor do they actually make policy in the sense of fashioning goals or programs unilaterally without approval of elected officials. Furthermore, if told they are filling a vacuum, CEOs would probably be incredulous when they think about the conditions in which they operate (even though they might agree in the abstract). CEOs hardly fill an empty or pressure-free space.

It is likely that roles have shifted, reflecting changes in the political process and in the problems cities confront. In an earlier time, elected officials were governors and CEOs were policy proposers operating within a framework of goals (Svara 2000). This division of leadership functions may also have been better suited for an earlier period in the development of the administrative state when a key governance task was to identify what problems government would address and how extensive services should be. It is natural that elected officials would take the lead in decisions to alter the purpose and scope of government.

The policy process is more open, and the issues to be resolved have changed. The council members are as attentive or more attentive to the citizens as they are to the CEO. They are often activists with their own political agenda. They are also more concerned with handling pressing but possibly ephemeral current issues than with confronting long-term problems. The council listens to what the CEO has to offer but is wary of accepting his or her advice and preoccupied with pressing issues that the CEO may not consider to be important. CEOs fill a vacuum in the sense that they are more vocal and visible and more often contribute ideas formerly offered by elected officials. They are influential—perhaps more so than in the past—but their impact on decision making is less predictable given the commitments elected officials have to specific policy outcomes and the wide array of media and constituency inputs they are processing. Thus, the CEO is competing with other sources of information and influence. The elected officials pay some attention to the CEO—the amount presumably reflects the CEO's influence—but they are attentive to other actors and other agendas as well.

Furthermore, CEOs will differ in their capacity to keep deliberations about policy in the open (or in administrative rooms) and out of the political room. Even independent CEOs are unlikely to be able always to determine the location or nature of the deliberations. Thus, all CEOs operate in settings they do not control. Although simple hierarchical direction is less likely as administrative influence increases, indeterminacy and unpredictability add to the capacity of elected officials to control administrators.

In view of these conditions, what contributions do and should elected officials make? Innovative or visionary mayors put new ideas onto the policy agenda; they do not just bring current problems to the table. Offering general proposals based on popular support exhilarates other elected officials and citizens, and articulating goals creates a heightened sense of common purpose. Still, with such leadership or without it, the basic course the city is on or the functions it performs continue. The "working vision" that reflects past political and administrative consensus persists.

All officials contribute to shaping, preserving, and adjusting the working mission of the city. The respective contributions vary across different institutional forms and with the characteristics of incumbents and communities. We should not stop encouraging elected officials, particularly mayors, to be visionaries, but we should not be surprised or distressed when they are not. As a U.S. county administrator from a very large jurisdiction observed, "Politicians do not run for office to be visionaries."[10] The emphasis on being "governors" may distance elected officials from their constituents (Bledsoe 1993). Council members now frequently are "electoral activists" who seek to serve their communities by pursuing elected office rather than trustees who seek to be detached governors of their communities (Svara 1999b).

Purpose is not lost and democracy is not threatened by periods of time without visionary elected leadership as long as creative ideas come from some source, including from administrators. In addition, democracy is protected as long as politicians continue to do the things they are likely to do as electorally accountable officials. These contributions include insuring that policy decisions are acceptable to voters, that pressing current issues are not ignored, and that citizens are not mistreated as the city carries out its work. Elected officials can and should affect the momentum and focus of government, but it is neither likely nor desirable to expect them to fundamentally redefine the purpose of government on a regular basis. We should give politicians credit for doing the job they do rather than finding fault with them for not meeting our heroic expectations for them.

Respective Contributions of Officials

Complementarity is sharing the functions of governance. Elected officials check and approve the policies of their cities, they bring current problems to the governmental agenda, they link citizens to government and investigate their complaints, they make some specific decisions, they act as ambassadors for their governments in dealings with the outside world, and some act as party spokespersons. Some leading politicians propose new policy initiatives and help to redefine the vision of their city.

CEOs bring professional norms to the governmental process and offer policy proposals on a regular basis for both specific projects and broad goals. In this sense they bring values and energy to the process. In view of the focus of elected officials on pressing issues and constituency concerns, it is important that CEOs organize a policy agenda with recommendations on how to meet prior commitments and proposals for meeting long-term needs. This is a key aspect of complementarity because administrators offer policy proposals that elected officials are unlikely to make on their own. When the mayor brings to the office visionary leadership and the capability to mobilize public and council support, the CEO can work even more effectively to help shape the specific content of the mayor's agenda. Beyond making specific proposals, administrators create a sense of purpose and coherence in the governmental process. They stress long-term solutions and adherence to previous commitments. They help to shape vision but do so more by making sense of the actual and linking specific choices in the present to long-term intentions for the future than by envisioning an ideal future. In this sense, they bring equilibrium and stability to the process. Beyond contributions regarding the content of policy and the impetus for making policy decisions, CEOs also contribute advice about the process of making policy and to differing degrees help elected officials deal with political problems. In their advice to politicians, CEOs help their partner in governance make difficult decisions and handle complex situations.

Differences between Top Administrators at the Local and Higher Levels of Government

The findings from this study further substantiate the importance of characteristics that may differentiate local administrators from those in provincial or national government. Local CEOs have a broad view of the governmental process and work to integrate its various parts, they are committed to ideals for the way government operates and what it accomplishes, and they have a long-term orientation. More research is needed to determine whether there are similarities or differences across levels when controlling for the scope of their position, their proximity to key politicians, the level of political leadership, and the trust in the relationship between politicians and administrators. It is possible that the importance of national culture will make officials in one country from different levels more alike than local officials from different countries.

The differences in the characteristics of political leaders at the national level and resources available to elected officials illustrate differences and similarities in the interactions of top officials at the national compared to the local level of government. Presumably, there is greater capacity for innovative leadership by politicians in national than in local government. The generalization that politicians provide energy to the governmental process and administrators provide continuity may be more appropriate to national than local government. In addition, roles may be somewhat more clearly separated and the potential for tension in the relationship may be greater in some countries than it is generally in local government. Still, even in the United States where separation of powers and divided governments can contribute to distrust of permanent staff at the national level, it is common that grudging respect develops between political appointees and civil servants over time as they have more experience working with each other (Aberbach and Rockman 2000, 171). Although interactions may be closer and interdependency greater at the local level, the fusion of perspectives and close connections observed in national governments by Self (1972), Aberbach, Putnam, and Rockman (1981), Mayntz and Scharpf (1975), and Aberbach and Rockman (2000) among others, suggests that complementarity in relationships is a general phenomenon at the apex of all governments.

Conclusion

This study of the role of administration in the political process establishes more clearly than do previous studies that top administrators are partners in leadership with the mayor and other leading politicians. Leadership in government arises from and is conditioned by a relationship that is generally characterized by interaction, interdependency, reciprocal influence, and mutual respect between politicians and administrators. Although there are differences in authority between the two sets of officials and formal subordination of the top administrator to elected officials, they have a complementary relationship in which each needs the other and each makes unique contributions to the other in conducting both shared and separate tasks. Although differences in relative influence divide CEOs into those who are dependent, interdependent, and independent compared to elected officials, virtually all the CEOs in the study operate within the boundaries of complementarity.

Despite these variations in the type of partner the CEO is, similarities among the types outweigh the differences. CEOs are a professional group that exhibits similar characteristics across country and governmental structure. They have presumably always operated in a complementary relationship with elected officials. Although we do not have systematic data to confirm it, it seems likely that there has been a shift from the dependent type to the interdependent and independent types as the capability of CEOs has increased, as the scope of government programs has expanded, and as the problems faced by local governments have become more complex.

This study reinforces the importance of complementarity as a framework for understanding the relationships among officials. Complementarity entails ongoing interaction between elected officials and administrators—a continuous dialogue among officials about governance. Administrators help to shape policy and give it specific content and meaning in the process of implementation. Elected officials oversee implementation and probe specific complaints about poor performance, and they seek to correct problems by fine-tuning either on the policy side or the administrative side. New policies and services are defined by elected officials with administrative input and initiative, and they are implemented or delivered by staff with continuous political oversight. With extensive interaction, the knowledge and values of those who do the ongoing work of government complement the knowledge and values of those who ultimately set the course for government and ensure that it remains on course. The complementarity of politics and administration holds that elected officials and administrators—both in regular communication with citizens—need and help each other in a partnership for governance. Dividing the partners or skewing the relationship in one direction or the other means that an important contribution is missing.

The partnership between officials realizes the potential in the modern administrative state to combine the qualities of political and professional leadership, each of which is democratically grounded in distinctive ways. The balance of the two elements can easily be tilted in one direction or the other, compromising either democratic or professional values, but the two are not inherently in conflict.

Rather, political and professional elements are held together by mutual dependency and dynamic tension. They come together in resolving questions about policy and the direction of city government. They interact extensively—probably more than CEOs would like—in dealing with problems of service delivery. CEOs empathize with politicians over how to handle sensitive political situations. Most are willing to help politicians work their way through political problems as long as doing so does not cause harm to other political actors. Although they may not acknowledge it, professional administrators surely gain increased sensitivity to the public opinion and political forces by their exchanges with elected officials over the problems that politicians encounter.

To meet the increasing challenges faced by local government, elected officials together with administrators need to make policy that is more clear, focused on results, and strategic. CEOs are uniquely qualified and situated to help elected officials to do this. Administrators guided by elected officials and their own interactions with citizens need to carry out policies with even greater and more clearly demonstrated attention to effectiveness, efficiency, responsiveness, and equity. Together, officials need to search for an appropriate and democratically acceptable determination of the scope of governmental services and the most accountable and cost-effective modes for delivering them. Governance at all levels of government is advanced, not by ignoring or dismantling the relationship between politicians and bureaucrats, but by recognizing and enhancing their shared leadership.

This study supports a number of important claims. Institutions matter, and the choice of political-administrative structure makes a difference. Leaders vary in their characteristics and performance, and these variations matter within the broad parameters set by structure. When explaining motivations for behavior, one should look for a blend of exogenous interests and endogenous norms rather than using one explanation to the exclusion of the other. Rather than approaching public administration with a conceptual framework of dichotomy and looking for exceptions to it, it is more appropriate to use a framework of complementarity and examine variations within it. Finally, we immodestly propose that the characteristics of top administrators we have identified be used as the basis for developing hypotheses about the values and behavior of public administrators generally. Further research that compares officials within and across institutions, levels of government, and countries can extend or revise these generalizations drawn from observing officials at the apex of local government.

Technical Appendix

This appendix contains additional information concerning the survey, the intensive interviews, chapters 3–8, and a list of participants in the U.Di.T.E. Leadership Study.

The Survey

The surveys in the fourteen countries were conducted from November 1995 until May 1997.[1] A joint questionnaire was prepared during 1995 by the European countries involved in the U.Di.T.E. Leadership Study. In January of that year the first joint meeting of the researchers was held in Odense, Denmark. At the meeting, the attendees agreed about terminology and the type of questions to be included in the survey. During the following months, the team at Odense University prepared a draft of the questionnaire, which was reviewed at a meeting in Bordeaux, France, at the end of April. The comments and ideas from the Bordeaux meeting were incorporated into the questionnaire during the summer. Each country team translated the questionnaire into the national language, and the first surveys were conducted by the end of 1995.

The joint questionnaire consists of 54 core questions with 254 variables. Each country was allowed to add specific questions. The responses to these questions, however, are not part of the joint datafile.

The third joint project meeting was held in Odense in January 1996. At this meeting a coding workshop was conducted with student assistants from nine countries. During the week in Odense, the coders participated in the development of general coding principles as well as in the development of categories for open-ended questions. The trained coders returned to their countries to finish the job in an efficient way guided by the common principles. The researchers from countries who did not participate in the coding workshop were given individual instructions about how to code the questionnaires and how to work with the datafile. Researchers from the United States and Australia joined the project in 1996 and utilized the joint questionnaire and common coding scheme.

Table A.1 gives information about the survey in each of the fourteen countries. It is important to note that the response rates vary considerably across countries. In order to increase the representativeness of the samples, weights have been created along two dimensions. The first dimension assures representativeness within each country according to size of municipalities. The second dimension assures that all countries are weighted equally regardless of sample size.

Table A.1 Response rates in the national surveys

Country	Survey conducted	Sent out	Returned	Response rate	Comments on population
Australia	Oct. 96	670	246	37	All local governments with the exception of Aboriginal community governments in the Northern Territory
Belgium	Nov.–Dec. 95	589	351	60	All municipalities are included in the survey. Questionnaire mailed in both a Dutch and a French version
Denmark	Nov. 95	275	200	73	All Danish municipalities
England	Dec. 95–Feb. 96	511	284	56	Total population less city of London
Finland	Mar.–Apr. 96	439	308	70	All municipalities except those of the Åland Islands
France	Dec. 95–Jan. 96	772	266	35	A stratified disproportionate sampling drawn from municipalities with more than 5,000 inhabitants
The Netherlands	Mar.–May 96	584	404	69	All municipalities, except 59 that do not have an appointed CEO
Ireland	May–June 96	34	21	62	All municipalities included
Italy	Dec. 95–Mar. 96	2,000	541	27	Italy has 8,100 municipalities, but only 6,100 CEOs. Several CEOs work in two or three small municipalities. The sample is 50% of all municipalities with more than 10,000 inhabitants, and 50% of a random sample of municipalities with less than 10,000 inhabitants.
Norway	Jan. 97	434	325	75	All municipalities included
Portugal	Dec. 95	275	104	38	All municipalities except the Islands of Madeira and the Azores
Spain	Nov. 95	5,000	366	7	The actual population is 8,120. Questionnaire distributed with newsletter to CEOs
Sweden	Nov.–Dec. 95	279	224	80	The actual population is 288, but 9 municipalities did not have an appointed CEO at the time.
USA	Jan.–May 97	1,178	697	59	CEO/CAO in all cities with more than 50,000 inhabitants and a sample of one-quarter of the cities with a population between 2,500 and 50,000

In creating the weights a special issue concerning the many small municipalities in the Southern European countries had to be resolved. As discussed in chapter 3, these countries also assign fewer functions to municipalities than in other countries. Consequently, very small communities have few employees, and the CEOs' responsibilities are limited. In France, no questionnaires were sent to municipalities with less than 5,000 inhabitants. In Italy and Spain, cities of all sizes were surveyed, but only cities with a population of 2,000 or greater are included in the weighed dataset used for the analysis in this book.

Intensive interviews

To get a more detailed knowledge of the work of a CEO, a series of intensive interviews were conducted in some of the participating countries. Most of the interviews were taped and transcribed. In some cases English summaries were made and distributed among participants. For a summary of the number of interviews and the interview guide, see Klausen and Magnier (1998, 288–89).

Chapter 3

The Leadership Variables

In order to tap the four dimensions of leadership the U.Di.T.E. Leadership Study made use of a battery of six items:

1. The mayor is very much engaged in the details of the daily work of the administration.

2. The mayor is a visionary person who constantly initiates new projects and policies in the locality.

3. The mayor has excellent relations with the public and knows what concerns the citizens.

4. The mayor is primarily a politician engaged in policy making rather than administrative details.

5. The mayor merely reacts to circumstances when new policies are formulated.

6. The mayor emphasizes the promotion of the party program and the interests of his fellow party members.

The response categories for all six items were "to a very high extent," "to a high extent," "to some extent," "to a little extent," and "not at all." Based on a factor analysis as well as substantive considerations, four leadership variables were constructed based on the six items. These variables follow:

Public leadership measures the extent to which the mayor is considered a visionary person who initiates change in the community and has positive relations with citizens. This is a three-point ordinal scale with values of high, moderate, and low.

Policy leadership measures the extent to which the mayor is engaged in the detailed work of government and focused on policy making. This is a four-point nominal scale with the values innovator, administrator, designer, and caretaker that are defined in the text.[2]

Partisan leadership is a measure of the extent to which the mayor promotes the party program and the interests of the party members. This is a three-point ordinal scale with values high, moderate, and low.

Proactive leadership measures the extent to which the mayor's style of leadership is considered proactive rather than reacting to circumstances in formulating policy. This is a three-point ordinal scale with values proactive, mixed, and reactive.

The distribution by country and form of government of the four leadership variables is found in table A.2.

Table A.2 CEOs' Perceptions of Mayors as Leaders by Country and Form of Government *(percent)*[a]

	Public Leadership[b]				Policy Leadership[c]				
	High	Moderate	Low	%	Innovator	Administrator	Designer	Caretaker	%
France	23	24	53	100	11	23	39	28	100
Italy	63	24	13	100	19	43	16	22	100
Spain	26	51	23	100	28	14	34	24	100
US-MC	41	46	13	100	19	12	41	28	100
Denmark					21	22	35	21	100
Great Britain	30	38	32	100	4	17	48	31	100
Sweden	27	52	20	100	5	27	38	30	100
Belgium	48	40	12	100	12	27	33	28	100
The Netherlands	33	39	28	100	3	9	50	37	100
Australia	42	42	15	100	3	8	45	45	100
Finland	14	39	47	100	2	7	22	69	100
Ireland	15	59	26	100	0	0	55	46	100
Norway	31	48	21	100	0	15	53	32	100
US-CM	32	47	21	100	8	6	62	25	100
Strong-mayor	38	34	28	100	19	25	31	25	100
Committee-leader	29	46	26	100	11	22	40	27	100
Collective	40	40	20	100	8	18	42	32	100
Council-manager	26	47	27	100	3	7	46	45	100
Total	32	42	26	100	9	17	40	34	100

	Partisan Leadership[d]				Proactive Leadership[e]			
	High	Moderate	Low	%	Proactive	Mixed	Reactive	%
France	44	35	22	100	56	28	16	100
Italy	29	31	40	100	37	40	24	100
Spain	24	32	44	100	33	40	26	100
US-MC	6	19	76	100	44	45	11	100
Denmark								
Great Britain	46	33	21	100	53	26	22	100
Sweden	26	39	35	100	41	37	22	100
Belgium	17	34	48	100	53	28	19	100
The Netherlands	1	2	97	100	52	34	14	100
Australia	9	10	82	100	53	32	15	100
Finland	7	10	84	100	57	23	21	100
Ireland	15	37	48	100	34	41	25	100
Norway	5	35	60	100	16	42	42	100
US-CM	5	5	90	100	33	46	20	100
Strong-mayor	30	31	38	100	42	36	22	100
Committee-leader	35	36	29	100	47	32	21	100
Collective	9	18	73	100	53	31	16	100
Council-manager	8	21	71	100	41	34	25	100
Total	19	26	55	100	44	34	22	100

NOTES: a. Data for Portugal are not available. Only policy leadership was assessed for Denmark.

b. $N = 3278$, chi-square for form of government = 73.2, significant at the .00 level

c. $N = 3608$, chi-square for form of government = 382.4, significant at the .00 level

d. $N = 3266$, chi-square for form of government = 497.0, significant at the .00 level

e. $N = 3293$, chi-square for form of government = 33.4, significant at the .00 level. If Belgium and the Netherlands are left out, chi-square = 10.1, significant at the .04 level.

The Cultural Variables

The calculation of the power distance index (PDI) and uncertainty avoidance index (UAI) is based on the Values Survey Module 1994 (VSM 94) as documented in Hofstede (no year). The following is a minimal documentation of the survey instrument and its background that is necessary to understand the basic features. For more detailed understanding the reader is referred to Hofstede (1980; no year).

The VSM 94 generates scores on five dimensions of national cultures on the basis of four items per dimension. The items used and the exact weighting of each item are based on experience over a twenty-five-year period. The twenty items have been shown to produce five independent factors which vary across countries. Independence between factors is only obtained with the full range of countries in Hofstede's original sample of countries. The fourteen countries covered by the U.Di.T.E. Leadership Study are a subset of the original sample, and the PDI and UAI correlate ($r = .54$).

The five cultural dimensions are found only in analysis with countries as units of analysis. In samples of respondents from the same country the same dimensions are not found. The PDI and UAI are supposed to be used only at the country level, not at the level of individuals, for reasons explained by Hofstede, Bond, and Luk (1993). For all the variables used to construct the indices, the responses are chosen from a five-point scale ranging from 1 (never) to 5 (always).

The index formula for calculating the power distance index is:

$$\text{PDI} = -35^\star(m v1) + 35^\star(m v2) + 25^\star(m v3) - 20^\star(m v4) - 20$$

where $m v1$–4 stand for the country mean scores on the following four variables:

$v1$: In choosing an ideal job, how important would it be to you to have a good working relationship with your direct superior? (five-point scale from 1 [of utmost importance] to 5 [of very little importance])

$v2$: In choosing an ideal job, how important would it be to you to be consulted by your direct superior in his/her decisions? (five-point scale from 1 [of utmost importance] to 5 [of very little importance])

$v3$: How frequently, in your experience, are subordinates afraid to express disagreement with their superiors? (five-point scale from 1 [very seldom] to 5 [very frequently])

$v4$: To what extent do you agree or disagree with the following statement: An organization structure in which subordinates have two bosses should be avoided? (five-point scale from 1 [strongly agree] to 5 [strongly disagree]).

The index formula for calculating the uncertainty avoidance index is:

$$\text{UAI} = 25^\star(m v5) + 20^\star(m v6) - 50^\star(m v7) - 15^\star(m v8) + 120$$

where $m v5$–8 stand for the country mean scores on the following four variables:

$v5$: How often do you feel nervous or tense at work? (five-point scale from 1 [very seldom] to 5 [very frequently]).

$v6$: To what extent do you agree or disagree with the following statement: One can be a good manager without having precise answers to most questions that subordinates may raise about their work? (five-point scale from 1 [strongly agree] to 5 [strongly disagree]).

$v7$: To what extent do you agree or disagree with the following statement: Competi-

Table A.3 Values on Power Distance (PDI) and Uncertainty Avoidance (UAI) in Hofstede's Study and the U.Di.T.E. Leadership Study

	Hofstede index		U.Di.T.E. index		
	PDI	UAI	PDI	UAI	N[a]
France	68	86	34	89	251
Belgium	65	94	31	104	333
Portugal	63	104	35	73	97
Spain	57	86	31	120	328
Italy	50	75	14	90	522
United States	40	46	19	29	672
The Netherlands	38	53	30	18	398
Australia	36	51	22	21	239
Britain	35	35	12	22	280
Finland	33	59	27	10	311
Norway	31	50	20	−27	316
Sweden	31	29	25	−8	219
Ireland	28	35	21	−8	20
Denmark	18	23	10	−34	195

Source: Hofstede (1997, 26 and 113) and the U.Di.T.E. Leadership Study.

NOTES: a. The number of respondents refer to the minimum *N* on the two measures (unweighted, although the index values are based on a weighted calculation).

tion between employees usually does more harm than good? (five-point scale from 1 [strongly agree] to 5 [strongly disagree]).

v8: To what extent do you agree or disagree with the following statement: A company's or organization's rules should not be broken—not even when the employee thinks it is in the company's best interest? (five-point scale from 1 [strongly agree] to 5 [strongly disagree]).

The indices will normally have a value between 0 (small power distance) and 100 (large power distance), but values below 0 and above 100 are technically possible. For documentary purposes we list Hofstede's values as well as the values obtained from the U.Di.T.E. Leadership Study (table A.3).

In the book, we have used the indices calculated from the U.Di.T.E. data. The major relationships, however, have been checked using Hofstede's original values also. For all practical purposes the results are the same. The difference in the correlation coefficients rarely exceeds .10 with no consistent pattern implying that one of the measures would be better than the other.

A complete breakdown of the attitudes of CEOs about neutrality and orientation to the political process by county and form of government is presented in table A.4.

Table A.4 Attitudes of CEOs about Neutrality and Orientation to Political Process by Country and Form of Government *(percent who agree and index values)*

	Percent who agree			Mean
	CEO should be nonpartisan expert	Activist role for administration	Spokesperson for poor	Advocacy index[a]
France	80	81	67	68
Italy	97	72	60	65
Portugal	74	90	71	78
Spain	87	81	62	70
US-MC	80	83	39	61
Denmark	73	95	52	72
Great Britain	62	91	72	74
Sweden	86	69	26	56
Belgium	95	67	45	63
The Netherlands	75	75	46	61
Australia	89	89	56	70
Finland	80	88	71	71
Ireland	86	100	66	78
Norway	86	89	65	74
US-CM	84	87	43	62
Strong-mayor	84	81	64	70
Committee-leader	74	85	50	68
Collective	85	71	45	62
Council-manager	85	91	61	72
N	4024	4037	4036	4022
Chi-square for form of government	111.5**	209.6**	157.8**	F = 38.0**
Total	82	84	57	69

NOTES: **Significance <.01

a. Advocacy index is the average index score for the two items "activist role for administration" and "spokesperson for poor." Since it is based on index values it is not directly comparable to the scores shown in the table for these two variables.

Chapter 5

The CEOs were asked to indicate how much importance they placed on sixteen different tasks. The list of tasks has been developed over a number of years and is based partly on previous research (Mouritzen et al. 1993).

The sixteen items were subjected to a factor analysis with oblique rotation which yielded four underlying dimensions with an eigenvalue larger than one. The resulting pattern matrix is shown in table A.5. The fourth factor, "the organizational integrator," is not used in the analysis in this book. The factor scores are not used directly in the analysis. The factor analysis helped identify items that belong to the same underlying dimensions, and once identified, the indices used in chapter 5 are based on a simple average of the index values on the relevant items.

Table A.5 Factor Analysis of Sixteen Activities of CEOs *(Pattern Matrix[a])*

	Component			
	1	2	3	4
Attract resources from external sources	.777			
Promote and encourage new projects in community	.677			
Make sure that resources are used efficiently	.611			
Formulate ideas and visions	.535			
Be informed about citizens' viewpoints				
Ensure that rules and regulations are followed		−.851		
Guide subordinate staff		−.703		
Give the mayor technical advice		−.576	.548	
Manage economic affairs, accounts, and budgetary control	.490	−.561		
Develop and implement new routines and work methods		−.527		
Give the mayor political advice			.707	
Shape norms concerning the proper roles of politicians			.628	
Influence decision-making processes			.562	
Solve human relationships				−.764
Promote cooperation between departments				−.678
Be informed of the viewpoint of employees				−.569

Extraction method: principal component analysis
Rotation method: Oblimin with Kaiser normalization
    NOTES:a. Rotation converged in 18 iterations

Chapter 6

The special study was conducted in three countries: Denmark, the Netherlands, and the United States. Because of the differences in form of government, distribution of tasks, and so on, the items covering the various hypothetical situations had to be adapted to the particular national setting. The exact wording of the items for the three countries is available from the local government research unit at the University of Southern Denmark, Odense (politics@sam.sdu.dk).

Chapter 7

The CEOs were asked to indicate in their opinion how much importance leading politicians ought to attach to fourteen different tasks. The fourteen items were exposed to a factor analysis with oblique rotation which yielded four underlying dimensions with an eigenvalue larger than one. The resulting pattern matrix is shown in table A.6.

The roles as governor (factor 4), stabilizer (factor 3), and ambassador (factor 2) represent three of the four dimensions. The first factor in table A.6 includes two items covering the administrator role (making decisions and laying down rules) as well as two of the items from the representative role (implement program on which elected and spokesperson for groups or individuals). For analytical reasons it was decided to split up this fourth factor into two for the roles of administrator and representative.

Table A.6 Factor Analysis of Fourteen Items Concerning the Ideal Politician as Perceived by the CEO *(Pattern Matrix[a])*

	Component			
	1	2	3	4
Be aware of citizens' views		.445		
Represent the municipality to the outside world		.795		
Create stability for the administration			.718	
Formulate exact and unambiguous goals for the administration			.607	
Defend decisions and policies		.601		
Implement the program on which he/she was elected	.622			
Spokesperson for local groups of individuals	.665			
Decide major policy principles				.820
Spokesperson for their political party			−.546	
Vision of the long-run development of municipality				.730
Lay down rules and routines for the administration	.665			
Make decisions concerning specific cases	.630			
Be a spokesperson for the press		.532		
Procure resources from higher-level governments	.455			

Extraction method: principal component analysis
Rotation method: Oblimin with Kaiser normalization
   NOTES: a. Rotation converged in 18 iterations.

Chapter 8

A complete breakdown of the influence ratings given by the CEOs to five official actors by county and form of government is presented in table A.7.

Table A.7 Budget and Economic Development Influence by Country and Form of Government
(index)

	Budget					Economic Development				
	Mayor	Council	Committee chairs	CEO	Department heads	Mayor	Council	Committee chairs	CEO	Department heads
France	95	69	56	70	56	87	55	39	55	33
Italy	87	60	33	56	59	100	75	75	75	50
Portugal[a]	96	51	76	52	53					
Spain	90	83	51	58	41	78	63	37	41	26
US-MC	75	67	50	88	81	77	55	43	73	43
Denmark	91	85	73	73	71	62	59	40	45	35
Great Britain	83	85	72	73	69	68	70	56	75	63
Sweden	93	85	72	67	71	83	69	56	62	59
Belgium[a]	87	66	83	65	55					
The Netherlands	62	60	50	57	62	61	42	35	42	42
Australia	63	62	46	85	75	67	55	40	76	55
Finland	71	73	52	90	78	64	66	45	86	67
Ireland	42	48	30	91	66	47	45	27	90	65
Norway	77	87	55	81	69	51	56	29	51	36
US-CM	63	74	36	92	79	67	63	34	78	46
Strong-mayor	91	66	54	61	54	82	59	39	51	31
Committee-leader	89	85	72	71	71	71	66	51	61	52
Collective	74	63	66	61	59	61	42	35	42	42
City manager	63	69	44	88	73	59	57	35	76	54
F score[b]	380.5	102.9	234.1	357.6	180.3	125.0	50.9	73.5	227.9	136.8
Significance	<.00	<.00	<.00	<.00	<.00	<.00	<.00	<.00	<.00	<.00
Overall mean	79	71	56	72	65	67	58	40	64	48
N	4008	3994	3993	4026	4014	3126	3106	3129	3146	3144

NOTES: a. Data not available for Belgium and Portugal concerning economic development.
    b. Test of significance for difference between forms of government

Participants in the U.Di.T.E. Leadership Study

Australia: Rolf Gerritsen, Michelle Whyard—Australian Centre of Regional and Local Government Studies, University of Canberra

Belgium: Thierry Laurent, Rudolf Maes, Yves Plees—Department of Politieke Wetenschappen, Katholieke Universiteit Leuven

Denmark: Lene Anderson, Peter Dahler-Larsen, Niels Ejersbo, Morten Balle Hansen, Kurt Klaudi Klausen, Poul Erik Mouritzen, Mikael Søndergaard—Department of Political Science and Public Management, Odense University

England: Michael Goldsmith, Jon Tonge—Department of Politics and Contemporary History, Salford University

Finland: Sari Pikkala, Siv Sandberg, Krister Ståhlberg—Department of Public Administation, Äbo Akademi

France: Katherine Burlen, Jean-Claude Thoenig—GAPP (Groupe d'Analyse des Politiques Publiques), Cachan

Ireland: Andy Asquith—Department of Politics and Public Policy, University of Luton; Eunan O'Halpin—Dublin City University Business School

Italy: Maurizio Gamberucci, Annick Magnier—Dipartimento di Scienzs delle Politico e Sociologi Politica, Universita degli studi di Firenze

The Netherlands: Marcel van Dam, Geert Neelen, Anchrit Wille—Department of Public Administration, University of Leiden; Jaco Berveling—Dutch Transport Research Centre

Norway: Harald Baldersheim, Morten Øgaard—Department of Political Science, Oslo University

Portugal: Manuel da Silva e Costa, Joel Filizes, José P. Neves—Instituto de Ciências Sociais, Universidade do Minho

Spain: Irene Delgado, Eliseo López, Lourdes López Nieto—Departmento de Ciencia Politica, Universidad Nacional de Educacion a Distancia

Sweden: Roger Haglund, Folke Johansson—Department of Political Science, University of Gothenburg

United States: James Svara—North Carolina State University

Notes

Chapter 1

1. We borrow this term from Peter Self (1972). An explanation of the term and what it signifies is provided later in this chapter.

2. As a characteristic of bureaucracy as an ideal type, it is impersonal rules that should be dominant. In practice, Weber (Gerth and Mills 1946, 229–32) observed, a bureaucracy may be made into the tool of a political master or become its own master.

3. The Nordic comparative project on local government CEOs reported in Rose (1996) was a source of inspiration for a special Danish study conducted in the early 1990s (Mouritzen et al. 1993), which again was a forerunner of the present study.

4. In the 1999 local elections, 20 municipalities had direct election for the mayoral position, evidently with no perceptible effect on electoral turnout (Larsen 1999).

5. An overview of efforts to introduce directly elected mayors in Europe is found in Larsen (2000).

6. The revisions that passed were claimed by proponents to be consistent with the council-manager form, but critics charged that new provisions represented the de facto creation of the strong mayor-council form of government (Wilkinson 1999). The new features include directly electing the mayor, making the mayor presiding officer of the council without a vote, and giving the mayor veto power, the power to transmit with comment the budget prepared by the city manager, the power to initiate the hiring and firing of the city manager (subject to council approval), and the power to appoint council committee chairs and assign legislation to council committees. The city manager is the "chief executive and administrative officer of the city."

7. Due to misunderstandings, the first effort to include Germany in the study did not succeed. At the time of finalizing the book, the German team at Stuttgart University had successfully completed the survey with German CEOs.

8. Our previous experience with cross-national research taught us that the chances of failure increase exponentially with the number of countries and teams to be coordinated.

9. After extensive discussions among the participating researchers it was decided to choose the label CEO, because this was considered to be the best generic term with the fewest connotations in all the participating countries. The term *city manager* might well have been used in many European countries, but in some contexts (notably the American, Australian, and Irish) this term identifies a particular form of government and has, therefore, specific

connotations attached to it. This form is also associated with specific definitions in the authority and role of elected officials in general and the mayor in particular.

10. We acknowledge that in some countries, e.g., New Zealand, the term is applied to department heads.

11. The quotation and the interpretation by the former CEO stem from an informal interview conducted on November 16, 2000. The name of the CEO has been changed.

12. The framework is developed in Mouritzen (1995). All the participants in the study are listed at the end of the book.

13. Job motivation and career patterns are examined in Dahler-Larsen (2001). Organizational change will be covered by a fourth book with the working title, *New Public Management and the CEO: Managing Change in Western Local Governments*, edited by Michael Goldsmith.

14. Fesler (1957) notes the "swing away from the simple, overly mechanical view of administration" but warns that it could go so far as to be destructive to our understanding of government and to public administration itself (139). Anticipating the sentiment that would soon become dominant in political science, he notes the argument that "all the *important* problems of administration are really problems of politics" (140). To those who accept this line of reasoning, "the administrative problems that matter are not problems of administration proper. And the administrative problems that don't matter don't matter" (140).

15. A disadvantage of this approach is that it gives very great weight to one country with a small actual number of respondents. In Ireland, the number of local governments is small because of low population overall and because governments have been consolidated into large units. There are only 34 CEOs in Ireland of whom 21 returned a questionnaire. Under the weighting formula, the total number of Irish CEOs is 291. Normally, this is not a problem. When Irish CEOs represent a disproportionate portion of a subcategory, however, we will consider the Irish responses separately.

16. Hofstede, Bond, and Luk (1993) refer to these levels as ecological, pancultural, and individual analysis. A fourth level of analysis is examination of characteristics within each country with no comparative dimension. This is the common mode of political science and public administration research. This kind of analysis is found in the first published book from the U.Di.T.E. Study, *The Anonymous Leader* (Klausen and Magnier 1998), which contains fourteen separate country chapters that describe the local government system and characteristics of CEOs within each of the countries. Because this study is available, country-by-country descriptions are not offered in the present book.

17. Since the US sample contains data from two forms of government, N in these analyses is 15.

18. When the question calls for an agree/disagree response, the scale is based on the following values: agree completely = 100, agree = 75, undecided = 50, disagree = 25, completely disagree = 0. The exact frequencies for the whole questionnaire, divided by country, are available from the local government research unit at the University of Southern Denmark, Odense (politics@sam.sdu.dk).

Chapter 2

The opening quotation is from Ted A. Gaebler, City Manager, San Rafael, California (interview in Nalbandian and Davis 1987, 79).

1. There are two other approaches that match certain of the four models developed. Riggs (1997) broadens the range of variation with a scale that extends from powerless administrators (an extreme version of the responsive administrator model) to bureaucratic dominant, a bureaucratic dictatorship that would represent an extreme version of the autonomous model. In between, administrators are "semipowered," a blend of separate roles and responsive administrators, or "powerful," comparable to either the overlapping roles or autonomous administrator models. Peters (1997) offers an interesting variation on the multimodel approach. At one end is complete separation of politics and administration and at the other end of a continuum is the "administrative state." In this latter model, there is also separation between politics and administration but the bureaucracy is the dominant force. An approach that blends roles is the "village life" model. In it, civil servant and politician are both part of a unified elite, and there is no conflict over power or policy.

2. Thompson offers arguments to counter the presumption that administrators are not capable of making independent moral judgments.

3. In Sayre's view, the founders of the field perceived administration to be in a "self-contained world of its own, with its own separate values, rules, and methods" (1958, 102). Svara (1999a) contends that Sayre misrepresented the position of the early contributors as we have argued here.

4. The point of the nonpartisanship of classical bureaucrats, Putnam (1975, 90–91) argues, "is not to deny that these officials have often been deeply involved in what we might term political activity in a broad sense, but rather to affirm that they interpreted their own motives and behavior as 'above politics.'"

5. This is one of four images in Aberbach, Putnam, and Rockman (1981, 4). Image I is essentially the dichotomy model, i.e., a divided world in which the "politicians make decisions; bureaucrats merely implement them."

Chapter 3

The first quotation is from Thomas Downs, City Administrator and Deputy Mayor, District of Columbia (interview in Nalbandian and Davis, 1987, 33).

1. The following description of the individual countries is based on different sources: The first book from the U.Di.T.E. project, *The Anonymous Leader* (Klausen and Magnier 1998), has proved to be an invaluable source with its many detailed descriptions of the various countries drawn upon the same conceptual framework. Also Clarke et. al (1996), Harloff (1987), Det Fælleskommunale EF-sekretariat (n.d.) as well as personal communications from the national teams of the project have been used as sources for the country descriptions.

2. Not all the study countries have an appointed CEO in all municipal governments, for example, the United States and small towns in France and Italy, but all the cities chosen for inclusion in the study have a top administrator.

3. A related concept in the United States is political supremacy: elected officials are ultimately in charge of government (Henry 1975).

4. In many European countries political parties hardly existed when local government was conceived in the nineteenth century. Elections were based on individuals running for office or were based on nonpartisan lists. Over the years, political parties have increasingly

dominated local elections, however. In some cities in the United States, elections are non-partisan by statute or by tradition.

5. The form of government with an elected executive mayor in the United States is called the mayor-council form. It may be further differentiated as "strong" or "weak" mayor-council forms. When a city administrator is appointed, the form is sometimes but not always referred to as the mayor-council-CAO form of government in the United States.

6. The four largest cities in Denmark did not at the time of the survey have a committee-leader form of government, but rather a "magistratsstyre" with full-time politicians forming the executive committee while individually heading the various departments. Three of the four cities participated in the U.Di.T.E. Leadership Study. With 200 respondents, their effect on the Danish results is negligible.

7. In 2000, Great Britain began introducing structural change in local governments, including the option of directly electing a mayor with executive authority.

8. Richard Childs—the great promoter of the council-manager form in the United States—did not want the chairman of the council to have the title mayor in order to avoid having any single identifiable political leader (Svara 1990b). Most cities in the United States did not follow this approach, although Irish mayors approximate Childs's ideal.

9. Interview with Norwegian CEO.

10. For a discussion of how governments can shape preferences through social engineering (and other strategies) see Dunleavy (1991, 117ff.).

11. The formation of the indicators used to measure leadership is explained in the technical appendix.

12. The labels chosen for the four categories have been influenced mostly by the American literature on mayoral leadership. See Svara (1990a, chap. 4).

13. The two items are positively related and the factor analysis seems to confirm that they belong to the same underlying dimension. This justifies the construction of a single indicator of public leadership that divides the individual mayors into categories of high, moderate, or low public leaders.

14. The leadership items were one of the few batteries of items which were labeled optional in the U.Di.T.E. Leadership Study. Only Portugal and Denmark chose to disregard these items, although the two policy-leadership items were included in the Danish questionnaire.

15. For the full U.S. sample, significant at a .01 level, N = 648.

16. The difference is significant at a .00 level.

17. In the U.Di.T.E. Leadership Study it was decided at an early point to include Hofstede's cultural dimensions, particularly power distance and uncertainty avoidance. There is a substantive as well as methodological reason for this. First, the two dimensions have, to our knowledge, never been used by political scientists in comparative analyses. Second, the U.Di.T.E. survey was a unique chance to replicate Hofstede's 25-year-old research from the private sector—specifically IBM's international branches—in public sector organizations. Like the IBM employees, the CEOs from the fourteen countries represent almost perfectly matched samples, i.e., they are similar in all respects except nationality (see Hofstede 1980, 37f.). Of course there are gender, educational, and age differences across countries in the U.Di.T.E. samples, but for all practical purposes they are negligible. Three other dimensions are not included in the present study, although they were included in the survey of the CEOs.

These include Hofstede's two original dimensions, masculinity versus femininity and individuality versus collectivism, as well as the later dimension, long-term versus short-term orientation.

18. An important outlier on the power distance index is Italy, which came close to Portugal, Spain, France, and Belgium in Hofstede's study but exhibits a rather low score, on par with Denmark and Britain in the U.Di.T.E. study.

19. For example, police services are provided by municipalities in the United States but by higher level governments in most European countries. Social services are distributed by municipalities in Scandinavia but are provided by the national Social Security Administration or county departments of welfare in the United States.

20. Median population (col. 2) and workforce in municipality with 10,000 inhabitants (col. 3) explain 87 percent of the variation in median workforce (col. 4) (adjusted R-square, N = 14).

21. For comparison with cities in the United States that are representative of urban support system cities, the city of Phoenix, Arizona, with twice the population of Copenhagen, had total expenditures of $1.8 billion in 1999–2000. Seattle, Washington, with a population of 541,500, had total expenditures of $2.1 billion.

Chapter 4

1. In strong mayor cities, 84% agree that the CEO should be a nonpartisan expert. The percentage in collective and in council-manager cities is 85%. In committee-leader cities, 74% agree.

2. The correlation is .16, significant at a .00 level.

3. When cluster analysis is conducted on these two variables, half of the respondents are in a cluster with high mean index scores on both (prime mover = 87; speak for poor = 81), one-third score high on being a prime mover (84) and low on speaking for the poor (31). Low scores on both are found for 6% of the CEOs, and 11% score moderately high on speaking for the poor (70) and low on being a prime mover (31).

4. F = 38.0, significant at the .01 level. The average value for the advocacy index is 69.

5. For both items, respondents could choose whether they strongly agreed or agreed, were undecided, disagreed, or strongly disagreed. The responses were converted to a 100-point scale with zero indicating strong disagreement and 100 indicating strong agreement.

6. The following are the mean values on each variable for the four clusters. Congruent means agreement that it is advantageous for the CEO to be of the same political opinion as the majority of the local council. Accountable to politicians means agreement that the CEO should be primarily responsible to the political leadership and only secondarily to the local population.

	Congruent/ accountable to politicians	Noncongruent/ accountable to politicians	Congruent/ accountable to public	Noncongruent/ accountable to public
CEO same opinion	69	12	69	11
Primarily responsible to elected officials	87	85	23	18
Percent (number)	% (1023)	28% (1095)	18% (692)	29% (1149)

7. The question on which this index is based is, "To what extent has your ability to perform your job as CEO been affected negatively by the following factors during recent years?" The choices included "lack of clear political goals" and "unclear division of labor between elected officials and the administration." The response options ranged from "to a very high extent" to "not at all."

8. Chi-square for form of government and uncertainty is 198.2, significant at the .00 level.

9. The variation in uncertainty is based primarily on role confusion. The council-manager cities also have slightly lower uncertainty with regard to goals.

10. The range in the proportion of strong-mayor cities that report high uncertainty is from 46% when the mayor is a detached caretaker to 34% when the mayor is a policy designer.

11. In this form, the second highest level of uncertainty is found in cities with a caretaker mayor. This appears to be an indicator that active policy leadership is expected.

12. In the collective cities, the proportion of CEOs reporting high uncertainty is 38% when the mayor is classified as an administrator and 30% when the mayor is an innovator, compared to 22% when mayors are designers or caretakers. In council-manager cities, the comparable percentages are administrator (35% high uncertainty), innovator (28%), designer (14%), and detached (18%).

13. In committee-leader cities, the gamma measure of association between the ordinal measures for uncertainty and public leadership is .26 (significant at a .00 level). In collective cities, gamma is .22 (significant at a .00 level).

14. The gamma between uncertainty and proactive leadership in strong-mayor cities is .21 (significant at a .00 level), in committee-leader cities it is .18 (significant at a .00 level), and in council-manger cities it is .27 (significant at a .00 level). In collective cities, gamma is only .10 (significant at a .10 level).

15. This option was "conflicts between the political parties." Of the respondents 17% reported that this factor affected them to a high extent, 28% to some extent, and 56% to little extent or not at all.

16. This is an excerpt from the 1989 annual report from the city manager in Tromsø, Norway. Cited from Lyngstad (1999).

17. Chi-sqare is 210.1, significant at the .01 level.

18. The gammas between uncertainty and negative impact of party conflict are as follows: strong-mayor, .39; committee-leader, .37; collective, .38; council manager, .47. All are significant at the .00 level.

19. The gamma measure of association for community pressures and uncertainty is .15 (significant at a .00 level) and for intergovernmental pressures and uncertainty is .15 (significant at a .00 level). The association is fairly uniform across the four types of cities.

20. A systematic profile of the networks of CEOs—characterized by frequency, importance and cooperation—is presented for each country in the first book from the U.Di.T.E. Leadership Study (Klausen and Magnier 1998).

21. Svara (1990a) makes the same distinction in the behavior of mayors—some of whom focus on process and others who also focus on the ends they wish to accomplish. For a more detailed discussion of the brokerage activity as a basic network function, see Knoke (1990, 144).

22. The standard deviations are 29 and 25, respectively, compared to 17 for the mayor.

23. The correlation between the extent to which the CEO emphasizes promoting new projects in the community and the importance of community leaders is .23, whereas the correlation with the importance of citizens is .16. Correlations are calculated at the individual level. Significance for all correlations is .00.

24. Interview with Danish CEO in a fairly small municipality.

25. The correlation between the extent to which the CEO emphasizes securing resources for the community and the importance of national and state officials is .33 and .27, respectively, whereas the correlation with the importance of other CEOs is .13. Correlations are calculated at the individual level. Significance for all correlations is .00.

26. The correlation between the level of community pressures and the importance assigned to community leaders is .25, the correlation of community pressures and the importance of higher level governments is .16, and the correlation between intergovernmental pressures and importance of higher level governments is .15. Correlations are calculated at the individual level. Significance for all correlations is .00.

27. As noted earlier, they consider the board of aldermen to be as important as the mayor in the Netherlands, but this category of officials was not included in the survey in any other country.

28. Including both sets of elected officials in the cluster analysis simply reconfirms that committee-leader CEOs are distinctive in their emphasis on both. It is more useful to distinguish CEOs that stress the importance of council members from those who do not, regardless of which council members they view as the more important referent.

29. The following are the mean values on each variable for the four clusters.

Importance of:	Isolated	Intergovernmental	Internal	Inclusive networkers	Total
Council members	41	45	82	81	64
Community leaders	26	33	33	58	38
Higher government officials	18	56	22	57	38
Percent in each cluster	24.3%	21.4%	27.2%	27.1%	100.0%
N	923	813	1035	1031	3802

30. These four types of networks have relevance to the way that the CEO views the other actors that were excluded from the cluster analysis. The isolated CEOs also assign the least importance to each of the other sets of actors. The intergovernmental orientation in network building carries over to other local governments. The internal networkers give relatively more emphasis to the mayor and less to the other CEOs. Finally, the inclusive networkers place strong emphasis on all these actors as well as the groups used in the cluster analysis.

Chapter 5

The opening quotation is from Ted A. Gaebler, City Manager, San Rafael, California. Interview in Nalbandian and Davis (1987, 80).

1. There is a large body of literature in the United States on the role of the city manager in policy making that includes Ammons and Newell (1988), Bosworth (1958), Ellis (1926), Fan-

nin (1983), Harrell (1948), Kammerer et al. (1962), Loveridge (1971), Montjoy and Watson (1995), *The Municipal Year Book, 1953* (1953), Newell and Ammons (1987), Price (1941), Ridley and Nolting (1934), Stillman (1974; 1977), Stone, Price, and Stone (1940), Svara (1985; 1989), White (1927), and Wright (1969).

2. The questionnaire item was as follows: "CEOs must necessarily decide the priority of various tasks. Please indicate how much importance you regularly place on each of the tasks listed below." The response choices and the points assigned to each response in constructing an index for each activity were as follows: very little or no importance (0), little importance (25), moderate importance (50), great importance (75), utmost importance (100).

3. A fourth dimension is the organizational integrator. It is based on three of the sixteen activities: solving problems and conflicts of human relationships, stimulating cooperation between departments, and being informed about the viewpoints of employees. (See the technical appendix.) It will not be discussed in this book because it focuses on the internal leadership of the organization rather than tasks that involve interaction with elected officials or the public.

4. Interview with American city manager.

5. The Pearson product correlation in individual-level analysis between promoting efficiency and attracting resources was .47 and with promoting new projects was .29. This is higher than the correlation with all of the activities in the administrative dimension except one—fiscal management at .33. All these correlations are significant at a .00 level.

6. There is a moderate correlation in the scores for the policy innovation and the political advice dimensions (Pearson product correlation is .37 at the individual level of analysis). There is a modest relationship between innovation and classical administration (.27), but the latter is only weakly related to political advice. The positive correlation between policy innovation and classical administration indicates that higher activity shows up in both dimensions.

7. The average score for the creating vision activity is 78 compared to the overall index average score of 72.

8. There is no difference in the CEO's involvement related to the leadership behavior of strong mayors. The difference in the policy innovation and administrative function scores for CEOs who work for mayors with different levels of public leadership and different types of policy leadership are not significant at the individual level of analysis.

9. The advice index score is 60 when there is a party dominant mayor and is 49 in other committee-leader cities (significant at a .00 level).

10. As indicated in chapter 3, these mayors are most likely to be innovators and administrators compared to mayors in other forms. They are also ranked top in influence among mayors in the four types of cities (chapter 8).

11. Pearson correlations for fifteen countries with one-tailed test of significance: policy innovation and power distance index (PDI) $r = -.33$ (significant at a .11 level) and uncertainty avoidance index (UAI) $r = -.45$ (significant at a .05 level); advice to politicians and PDI $r = -.55$ (significant at a .02 level) and UAI $r = -.44$ (significant at a .06 level); and classical administration and PDI $r = .36$ (significant at a .10 level) and UAI $r = .64$ (significant at a .01 level).

12. The Pearson correlation between UAI and relative emphasis on administration compared to policy is .80 (significant at a .00 level).

13. The size of government and the transfer of resources to local governments have been dropping in Great Britain. The score for attracting external resources is also high (73) suggesting that reduced resources produce greater competition and effort to secure what is left.

14. The differences are as follows: classical administration, Belgium 59, Netherlands 51; technical advice, Belgium 73, Netherlands 46; political advice, Belgium 27, Netherlands 48. All these are significant at the .00 level.

15. For a discussion of this type of analysis, see the introductory chapter and Hofstede et al. (1993).

16. In this example, the correlation of advice to politicians and networking with opposition is .18 with individual-level analysis and .13 using difference from the country mean to measure the variables.

17. The factors related to the classical administrator dimension have not been analyzed because of the discovery that it is not the level of administrative involvement per se that is most important in defining the CEO's roles, but rather the relative emphasis on administration compared to policy. Obviously, the measure of relative emphasis reflects in part variation in the level of policy activity that is analyzed separately.

18. Dummies for high party conflict and high uncertainty are not significantly related to advice at a .01 level.

Chapter 6

1. Indeed, some would contend that administrators do all these things in order to shape the policies of the government, at least as they pertain to bureaucratic interests.

2. Administrators could be involved in the politics of power at another level, i.e., the struggle for power between bureaucrats and administrative units. Often the politics of power at the two levels will be intermingled. The data available in this study do not permit examination of intra-organization conflicts among administrators to gain power.

3. Political advice to the mayor was one of four items entering into the "advisor to elected officials" dimension analysed in chapter 5.

4. Plotting uncertainty avoidance and political advice presents a similar picture. This factor discriminates between Netherlands and Belgium, which are clearly separated as well as being different in the level of political advice.

5. The adjusted R-square for the form of government dummies (with strong-mayor cities as the reference group) was .39 and for the two cultural variables it was .26. The combined equation, which included committee-leader (beta = .45), collective leadership (beta = .37) cities, power distance (beta = −.28), and uncertainty avoidance (beta = −.27), resulted in an adjusted R-square of .46. It was significant at a .05 level.

6. The Danish CEOs were at the start of the questionnaire asked to report the name of their municipality or the municipality's official code. This procedure have been used extensively over the years without negative effects on response rates or willingness to respond to even controversial questions.

7. The respondents were selected to represent contrasting cases in terms of geography, city size, and the political climate. In one country (Denmark) the selection of cases was based on a systematic study of the responses to the survey or was based on knowledge obtained from previous studies. The interviews were taped. In some countries the interviews

were transcribed in the native language and translated word for word to English. In other cases an English resume was developed, and in France the source material consists of a transcription in French. In the United States the tapes were reviewed directly.

8. During the discussions in Denmark and the Netherlands, the discussion was carefully monitored and notes prepared subsequently. In the United States, the discussion was taped. In Denmark all 20 respondents participated in the seminar; in the Netherlands 13 out of the 16 respondent showed up while in the United States only one CEO participated. Although this situation was different from the one planned, it turned out to be an intensive examination of the results with a CEO who has worked in a number of communities which yielded useful insights. In addition, a number of U.S. CEOs added comments to the questionnaire that have been incorporated into the review of the survey findings.

9. This was one of the items constructed on the basis of a real event. On election eve after the outcome was known, a CEO approached the mayor and all the other party leaders and urged them to form a broad coalition.

10. The American CEO who provided equal information to incumbent and nonincumbent candidates indicated that if he liked a candidate, he would meet with him or her to discuss campaign proposals if asked.

11. At the individual level of analysis, there is a positive relationship between the importance of the opposition and the level of political advice to the mayor in ten of the fifteen countries (with the U.S. cities split) with levels of significance below .05 in five countries. The highest correlations are found in Portugal ($r = .34$) and Denmark ($r = .22$).

12. For a comparative analysis of de-recruitment of local government CEOs based on the U.Di.T.E. Leadership Study, see Ejersbo and Dahler-Larsen (2001).

13. Observation by Jean Claude Thoenig in a communication with the authors. He also suggested that certain options contained in the situation are not likely to be present in France. For example, there is no way to broaden the majority immediately after the election. The only way to do so is by pushing policies that attract broad support.

Chapter 7

1. The modern study of legislative roles dates back to the landmark book by Wahlke et al. (1962) in which legislators in four American states were analyzed. Local councilors have been the focus of analysis in several within-country studies in the United States (Eulau and Prewitt 1973; Zisk 1973; Svara 1990a; Welch and Bledsoe 1988; Bledsoe 1993), Denmark (Bentzon 1981; Berg 1999), Britain (Young and Rao 1994; Rao 2000), Sweden (Lundquist 1989; Wallin, Bäck, and Tabor 1981), and Norway (Larsen and Offerdal 1992). What is characteristic of most of these studies is a focus on the roles of elected officials vis-à-vis citizens and voters, that is, a focus on the environment of the political-administrative organization. Few scholars have studied the role of elected officials in relation to the executive (Berg 1999 and Lundquist 1989 are exceptions), and no one has—to our knowledge—studied the role of local politicians across countries.

2. The groupings in table 7.1 are based in part on a factor analysis, which yielded four underlying factors described in the technical appendix. The roles as governor, stabilizer, and ambassador directly match three of the four dimensions identified in the factor analysis. For analytical reasons it was decided to divide the items in the fourth factor between the administrator and representative roles, as indicated in table 7.1. The two remaining items in the

administrator role are part of the same dimension. Two other items were added to the representative role—"implement program on which elected" and "spokesperson for groups or individuals." When the items connected to one of the five roles belong to the same dimension identified in the factor analysis, it is appropriate to calculate a composite score (boldfaced in the table). This is not the case for the representative role, and no composite score is calculated. An additional item "procure resources from upper-level governments" was left out of the factor analysis. The factor analysis, which was done at the country level, was carried out with oblique rotation.

3. To measure the significance of differences between categories in the analysis, regression analysis is used either with or without controlling for uncertainty avoidance (UAI). The test of significance is relaxed to the .10 level in view of the small number of country cases.

4. Theoretically one should expect uncertainty avoidance to be more relevant than power distance (PDI) as an explanation of preferences for the ideal politician. The basis for this expectation is that elected officials are potentially a major source of uncertainty for CEOs. Empirically this expectation seems to hold true. The PDI correlates significantly with the thirteen items in only three instances, whereas the relationship between UAI and the individual items is significant in nine out of thirteen instances. For this reason we focus on the UAI only.

5. The dummy for committee-leader government and the UAI explain 31 percent of the variation in the governor role index (adjusted R-square). Only the first variable is significant at a .10 level. The inclusion of UAI decreases the adjusted R-square from 33 to 31.

6. The simple correlation coefficient between UAI and the stabilizer index is .62. A model with UAI and three dummies for form of government yields an adjusted R-square of .34. Only one dummy (for committee-leader) is introduced together with UAI. Additional dummies result in a decrease in adjusted R-square. In the two-variable model only UAI is significant (significant at the .06 level), whereas the level of significance for the committee-leader dummy is .36 (overall significance .03). A model with the form-of-government dummies produces an adjusted R-square of .23, with none of the dummies being significant. A model with a dummy for strong-mayor is significant at the .04 level with an adjusted R-square of .23.

7. R-square is .65 for UAI alone. In a multivariate analysis, form of government comes close to playing an independent role, being .01 point short of meeting the .10 significance level. For the composite measure of the administrative role, this is solely attributable to the Portuguese outlier (figure 7.2). It might appear that the differences in preferences regarding the elected officials filling the administrative role is for all practical purposes a cultural phenomenon, that is, an effect of uncertainty avoidance. After the fourth variable is introduced in the model, the adjusted R-square starts to fall. In the three-variable model, with UAI and dummies for strong-mayor and committee-leader, the adjusted R-square stands at .69. The model yields the following estimates in the accompanying table.

	B	Beta	Signif.
UAI	.128	.47	.06
Strong-mayor	9.9	3.7	.11
Committee-leader	−6.1	−.19	.28

8. The separation would not be complete even if substantiated. We established in chapter 5 that the CEOs in strong-mayor cities are extensively involved in policy innovation.

9. The correlation is present at the individual level as well: classical administration index and "elected officials should establish rules" = .38; classical administration and "elected officials should make specific decisions" = .28. When individual differences from mean variables are used, the association is weaker but still present: classical administration and "elected officials should establish rules" = .21; classical administration and "elected officials should make specific decisions" = .15. All correlations are significant at a .01 level.

10. For decisions in specific cases, UAI alone has an adjusted R-square of .65. A committee-leader government dummy improves the adjusted R-square to .67, but is significant at a .18 level. For establishing rules, a strong-mayor government dummy alone has an adjusted R-square of .53. Adding UAI reduces the adjusted R-square to .52; it is significant at a .41 level.

11. Appointed by the council: guide subordinates = 55; establish routines = 57. Appointed by the mayor: guide subordinates = 61; establish routines = 63. The differences based on method of appointment are both six points. When expressed in percentages, 47% of those appointed by the mayor feel that it is very important to supervise subordinates versus 29% of those appointed by the council. Fifty-eight percent versus thirty-seven percent feel that establishing routines is very important. Because of the small number of respondents, the differences are not significant at a .05 level.

12. Banfield and Wilson (1963, 148–49) point out the anomalies in the record of the reform movement. Although in the early decades of the twentieth century the form was primarily adopted by smaller communities in which party dominance and corruption were uncommon, the antipartisan spirit animated the reform movement.

13. Excerpt from summary of interview with Irish city manager.

14. In the U.S. survey, two additional items were added that measure the ombudsman activity more fully. Preference for elected officials securing services for constituents and helping to resolve citizen complaints correlates strongly with acting as spokesperson for individuals and groups, .40 and .37, respectively. (The two additional items have a .59 correlation with each other.) Thus, it appears appropriate to consider the spokesperson-for-individuals-and-groups item as an indicator of the ombudsman activity. All correlations are significant at a .01 level.

15. Correlation –.59 at the country level of analysis (p < .01). See also figure 7.3.

16. Correlation .75, significant at a .01 level.

17. The form-of-government dummies alone explain 36% of the variation while the cultural variables alone explain 58% (adjusted R-squares). The model yields the accompanying table. The betas for the two cultural factors suggest a problem of multicollinearity. However, the simple correlations between UAI and PDI on the one hand and the ombudsman index on the other are very different, .74 for UAI and only .14 for PDI. An inspection of the tolerance levels and simple correlations suggests that multicollinearity is not a problem here.

	B	Beta	Signif.
UAI	.192	.85	.01
PDI	−.565	−.41	.07
Committee-leader	− 9.1	−.35	.09
Collective	− 6.8	.22	.21

18. The concepts of trustee and delegate were originally conceived to describe style of representation rather than foci, two separate dimensions in the sense that "the style of the representative's role is neutral as far as [the] different foci of representation are concerned," at least as seen from an analytical point of view (Wahlke et al. 1962, 270). Empirically, it is likely that they are interrelated in the sense that strong emphasis on party and/or groups and individuals as foci of representation may tend to go hand in hand with a delegate-role orientation; that is, the idea that elected officials should take orders or follow instructions from certain groups. If party and groups or individuals (and other specific publics such as geographical interests) are not part of a politician's focus, he or she may be more likely to believe in the trustee style of representation, where political stands follow from personal conviction.

19. In the United States, this item read, "Based on your experience, please indicate the extent to which council members engage in the following tasks."

20. This case was documented in Berg (1995).

21. The second possible explanation of the commonalties indicated at the beginning of the chapter rests in the possible existence of a "cross-national organizational field." According to this explanation certain ideas about the proper behavior of politicians would develop and spread in a global field and be interpreted and adapted by individual countries and municipalities. It seems unlikely, however, that this explanation can be defended, as it is difficult to point at global agents or sources of institutional innovation.

Chapter 8

1. The questionnaire items were as follows: "Many actors may influence local policymaking. Please indicate how influential the following actors are regarding the budget [or] economic development. Make your entries on a scale from 1 (high influence) to 5 (no influence)." The values were converted to 100 for high influence; 75, 50, and 25 for values 2, 3, and 4, respectively; and 0 for no influence.

2. As indicated in table 8.1, the collective cities differ. In Belgium, the mayor is the leading politician in budgeting, but the committee chairs are almost as influential. Two factors may account for these differences from the Netherlands. In Belgium, the mayor is chosen by the crown following the recommendation of the majority party. The board of aldermen was not presented as an option on the questionnaire in Belgium, and it may be that the CEOs had the aldermen in mind when they assigned high scores to the committee chairs.

3. The influence level of officials in each of the clusters is as follows:

All officials influential		Mayor centered		Administrator centered	
Budget	ED	Budget	ED	Budget	ED
Mayor 89*	Mayor 85	Mayor 88	Mayor 53	CEO 84	CEO 87
Council 86	Council 79	Council 64	Council 40	Dept. heads 70	Dept. heads 63
CEO 81	CEO 74	Chairs 55	CEO 36	Mayor 50	Mayor 49
Dept. heads 75	Dept. heads 59	CEO 41	Chairs 24	Council 49	Council 44
Chairs 71	Chairs 58	Dept. heads 38	Dept. heads 24	Chairs 29	Chairs 29
50%		23%		27% = 100%	
	45%		35%		20% = 100%

NOTE: *Influence rating for officials in this cluster

4. The administrators equal the innovator in budgetary influence in strong-mayor (93) and council-manager cities (75). They exceed the innovators' economic development influence in strong-mayor and committee-leader cities.

5. For budgeting, significant at a .05 level, but the difference between the average influence in high and low party promotion is only six points in mayor-council and committee-leader cities and 14 in collective cities.

6. Significant at a .00 level, N = 1248.

7. Significant at a .00 level for both budgeting and economic development.

8. The proportion of mayors with less than five years experience in the four types of cities is as follows: strong-mayor, 55%; committee-leader, 60%; collective, 44%; and council-manager, 70%.

9. The correlation of involvement in policy innovation with budgetary influence is .26 and with economic development influence is .42, both significant at the .00 level.

10. The correlation of involvement in advice to politicians with budgetary influence is .06, significant at the .00 level, and with economic development influence is .03, not significant. In committee-leader cities the correlation with budgetary influence is .19, with a partial correlation of .12 (both significant at the .00 level), controlling for involvement in policy innovation. The committee-leader cities are the only ones with a partial correlation over .10.

11. In strong-mayor cities the correlation with economic development influence is .23, with a partial correlation of .10 (the latter significant at the .02 level), controlling for involvement in policy innovation. The strong-mayor cities are the only ones with a partial correlation over .10.

Chapter 9

1. Rohr (1990, 80–82) and Terry (1995, 18 and 50) argue that public administrators combine autonomy and constitutional subordination in the United States.

2. In designating the most influential, the mayor received the nod if he or she was more influential than or equal to the other officials. The others needed to have superior influence to be classified as most influential.

3. The dataset has been prepared as a sample of national CEOs from the fourteen countries. Across the countries, respondents have been weighted so that there is an equal number of respondents from each country. This approach creates a sample of Western countries in which each country has equal weight. By preparing the data in this way, it is possible to make comparisons across countries without the relative size of the country sample distorting the results. In this case distortion results from the weighting, since the Irish CEOs are so heavily skewed toward the independent type. This type represents 64% of the Irish CEOs but only 13% of the CEOs in all other countries.

4. These comparisons of means and those in figure 9.1 are all significant at a .01 level. The strength of association, however, varies considerably. The rank order of F scores from lowest to highest is as follows: CEO nonpartisanship (3.5), importance of higher governmental actors (5.0), council members decide specific matters (7.3), advocacy by CEO (8.2), classical manager scale (12.8), council members decide principles (15.08), council members formulate exact goals (23.1), political adviser scale (23.9), council members establish rules and routines (37.7), council members party spokesperson (42.3), policy innovator scale

(53.3), importance of community actors (60.0), council members keep election promises (115.5).

5. There is much less variation in preferences regarding elected officials serving as spokespersons of local groups or individuals who have issues pending decision by the municipality. The scores are 43 for the political agents, 41 for the professional agents, 39 for the interdependents, and 36 for the independents. The F score is 6.24, significant at a .00 level.

6. The exact percentages are political agent, 33%; professional agent, 34%; and interdependent, 29%.

7. If the standard is relaxed to include CEOs who are more influential in both (25 points or higher), 4 percent of the CEOs outside of Ireland meet this criterion compared to 30 percent in Ireland.

8. In the overall sample, excluding Ireland, the breakdown of mayors is as follows: hands-on visionary leader, 32%; visionary, 12%; checker (detail-oriented/nonvisionary), 16%; nonleader, 40%. In Ireland, 15% are hands-on leaders, 5% are visionaries, 0% are checkers, and 79% are nonleaders.

9. Chi-square is significant at a .01 level or less in cities divided by each form of government except the collective form. Ireland is excluded from the council-manager cities.

10. The contribution is partial and indirect. The key factor in determining the CEO types is the CEO's influence compared to the influence rating of the most influential elected official, who is likely to be the mayor, and influence is related to the effectiveness of mayoral leadership, as we saw in chapter 8.

11. When the mayor is the most influential elected official, 49% are "effective," i.e., either hands-on leaders or visionaries. When committee chairs are the most influential politicians, 35% of the mayors are effective leaders. When the council is most influential, 30% of the mayors are effective. (Chi-square is significant at a .00 level; N = 2845, with Ireland excluded from calculations.)

12. There is no variation in the level of the CEO involvement in policy innovation related to the mayor's leadership effectiveness.

Chapter 10

1. The gap between preferences and performance among the partners in governance is probably found in all countries, although we only had data from Denmark and the United States to substantiate this conclusion.

2. Waterman and Meier (1998) argue that issues of control in the classic principal-agent relationship arise only when goals are in conflict and agents have superior knowledge.

3. "Lack of clear political goals" and "unclear division of labor between politicians and the administration" rank as the third and sixth most important negative forces affecting performance from a list of twelve.

4. The correlation between uncertainty index and influence in budgeting is −.15 and in economic development is −.16, significant at a .01 level.

5. Consistent with this view of strong mayor cities, political agents who are more responsive to political direction have a lower score on an uncertainty index (42) than do the professional agents (55).

6. See Pratchett and Wingfield (1996) who identify the "public service ethos" as an institution.

7. For a discussion of those differences, see Nalbandian (1994).

8. This measure, not used previously in the analysis, measures the elements that are important in an ideal job. Seventy-three percent considered the opportunity to influence the future development of their community to be very or extremely important.

9. In our time, there is emphasis on the view that many actors, including those in the nonprofit sector, provide social opportunity and resolve or ameliorate the problems of society, not government alone (Frederickson 1996).

10. Presentation by David Jannsen, County Administrator, Los Angeles County, at the Annual Meeting of the American Society for Public Administration, April 2, 2000.

Technical Appendix

1. In the spring of 2000 a German team at the University of Stuttgart surveyed the German CEOs, unfortunately too late to be incorporated in the book.

2. The labels chosen for the four categories have been influenced mostly by the American literature on mayoral leadership (cf. Svara, 1990, ch. 4).

References

Aberbach, Joel B., Robert D. Putnam, and Bert A. Rockman. 1981. *Bureaucrats and Politicians in Western Democracies.* Cambridge: Harvard University Press.

Aberbach, Joel D., and Bert A. Rockman. 1993. *Civil Servants and Policy Makers: Neutral or Responsive Competence.* Paper delivered at the APSA annual meeting.

———. 2000. *In the Web of Politics: Three Decades of the U.S. Federal Executive.* Washington, D.C.: Brookings Institution Press.

Adams, Guy B., and Danny L. Balfour. 1998. *Administrative Evil.* Thousand Oaks: Sage Publications.

Adrian, Charles. 1987. *A History of American City Government.* New York: University Press of America.

Asmeron, Haile K., and Eliza P. Reis, eds. 1996. *Democratization and Political Neutrality.* London: MacMillan Press.

Ammons, David N., and Charldean Newell. 1988. "City Managers Don't Make Policy:" A Lie; Let's Face It. *National Civic Review* 57: 124–32.

Asquith, Andy, and Eunan O'Halpin. 1998. Power and Responsibility: The Role of the Manager in Irish Local Government. In *The Anonymous Leader, Appointed CEOs in Western Local Government,* edited by Kurt Klaudi Klausen and Annick Magnier. Odense: Odense University Press.

Axelrod, Robert. 1984. *The Evolution of Cooperation.* New York: Basic Books.

Baldersheim, Harald, ed. 1990. *Ledelse og innovasjon i kommunerne.* Oslo: Tano.

Baldersheim, Harald, and Morten Øgaard. 1998. The Norwegian CEO: Institutional Position, Professional Status, and Work Environment. In *The Anonymous Leader, Appointed CEOs in Western Local Government,* edited by Kurt Klaudi Klausen and Annick Magnier. Odense: Odense University Press.

Banfield, Edward C. 1961. *Political Influence.* New York: Free Press.

Banfield, Edward C., and James Q. Wilson. 1963. *City Politics.* New York: Vintage Books.

Banks, Jeffrey S., and Barry R. Weingast. 1992. The Political Control of Bureaucracies under Asymmetric Information. *American Journal of Political Science* 36: 509–24.

Batley, Richard, and Adrian Campbell. 1992. *The Political Executive: Politicians and Management in European Local Government.* London: Frank Cass and Co., Ltd.

Bennett, Robert J. 1993. *Local Government in the New Europe.* London: Belhaven Press.

Bentzon, Karl Henrik. 1981. *Kommunalpolitikerne*. Copenhagen: Samfundsvidenskabeligt Forlag.

Berg, Rikke. 1995. *En ny politikerrolle i kommunerne—et studie af byrådspolitikere i Odense Kommune*. Odense: Faculty of Social Sciences, University of Southern Denmark.

Berg, Rikke. 1999. *Den 'gode' politiker. Et studie af politiske ledelsesværdier i kommunerne*. Ph.D. diss. Odense: University of Southern Denmark.

Berg, Rikke, and Ulrik Kjær. 1997. Afspejler kommunalpolitikerne vælgerne? In *Kommunalvalg*, edited by Jørgen Elklit and Roger Buch Jensen. Odense: Odense Universitetsforlag.

Berveling, J., Marcel van Dam, and Geert Neelen. 1997. *"De deugd in het midden," Over de sleutelpositie van de gemeentesecretaris*. Delft: Eburon.

Berveling, J., M. van Dam, G. Neelen, and A. Wille. 1998. No More Double Dutch: Understanding the Dutch CEO. In *The Anonymous Leader, Appointed CEOs in Western Local Government*, edited by Kurt Klaudi Klausen and Annick Magnier. Odense: Odense University Press.

Bledsoe, Timothy. 1993. *Careers in City Politics*. Pittsburgh: University of Pittsburgh Press.

Bosworth, Karl. 1958. The Manager Is a Politician. *Public Administration Review* 18 (summer): 216–22.

British Council. 1999. *The Evolution of the UK Civil Service, 1848–1997*.
http://www.britishcouncil.org/governance/manag/civil/civil01.htm

Buck, Marcus, Helge O. Larsen, and Helen Sagerup. 2000. *Demokratisk nyskapning eller mislykket eksperiment? En evaluering av forsøket med direktevalg av ordfører i 20 kommuner*. Stencilserie A, nr. 94, Institut for Statsvitenskap, Universitetet i Tromsø.

Caiden, Gerald E. 1996. The Concept of Neutrality. In *Democratization and Political Neutrality*, edited by Haile K. Asmeron and Eliza P. Reis. London: MacMillan Press.

Clark, Terry Nichols, and Vincent Hoffmann-Martinot, eds. 1998. *New Political Culture*. Boulder: Westview Press.

Clarke, M., H. Davis, D. Hall, and J. Stewart. 1996. *Executive Mayors for Britain: New Forms of Political Leadership Reviewed*. Birmingham: The University of Birmingham.

Clarke, Susan, ed. 1989. *Urban Innovation and Autonomy: The Political Implications of Policy Change*. Newbury Park: Sage Publications.

Cook, Brian J. 1996. *Bureaucracy and Self-Government*. Baltimore: Johns Hopkins University Press, 1996.

Cooper, Terry L. 1987. Hierarchy, Virtue, and the Practice of Public Administration. *Public Administration Review* 47: 320–328.

Cooper, Terry L. 1998. *The Responsible Administrator*. San Francisco: Jossey-Bass.

da Silva e Costa, Manuel, Joel Felizes, and José P. Neves. 1998. Portuguese Chief Administrative Officers: Between Rationalization and Political Struggles. In *The Anonymous Leader, Appointed CEOs in Western Local Government*, edited by Kurt Klaudi Klausen and Annick Magnier. Odense: Odense University Press.

Dahler-Larsen, Peter, ed. 2001. *Social Bonds to City Hall: How Appointed Managers Enter, Experience, and Leave their Jobs in Western Local Government*. Odense: Odense University Press.

Dahler-Larsen, Peter, and Niels Ejersbo, 2001. Leaving the Job as CEO. In *Social Bonds to City Hall: How Appointed Managers Enter, Experience, and Leave Their Jobs in Western Local Government*, edited by Peter Dahler-Larsen. Odense: Odense University Press.

Delgago, Irene, Lourdes López Nieto, and Eliseo López. 1998. Functions and Duties of Funcionarios Directivos Locales (Local Chief Officers). In *The Anonymous Leader, Appointed CEOs in Western Local Government*, edited by Kurt Klaudi Klausen and Annick Magnier. Odense: Odense University Press.

Det fælleskommunale EF-sekretariat. n. d. *Regional- og lokalstyret i EF-Europa*, Copenhagen: Det Fælleskommunale EF-sekretariat.

DETR. 1998. *Modern Local Government in Touch with the People*. London: Department of the Environment, Transport and Regions, HM Government.

Diamant, Alfred. 1962. The Bureaucratic Model: Max Weber Rejected, Rediscovered, Reformed. In *Papers in Comparative Public Administration*, edited by Ferrell Heady and Sybil L. Stokes. Ann Arbor: Institute of Public Administration.

Dobel, J. Patrick. 1984. Doing Good by Staying In? *Public Personnel Management* 13: 126–38.

Doig, J. W., and E. C. Hargrove, eds. 1990. *Leadership and Innovation, Entrepreneurs in Government*. Baltimore/London: Johns Hopkins University Press.

Downs, Anthony. 1967. *Inside Bureaucracy*. Boston: Little, Brown.

Dubnick, Melvin J. 1999. Demons, Spirits, and Elephants: Reflections on the Failure of Public Administration Theory. Paper presented at the Annual Meeting of the American Political Science Association.

Dunleavy, Patrick. 1991. *Democracy, Bureaucracy and Public Choice: Economic Explanations in Political Science*. London: Harvester Wheatsheafs.

Dunn, Delmer. 1997. *Politics and Administration at the Top: Lessons from Down Under*. Pittsburgh: University of Pittsburgh Press.

Easton, David. 1965. *A Systems Analysis of Political Life*. New York: Wiley.

Eggers, William D., and John O'Leary. 1995. *Revolution at the Roots*. New York: Free Press.

Eldersveld, Samuel J., Lars Strömberg, and Wim Derksen. 1995. *Local Elites in Western Democracies. A Comparative Analysis of Urban Political Leaders in the U.S., Sweden, and the Netherlands*. Boulder: Westview Press.

Ellis, Ellen Deborah. 1926. The City Manager as a Leader of Policy. *National Municipal Review* 15: 204.

Eulau, Heinz, and Kenneth Prewitt. 1973. *Labyrinths of Democracy*. Indianapolis: Bobbs-Merrill.

Fannin, William R. 1983. City Manager Policy Roles as a Source of City Council/City Manager Conflict. *International Journal of Public Administration* 5, no. 4: 381–99.

Farazmand, Ali. 1997. Introduction. In *Modern Systems of Government Exploring the Role of Bureaucrats and Politicians*, edited by Ali Farazmand. Thousand Oaks: Sage Publications.

Fesler, James W. 1957. Administrative Literature and the Second Hoover Commission Reports. *American Political Science Review* 51:135–57.

Finer, Herman. 1941. Administrative Responsibility in Democratic Government. *Public Administration Review* 1: 335–50.

Frederickson, H. George. 1980. *The New Public Administration*. Tuscaloosa: University of Alabama Press.

Frederickson, H. George. 1997. *The Spirit of Public Administration*. San Francisco: Jossey-Bass.

Friedrich, Carl J. 1940. Public Policy and the Nature of Administrative Responsibility. *Public Policy* 1: 1–24.

Gaardsted Frandsen, Annie. 1998. *Landspolitik eller lokalpolitik? Et studie af danske kommunal-valg.* Odense: Faculty of Social Sciences, University of Southern Denmark.

Gabriel, Oscar W., Vincent Hoffmann-Martinot, and Hank V. Savitch, 2000. *Urban Democracy.* Leske and Budrich, Opladen.

Gardner, George W. 1990. *On Leadership.* New York: The Free Press.

Gerth, H. H., and C. Wright Mills, trans. 1946. *From Max Weber: Essays in Sociology.* New York: Oxford University Press.

Gibbon, I. G. 1925. Municipal Government in the United States: Some Impressions. *National Municipal Review* 14: 78–81.

Goldsmith, Michael. 1992. Local Government. *Urban Studies* 29, no. 3/4: 393–410.

Goldsmith, Michael, and Edward Page, eds. 1987. *Central and Local Government Relations.* London: Sage.

Goldsmith, Michael, and Harold Wolman. 1992. *Urban Politics and Policy.* London: Blackwell.

Goldsmith, Michael, and Poul Erik Mouritzen, eds. 1997. *The U.DI.T.E. Leadership Study. Report from the 3rd Congress 6–7 September 1996.* Odense, Denmark. (Available in English, French, and Danish from the National Association of Chief Executives in Denmark.)

Goldsmith, Michael, and Kurt Klaudi Klausen, eds. 1997. *European Integration and Local Government.* Cheltenham: Elgar.

Goodnow, Frank J. 1900. *Politics and Administration.* New York: Macmillan.

Green, Richard. 1998. Impartiality and Administrative Statesmanship. In *Active Duty: Public Administration as Democratic Statesmanship,* edited by Peter A. Lawler, Robert M. Shaefer, and David L. Schaefer. New York: Rowman & Littlefield Publishers.

Gruber, Judith E. 1987. *Controlling Bureaucracies.* Berkeley: University of California Press.

Gurr, Ted Robert, and Desmond S. King. 1987.*The State and the City.* Chicago: University of Chicago Press.

Haglund, Roger. 1998. Turbulence As a Way of Life: The Swedish Municipal CEO. In *The Anonymous Leader, Appointed CEOs in Western Local Government,* edited by Kurt Klaudi Klausen and Annick Magnier. Odense: Odense University Press.

Hall, Peter A., and Rosemary C. R. Taylor. 1996. Political Science and the Three New Institutionalisms. *Political Studies* XLIV: 936–57.

Hambleton, Robin, 2000. Modernising Political Management in Local Government. *Urban Studies* 37, no. 5–6: 931–50.

Hansen, Morten Balle. 1997. *Kommunaldirektøren—Marionet eller Dirigent.* Odense: Faculty of Social Sciences, University of Southern Denmark.

Harloff, Eileen Martin. 1987. *The Structure of Local Government in the European Community.* The Hague: IULA.

Harrell, C.A. 1948. The City Manager as a Community Leader. *Public Management* 30: 290–94.

Heady, Ferrel. 1984. *Public Administration: A Comparative Perspective.* New York: Marcel Dekker.

Heclo, Hugh. 1975. OMB and the Presidency—the Problem of "Neutral Competence." *The Public Interest* 38: 80–98.

Henry, Nicholas. 1975. Paradigms of Public Administration. *Public Administration Review* 35: 376–86.

Hofstede, Geert. 1980. *Culture's Consequences. International Differences in Work-Related Values.* Beverly Hills: Sage Publications.

Hofstede, Geert. 1997. *Cultures and Organizations. Software of the Mind.* New York: McGraw-Hill.

Hofstede, Geert. (no year). *Values Survey Module 1994 Manual.* Maastricht: University of Limburg.

Hofstede, Geert, Michael Harris Bond, and Chung-leung Luk. (1993). Individual Perceptions of Organizational Cultures: A Methodological Treatise on Levels of Analysis. *Organization Studies* 14/4: 483–503.

Kaarsted, Tage. 1992. *De danske ministerier 1953–1972.* Copenhagen: PFA.

Kammerer, G. M., C. D. Farris, J. M. DeGrove, and A. B. Clubok. 1962. *City Managers in Politics.* Gainesville: University of Florida.

Kettl, Donald F. 2000. Public Administration at the Millennium: The State of the Field. *Journal of Public Administration Research and Theory* 10: 7–34.

Klausen, K. K., and A. Magnier, eds. 1998. *The Anonymous Leader: Appointed CEOs in Western Local Government.* Odense: Odense University Press.

Knoke, D. 1990. *Political Networks, The Structural Perspective.* Cambridge: Cambridge University Press.

Krause, George A. 1999. *A Two-Way Street: The Institutional Dynamics of the Modern Administrative State.* Pittsburgh: University of Pittsburgh Press.

Larsen, Helge O. 1990. Ordføreren—handlekraft eller samlende symbol? In *Ledelse og innovasjon i kommunerne,* edited by Harald Baldersheim. Oslo: Tano.

Larsen, Helge O. 2000. *Directly Elected Mayors—Democratic Renewal or Constitutional Confusion.* Paper presented at Convegno Annuale, Sociatà Italiana di Scienza Politica, Università di Napoli, September.

Larsen, Helge O., and Audun Offerdal. 1992. *Demokrati uten deltakere.* Oslo: Kommuneforlaget.

le Maire, Emil, and Preisler, Niels. 1996. *Lov om kommuners styrelse med kommentarer.* Copenhagen: DJØF Forlaget.

Lepawsky, Albert. 1949. *Administration: The Art and Science of Organization and Management.* New York: Alfred A. Knopf.

Lidström, Anders. 1996. *Kommunsystem i Europa.* Stockholm: Publica.

Lineberry, Robert L., and Edmund P. Fowler. 1967. Reformism and Public Policies in American Cities. *American Political Science Review* 61 (September): 701–16.

Lineberry, Robert L., and Ira Sharkansky. 1978. *Urban Politics and Public Policy.* New York: Harper and Row.

Long, Norton E. 1954. Public Policy and Administration: The Goals of Rationality and Responsibility. *Public Administration Review* 14: 22–31.

Long, Norton E. 1965. Politicians for Hire. *Public Administration Review* 25: 115–19.

Loveridge, Ronald. 1971. *City Managers in Legislative Politics.* Indianapolis: Bobbs-Merrill.

Lundquist, Lennart. 1989. Lederskapet och följarna. *Statsvetenskaplig Tidskrift* 92: 149–71.

Lyngstad, Rolf. 1999. *Den kommunale tenkemåte. Ein case-studie av makt og innflytelse i ein norsk kommune—belyst gjemme ein prioriteringskonflikt mellom tre kommunale utbyggingsprosjekt,* Ph.D. diss., Tromsø: University of Tromsø.

March, James G., and Johan P. Olsen. 1989. *Rediscovering Institutions: The Organizational Basis of Politics.* NewYork: The Free Press.

March, James G., and Johan P. Olsen. 1995. *Democratic Governance*. NY: Free Press.

Marini, Frank, ed. 1971. *Toward a New Public Administration: The Minnowbrook Perspective*. San Francisco: Chandler Publishing.

Martin, Daniel W. 1987. Déjà Vu: French Antecedents of American Public Administration. *Public Administration Review* 47: 297–303.

Mayntz, Renate, and Fritz W. Scharpf. 1975. *Policy-Making in the German Federal Bureaucracy*. Amsterdam: Elsevier.

Meier, Kenneth J. 1997. Bureaucracy and Democracy: The Case for More Bureaucracy and Less Democracy. *Public Administration Review* 57: 193–99.

Miller, Gary, 2000. Above Politics: Credible Commitment and Efficiency in the Design of Public Agencies. *Journal of Public Administration Research and Theory* 10: 289–327.

Meltsner Arnold J. 1971. *The Politics of City Revenue*. Berkeley: University of California Press.

Moe, Terry M. 1985. The Politicized Presidency. In *The New Direction in American Politics*, edited by John E. Chubb and Paul E. Peterson. Washington: The Brookings Institution.

Moe, Terry M. 1989. The Politics of Bureaucratic Structure. In *Can the Government Govern?* edited by John E. Chubb and Paul E. Peterson. Washington: The Brookings Institution.

Montjoy, Robert S., and Douglas J. Watson. 1995. A Case for Reinterpreted Dichotomy of Politics and Administration as a Professional Standard in Council-Manager Government. *Public Administration Review* 55: 231–39.

Mouritzen, Poul Erik. 1991. *Den politiske cyklus. En undersøgelse af vælgere, politikere og bureaukrater i kommunalpolitik under stigende ressourceknaphed*. Aarhus: Forlaget Politica.

Mouritzen, Poul Erik, ed. 1992. *Managing Cities in Austerity*. London: Sage Urban Innovation Series.

Mouritzen, Poul Erik. 1995. A Comparative Research Project on Chief Executives in Local Government. The U.D.I.T.E. Leadership Study. *Local Government Studies* 5. Odense University, Department of Political Science and Public Management.

Mouritzen, Poul Erik. 1996. *Politicians As a Source of Bureaucratic Frustration*. Paper presented at the conference on The Executive at the Political Vortex, Canberra, August 1–3.

Mouritzen, P. E., H. Larsen, H. Ragn Hansen, and A. Storm. 1993. *Mod en fælles fremtid. De kommunale chefforeninger i en brydningstid*. Odense: Odense Universitet.

Municipal Highlights of 1952, 1953. *The Municipal Year Book, 1953*. Washington: ICMA: 3.

Nalbandian, John. 1987. The Evolution of Local Governance: A New Democracy. *Public Management* 69: 2–5.

Nalbandian, John. 1994. Reflections of a "Pracademic" on the Logic of Politics and Administration. *Public Administration Review* 54: 531.

Nalbandian, John. 2000. The Manager as Political Leader: A Challenge to Professionalism. *PM* 82 (March): 7–12.

Nalbandian, John, and Raymond G. Davis, eds. 1987. *Reflections of Local Government Professionals*. Lawrence: The University of Kansas.

Nardulli, Robert F., and Jeffrey M. Stonecash. 1981. *Politics, Professionalism, and Urban Services*. Cambridge: Oelgeschlager, Gunn and Hain, Publishers.

Newell, Charldean, and David N. Ammons. 1987. Role Emphasis of City Managers and Other Municipal Executives. *Public Administration Review* 47: 246–52.

Newton, Kenneth, ed. 1980. *Balancing the Books. Financial Problems of Local Government in West Europa*. London: Sage Publications.

Niskanen, William. 1971. *Bureaucracy and Representative Government*. Chicago: Aldine.

North, Douglas C. 1990. *Institutions, Institutional Change, and Economic Performance*. Cambridge: Cambridge University Press.

Norton, Alan. 1991. *The Role of Chief Executive in British Local Government*. Birmington: University of Birmington, Institute of Local Government Studies.

Ostrom, Elinor. 1986. An Agenda for the Study of Institutions. *Public Choice* 48: 3–25.

Peters, B. Guy. 1995. *The Politics of Bureaucracy*. White Plains: Longman.

Peters, B. Guy. 1997. Bureaucrats and Political Appointees in European Democracies: Who's Who and Does It Make Any Difference? In *Modern Systems of Government Exploring the Role of Bureaucrats and Politicians*. Edited by Ali Farazmand. Thousand Oaks: Sage Publications.

Peters, B. Guy. 1999a. *Institutional Theory in Political Science. The 'New Institutionalism'*. London and New York: Pinter.

Peters, B. Guy. 1999b Institutional Theory and Administrative Reform. In *Organizing Political Institutions: Essays for Johan P. Olsen*, edited by Morten Egeberg and Per Laegreid. Oslo: Scandinavian University Press.

Peters, B. Guy, and John Pierre. 1998. Rethinking Public Administration. *Journal of Public Administration Research and Theory* 8: 223–43.

Peterson, Paul. 1981. *City Limits*. Chicago: University of Chicago Press.

Plees, Yves, and Thierry Laurent. 1998. The Belgian Municipal Secretary: A Manager for the Municipalities. In *The Anonymous Leader, Appointed CEOs in Western Local Government*, edited by Kurt Klaudi Klausen and Annick Magnier. Odense: Odense University Press.

Practhett, Lawrence, and Melvin Wingfield. 1996. Petty Bureaucracy and Woolly-Minded Liberalism? The Changing Ethos of Local Government Officers. *Public Administration* 74 (Winter): 639–56.

Prewitt, Kenneth. 1970. *The Recruitment of Political Leaders*. Indianapolis: Bobbs-Merrill.

Price, Don K. 1941. The Promotion of the City Manager Plan. *Public Opinion Quarterly* (Winter): 563–78.

Price, Don K. 1985. *America's Unwritten Constitution*. Cambridge: Harvard University Press.

Przeworski, Adam, and Henry Teune. 1970. *The Logic of Comparative Social Enquiry*. New York: Wiley-Interscience.

Putnam, Robert D. 1975. The Political Attitudes of Senior Civil Servants in Britain, Germany, and Italy. In *The Mandarins of Western Europe: The Political Role of Top Civil Servants*, edited by Mattei Dogan. New York: John Wiley & Sons.

Rao, Nirmala. 2000. Representation under Strain: The British Experience. In *Representation and Community in Western Democracies*, edited by Nirmala Rao. London: Macmillan Press.

Rao, Nirmala, ed. 2000. *Representation and Community in Western Democracies*. London: Macmillan Press.

Rhodes, R.A.W. 1997. *Understanding Governance, Policy Networks, Governance, Reflexivity and Accountability*. Buckingham, Philadelphia: Open University Press.

Ridley Clarence C., and Orin Nolting. 1934. *The City Manager Profession*. Chicago: University of Chicago Press.

Riggs, Fred W. 1997. Coups and Crashed: Lessons for Public Administration. In *Modern Systems of Government Exploring the Role of Bureaucrats and Politicians*, edited by Ali Farazmand. Thousand Oaks: Sage Publications.

Rohr, John A. 1989. *Ethics for Bureaucrats*. New York: Marcel Dekker.

Rohr, John A. 1990. The Constitutional Case for Public Administration. In *Refounding Public Administration*, edited by Gary Wamsley. Newbury Park: Sage Publications.

Rose, Larry, ed. 1996. *Kommuner och kommunala ledare i Norden*. Åbo: Åbo Akademi.

Rourke, Francis E. 1992. Responsiveness and Neutral Competence in American Bureaucracy. *Public Administration Review* 52: 539–46.

Sayre, Wallace S. 1958. Premises of Public Administration: Past and Emerging. *Public Administration Review* 18:102–05.

Schneider, Mark, and Paul Teske. 1992. Toward a Theory of the Political Entrepreneur: Evidence from Local Government. *American Political Science Review* 86: 737–47.

Self, Peter. 1972. *Administrative Theories and Politics: An Inquiry into the Structure and Processes of Modern Government*. London: George Allen & Unwin Ltd.

Sharpe, L. J., ed. 1981. *The Local Fiscal Crisis in Western Europe*. Beverly Hills & London: Sage Publications.

Smith, John, 1991. The Public Service Ethos. *Public Administration* 69: 515–23.

Sparrow, Glen. 1984. The Emerging Chief Executive: The San Diego Experience. *Urban Resources* 2: 3–8.

Stein, Lana. 1991. *Holding Bureaucrats Accountable: Politicians and Professionals in St. Louis*. Tuscaloosa: University of Alabama Press.

Stillman, Richard J., II. 1974. *The Rise of the City Manager*. Albuquerque: University of New Mexico Press.

Stillman, Richard J., II. 1977. The City Manager: Professional Helping Hand, or Political Hired Hand? *Public Administration Review* 37: 659–70.

Stone, Harold A., Don K. Price, and Kathryn H. Stone. 1940. *City Manager Government in the United States*. Chicago: Public Administration Service.

Story, Russell McCulloch. 1918. *The American Municipal Executive*. Urbana: University of Illinois. [Reprinted by Johnson Reprint Corporation, New York, 1970.]

Svara, James H. 1985. Dichotomy and Duality: Reconceptualizing the Relationship Between Policy and Administration in Council-Manager Cities. *Public Administration Review* 45: 221–232.

Svara, James H. 1989. Policy and Administration: City Managers as Comprehensive Professional Leaders. In *Ideal and Practice in City Management*, edited by H. George Frederickson. Washington: International City Management Association.

Svara, James H. 1990a. *Official Leadership in the City: Patterns of Conflict and Cooperation*. New York: Oxford University Press.

Svara, James H. 1990b. The Model City Charter: Innovation and Tradition in the Reform Movement. *Public Administration Review* 50: 688–92.

Svara, James H. 1991. *A Survey of America's City Councils: Continuity and Change*. Washington: National League of Cities.

Svara, James H., 1998a. The Politics-Administration Dichotomy Model as Aberration. *Public Administration Review* 58: 51–58.

Svara, James H. 1998b. United States of America. Similarity Within Diversity. In *The Anonymous Leader, Appointed CEOs in Western Local Government*, edited by Kurt Klaudi Klausen and Annick Magnier. Odense: Odense University Press.

Svara, James H. 1999a. Complementary of Politics and Administration as a Legitimate Alternative to the Dichotomy Model. *Administration & Society* 30: 676–705.

Svara, James H. 1999b. The Shifting Boundary Between Elected Officials and City Managers in Large Council-Manager Cities. *Public Administration Review* 59: 44–53.

Svara, James H. 2000. Representation and Governance: Redefining Roles for Large Council-Manager Cities in the United States. In *Representation and Community in Western Democracies*, edited by Nirmala Rao. London: Macmillan Press.

Svara, James H. 2001a. The Myth of the Dichotomy: Complementarity of Politics and Administration in the Past and Future of Public Administration. *Public Administration Review* 61: 164–71.

Svara, James H. 2001b. Do We Still Need Model Charters? The Meaning and Relevance of Reform in the Twenty-First Century. *National Civic Review* 90: 19–33.

Svara, James H., and Associates. 1994. *Facilitative Leadership in Local Government: Lessons from Successful Mayors and Chairpersons in the Council-Manager Form*. San Francisco: Jossey-Bass.

Terry, Larry. 1995. *Leadership of Public Bureaucracies: The Administrator as Conservator*. Thousand Oaks: Sage Publications.

Thoenig, Jean-Claude. 1995. De l'incertitude en gestion territoriale. *Politiques et Management Public* 13: 1–27.

Thoenig, Jean-Claude, and Katherine Burlen. 1998. The Asymmetric Interdependence Between two Powerful Actors: The CEO and the Mayor in French Cities. In *The Anonymous Leader, Appointed CEOs in Western Local Government*, edited by Kurt Klaudi Klausen and Annick Magnier. Odense: Odense University Press.

Thomas, Rosamund M. 1978. *The British Philosophy of Administration: A Comparison of British and American Ideas 1900–1939*. London: Longman.

Thompson, Dennis. 1985. The Possibility of Administrative Ethics. *Public Administration Review* 45: 555–61.

Tullock, Gordon. 1965. *The Politics of Bureaucracy*. Washington, D.C.: Public Affairs Press.

Urban, Brian. 1999. *Kommunestørrelse og demokrati—en undersøgelse af den politiske mistillids omfang, årsager og konsekvenser for en fremtidig kommunalreform*. Thesis, Department of Political Science and Public Management. Odense: University of Southern Denmark.

Wahlke, J. C., H. Eulau, W. Buchanan, and L. C. Ferguson. 1962. *The Legislative System*. New York: Wiley.

Wallin, Gunnar, Henry Bäck, and Merrick Tabor. 1981. *Kommunalpolitkerna. Rekrytering—arbetsförhållanden - funktioner*. Ds Kn 1981: 17–18.

Wamsley, Gary L., Robert N. Bacher, Charles T. Goodsell, Pailip S. Kronenberg, John A. Rohr, Camilla M. Stivers, Orion F. White, and James F. Wolf. 1990. *Refounding Public Administration*. Newbury Park, CA: Sage Publications.

Waterman, Richard W., and Kenneth J. Meier. 1998. Principle-Agent Models: An Expansion? *Journal of Public Administration Research and Theory* 8: 173–202.

Welch, Susan, and Timothy Bledsoe. 1988. *Urban Reform and Its Consequences*. Chicago: University of Chicago Press.

West, William F. 1995. *Controlling the Bureaucracy*. Armonk: M.E. Sharpe.

White, Leonard. 1927. *The City Manager*. Chicago: University of Chicago Press.

Wilbern, York. 1973. Is the New Public Administration Still With Us? *Public Administration Review* 33: 373–78.

Wildavsky, Aaron B. 1984. *The Politics of the Budgetary Process*. Boston: Little, Brown.

Wilkinson, Howard. 1999. *Debate on Mayor's Powers Makes for Lively Live Radio* [Online].

Cincinnati Enquirer [cited 29 April 1999]. Available from World Wide Web: (http://enquirer.com/editions/1999/04/29/loc_debate_on_mayors.html)

Wilson, Woodrow. 1887. The Study of Administration. *Political Science Quarterly* 2: 197–222.

Wolf, Patrick J. 1999. Neutral and Responsive Competence—The Bureau of the Budget, 1939–1948, Revisited. *Administration & Society* 31: 142–67

Wolman, Harold, John Strate, and Alan Melchior. 1996. Does Changing Mayors Matter? *Journal of Politics* 58: 201–23.

Woodruff, Clinton Rogers, ed. 1919. *A New Municipal Program*. New York: D. Appleton and Company.

Wright, Deil. 1969. The Manager as a Development Administrator. In *Comparative Urban Research*, edited by Robert T. Daland. Beverly Hills: Sage Publications,

Yates, Douglas. 1977. *The Ungovernable City*. Cambridge: MIT Press.

Yates, Douglas. 1982. *Bureaucratic Democracy*. Cambridge: Harvard University Press.

Young, K., and Nirmala Rao. 1994. *Coming to Terms with Change: The Local Government Councillor in 1993*. York: Joseph Rowntree Foundation.

Zisk, Betty H. 1973. *Local Interest Politics: A One-Way Street*. Indianapolis: Bobbs-Merrill.

Index